RESTLESS EMPIRE

CHINA
AND THE WORLD
SINCE 1750

ODD ARNE WESTAD

THE BODLEY HEAD
LONDON

Published by The Bodley Head 2012

2 4 6 8 10 9 7 5 3 1

First published in Great Britain in 2012 by
The Bodley Head
Random House, 20 Vauxhall Bridge Road,
London SW1V 2SA

www.bodleyhead.co.uk
www.vintage-books.co.uk

Addresses for companies within The Random House Group Limited can be found at:
www.randomhouse.co.uk/offices.htm

The Random House Group Limited Reg. No. 954009

A CIP catalogue record for this book
is available from the British Library

ISBN 9781847921970 (HBK)
ISBN 9781847921987 (TPB)

The Random House Group Limited supports The Forest Stewardship
Council (FSC®), the leading international forest certification organisation.
Our books carrying the FSC label are printed on FSC® certified paper.
FSC is the only forest certification scheme endorsed by the leading
environmental organisations, including Greenpeace.
Our paper procurement policy can be found at:
www.randomhouse.co.uk/environment

Printed and bound in Great Britain by
Clays Ltd, St Ives Plc

For Michael
and Paula Hunt

CONTENTS

A NOTE ON CHINESE PRONUNCIATION

CHINESE IS WRITTEN IN IDEOGRAPHIC CHARACTERS, not letters as most Indo-European languages are. The pronunciation of these characters differs greatly among people in China, not to mention with Koreans and Japanese, who also in part use them. The character 江, for instance, meaning "river," is pronounced something like djiang in the north, kiang in central China, kang in Fujian, and gong in Cantonese.

This book uses the system of transliteration from Chinese known as *hanyu pinyin* (Chinese phonetics). The only exceptions are personal names well known in English in other transliterations, such as Chiang Kai-shek (who would be Jiang Jieshi in pinyin) or Sun Yat-sen. Developed by linguists working in Moscow in the 1930s, pinyin has become standard in the People's Republic of China and increasingly elsewhere, replacing earlier systems. It is based on how people speak in north China.

In most cases the intuitive pronunciation of an English speaker comes close to imitating the sound as intended in pinyin. But in a few cases it is more difficult. Q is generally pronounced "ch," x is "sh," zh is "j" (as in Joe), and c is "ts." Deng Xiaoping's given name (Xiaoping) is therefore pronounced something like Shaoping. The city Chongqing is Chongching. Zhou Enlai's surname (Zhou) is Joe. And Cixi, the empress dowager, is Tseshi. Accurate pronunciation is of course a bit more difficult than that. All Chinese characters are tonal as well, but no need to worry about that unless you want to study the language.

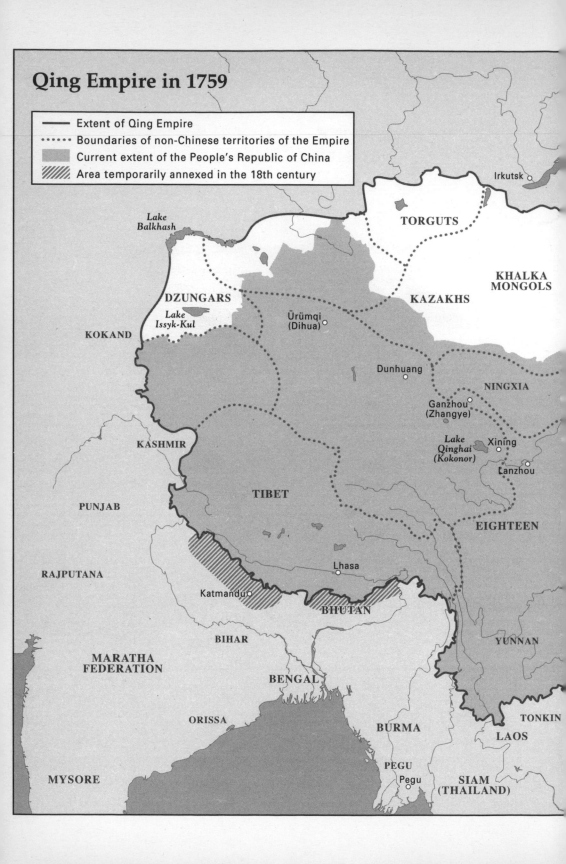

Qing Empire in 1759

Legend:
- Extent of Qing Empire
- Boundaries of non-Chinese territories of the Empire
- Current extent of the People's Republic of China
- Area temporarily annexed in the 18th century

Irkutsk

Lake Balkhash

TORGUTS

KHALKA MONGOLS

DZUNGARS

KAZAKHS

Lake Issyk-Kul

Ürümqi (Dihua)

KOKAND

Dunhuang

NINGXIA

Ganzhou (Zhangye)

KASHMIR

Lake Qinghai (Kokonor)

Xining

Lanzhou

PUNJAB

TIBET

EIGHTEEN

RAJPUTANA

Lhasa

Katmandu

BHUTAN

PUNJAB

BIHAR

YUNNAN

MARATHA FEDERATION

BENGAL

ORISSA

BURMA

TONKIN

LAOS

MYSORE

PEGU

Pegu

SIAM (THAILAND)

EMPIRE

AT THE BEGINNING OF THE TWENTY-FIRST CENTURY, China is moving ever closer to the center of global affairs. As the most populous country on earth, and one of the largest, it has always commanded the attention of others, even in those rare periods in its history when it has been weak, divided, or poor. Today many Chinese and foreigners believe that China has emerged from an era of relative impotence to amass extraordinary international power. It is often predicted that within two decades it will become the world's largest economy, overtaking the United States. The Chinese Academy of Sciences anticipates that, around that time, China will have become the world's technological powerhouse and that it will have eradicated poverty among its more than 1.5 billion citizens, while increasing their life expectancy to eighty years.[1] Meanwhile, some, especially in neighboring countries, fear that China will strengthen its military might in order to bend others to its will.

But even though China's economic output has soared over the past thirty years, its history indicates that the march into the future may be less unilinear than some experts would have us believe. Both the period of Communist rule and China's deeper history—the centuries of distinctive development under imperial and dictatorial rulers—have left deep historical fissures that future leaders will have to navigate in order to reach their political, economic, and social goals. Beneath the surface of today's frenzied quest for progress lie currents and fault lines that could take China in very different directions from those we are seeing at present. These alternative paths may be positive or negative for China and the world. But with the significance that the country has already

1

achieved in international affairs, we ignore the topography that made them only at our peril.

Some of this topography lies within today's People's Republic and some lies outside it. China's relationships with its many neighbors and with the United States are essential to understanding its trajectories, as are the beliefs and worldviews of the Chinese people, China's particular way of organizing the state and social affairs, and its economic and resource needs. But the boundaries between China and rest of the world are themselves not always clear or distinct. In the intersection between the internal and the external lie some of the most important aspects of China's mental maps: borders, diasporas, ethnicities, trade, and the exchange of ideas. As often happens when dealing with great powers, the boundaries of this landscape become blurred when you look closely at them. The division lines between inner and outer fade away, and what remains is a China that is, to some extent, transnational and even global.

If border demarcations are blurred, so even more are time distinctions. The past is inscribed in China's mental terrain in a calligraphy so powerful that it determines most of its approaches to the present. History therefore influences Chinese ways of seeing the world in a more direct sense than in any other culture I know. Today, little of this is mechanical—the Chinese do not necessarily draw explicit parallels between events of the past and those of the present. Very few Chinese—certainly of the present generation—think, for instance, about events from the Warring States period (475–221 BC) when reflecting on the current international situation. But they do carry with them concepts of justice, rules of behavior, and views of China's place in the world that have been shaped by practices developed centuries ago. Although it is impossible to predict the future based on this past, it is necessary to understand it in order to have at least some means of navigation at hand.

THIS BOOK ATTEMPTS TO GIVE a brief overview of China's relationship to its outside worlds over the past 250 years, but it might be useful, in the beginning, to dwell briefly on what the legacies of the even deeper past are. In doing so, we first have to tackle the big question: What exactly is this "China" that we are discussing here, historically, geographically, and culturally? Frankly, the more I have learned about China, the more elusive a clear definition becomes. Over the past two millennia it has been an empire rather than a country, but an empire with very open and very fluid borders. Its inhabitants have, until very recently, been defined by the civilization they were part of rather than by the way they look or the ancestors they have. Reading and writing Chinese script (but not necessarily speaking whatever form of the language was in vogue at Court) have been the key to this culture—whoever mastered written Chinese were *inside*; whoever did not were *outside*, or, at best, peripheral, whether they were foreigners, slaves, peasants, women, or conquered tribes.

Perhaps because of their cultural elitism, the state has always been a central concern for the Chinese. Benjamin Schwartz, a Harvard intellectual historian who rightly warned against seeing all things in contemporary China as rooted in the past, has put it well: "One of the most striking characteristics of Chinese civilization is what might be called the centrality and weight of the political order."[2] Identifying with that state and, if possible, improving it have been central to being Chinese for more than two thousand years. Even those who persistently attempted to escape from the state's reach—whether they were Buddhists in the tenth century or anarchists in the twentieth—had to contend with the political order. There is no organizational project quite like it anywhere else in the world, including Russia, which has its own kind of state veneration, or China's Asian neighbors, who all have taken up some of the Chinese concepts of the state.

China originated in the Yellow river valley, first as many states that collectively called themselves the Central Kingdoms, Zhongguo—

today's Chinese name for China. Then there was a unified empire under the Han dynasty, which ruled for most of the period from 206 BC to AD 220, roughly coinciding in time with the Roman empire in the west. The core parts of China have always faced eastward, toward the Yellow Sea, even after the vast regions south of the Yangzi river had been fully integrated during the Tang and Song dynasties some thousand to twelve hundred years ago. I always use a raised-relief map to explain to students how the state viewed its empire from its eastern capitals. The far west was mountains and deserts. Sichuan—the rich province in the southwest— was only accessible from the east through narrow mountain passes. The south was very far away, across rivers and valleys. The north held count- less enemies, strong ethnic groups that could challenge the empire even when it was expanding. With few exceptions, the epicenter of power would therefore remain in the east, with most dynasties setting up their capitals around the Yellow river. Since the fourteenth century, the po- litical center has moved between Beijing, the Northern Capital, in the northeast, and Nanjing, the Southern Capital, on the Yangzi, upriver from the central eastern coast. In essence, China has had its back on the middle part of the Eurasian continent, and that orientation has had enormous consequences for the country as it has approached the rest of the world.

Granted, it is a sketchy definition of a country, but here is mine: China is a culture, a state, and a geographical core, around which iden- tities, boundaries, and definitions of purpose have shifted and adjusted for a very long time. Indeed, perhaps one of the reasons why the con- cept of China has been so durable is that it is so amorphous and so contentious. Generations after generations have struggled to give their own meaning to it and to its place in the world, while drawing on the history that preceded them. Over the past 250 years, the deeper his- torical legacies—the state, Confucian culture, geography—appear in battles over crucial terms that define and give a sense of direction to the Chinese.[3]

The concept of justice is one of these essential terms. It is key to the Confucian influences that have shaped Chinese politics since the early Han dynasty. To the philosopher Confucius (551–479 BC), as to his Greek contemporary Plato, justice meant a proper, harmonious relationship within a family, within a state, and between states. The sincerity of the ruler, according to Confucian tradition, is more important than any form of procedural justice. "He who exercises government by means of his virtue may be compared to the north polar star, which keeps its place and all the stars turn towards it," Confucius said.[4] In the Chinese view today, the outside world over the past two hundred years has treated China unjustly, and this grievance remains a leitmotif in China's international affairs.

Rules and rituals are central to many Chinese systems of thought, including but not limited to Confucianism. These rules were created by Chinese elites for their own use, and to regulate conditions for those who were subservient to them. Most of the concepts clearly define hierarchies, but they also set out the mutual duties and obligations of various members of society. As the world changed in the nineteenth century, many Chinese felt that the new Western-led international society they were being forced into was characterized more by chaos than by rules. The search for general principles in international affairs has therefore been a staple of Chinese foreign policy, even though China, like all states, accepts those rules that are to its advantage more easily than those that are not.

A sense of centrality is also a crucial component of the Chinese mindset. The ease with which its neighbors have, throughout history, accepted elements of Chinese culture has served to confirm a cosmology in which China always stands at the center. With the belief in an essential role for their country in Eastern Asia came a sense of responsibility in systemic terms, of China as the indispensable nation for its region. For this reason, some Chinese have found it difficult to understand alternative visions of how the world works and how societies should be organized. There is an irony here. For most of its history, China has been open to the importing of ideas without, however, relinquishing the sense that Chinese thought has absolute universal applications. The parochialism and intolerance that sometimes come out of a belief in one's own centrality have plagued China's foreign affairs at crucial moments in its history.

Justice, rules, and centrality—these three crucial concepts should always be borne in mind when considering the past, present, and future of Chinese foreign policy. But they are, however, broad preoccupations rather than concrete prescripts. And although China's written tradition can help us understand these concerns, the belief that we can fathom more of what China will do in a conflict today through studying, for instance, Sun Zi's *The Art of War*—a key text of the late sixth century BC—is a far-fetched proposition.[5] Present-day Chinese, whatever their background, do not set their personal priorities or those for their state and its international affairs by studying their ancient texts any more than Europeans or Americans study Plato or Aristotle before making a decision. But the social and cultural concepts developed and contested over time color their concerns and help set the agenda for people's views of what their country ought to do.

THE HISTORY OF MODERN CHINA'S foreign relations began with the Qing dynasty, which ruled for almost three hundred years, from 1644 to 1912. Under the Qing, China saw the peak of its power. By the 1750s, it had crushed the political and military independence of all the smaller nations on its northern frontier and begun incorporating them into a much-enlarged China. It had regulated its relations with its remaining neighbors, from the Russian empire in the north to the kingdoms in Southeast Asia and in the Himalayas, according to Chinese preconditions and based on a Chinese sense of superiority. By the middle part of the eighteenth century, the Qing empire had created a world in eastern Asia that was almost entirely its own.

The unlikely story of the Qing empire originates in the beginning of the seventeenth century. At that time, a motley crew of princes from north of the border began to take power in parts of the territory belonging to the Ming dynasty, which had ruled China since 1368. The professed goal of the invaders was to conquer all of the country and restore Confucian rectitude, which they believed had been lost under the Ming emperors, whom they saw as unrighteous and decadent. The leaders of the conquering army came from a Tungusic tribe which in the past had been known as Jurchen and now called themselves the Manchu. As they expanded southward, they were joined by many Mongols, Koreans, and Chinese, as well as people from smaller tribes in the northeast, the territory we now call Manchuria. In 1636, they created a separate polity, a state and a dynasty they called Qing, meaning bright or pure. By 1644 they had taken the Chinese capital, Beijing, and began to pacify the rest of the country. The last Ming dynasty pretender was hauled back from Burma and executed in 1662.

The Qing's announced goal was to rule according to ancient wisdom as set out in the classic works of Confucianism. The Ming had failed, they declared, because its rulers had become lax and equivocal; they had seemed weak and without a sense of direction for generations. Now the Manchus, the outsiders, had arrived in order to rectify China and bring back its greatness. But as with many political leaders who appeal to traditions and values, the Qing emperors' message hid the fact that they were setting out to remake China in their own image, as a great multicultural dynastic state with universalist pretensions. Their forms of organization were modern, in the sense that they were different from anything that had existed before, stressing coordinated use of economic, technical, and ideological resources. Their armies, through which they ruled, had more in common with those of the Ottoman, Russian, or even the Austro-Hungarian empires than with those of the Ming; they relied on highly mobile cavalry, firearms and artillery, and well-developed logistics. Their intention was to form a super state in which peoples of all ethnic backgrounds and faiths should find their obedient place.[6]

In spite of its ideological and military power, the Qing might not have been such a success were it not for the longevity of two remarkable emperors: Kangxi (Abundant Prosperity), who ruled from 1661 to 1722, and his grandson Qianlong (Heavenly Greatness), who ruled from 1736 to 1796.[7] Between them they governed China for more than 120 years and solidified Qing rule to an extent that few who were living in the 1650s would have thought possible. They also embedded their personal characteristics in the empire they created. Kangxi was mercurial and dynamic, curious about the outside world but fiercely protective of his power and that of the Manchus. Qianlong was cultured and hard-working, but he was not as intelligent as his grandfather and was therefore more doctrinaire on civil and political matters. Both were knowledgeable about the peoples they ruled and about the world that surrounded them, and adept at the diplomatic and military tools needed to navigate a complex region.

By 1750, the fourteenth year of Qianlong's reign, the Qing empire had consolidated its rule over all of China and was expanding its imperial government into Central Asia, Tibet, and Mongolia. Unlike their predecessors, the Manchu emperors regulated the empire's foreign relations, so that all smaller states in the region, from Korea to Burma, explicitly recognized the preeminence of the Central Kingdom and of the Qing. At home the empire was at peace, with considerable economic expansion, especially in agriculture (although China also had a large manufacturing sector, some of which specialized in porcelain and silk for export). Irrigation and transport were well developed, and markets had begun to emerge, dealing in everything from land to tools to candlesticks for the afterlife. It was an increasingly specialized society, in which written contracts and agreements between individuals and families were taking on major roles.[8]

The impact of the state could be seen in all walks of life. A bit like the absolutist kings of the French prerevolutionary era, the Qing aspired to control every aspect of the lives of their subjects and to regulate those they could not directly control. Like their European counterparts they of course failed in many of these pretensions, but they did set a pattern in ideological terms that the Qing state continued to adhere to up to its collapse in the twentieth century. This pervasiveness of the state was closely linked to dreams of expansion. Qianlong believed that Qing rule was in form universal, in the sense that its principles should be applied by all peoples who were culturally advanced enough to appreciate and use them. It was this universalism, more than anything else, that in the late eighteenth century drove the empire to engage in costly military expeditions at its frontiers. These excursions would, by the early nineteenth century, empty the imperial coffers and contribute to a general sense of exhaustion and malaise.

Qing China is often presented by historians, even today, as insular and inward looking. But nobody within their region who came up against Kangxi or Qianlong in real time would have viewed them as looking inward. The Qing were continuously expanding outward. They focused primarily on their land borders, though Kangxi conquered Taiwan in 1683. By 1750, the Qing operated in three distinct spheres of foreign affairs: Central Asia, where the theme was expansion; coastal Asia, where the theme was trade and tribute; and Russia, where the theme was diplomacy. Policy on all of these fronts was coordinated to leave the Qing emperors time to fully impose their rule on China, while exterminating those enemies at the frontiers whom Beijing thought capable of threatening its rule. Having themselves taken China by force, the Qing wanted to prevent any new contenders from doing the same to them.

The dramatic Qing penetration of Central Asia is a story of intense conflict and, eventually, of genocide. In the early eighteenth century, Zungharia was a mighty khanate led by Mongols, covering all the territory between western Central Asia and the Mongolian heartland, down to the Tibetan borders, an area roughly similar to modern India in size. It had been intermittently at war with the Qing for more than seventy years. In the 1750s Qianlong unleashed what he called "the final solution" to the Zunghar problem. After having defeated Zungharia in battle, he ordered his army to kill all of the Zunghar elite whom they could lay their hands on, causing what has been called the eighteenth-century genocide par excellence. Then he incorporated most of eastern Zungharia and the minor khanates to its south into China, creating one region that Qianlong, triumphantly, referred to as China's new frontier (Xinjiang).[9]

Along the Asian coastline, the Qing were equally forceful but less violent. In the south and east, China was surrounded by states that all stood in some form of tributary relationship to the emperor in Beijing. (The only exception was Japan. The Qing regarded it as a tributary state but in reality had no authority over it.) Countries from Korea to Nepal had dynamic affiliations with China based on some form of ritual sub-servience, such as the regular paying of tribute to the emperor.[10] All of these relationships were different in character, though, and there was no overall "tributary system," unlike what some historians have claimed. Instead it makes sense to talk of a Sino-centric system, in which Chinese culture was central to the self-identification of many elite groups in the surrounding Asian countries. China was a constant reference point in their orientation (much like the United States is now for Europeans). But the states that paid tribute were generally good at using the rela-tionship for their own purposes. Very often the suzerainty of the em-peror was invoked by smaller countries to secure trading privileges for themselves, sometimes disguised as tribute, or assistance from China in local power struggles.

Until the arrival of the British and the French in the nineteenth century, Russia was China's only imperial neighbor. But in spite of the Qing determination to respect Russian territory to the north, it was a very unequal relationship. Distance and overall strength did not favor the Russians, so they were careful not to provoke quarrels with the Qing. The treaty of Nerchinsk in 1689 (the twenty-eighth year of the mighty

Kangxi's reign) drew a borderline more or less straight east from where the northern Mongolian frontier is today. It gave China the whole Amur basin and what is now the Russian maritime province, including the island of Sakhalin. The agreement helped to keep the peace and allowed licensed trade along the borders. It gave the Qing free hand to expand westward in return for renouncing rights to what they considered the frozen wastes of the north. The treaty with Russia was China's first with a European power and was for the Qing a useful introduction to the practice of European diplomacy. They already had decent introductions to the subject from two of Kangxi's top diplomatic advisers, the French Jesuit Jean-François Gerbillon and his Portuguese colleague Tomas Pereira.[11]

Aside from Russia and eastern Asia, in 1750 the rest of the world mattered less to China in security terms than it did in terms of cultural knowledge. Kangxi had received at Court Asian islanders, Indians, Arabs, and Persians and ordered his scholars to expand their knowledge about these foreign domains. For a while some of his favorite companions were European Jesuit priests, such as Gerbillon and Pereira, who could present the latest findings on astronomy, military affairs, architecture, and painting. Kangxi guarded against any proselytizing by them or by Muslims or Buddhists that could undermine the primacy of the Qing state. But while Christian preaching had been prohibited in 1721, after a narrow-minded decree from Pope Clement XI had forbidden Chinese Christians from participating in the state rituals of the Qing, Jesuits stayed in China up to the suppression of the Jesuit order in 1773. Some even stayed on after that, such as Qianlong's European translator Jean Amiot, who died in Beijing in 1793, only six years before the emperor's own death.

By 1750 the Qing dynasty had reached the peak of its position in Asia. It was, as its emperor liked to emphasize, secure against invaders and broadly self-sufficient in terms of agricultural supplies. Its forms of interaction with the rest of the continent were decided in Beijing, and even though its imperial court could not determine the policies of other courts, it often had a decisive influence on them through diplomacy, education, or culture. The Qing capital was recognized as the center of the eastern Asian region, the city to which outsiders were drawn and from which important judgments on thinking, taste, and style emanated. Moreover, its elite was firm in its conviction that the Qing political system was the only rational way of administering the empire, and that it served as a model for how states should be organized not just in Asia but worldwide.

COMPLETED IN 1750, the Gardens of Perfect Brightness (Yuanmingyuan) in northwestern Beijing were the great symbol of Qing power and its universalist urges. Qianlong commissioned the vast pleasure park to demonstrate his esthetic knowledge and the power of his empire. Five times bigger than the Forbidden City (the massive palace complex in central Beijing where the imperial family lived), the park was intended to show everything under heaven, a kind of eighteenth-century World's Fair. In its sprawling collection of palaces and gardens, there were Chinese-style buildings from various dynasties and structures and landscapes from the Chinese hinterlands, Korea, and Southeast Asia. But strangest for Chinese visitors were the buildings at the back of the park, which had been designed by the Milanese painter and architect Giuseppe Castiglione in Italian baroque style. The main edifice, a large building overlooking the central fountain, was called the Hall of Calm Seas. It housed the emperor's collection of European works of art, including the French clocks that particularly fascinated him.

The Yuanmingyuan symbolized the pretensions of the Qing and the centrality of their capital until it was plundered and destroyed by British troops when they invaded Beijing during the Opium Wars in 1860. When I first came to the Chinese capital as a student 120 years later, the ground where it had stood was almost empty, except for a few scattered anti-imperialist billboards at the entrance ("Beat Down All

Imperialists and Their Running Dogs!") and skimpy vegetable plots of poor peasants. For me, it was a good spot for an afternoon's stroll and the ideal place to meet friends and girlfriends, providing shelter from the prying eyes that populated Beijing. But some local people refused to go there because it was ridden with ghosts of a past best forgotten.

The idea for this book came during one of my hikes through the remains of the Gardens of Perfect Brightness in 2006. I had been at Peking University, across from the ruined gardens, lecturing on the relationships between China and the rest of the world. Once started, the book took a considerable while to complete—the amount of reading that had to be done was large and, worse, seemed to double every six months or so, given the interest China stirred in the 2000s. What drove me on was a need to present my students and other readers with a somewhat revisionist take on China's foreign relations—one that stresses cultural transformations and hybrid identities as much as conflicts and nationalisms, and one that gives equal treatment to missionaries and diplomats, businessmen and revolutionaries, workers and bosses. Most conventional histories of Chinese international affairs have, until very recently, centered on relations between states in one form or another. While there is nothing wrong in discussing how governments develop their foreign policies, such presentations do not give us a full picture of how the relationships between the international and the domestic evolve, or how different groups of people interact. They focus much too narrowly on the central functions of the state—administration, communications, war—and thereby build up an image of construction and destruction that does not always coincide with how most people have seen their own interaction with the international or the foreign.

This fixation on the state within Chinese historiography has challenged me to try to tell a story that is not teleological, that does not move from the Qing collapse to the establishment of the People's Republic with the resurrection of the state as the central, necessary aim and outcome. At the same time I also want to explain why (contested) images of the state have been so important to many Chinese for a very long time—it is much easier to complain about the state when you have it than when you do not. But I did not want readers to believe that state weakness and power were the only key lines in the history of China's modern international affairs.

Instead of discussing only diplomacy and wars, in this book I try to take readers on a much deeper journey into China's international past. *Restless Empire* deals with history very much as the lived experience of different groups in society, from top to bottom. When it focuses on the state, as it does during periods when the state was strong, it is in order to give an overview of how Chinese elites saw their own role and that of the outside world. While it has no overall hypotheses of single factors that have driven China's interaction with the world, the book does emphasize the rapidity of change in the modern era and China's unique ability to absorb such change. It also argues for China's capacity to form hybrid or at least eclectic forms of social identities, and its propensity for internalizing worldviews created elsewhere. These points are not drivers of history, but they are helpful indications of where I want to go in order to explain what happened.

A T THE CENTER OF THIS BOOK is the tale of China's metamorphoses in the nineteenth and twentieth centuries. It was a time when people who viewed themselves as Chinese transformed their lives and practices into those of participants in global forms of modernity. Chinese who embraced the new—when given a chance to do so— always far outnumbered those who did not. Chinese traveled, studied, and settled abroad in order to understand and benefit from the new world that was opening to them. In many ways their experience with the international was very similar in timing and significance to that of European peasants (my grandparents, for instance) who entered a new world of capitalist markets. The market was harsh and exhilarating at the same time. It presented opportunities and dangers, attractions and horrors, and it increasingly preoccupied even those who stood apart from it either geographically or ideologically. China's international history over the past 250 years is the story of its encounter with capitalist modernity and of how Chinese shaped that modernity and were shaped by it in roughly equal turns.

Destruction and violence also play important roles in this story. As the history of the Gardens of Perfect Brightness shows, the incursions of Western armies into China in the nineteenth and early twentieth centuries were immensely destructive for those regions that were hit by them.[12] But the real disasters in terms of destruction and violence came from the middle of the twentieth century on, when the Japanese attack on China set off wars and terror that—for the Chinese peasantry, especially—lasted up to the mid-1970s.

For many Chinese, the combination of war and Maoism came as the perfect storm. War confirmed that the outside world hated China. Mao Zedong's Communism confirmed that there was a way to modernity beyond capitalism and foreign influence. The latter could not have thrived without the former. But as things were, China set its course in the bloody 1940s toward what would become the greatest tragedy of its modern history: the mass killings, the terror, and the self-humiliation of the Maoist years, in which twenty million died and countless more lives were wrecked. These were crimes mainly committed by Chinese against other Chinese—so awful that most people in China still prefer not to talk about them—but they were inspired by the ideas of Communist shortcuts to modernity that also wreaked havoc elsewhere in the twentieth century.

When Maoism died with Mao in the 1970s, China began its tortuous road back toward international capitalist modernity that its leaders had tried to circumvent for a generation. Some historians of China say that the work of building a new country today was made easier by Maoist destruction in previous decades: Mao killed off Old China and, unintentionally, left a blank slate on which the laws of market development could be written. I am not so sure. China in the 1970s could have gone in many different directions—from genocidal terrorism of the Cambodian kind to democratic development such as on Taiwan. The potential for market developments was there, not because of the destructiveness of the Chinese Communist Party (CCP), but despite it, since China had experimented with integrated markets for a long time before the Communists attempted to destroy them. These origins are a central part of the story told in this book, not just because of their significance for the present, but also because they created so much of China's journey through the nineteenth and twentieth centuries.

The past shapes the present. Today's China is shaped by its modern metamorphosis, by the transformations wrought by both external and internal pressure. History is therefore the most fundamental background on which to understand present-day Chinese foreign relations. In our own time, some use China's troubled past as an excuse for its authoritarianism or its occasional international power-mongering. That should not be so. China's bloody twentieth century saw Chinese do far more damage to themselves than foreign powers managed to do, and in far more harmful ways for the longer term. China can take this lusterless legacy and turn it in either of two very different directions. It could behave with increasing aggression as its power grows, in the way that many Chinese feel China was treated by others when it was weak. But such outward hostility would most likely be a sign of continued weakness at home, a China that struggles with its past without coming to terms with it, and which is inherently unstable as a result. The other option is a China that seeks cooperation with others based on its own values and lessons of the past. Such a China would likely be stable at home, because it could focus attention on peaceful political change and thereby achieve a more legitimate and more dynamic government. Only time will tell which direction China will go in, but wherever it moves, its history will set the fissures in the terrain that it moves across.

Some Chinese like to see their country's history as cyclical: Over thousands of years China has gone from splendor to decay to regeneration. They believe that we are now at the beginning of a regeneration phase: China will, in the future, become increasingly central and powerful. And they take great pride in the fact that China in so many fields is now steaming toward becoming the world's preeminent power. Whichever way one wants to approach history, there is, though, one fundamental change from the eighteenth century, when our story begins: Nobody today expects the past to return, at least not in the exact form that it once had. It is part of the modern condition to look more to the future than to the past, and so do the Chinese, even those who believe in great cycles of development. China's future relations with the world may in form constitute a return to some of what has gone before, but in content they will undoubtedly be altogether new.

CHAPTER 1

METAMORPHOSIS

IN THE FIRST PART OF THE NINETEENTH CENTURY, China began a series of transformations that would change the country forever. Although some of these changes had domestic roots, most were linked to new contacts with the West. But this evolving relationship was not simply an issue of Western impact and Chinese response. For China, it was a complex period of change, in which new practices were formed out of established Chinese patterns. As the Qing state came under pressure from within and without, the room for families and individuals to engage in forms of activity—trade, studies, religious affairs—that took them abroad or at least introduced them to foreigners or foreign ideas in China increased. The story of China's ninteenth century is therefore not just about imperialism and destruction but also about something new being born, something that is a hybrid of what comes from the inside and from the outside. Some of this hybridity flourished while the Qing empire stumbled from one crisis to the next and came to set the stage for much of what happened later.

The decline in the position of the state in China was crucial to the country's nineteenth-century metamorphosis. The Qing's humiliation in its military encounters with the West was one part of this story, but there were also important historical links with the troubled position of the dynasty after the Qianlong emperor's death in 1799. The Manchus had attempted to control the country and its neighbors in ways that no other rulers had done before, and by the early nineteenth century they were suffering the consequences of imperial overstretch: The coffers were emptying out, the military was tired of engagements abroad, and the population was becoming weary of a police state that was less and less effective. The framework within which the Qing dynasty had to rule was changing, and it would have taken strong emperors and significant modification of policies to overcome the challenge posed by the new conditions. The Western attacks on China, beginning with the Opium War in 1839, meant that the empire had much less time to change than most people would have expected as the century began. Still, the Qing fought for its position both within China and outside; it was no pushover for its domestic enemies or its international rivals, even when these combined against them. As China's political crises unfolded, the dynasty learned much about how it could cling to power and about how it could turn new ideas to its advantage. But the state could no longer control knowledge the way it had done in the eighteenth century. Instead, it had to face a revolution in information and practices that gradually spread throughout the country. This revolution in thought and behavior was the early breakthrough of a new form of Chinese modernity, created in constant interaction with the outside world.

CHINESE WHO ENCOUNTERED FOREIGNERS in the year 1800—the fourth year of the Jiaqing emperor's reign—would in most cases have regarded them as yet another group of Qing dynasty subjects. The empire was vast and contained people of different skin colors, different languages, and different faiths. Although its physical borders were ill-defined, China's political power covered much of Asia from the Korean peninsula to the Tianshan mountains in Central Asia and from Lake Baikal in Siberia to the coasts of Burma. Immediately outside the main circle of imperial control were the tributary states. All of these accepted, in some form or the other, the suzerainty of the Qing emperor, but mostly managed their own affairs themselves. In Korea, the Qing emperor had direct political influence. In faraway Thailand and Nepal, the tribute relationship was more ceremonial, though still adhered to. But Qing power was fraying at the edges. In Vietnam, officially a Chinese tributary state, the Qing had recently lost most of their sway by backing the losing side in a long civil war.

The situation on the southern borders in 1800 was typical of the ups and downs of China's relationship with its neighbors. On the one hand, the empire was generally regarded by Chinese and foreigners alike as the center of the larger region, first and foremost in terms of culture and politics. On the other, a Chinese emperor could easily overreach when throwing his weight around in local contests for power within a tributary state. By the late eighteenth century, the Qing dynasty was already less than successful in some of these expeditions: In the 1760s, Qianlong had tried to intervene in Burma to keep the country within the Chinese zone of influence. The expedition was ineffective and costly—at least 70,000 Chinese soldiers died—and the Burmese kept their independence. A war with a newly unified Vietnam in the 1780s was disastrous (as a similar engagement would be two hundred years later): China lost several thousand men in a badly planned and ultimately futile attempt at influencing the outcome of Vietnam's civil strife. The Vietnamese king soon sought imperial pardon, however, and emphasized his country's desire again to be allowed to pay tribute to the Court in Beijing. But the Qing's loss of prestige was considerable.

Some historians see China's feebleness in tending its regional hegemony in the late eighteenth century as a consequence of domestic weakness. Most of these arguments are unlikely to hold up to historical scrutiny, just as America's loss in Vietnam two hundred years later is difficult to explain as a by-product of internal decline. Qing China would have prevailed in these engagements, if it had not been for political aimlessness and strategic folly. There were indeed difficulties emerging in a domestic context toward 1800, but none of these had any major impact on China's foreign affairs. The main reason for the decline in foreign policy prowess was the feebleness of decision making as the Qianlong emperor had become old and closed-minded, leaving a vacuum at the center of the small group who made foreign policy decisions. As with all authoritarian political systems, Qing China was only as strong as a narrow ruling elite allowed it to be.

Qianlong had ruled for sixty years when he abdicated in 1796, but the old man had no intention of giving up power even then. He only stepped down in order not to insult the memory of his illustrious grandfather, the Kangxi emperor, by ruling longer than he had done. Increasingly feeble, Qianlong remained the source of all authority until he died at eighty-eight, in 1799. All through his life, Qianlong had believed in military solutions to China's many border problems. At first, his campaigns had generally been successful. Claiming (and probably believing) that he was simply acting to secure China's borders, rather than expanding the empire, by the 1750s he had taken control of much of Central Asia and sent his military to oversee the mountain passes into India, forcing Nepal to accept China's suzerainty. Inside the empire, he had brought Tibet and Mongolia, as well as the rich province of Sichuan, more firmly under Beijing's control. But the military expeditions had been costly and had taken their toll on the emperor himself. By the late 1760s Qianlong had lost the genius for deal-making and compromise that in the past had so often made it possible for him to claim great victories. His increasing inflexibility and isolation from the world outside the Qing Court made him a lesser ruler than what he had once been.

Qianlong's son and grandson, the Jiaqing (1796–1820) and Daoguang (1820–1850) emperors, were ineffectual leaders, who had none of the nous of the first Qing emperors. Jiaqing, the fifteenth son of Qianlong, was a very earnest and rather square ruler, in both body and mind, when he finally became the real emperor of China at the age of thirty-nine. He had been his father's third choice for successor (both of his predecessors had died before the end of Qianlong's rule).

Jiaqing spent his first years in power dealing with what he saw as the twin misfortunes of the past reign: official corruption within the regime and religious fanaticism among some of his subjects. His limited success in stamping out graft gave him some popularity, but reduced his personal power. His efforts to contain religious zealotry were less successful, especially his preoccupation with suppressing the White Lotus Society, a Buddhist millenarian sect with much support among poor settlers in central China. The campaign drained the treasury and dragged on for eight years, up to 1804, before his father's generals took charge with their old methods of combining resettlement, protected villages, and the use of local militia to fight insurgents.

In the end, Jiaqing crushed the White Lotus Society. But he was criticized both for having exaggerated its significance to begin with and for ham-fistedness in putting down what, in the end, had begun to look like a large-scale rebellion against Qing rule. The White Lotus upheaval was seen by many as self-inflicted damage by the Qing. While his father had been able to spin his most mindless interventions as victories, Jiaqing could not present even his victories as victories, and his personal prestige deteriorated. In 1803 a mob attacked him in the street, and in 1813 a band of conspirators attempted to storm the Forbidden City. When Jiaqing died suddenly in 1820—struck by lightning, it was said, on his way to one of his summer palaces—one of his advisers remarked that his manner of departure was the most exciting initiative the emperor had ever undertaken.

Jiaqing's rule had diminished the stature of the emperor, and the weakness of the office haunted his son and successor, Daoguang, during his thirty-year reign. Daoguang was a well-meaning but weak-willed man, often ill and given to sudden reversals of policy dependent on the content of the most recent report or recommendation to reach him. As his reign wore on, he increasingly became hostage to powerful factions at Court. His uncles, cousins, consorts, ministers, and palace servants formed strong groups that fought among themselves for power and influence. The emperor himself sought guidance from the practice of his great forebears—his grandfather Qianlong and his great-great grandfather Kangxi especially—and from established ritual and routine. But while the Qing founders had been innovators (though masking their innovations as a return to the great tradition), Daoguang labored helplessly with returning China to a glorious past he did not understand, while observing his empire sliding into disarray and subjugation.

HISTORIANS HAVE DEVELOPED a number of explanations for China's nineteenth-century economic and social difficulties, few of which now seem to hold up to source-based examination. Among them are the effects of excessive population growth, exhaustion of resources, inherent technological backwardness, and a lack of market mechanisms. The problem with all of these views is that they find little support in the evidence that has become available recently. New research shows, for instance, that during the eighteenth century, China's agricultural productivity compared well with any other major part of the world. The rural standard of living in the most productive regions of China (the lower Yangzi river area) was approximately the same as that in the most productive regions in Europe (England) in the same period. In terms of population growth, fertility rates in China seem to have increased in ways comparable to those of European populations, with the economically successful regions becoming the most populous. Although economic growth and population growth put pressure on available resources, the ecological situation in China was not much worse than that in Europe. In some areas it was far better, in part due to efficient and cheap transport. The technology available to farmers and artisans was advanced enough to sustain high productivity (in global comparative terms) and a high level of output in agriculture and handicrafts.

By the early nineteenth century, the Chinese economy was stable but not flourishing. It had reached a plateau in productivity that only a technological transformation could transcend. As long as domestic politics remained relatively stable and major war was avoided, a dramatic increase in poverty was unlikely. But so was cataclysmic change of the kind that overtook Europe between 1750 and 1850. There political ferment, interstate wars, cheap and accessible energy, and resources from the Americas combined to favor new technologies over old and begin the expansion of an integrated capitalist market. It was, in other words, Europe—and especially England—that was the exception, not China.

While quite a few of the disasters that befell China in the nineteenth century were economic or social, almost none seem to have originated from built-in weaknesses in the development of the empire. Quite the contrary, they were the products of misrule, foreign invasion, wars, and rebellions. There were two major trends in the domestic economy of nineteenth-century China that need some attention, though, so that we may understand their implications for foreign affairs. One was the relative impoverishment of the periphery as the state disintegrated. The other was the shift in patterns of trade in the rich Chinese coastal areas from the interior of China to abroad, mainly (but not exclusively) to Southeast Asia. Both of these trends were, of course, intimately linked to political events. But they combined to create a China that in the mid and late nineteenth century was much more unequal and much less integrated than it had been a century earlier. The disappearance of state-organized transport disadvantaged regions along the economic frontier from Shandong through North China and the middle Yangzi to the great rivers in the south, where Chinese had been moving in large numbers in the eighteenth century to extract raw materials for the economic center. Meanwhile, the increase in foreign trade outcompeted some of these areas; rice from Southeast Asia, for instance, replaced rice from Hunan in feeding the growing cities along the coast and on the Yangzi river.

The overall economic pattern in nineteenth-century China was what economists call uneven growth. Some parts of the economy grew quite rapidly, while others stagnated or even disappeared. Geography became destiny as the rich coastal zones tended to get richer, even when they were temporarily held back by the effects of war, while poor areas and the periphery tended to get poorer, at least relatively speaking, and were especially vulnerable to armed conflict and the social dislocation that followed.

Uneven growth was a major factor in development of the Chinese economy during the nineteenth century, but more crucial still were Western incursions into the country, which divide the century in two halves. The establishment in the 1840s and 1850s of foreign-run capitalist nuclei inside China was key to the country's economic development. While it would take yet another century for foreign products and methods of production to reach the majority of Chinese, and while the country's economy would remain predominantly agricultural almost up to today, the contact with foreign lands and peoples began a profound transformation not just of products, workplaces, and consumption but of the way the Chinese thought about their economy.

This profound change was not just to take place within China; it would happen among Chinese abroad as well. Since the beginning of China's history, its people have been leaving in search of trade, adventure, or a better life for themselves and their families. Just as with people elsewhere, a mixture of human curiosity and the search for gain have driven some to take extraordinary risks in exploring and settling unknown countries. For the Chinese, the first major wave of emigration began in the late fifteenth century, as trade with Southeast Asia expanded. The original Chinese settlements in Vietnam, Cambodia, the Philippines, Java, Malaya, and Thailand were all commercial and followed the trade routes that linked China with the countries to its south. In spite of the Chinese state's various attempts at discouraging both foreign trade and emigration—attempts at unofficial travel abroad was punishable with beheading during the early Qing dynasty—there were enough of both push and pull factors to make people want to go abroad in increasing numbers. After the Qing relaxed travel restrictions in the mid-eighteenth century, a second wave of emigration created large Chinese towns all over Southeast Asia.

During the hundred years that followed, up to the mid-nineteenth century, at least a million people left southern China and attempted to settle in areas outside the immediate reach of the empire. This number is not large compared to the massive outward emigration of Europeans, but it had significant effects both for China and for the recipient countries. In most cases the new emigrants went to places that already had small Chinese populations and often—as in the case of emigrants elsewhere—they tried to find kinsmen from their home region, village, or clan. In some regions of Thailand and Java, new immigrants outnumbered the local people. While intermarriage with locals started almost immediately, many Chinese families have kept their distinctly Chinese identity up to our own time. They have formed strong social and trade networks, linking their home regions in China with the areas where they settled.

Patterns of emigration changed after 1850, as the Qing state became increasingly weak. Because of new contacts with foreigners and the disappearance of emigration control, Chinese began leaving for new regions and for new purposes. In addition to the large numbers leaving for Southeast Asia, the new destinations between 1850 and 1875 included Hawaii, the United States, and Canada (seventeen percent of all Chinese emigrants combined), Cuba (eleven percent), and Peru (nine percent). Those who left were often contracted to foreign companies and went to work in plantation agriculture or mining. In most cases it was a tougher life than earlier emigrants had experienced. But then life at home was tougher still, making for large numbers of people who were willing to take the risk of moving, at least temporarily, to foreign parts.

Throughout the eighteenth and nineteenth centuries, most of China's emigrants came from the south, especially the coastal provinces of Guangdong and Fujian. Emigration from these parts created a kind of pendant to the establishment of Western strongholds inside these regions of China, through which people from the coastal areas of the south were doubly linked to the expanding world economy. The emigrants served that economy at home, as traders, workers, and consumers. They also manned the new trade routes, using their local knowledge to carve out an often precarious role for themselves among foreign traders and colonists. By the late nineteenth century, all over the eastern parts of Asia and in some parts of the Americas as well, it was Chinese labor and Chinese tradesmen who provided the glue that kept both the local and the trade economies together. These diasporic communities were to play decisive roles in China's foreign affairs and sometimes in China's own history. They established a global China—often frowned upon by Westerners and Chinese alike—and served in key roles as middlemen, transmitting practices and ideas between alien worlds.

C HINESE GOING ABROAD ENTERED into a complex world of competing ethnic and social groups, rival cultures, and chaotic forms of governance, but the situation they left behind in China was also complicated in terms of identifications and representations. We now know that the populations in and around the Chinese core area have defined themselves ethnically in many different ways over the past 5,000 years. The group that today increasingly sees itself as "Han" Chinese, and which the present Chinese government believes includes up to ninety-two percent of the people who live in their country (and almost twenty percent of the global population), originated in the central northern areas of today's China, mostly along the Yellow river, and became the culturally dominant group for a much larger area in the Han Dynasty from around 200 BC. During and after that dynasty its culture spread to other parts of what is currently China, especially the south and the west. Some of this dissemination occurred through conquest, some by assimilation, and some—especially after the breakdown of the Han empire—by involuntary migration from the core areas. The Sinification of south China was to a large degree a product of refugees from the north who fled the collapse of the northern states in the post-Han era. By 1800 this process of cultural and ethnic unification was well advanced (although in some parts of the country it is still continuing today).[1]

For the Qing state, ethnicity was a troublesome issue. The imperial family had its own origins in a non-Chinese population, termed the Manchu, and liked (at least when it served its purposes) to flaunt its "otherness." The cohesion of the inner group within the Qing project to some extent depended on its setting itself apart from the ocean of Chinese over which it ruled. But at the same time the Qing state was an empire, comprised of a myriad of different groups within its realm, and worked out a complicated set of rules for how to deal with each of them. Some of these defined groups were identified according to language and culture, such as the Manchus themselves, Mongols, or Tibetans, or the multifarious populations of the south, such as the Miao (called Hmong in Indochina), Bai, or Dai (Thai). Others were seen through the prism of religion: Muslims who were culturally Chinese, Kazakhs who happened to be Lamaist Buddhists, and the variety of religious practices among groups in Yunnan, Guangxi, Guizhou, or Taiwan. Most Qing emperors struggled bravely to extend their knowledge of all these groups, including their languages and religions, but even the hard-working Qianlong had to admit that he sometimes got his Kazakhs mixed up with his Turks and therefore could not treat them all according to the established protocol of the Qing.

Definitions were not easy. Even the elites among those who were defined as the numerically dominant population—those who possessed Chinese written culture, Confucian social organization, and ancestral links to the Chinese heartland—would in the early nineteenth century have found it difficult to define exactly what a "Chinese" person was. Since China had no concept of nation similar to what was slowly being developed in Europe, terms such as "us" and "our land" referred to one's villages, region, or province and not to the country—to an even greater extent than what was common among peasants further west in Eurasia.

Core Chinese culture was not exclusive. The imperial examinations, the essential prerequisite for serving the empire, remained remarkably open up to the late nineteenth century. The elites of all groups could put their best sons forward, as long as they had embraced Chinese culture and were willing to keep their beliefs and ethnicity to themselves. The empire pretended to be universal and the key to all meaningful civilization. But for most people, as an ancient saying goes, "Heaven is high and the emperor far away": While accepting the legitimacy of the imperial state, their primary identities were local or clan-oriented.

There is no simple answer to the question of what it meant to be Chinese during this period. Most people had multiple identities. Judging from written testimony, it was quite possible to be a little bit Chinese, a larger portion Sichuanese or Cantonese, and a servant of the empire (or its sworn enemy) all within the span of a day. Identities and loyalties were much like the eclectic religion practiced in country temples all over China. There were many deities and many forms of worship, but what was closest to you were your ancestors and your local heroes, symbolizing your land and your ancestral village. And if at the heart of the empire, identities were complex, they were transmuted at its edges. People could be very Chinese one day and much less so the next, depending on what opportunities or protection China gave them.

So, who were foreigners in the Chinese view? The answer depended of course on whom you asked. For most of those who lived in or originated from the Chinese core area, foreigners were people who were not culturally Chinese, even though the definition of "culturally Chinese" was itself highly contested. Lacking a modern nationalism—and living under a dynasty that at times prided itself on its foreignness, a narrow definition of what was *nei* (inside) or *wai* (outside) was not fruitful for people in eighteenth- and nineteenth-century China. Yet the Qing inherited from earlier states a value system that the Chinese often called *Huayiguan*, meaning—in a cultural context—"Chinese superior, others inferior." Over centuries this worldview had influenced the Chinese eye in seeing other peoples and their behavior. As a form of cultural ethnocentrism, it was probably stronger at the time than any similar European phenomenon, not least because it had been shared for half a millennium or more by large parts of the elites of China's immediate neighbors.

During the Ming and Qing dynasties, the Chinese view of foreigners was influenced by two main sources: Chinese travelers who returned from abroad and foreigners who settled in China. From the former came a number of written accounts of foreign lands. In most cases these books were stories retold several times over, and—like volumes published in Europe, especially in the eighteenth century—they often commented as much on China as on the ostensible subject of their investigations. In general they represented the empire as being at the center of three concentric circles. Immediately outside the center were the peoples and countries on the edges of China—those colonized and those influenced by Chinese civilization. The second circle contained those who were outside Chinese culture, but still, at least occasionally, paid tribute to the emperor. The third included those who had no relationship with China and its civilization, unknown peoples of whom only few accounts existed. Perhaps not surprisingly, those farthest away from the core were represented as the most strange and barbaric. Tales of madcap beliefs, sexual perversions, and cannibalism abounded. "Outer barbarians" smelled bad, dressed inappropriately, and were strange in appearance. In some cases these "wild men" were closer to animals than to humans. For such peoples, the Qing state believed in the ancient saying of "leaving them outside, not inviting them in, not governing or educating them, not recognizing their countries."[2]

China's knowledge of the geographical world increased sharply in the eighteenth century. Although Asian geography had been mapped since the twelfth century and a succession of complete European world maps had been available at least since the late sixteenth century, it was during Qianlong's reign that scholars began to incorporate a more accurate sense of where Europe was and what it looked like into their publications. Whereas all imperial cartography up to the mid-1800s understandably centered on the world with which China interacted—the magnificent ten-volume *Huang Qing zhigongtu* (Chart of the Tribute-Bearing People of the Imperial Qing, from 1761) is a good case in point—newer atlases included more information on European countries, some of it quite accurate. In 1794 the geographer Zhuang Tingfu printed a scroll that not only gave an exact account of Europe's geography but discussed the countries there and the relationships between them. A masterful cultural compromise, Zhuang's work puts China at the center of the earth, while praising Western cartography as an instrument in the world-historical process of allowing all peoples to pay homage at the imperial court.[3] As in the West, mapmaking in imperial China was not just about accurate renditions but about centrality, culture, and power.

In the eighteenth and the early nineteenth centuries, images of foreigners in China blended stereotypes of those well-known through Asian land-borders with those of the emerging sea-based periphery. In ways similar to the European encounter with peoples from the outer world, the definitions of what was civilized or barbaric behavior were seen through a prism of judgments already established in dealing with European "others." It is remarkable to see the degree to which traits already assigned to Mongols or Kazakhs reappear in early Chinese descriptions of the Dutch or Swedes. Just as established stereotypes of the Irish often were transferred by English writers to Native Americans or Africans, Chinese stereotypes of the known world were transferred onto the newly emerging one. As China's world was becoming bigger, its ethnographers tried to explain it by recognizable though slightly shopworn habits of mind. When more became known about them, Europeans were established as "wild men" of new kind. They were China's "others"—faraway peoples who were the objects of Chinese "occidentalism," fascinating because they were different, threatening because they were outside the realm of civilization.

OF ALL THE EUROPEAN STATES, China's first regular foreign relations were with Russia. Indeed, it can be argued that China's first foreign relations—in anything approaching the Western sense—with any country were with that other expanding empire moving into East Asia from the north. Already by the early Qing period, hunters and traders claiming some form of allegiance to the Russian Tsar had appeared on China's frontiers. Kangxi was engaged in the massive attempt to control all of eastern Central Asia that his grandson Qianlong would complete. He knew enough about the West and worried enough about Russian power to decide to pacify this new group of barbarians in ways different from those used before.

In 1689, against the advice of many of his counselors, Kangxi entered into the Treaty of Nerchinsk, China's first-ever treaty in any way similar to European treaties between states. In doing so, not only did he recognize a foreign monarch, the Tsar, who was not in an express tribute relationship to himself, but he agreed—at least in principle—to a border demarcation line between the two states along the Amur river. The greatest of the Qing emperors was a practical man: It was crucial that Russia remain neutral while he moved to crush the western Mongols, the Zunghars. In ways similar to today's Shanghai Group—the twenty-first-century Sino-Russian collaboration against Central Asian Muslim "terrorists"—Kangxi and his successors wanted to see Russia get enough, in terms of trade and territory, so that it would be willing to stand aside while the Qing colonized the land from Kashgar to Ulaanbaatar. It turned out to be a remarkably successful grand bargain from the perspective of both empires, though the Zunghars, slaughtered to almost the last man, woman, and child by the 1750s, would have disagreed.

From the late seventeenth to the mid-nineteenth centuries, China and Russia—the two great imperial projects of north and east Asia—managed not only to avoid war but to cooperate, at least to a limited extent. In 1727, they signed the Kiakhta Treaty, which reaffirmed and regularized the stipulations of the earlier agreement: Beijing would accept two hundred Russian merchants into the capital every third year, while also allowing for a flourishing border trade (which by the late eighteenth and early nineteenth century turned increasingly private). The economic importance of this trade was not negligible, especially for Russia. By the end of eighteenth century, ten percent of its foreign trade came and went across the border with China. All the way up to the late nineteenth century, the trade advantage was with the Chinese: The Russians sold fur (sable, tiger, and wolf were highly valued in China), and the Chinese exported manufactured goods: silk and porcelain, later cotton and furniture. The Tsar's general Alexander Suvorov rode against Napoleon under banners made from Chinese silk.[4]

While the Qing, at home, tried to pass its relations with the Russians off as tribute, it was clearly very different from the exchanges China had with any other country. Often in diplomacy, a little bit of make-believe can go a long way: The first Chinese "diplomatic" relations were remarkably stable because both sides read into them what they wanted to see. The Tsar's advisers believed that the Chinese would, over time, ally themselves with the Russians to the detriment of other European powers. The Qing nobles knew that keeping the Russians off their back would allow them to proceed with their colonization of China's Central Asian domains. And although the Chinese side benefited more from the trade, the Russians got products that they valued. The expanding trade did not lead to the kinds of political problems that we shall see later in the case of the Guangzhou trade with the West. Likewise, the Orthodox priests who served in Beijing were there for the small Russian community, not to proselytize among the Chinese. Like the Jesuits a century earlier, they were cultural interpreters, not collectors of souls. As a result, relations between the two empires remained remarkably nonconfrontational, until the Qing in the mid-nineteenth century—already wounded by its internal wars and its wars against Britain—became a tempting victim for a new round of Russian imperialism.

CHINA HAD BEEN A TRADING EMPIRE for a very long time by 1800, although—given its size—it was only natural that most of the trade took place inside its borders or with its immediate neighbors. Distances were vast and communications slow and cumbersome, but land and water transport compared favorably with that in the West. While the state controlled and regulated all forms of trade and provided supplies to the population in cases of emergencies or natural disasters, various forms of private or semiprivate trade were spreading throughout the empire, aided by tax incentives, or rather tax neglect. The Court's attitude to the merchant trade was snobbish, and so it neglected to impose comprehensive commercial taxation. As markets expanded in almost all parts of the country, so did private banking institutions and sophisticated brokerage practices.

Even in the field of foreign trade, in the early nineteenth century the Qing were ceding control to private interests. Part of the reason why China's hold on its region had been manifested through physical tribute was that this practice allowed rulers to show their magnificence through the display of foreign luxury goods. The emperors publicly proclaimed that China was entirely self-sufficient, but they loved having their portraits painted wearing furs from Siberia or holding a musical instrument from Southeast Asia.

In reality the Qing from the mid-eighteenth century gradually opened up for an extensive foreign trade, roughly divided into three zones. The first was based on the tribute relationships: Commerce in Thailand, for instance, grew along the routes originally developed for bringing presents to the emperor by sea through the Guangdong ports. After the Qing in the 1720s rescinded the prohibition on Chinese engaging in seaborne foreign trade, most of the shipping engaged was from Guangdong and Fujian, or from Chinese communities in Southeast Asia. By the early nineteenth century, the whole concept of tribute was mixed in with trade in a very pragmatic manner. The Thai kings, who attempted to run a monopoly on foreign trade, benefited from selling Chinese imports such as silk, tea, and copper. Chinese merchants prospered by reselling imported Thai dried goods and rice.

The two other zones of trade involved dealing with European powers. The Kiakhta system opened up and regulated trade with Russia along a border that from the late seventeenth century stayed remarkably stable. The third zone was more troubled: By the mid-eighteenth century the emperor tried to organize the seaborne trade by European merchants in a flexible system that borrowed elements of both the Russian trade and that with tributary states. The Canton system, as this routine was called, was based on setting up the port of Guangzhou (Canton) as the only harbor open to trade with Western ships. The foreigners, of whom most belonged to the British East India Company (EIC), could only come during the October to March trading season, get a Chinese permit when passing through Portuguese-held Macao, and then anchor at Huangpu just south of Guangzhou city. There they could establish contact with licensed Chinese merchants. On the Chinese side, the trade was organized by a superintendent of maritime customs for Guangdong province, appointed directly by the emperor. He licensed local merchants and collected duties and fees from them before each foreign ship was allowed to leave: The Chinese merchants, in other words, were responsible for the conduct of each ship with which they were trading.

By the late eighteenth century, the Guangzhou trade had begun to grow significantly, fueled to a great extent by the increasing British fondness for Chinese tea. As the EIC colonized India for Britain, a British-organized Asian trade began to integrate parts of South China with the emerging world market: Products from South Asia, such as cotton, were imported through Guangzhou, while British ships brought tea, porcelain, and silk back to Europe. The Chinese merchants and middlemen involved grew rich, and, more importantly, were able to set up their own trade links, which extended from the Pearl river delta upland, along the coast, and into the great rivers, as well as to parts of Southeast Asia where they had links already. As the modern world came into being, some Chinese were already finding their place in it. And the Qing, in spite of their mercantilist approach to foreign trade, found the taxes and duties earned through the Guangzhou system far too enticing to crack down on it, as long as the empire's sovereignty was not threatened.

As he lay dying, Qianlong lamented his failure to find the kind of balanced foreign relations he had sought since his early days in power. He had inherited a system in which rituals and institutions were well laid out, and which was reasonably well equipped to deal with China's mid-eighteenth-century world. But by the end of his reign, the old emperor saw that the world was changing, and in dealing with these changes Qianlong and his successors were drawn in two different directions. One was to take refuge in the established practices of the Qing when handling outsiders; another was to open up for new forms of interaction. On practical trade China chose change, though a change that was intended to be slow and measured. On diplomacy it moved back and forth between, at times, finding new forms within the ideological framework set and, at others, upholding supremacy, arrogance, and intransigence of the sort well-known to past and present imperial enterprises elsewhere.

B Y THE BEGINNING OF THE NINETEENTH CENTURY, China was running out of time to make changes in its approach to the world. In 1793, just at the outset of the wars that would engulf Europe over the next twenty years, the British government had sent its first formal representative to China to ask for trade and diplomatic relations. George Macartney was an Irishman who had been ennobled by the British after serving in the Caribbean and India (he was later governor in South Africa), and he and his adjutants were admitted to the imperial summer residence in Rehe on the assumption that they were there to present tribute on the occasion of the emperor's eightieth birthday. Qianlong and his advisers were curious about the newcomers and allowed them to circumvent regular Court ritual and be admitted to an audience with the emperor himself. But the mission misfired badly when Lord Macartney tried to impress the Court by showing off his astronomical instruments—impudent, thought the Chinese. It turned toward disaster when the British tried to obtain further concessions on ritual, including an unprecedented second meeting with the emperor himself. This was all before the delegation had got to the point of presenting their proposals to the Chinese. When Maccartney asked Qing officials for a general reduction in trade restrictions as well as a permanent British presence both in Beijing and at a depot along the coast, Qianlong's patience had run out. The group was returned home empty-handed.

The Macartney mission was a portent of things to come. In 1816, when the Napoleonic Wars were over, the British envoys returned. A new embassy headed by Lord Amherst in 1816 was even more of a fiasco than the previous one, but led to some concern among the advisers of the Jiaqing emperor about Britain's intentions in South China. They worried about unfettered commerce involving foreigners spreading from the coast to the interior. They also worried about foreign missionaries coming to China in increasing numbers. By the time of the Jiaqing emperor's death in 1820, they had become concerned about possible British attacks along the coast. One reason for the immediate concern with security was that the British-American War of 1812 had spilled over to Chinese waters with the British boarding US vessels off the Chinese coast. The emperor observed that "when two small countries have petty quarrels overseas, the Celestial Empire is not concerned with them." But if they brought their wars to China, "then not only shall we destroy their warships, but we shall also suspend their trade."[5]

In spite of increased concerns about the links between foreign trade and foreign power in the early nineteenth century, China wanted to keep some form of trading system in place. It was simply too profitable to give up on. In 1818 the Jiaqing emperor had decreed that "to the barbarians who obey our regulations, we offer kindness; to those who violate our regulations, we demonstrate our power. . . . We should not venture to start a war. [But] nor should we show cowardice which will encourage them to act lawlessly."[6] Those who advised his successor, Daoguang, followed the same strategy. But while commerce increased in the 1820s and 1830s, the Chinese state did not develop a foreign service to deal with the new circumstances, and the old institutions, the *Huitong siyiguan* or Common Residence for Tributary Envoys, superintended by a Board of Rites senior secretary, and the *Lifanyuan* or Court of Colonial Affairs, a special agency under the Grand Council, were not up to the task. As the Court most needed it, access to accurate intelligence on foreign powers became worse, if anything, because of the constant factional struggles during the Daoguang reign. At the same time, taking a tough line on all things foreign became a way of gaining influence with a narrow-minded emperor, especially since many advisers were increasingly concerned with certain products the foreigners were importing into China.

Opium was a primary concern to Daoguang and his advisers. Different forms of narcotic drugs had been consumed in China, as elsewhere, from time immemorial, and from the early Ming period opium, mainly arriving from Southeast Asia as trade or tribute, had become the drug of choice for much of the elite as a calmative or a painkiller. As use of the drug grew in the early nineteenth century—probably resulting from a combination of availability, fashion, and affluence—the authorities became increasingly concerned with its effects. Officials charged that drug users became lazy and effeminate and claimed that the spread of opium was a threat to the well-being of the state. The Jiaqing emperor complained in 1813 that "before only city rascals had opium and smoked it in private. But today, attendants, guards and officials, they all take it. This is truly sickening."[7]

By the latter half of the 1810s, Beijing began looking for more effective methods for upholding the emperor's 1796 total ban on opium import.[8] But the imperial administration's new concerns about the effects of opium came just as smuggling of the drug was becoming central to the British East India Company's China strategy. After almost two generations of a negative trade balance with China, the company had finally chanced upon a product that was not only popular there but also widely available from British India. For Britain, the China trade had suddenly turned both profitable and important in size. India had been a colonial enterprise whose cost-effectiveness many in Britain doubted, but now it began generating income through a government monopoly on opium production. Meanwhile, private investors profited from selling the drug in China, especially after the EIC's monopoly on trade was abolished in 1833. In the 1820s, the import of opium more than tripled. Beijing noted that large amounts of silver were flowing out of China as payment for opium and feared that inflation and state impoverishment would result.

Daoguang, who had taken over in 1820 after his father had been electrically discharged, believed strongly in opium prohibition, possibly because he had experimented with it and other drugs during his younger years. By his second decade in power, his war on drugs was becoming central to the emperor's rather indeterminate policies against decay, corruption, and disloyalty. While a few of his advisers proposed legalization—declare victory in the struggle against drugs and then tax importers, producers, and consumers—the emperor and the majority at Court would have nothing of it. They were afraid that opium import was part of a foreign plan to weaken China and dominate it. Like Christianity, drugs helped move people's attention from where it properly belonged: on service to the Qing state and loyalty to the emperor and his representatives.

After years of hesitation on the opium question, Daoguang decided to strike at the point of entry. In 1838 he sent an imperial commissioner to Guangzhou with vague orders to eliminate opium smuggling. But in the man they chose the Court may have got more than they bargained for: Lin Zexu, the former governor-general of Hunan and Hubei and one of China's top officials, had worried deeply about the impact of opium in the territories he had administered. When he arrived at Guangzhou in March 1839, Lin immediately began rolling up the domestic part of the operation by arresting 1,700 known Chinese opium smugglers. He then attempted to get the foreigners, mostly British and Americans, to trade their vast stores of drugs for tea at a fixed price. When they refused, Lin moved his troops into the Western enclave, confiscated all the opium he could find, and destroyed it outside the city walls. More than 1,200 tons were mixed with lime and salt and thrown into the Pearl river. Lin also demanded that foreigners who had injured or killed Chinese police during the upheaval be handed over and that all foreigners sign a promise never to smuggle opium again. The British authorities refused and ordered all foreign merchants to leave Guangzhou. They hoped that an embargo would hurt the Chinese more than it would hurt their own empire.

Lin was in no mood to cave in to an embargo, and neither was the Court in Beijing. The commissioner tried to appeal to reason by sending a letter to Queen Victoria. "Suppose the subject of another country were to come to England to trade," Lin wrote. "He would certainly be required to comply with the laws of England, then how much more does this apply to us of the celestial empire! Now it is a fixed statute of this empire, that any native Chinese who sells opium is punishable with death. . . . Pause and reflect for a moment: if you foreigners did not bring the opium hither, where should our Chinese people get it to resell?"[9] The British responded by changing the subject. For them, the conflict could not be presented as centering on the undignified subject of drug smuggling. It was, as the British Foreign Secretary Lord Palmerston put it, about the country's honor, trade access, and, ultimately, which empire's rules should reign supreme.

The Sino-British war, often called the Opium War, broke out in March 1839, not because of Chinese attacks on foreign shipping, but because the Qing authorities attempted to protect vessels from abroad that were willing to break the British embargo. When Commissioner Lin evicted merchants who obeyed the embargo from Guangzhou, they found refuge in the Portuguese-held port of Macao at the mouth of the Pearl river. But the authorities there dared not shelter them for long, and most of the merchants and their families ended up on the nearby island of Xianggang, which the foreigners called Hong Kong. The merchants were furious about what seemed to be a financially disastrous strategy by the British government and demanded that strict measures be taken against those who continued to trade with the Chinese. In November 1839 British warships attempted to stop one of their own barks called *The Royal Saxon* (no less), which was carrying rice from Java to Guangzhou on the first leg of its return journey after taking convicts to Australia. The Chinese navy moved in to protect the ship and the British opened fire, sinking four Chinese vessels. It was the grim beginning of a conflict that was to change China's foreign affairs forever.

Neither China nor Britain wanted full-scale war. But London was convinced it needed to protect British principles and interests, and Beijing was certain that Britain had to be contained. The British government, under attack from the opposition in the House of Commons, needed to come up with a response that supported free trade and protected commerce without being seen as a direct supporter of the opium business. Palmerston made military enforcement of the embargo the centerpiece of his policy. He and his colleagues were convinced that Britain was now a global power strong enough to impose progress on backward peoples. With naval bases in Aden, Singapore, India, and Sri Lanka, the British could send their warships into East Asia and have them supplied and re-equipped on the way. While uncertain about the prospects of engaging the imperial armies on land, Palmerston had no doubt about the superiority of the British fleet, even when fighting far away and without support on shore.

The negotiations that went on intermittently in early 1840 proved to be a dialogue of the deaf. When they failed, the British in the summer laid siege to Guangzhou and occupied key cities in the coastal provinces of Fujian and Zhejiang, heading north. Within twelve months, the foreign ships controlled the mouth of the Yangzi river and the southern entrance to the Grand Canal, as well as several small towns in the delta, among them what was to become Shanghai. Fighting in central China grew fiercer as Emperor Daoguang, fearing for the safety of his capital, threw in the Qing's best Manchu troops. But they could not prevent the British from using their fleet to take control of the economic lifelines at the core of the empire, while the chaos in the south increased by the day. In 1842 the emperor sued for peace, mostly out of dread for the domestic consequences of further war, including his dynasty's own survival.

The Qing empire lost a war for the first time because of its opponent's superior naval firepower, maneuverability, and organization. Chinese troops could hold their own in some engagements on land, in part because of their numerical superiority. But shallow-draught British iron steamers like the *Nemesis*, with accurate artillery, crushed all resistance on sea and on shore. The main Qing troops fought bravely and, mostly, with great discipline. Local forces, however, were less inclined to fight for a regime they felt was in trouble.[10] The technological superiority of the British fleet was obvious. And it was a form of warfare the Chinese had never seen before. But in spite of their obvious fighting abilities, most Qing observers thought of the British ships more as pirate vessels or, as we might say today, terrorists, than as an alternative to imperial rule. They were powerful, the Court believed, but unlikely to stay for long.

At least in the short run, Daoguang's Court was right about the future of the British fleet in Chinese waters. Britain had never intended to conquer large parts of China, and the Whig government in London was happy to accept peace as soon as Beijing had backed down on the principles that had precipitated the war in the first place. Britain and China signed the Treaty of Nanjing in August 1842. According to its

terms, the Qing accepted opening Guangzhou and four other ports
north to Shanghai for direct trade between foreigners and Chinese. The
island of Hong Kong was ceded to Britain in perpetuity, and China
agreed to pay 21 million silver dollars in reparations to the British merchants who had been driven out of Guangzhou. A treaty signed the following year gave Britain full extraterritoriality—that is, full exemption
from local laws—for all its subjects in China.

These treaties with Britain presented the Qing with a chance to re-
group and rethink its approach both to imperial defense and to its own
population. Many officials in the north and in the capital, who had not
yet witnessed British warfare, preferred to close their eyes to the implications of what had happened. That was a luxury unavailable to people
in the south, whether they supported the Qing or its increasing number
of enemies.

EIGHTEEN FORTY-TWO WAS NOT ONLY THE FIRST TIME in 200 years
that a Chinese regime had lost a war, it was also the first time for
more than 150 years that south China had seen major warfare. Among
a population that was socially and ethnically mixed, and where a residue
of resistance to Qing legitimacy remained, trouble soon broke out. Parts
of south China, particularly the edges of Guangdong province and
Guangxi, had something of a frontier feel to them—a rough-and-tumble
society with many groups and lots of conflict, rivalries, and resentments.
The emperor had always been far away. Now, in the wake of the Opium
War, he was not only distant but defeated. And stories, images, and rumors about the overwhelming might of the foreigners and the flaws of
the empire abounded.

The changing attitudes among people in south China were to have
a particular impact on the fate of the empire. But the first Qing defeat
had consequences all over the country. Officials and intellectuals began
questioning their belief in the Qing as authoritative and awe-inspiring.
From the very first moment when it became clear to those in the know

that the empire was losing the war against the foreigners—in spite of Beijing's very sophisticated and continuous public relations campaign to deny any losses at all—many Chinese took a step away from the Qing project. When losing, the Manchus were suddenly remembered to be a people apart who had usurped the Chinese throne. In many parts of the country, stories spread about how ordinary people had resisted the British, while the Manchus had fled (which is about the exact opposite of what foreign sources tell us happened). As they went from one loss to another during the war, the Manchus became the scapegoats for the decline of the empire they had put together, while many Chinese suddenly discovered that they disagreed with most things the Qing had ever attempted to do.

After the 1842 defeat, Chinese cities had to deal with an increasing foreign presence. Some members of the elite who came into contact with Westerners believed that their sheer presence was shameful and humiliating. Lin Changyi, a Fuzhou scholar and official—and a clansman of Commissioner Lin of Opium War fame—found himself living across from the British representatives in his home town in the late 1840s. He wrote in his diary:

> There is a pavilion to the northeast of my study. It faces the Jicui Temple on the Back Rock Hill which is now the hiding place of a flock of hungry eagles. They have built their nests and reside in them since. Whenever I rest my eyes upon the spot, the sight of it disgusts and embitters me. My first impulse is to snatch my strong-bow, and shoot a deadly arrow at them. But, alas. My dart will not be fatal, and I relinquish my purpose in despair. To console myself I have sketched a painting to which I have given the name *Shoot the Eagles and Chase the Wolves*. Hence I named my study the Pavilion of Eagle Shooting.[11]

The display of British power along the Chinese coast gave rise not only to a will to resist. It also created a sudden blossoming of interest in the West. Drawing on firsthand information from participants on both sides in the war, a number of Chinese publications from the 1840s dealt with Europe more deeply than ever before. In 1844, Wei Yuan, who had worked closely with Commissioner Lin Zexu in Guangzhou, published some of Lin's materials on the foreigners in the book *Illustrated Treatise on the Maritime Kingdoms.* (Lin himself had little use for them in the Xinjiang exile into which the Qing sent him after 1842 as punishment for his supposed failures in getting the war started.) Wei also became one of the first Chinese to urge the empire to equip itself with modern Western military technology to defend its coast. In the 1850s, the first translations of scientific texts began to appear, mostly in Shanghai and Hong Kong, often published by missionaries and their collaborators.

While the impact of missionaries on China's relations with and knowledge of the West had always been great, the number of Christian converts had been small. As the Qing perceived a rising threat from foreigners in the early 1800s, it attempted to crack down on missionary activities. But their efforts were largely in vain. The Protestant religious awakenings in Britain and the United States in the 1820s and 1830s, combined with the increase in trade, meant that many Christian missionaries were able to operate on the edges of the empire. The first complete Bible in Chinese was published in British India in 1822, and other versions appeared over the next thirty years. While the number of converts remained tiny, even after missionary activities expanded in the wake of the Opium War, it was large enough to irritate Chinese officials. With some reason one mandarin remarked that "most of these ignorant and deluded people attend these chapels out of necessity. They were driven to it by poverty and the need to relieve their distress."[12]

THE REAL THREAT TO THE ESTABLISHED ORDER, however, was not to come from missionary chapels, but from new and militant forms of religion born within China itself. Among the jetsam of the great turning of the tide in South China was a young man called Hong Xiuquan. Hong was born in 1814 in a village north of Guangzhou, nowadays close to the perimeter of the city's gleaming new international airport. But even in the early 1800s, Hong's birthplace was in touch with the outer world: It was emigrant country, with a population divided between Cantonese speakers and Hakkas, and already linked to international trade through the great port that it bordered.

Hong was a bright young man, the pride of his clan. He was sent to the city to sit for the first-degree Qing civil service examination in 1836, bringing with him his family's hopes for social betterment. Hong failed his exam and, the next year, went back and failed again. Returning to his village, heartbroken, Hong became ill, and, in between fits of what we would probably call psychotic depression, he read a set of tracts he had received from an American Protestant missionary in Guangzhou, a potted version of Christianity emphasizing God's call to man and religion as a moral endeavor. Over the next five years Hong reinvented himself to his Hakka neighbors as a religious guide, at least in his own eyes. In his village, he was mostly seen as an embarrassment to his clan. In 1843, with the local area in disarray after China's defeat in the Opium War, Hong Xiuquan announced that he was the son of God and the younger brother of Jesus Christ. He set out on a long march to Guangxi to win adherents for his heavenly father. Like so many founders of millenarian sects over the past two thousand years, Hong was an unbalanced man in unbalanced times; he and his gospel attracted the poor, the dispossessed, and the fearful, and made of them a formidable army that any earthly power would have found hard to put down.

Qing authorities tried to arrest Hong several times, but were driven away by his adherents. By 1850, he had turned the tables on those who persecuted him and his followers. Having mobilized 20,000 men and women as soldiers of God, he began laying siege to cities in south central China. The following year he announced the formation of a Christian state in China that he called Taiping Tianguo, the Heavenly Kingdom of Great Peace. Its twin goals were to drive the Manchus from power and establish Hong Xiuquan and his elder brother Jesus as the sources of all authority. The result was a thirteen-year war that killed at least twenty million people and laid waste to large parts of south, central, and eastern China.

Hong's message was based on a revisionist version of the Bible in which he himself played a primary role. The Manchus were devils who had to be driven away or killed. The Chinese had to reorganize their society based on their own traditions understood in light of Hong's Bible. The Taiping rebels believed that great peace would be established when the Heavenly Kingdom joined its foreign brethren overseas to form a universal Christian state. This was a message that won them many adherents in troubled times, not so much because of its religious content as because of its promise to set wrongs right. But the social aspect of their preaching also alienated most local elites, who by the late 1850s began to join the Qing to defeat the Heavenly Kingdom.

For most Westerners in China, Hong was a troublemaker as well as a blasphemer.[13] His Taiping movement prevented the expansion of trade that foreigners had been looking forward to, and most foreign countries and companies were happy to assist the imperial armies against him, at least for a good fee. In east China, the Qing were much aided by a mercenary army led, first, by the American Frederick Townsend Ward and then by the British Charles Gordon (who later lost his head to the Mahdi's army in Sudan). For the European governments—and for Britain especially—a weak Qing empire tied into international trade through accepted treaties was much preferable to a ferocious and fervent cult, albeit one underpinned by the Christian Bible.

As Hong's visions became more extreme and minor prophets of the Taiping began to fight among themselves, local elites in central China were finally able to mobilize enough support to destroy the movement in 1864. Other rebel groups that had risen in the wake of the Qing rout by Britain were also gradually defeated in the 1860s and early 1870s.

At tremendous cost to the empire, the Nian in east central China, Muslim rebels in Yunnan and Xinjiang, and local insurgents all over south China were gradually overpowered or forced into mountain areas or wildernesses, where some of them would survive to fight another day under other banners.

The people who had led these rebel movements had often been inspired by a mixture of Chinese and foreign ideas. They were "new" men, of a kind that the empire had not seen before. But if the rebels were a new breed, so were those who defeated them, men like the Hunanese general Zeng Guofan and his protégé, Li Hongzhang. First and foremost, they had battled the rebels not on behalf of the Qing but in order save their home provinces and thereby save China. They wanted to re-create China's greatness by learning from the West, while keeping a Chinese state and society in line with their traditions.

THE EXTENSION OF WESTERN-LED TRADE into China in the early nineteenth century led to a clash between the Chinese and the British empire that seriously weakened the Qing state. While some Chinese benefited from this waning of central power, others suffered as vital services disappeared. But at the same time as the Qing's troubles multiplied, a metamorphosis in economic and social relations within China was beginning. Carried out mostly from below, it originated from the strength and vitality of Chinese society coming out of the eighteenth century and the effects of the Western incursions in the nineteenth. These processes of change would have seemed far less painful if it had not been for the cataclysmic wars of the time. It was the wars and the misery that followed in their wake that split Chinese society open and made it more vulnerable to economic exploitation and social devastation.

In the first part of the nineteenth century, much of China's foreign relations and a reasonable amount of China's internal politics were ripe for change. In Europe and North America, a transformation in science and technology had helped create mighty military forces, which—in terms of power—favored the West over all other societies. In the early decades of the century, the Europeans had spent almost a generation tearing their own continent apart in the wars that followed the French Revolution. When these wars were over, China and Japan were at the top of the list of countries the leading Western states wanted opened to trade. There is also little doubt that both in China and Japan some sections of society were very well equipped to link into the trading networks that Western companies were setting up in the Indian Ocean and in the western Pacific. In China—and especially in the south—there were small groups of people who knew much about the changes that were taking place elsewhere in Asia and who wanted to profit from them.

The fact that the Qing could overcome the Taiping and other rebellions of the mid-nineteenth century is of central significance for understanding China's international affairs in the decades that followed. The Qing project showed that it had a good deal of life left. To many Chinese, the empire represented stability and certainty, even if they disliked the Manchus. The mix of "self-strengthening" (meaning mostly Westernization) and appeals to tradition and "Chineseness" that the Qing came up with after the defeat of the rebellions against them appealed to many, not least because several of the new initiatives were led by non-Manchu military heroes. And even in retreat the Qing were still more feared by the general population than rebels and foreigners combined; their immense brutality when threatened had been seen over and over again in China for more than 200 years.

D URING THE PERIOD OF THE QING'S maximum weakness in 1856, as Taiping troops were advancing north, the Western powers chose to continue their wars against China in order to force further trade concessions. When the Qing Court resisted, British and French troops landed at ports in the north and moved toward Beijing. Initially beaten back, the attacks were reinforced in 1860. At the western edges of Beijing, in a place called Baliqiao (Eight Mile Bridge), the Qing's Mongol cavalry made its last stand. It was destroyed by French artillery, which it confronted head-on. The Qing army may have lost 5,000 men, but there were considerable losses on the Western side too. Prisoners on both sides were killed, as were a large number of Chinese civilians who happened to get in the way of the Western advance.[14]

After occupying Beijing, the British and French generals decided to burn Yuanmingyuan, the Gardens of Eternal Brightness that the Qianlong emperor had built at the height of the Qing empire. The hundreds of palace buildings—art pavilions, pagodas, temples, and libraries—burned for several days, while soldiers and officers tried to get away with as much plunder as they could. A French soldier wrote: "I was dumbfounded, stunned, bewildered by what I had seen, and suddenly Thousand and One Nights seem perfectly believable to me. I have walked for more than two days over more than 30 million worth of silks, jewels, porcelain, bronzes, sculptures, [and] treasures! I do not think we have seen anything like it since the sack of Rome by the barbarians."[15]

CHAPTER 2

IMPERIALISMS

FOR THREE GENERATIONS FOLLOWING the Qing's defeat by Britain in the war of 1839–1842, imperialism and incursions by other states defined the framework for China's relations with the rest of the world. For some Chinese, the economic and social orders created by the overseas presence offered new opportunities for trade, travel, and social advancement. As we shall see, many of the networks—commercial and otherwise—that operated within the Western imperial structures were Chinese in origin and in operation. For the Confucian elite, however, the reach of foreign empires into East Asia was reason for despair. Westerners' contempt for Chinese tradition and their attacks on the Chinese state were appalling and humiliating. While it took another hundred years or so—right up to the end of the twentieth century—for values, products, and forms of exchange created by the encounter with the West to penetrate rural China, the stage was set for a transformation in ideas and politics that the country had not seen since the Buddhist revolution of the sixth century and the Qing revolution of the seventeenth respectively. And the first act within the new drama was the confrontation between the Qing empire and its imperial opponents, now established within the heart of Chinese territory.

The outcome of the confrontation between China and foreign empires was in no way a given in the mid-nineteenth century. There is reason to believe that if it had not been for the internal challenges that the

53

empire faced, it could have held its own for a longer time against its foreign challengers. As it were, the great rebellions had reduced the Qing to its lowest point ever, and the foreign empires recognized its weakness. Many Westerners were predicting the immediate collapse of the Chinese state, either through internal rebellions or external pressures. The fate of the Ottoman empire was the parallel often used, meaning the gradual breaking away of smaller parts of the whole until some form of "core only" remained.

But in the 1870s and 1880s, the Qing made a remarkable comeback. It was almost as if the elites within the empire had taken a hard look at their culture and decided to come out in its defense. Their Self-strengthening Movement was based on the idea that Western form—in defense and science, especially—could be combined with Chinese essence, meaning Confucianism. China could use Western weapons and technology to defend itself, but without losing its soul: Chinese culture would remain the unwobbling pivot of the empire. It is hard to say whether self-strengthening saved China from new levels of imperialist onslaughts—it is as likely that Western satisfaction with aims already achieved caused its temporary satiety after the end of the great rebellions. But there is little doubt that the policies developed by Li Hongzhang and other reformers saved the Qing from its domestic enemies and gave it—for a while—a new lease on life. Some proud Manchus called the first part of this era the Tongzhi restoration, for the five-year-old boy who became emperor in 1861. They hoped he could be thought of in the same way that the Japanese did with their emperor Meiji, who oversaw the revolutionary epoch that bears his name.

But the Tongzhi emperor was no Meiji, or, if he was, he did not get much of a chance to show it, since he died at nineteen in 1875. The empire was never to be ruled by an adult emperor again; Tongzhi's successor Guangxu was four years old when he took the throne, and his successor, the Xuangtong emperor—the last emperor, Puyi—was only two. The power behind the throne was increasingly Tongzhi's mother, the empress-dowager Cixi, a staunch conservative of no uncertain views. Like most of the imperial clan, Cixi detested Western influence—the more she knew about the West (and she came to know quite a bit) the less she liked it. Her, and the Court's, preference was for minimizing the impact of foreign learning and methods. Cixi argued that adopting the ways of the West—even in self-defense—would mean surrendering the culture that constituted the very meaning and essence of China. And the result would be certain disaster.

The predicament of the Qing is best understood in light of what was happening elsewhere in Asia in the late nineteenth century. While often following routes and practices established by Asians, Westerners were becoming central to the region's commerce and trade: Their companies and currencies gained predominance. In the Malay world (today's Malaysia and Indonesia), Britain and the Netherlands were expanding their influence, while France was taking over Indochina and the United States was occupying the Philippines. And only a generation after the West had forced it to open its borders to trade and Western influence, Japan became an imperialist power in its own right.

Meanwhile, Britain remained the major foreign power in China. Its control of the key bases and depots for the developing trade—Singapore, Hong Kong, and to a large extent Shanghai—anchored its primacy. But while the British controlled the structure, the Chinese supplied the infrastructure—the depots for East Asian trade were all Chinese cities, run as much by Chinese networks as by British authorities.

While the West inserted itself into China, the Chinese themselves, as travelers and emigrants, began reaching out to the rest of the world. The late nineteenth century saw not just the great encounter between China and the West in terms of war, diplomacy, science, and trade. It was also the decades in which China went global, with a sharp increase in emigration and travel. Increasingly, the world was seen through Chinese eyes in a direct sense, with travelers, sojourners, and emigrants covering the globe, with no area excepted. This Chinese diaspora posed new questions about what it meant to be Chinese, and about the distinctions between "Chinese" and "foreign." Therefore, most of this chapter deals with various forms of fluidity and hybridity, and the creation of new networks, communities, and institutions that would moderate relations between people who defined themselves in various ways and for various purposes somewhere on the scale between Chinese and non-Chinese.

THE GREAT REBELLIONS AGAINST QING rule in the 1850s and 1860s provided opportunities for Western powers to push for further concessions from the Chinese government. But even when the fortunes of the Qing seemed at their lowest, in the late 1850s, their princes were not willing to compromise their sovereignty further, at least not in formal terms. On the contrary, Beijing dragged its feet in implementing the 1842 agreement, which it had been forced to accept. And so, in 1857, the British again began military operations against China. Ostensibly they were retaliation against Chinese forces for having boarded a Hong Kong ship, the *Arrow*, but in reality they were used to extract more and more from a weakened Manchu government. By the end of the year, British forces under Lord Elgin, and French forces under Jean-Baptiste Gros seized Guangzhou against light resistance. The hapless Chinese governor, Ye Mingchen, was captured. Ye—who was to starve himself to death as a British captive in Calcutta two years later—somewhat unfairly became known to the Cantonese as "Six Nots": not negotiate, not defend, and not fight; not die, not surrender, and not flee.

After the allied forces moved north from Guangzhou, the Court in Beijing panicked and sent envoys, who agreed to extend the rights of foreigners in China. These included the right to embassies in Beijing, unrestricted travel for foreigners all over the country, and the opening of the Yangzi river to foreign navigation. The Chinese negotiators also accepted that the country should pay vast reparations. But when the British envoys in 1859 insisted on a military presence in Beijing, the

Chinese equivocated and the war resumed. In part as a result of having mobilized against the Taiping, this time the Qing were better prepared, and the first British attempt at reaching the capital was repelled, with four gunboats destroyed. But in the summer of 1860 nearly 20,000 British and French forces landed in North China. Against stiff resistance from Qing troops—this time mostly Mongols and Manchus—European artillery won the day, and the foreign forces fought their way to Beijing. Once there, they plundered the city and—in a deliberate act of destruction—razed much of the imperial summer palace to the ground. The 1860 looting of the Chinese capital was the greatest act of plunder of the nineteenth century, yielding treasure that still has pride of place in many a Western art museum.

While Britain used its victories over the Qing to solidify its hold on trade with China, Russia was expanding into outer Manchuria and along the Pacific coast. In 1858, at the height of the Taiping crisis and while China was at war with Britain and France, Russia presented its demands to Beijing. It was able to force a border revision that transferred to its control territory the size of France and Italy combined. For the Qing the new Russian expansionism was at least as threatening as that of the British, because it was overland and could potentially encroach on China along the 4,000-mile border from Central Asia to Korea. Thus, when Moscow tried to build up Muslim separatist regimes in Xinjiang in the 1860s, the Qing fought back, putting together what was to be its last major military campaign, culminating in the 1878 destruction of the pro-independence groups and—for the time being—a sharply reduced Russian influence there.

In the south, the Qing were confronted with an expanding French empire, which was laying claim to China's Indochinese tributaries. In 1874 France claimed a controlling influence in all of Vietnam, and—while the Qing was in no position to challenge it—local Chinese rebel movements operating in northern Vietnam soon came into conflict with the French. When Paris took formal possession of the whole country in 1883, Qing forces entered from the north. There followed a some-what confused war, in which French forces landed in Taiwan and on the Fujian coast, where they destroyed most of the newly built Chinese fleet. But given the tensions in European politics, France had to be careful not to be seen as challenging the position of other powers in China, first and foremost Britain. After having driven the Chinese forces out of Vietnam, the French commander attempted to enter Guangxi province, but a Qing counterattack in 1885 sent the invaders fleeing back to Hanoi. The defeat caused a major upheaval in French politics, forcing the resignation of prime minister Jules Ferry's government, and even if the threat of further military action led Beijing to concede control of Indochina to the French, the Tonkin and Xinjiang campaigns told both Chinese and foreigners that even when weakened, the Qing could be a formidable opponent for any enemy.

IT WAS IN HONG KONG that the colonial experience in China was formed. Even though Shanghai from the late nineteenth century became more important both for trade and industry, it was in the great harbor at the mouth of the Pearl river that the pattern for hybrid Chinese-European societies would be set. The city served both as a depot and a refuge. It facilitated British trade all over southern China, while becoming, in terms of its population, a Chinese city, attracting immigrants from all over the country: refugees, dissidents, entrepreneurs, and fortune hunters. After having swallowed up a number of Chinese settlements across the bay in 1860, Hong Kong had a population of more than 120,000, of whom only 3,000 were non-Chinese.

Like all British colonial cities, Hong Kong was basically well-run, but somewhat shoddy at the edges, where corruption and exploitation thrived. It was a city founded on enormous paradoxes and hypocrisies. The foreign missionaries preached virtue to the Chinese while the foreign merchants kept them addicted to opium. The British preached law and order, though they had taken the territory by brute force. The

Chinese came to Hong Kong to take advantage of the opportunities offered them in a city that was not theirs and bore the indignities of being second-class residents in a strict racial hierarchy in order to escape a world that was crumbling around them elsewhere in China. Over time, they built their own organizations, as the Chinese diaspora did elsewhere, even though the Hong Kongers had never left their own country.

The great trading houses stood at the center of foreign commercial activity in Hong Kong. Many of these companies—Jardine, Matheson, Butterfield & Swire, Hutchison—came out of British trade in India after the dissolution of the East India Company in 1834, and established a presence in many treaty ports in China. Still, they were nowhere more influential than in Hong Kong, where they not only ran the economy (and in effect also the politics) but also were the very raison d'être for the colony. From the beginning, these trading houses were international organizations, led by English (or in the case of Jardine's, Scots) businessmen but staffed by Chinese, Indians, Europeans, and Americans. By the late nineteenth century, they were the main mediators between Chinese and foreigners, not only in Hong Kong, but all over China, not least because of their increasing control of the Chinese banking system.

It was not just Hong Kong's economic opportunities that drew Chinese from all over but also its educational ones. To begin with, most of these were linked to the potential for economic gain. As elsewhere within Chinese societies, private schools were funded by families and organizations, but increasingly in the 1850s and 1860s, non-Chinese missions and foreign-run educational societies set up schools, too. Beginning in the 1870s, Hong Kong got a government-sponsored primary education system, which gradually expanded its enrollment among the Chinese. While to begin with, all of these schools emphasized Chinese classics, Bible study, and some English, from the late nineteenth century on they also made room for science. A teacher training college was set up in 1881, a medical school in 1887, and a university in 1910. For many Chinese parents, the relatively easy access to education in the colony became a massive argument in favor of entry into Hong Kong and contribution to its economy.

Hong Kong served as a convenient depot for British expansion in South China. But its economic role was—in the first hundred years of its existence—far inferior to that of the major foreign territorial concessions that were wrested from the Qing empire all over the country after the wars of the late nineteenth century. At the height of the system, just before World War I, there were forty-eight so-called treaty ports, where foreigners had the right to settle, conduct trade, and have extraterritoriality under their own consuls. In the main treaty ports, there were concessions or settlements that were almost entirely under foreign jurisdiction, with their own administrations usually answerable to a consul. This intricate system of exploitation produced micro-versions of informal empires within China. The concessions were almost entirely secured by blackmail: Most Western powers kept gunboats in Chinese waters and rarely hesitated to bombard Chinese cities if their conditions were not met. But some of the concessions became as important (and sometimes more so) for China and the Chinese as for their foreign inhabitants. And while unequal and oppressive in intent, they brought expanding concepts of Western law into China and helped globalize international law by attempting to regulate the multinational presence within the Qing empire.

There is a lot of nonsense about the role of the concessions that has been written both by Chinese and foreigners. Instead of a neat and tidy model created to subjugate China, the so-called treaty port system was an unwieldy, composite, and often unsuccessful response to events as they unfolded in the late nineteenth and early twentieth centuries. Most of the treaty ports and concessions played no role in furthering commerce. Some, such as the Italian concession in Tianjin, were set up for reasons of national pride by European powers that had almost no real

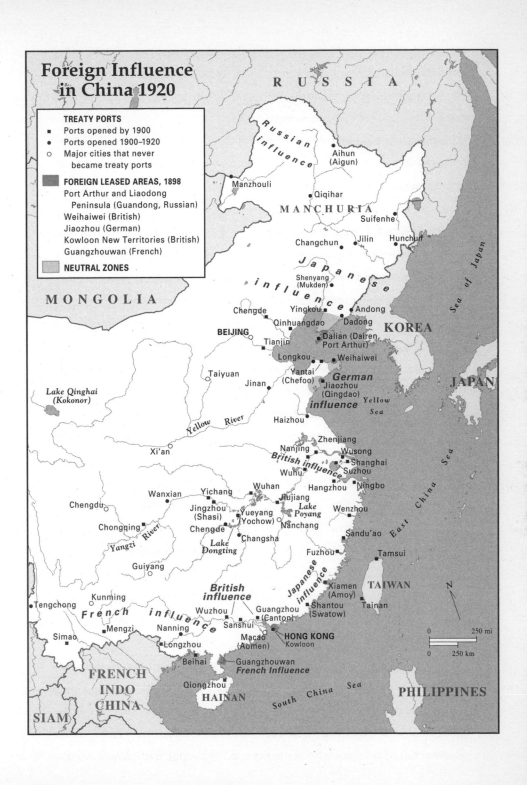

Foreign Influence in China 1920

TREATY PORTS
- ■ Ports opened by 1900
- ● Ports opened 1900–1920
- ○ Major cities that never became treaty ports

FOREIGN LEASED AREAS, 1898
Port Arthur and Liaodong Peninsula (Guandong, Russian)
Weihaiwei (British)
Jiaozhou (German)
Kowloon New Territories (British)
Guangzhouwan (French)

NEUTRAL ZONES

R U S S I A

Russian influence

MONGOLIA

MANCHURIA

Manzhouli

Aihun (Aigun)

Qiqihar

Suifenhe

Changchun   Jilin   Hunchun

Japanese influence

Shenyang (Mukden)

Chengde   Yingkou   Andong   KOREA

Qinhuangdao   Dadong

BEIJING   Tianjin   Dalian (Dairen, Port Arthur)

Longkou   Weihaiwei

Taiyuan   Yantai (Chefoo)

Jinan   *German*

Lake Qinghai (Kokonor)

Jiaozhou (Qingdao)   Yellow Sea

influence

Yellow   River

Haizhou

JAPAN

Xi'an   Zhenjiang

Nanjing   Wusong

British influence   Shanghai

Wuhu   Suzhou

Wanxian   Yichang   Wuhan   Hangzhou   Ningbo

Chengdu   Jiujiang

Jingzhou (Shasi)   Lake Poyang   Wenzhou

Chongqing   Yueyang (Yochow)   Nanchang

Chengde   Changsha   Sandu'ao

Lake Dongting   Fuzhou   Tamsui

Guiyang   *Japanese influence*

British influence   Xiamen (Amoy)   TAIWAN

Kunming   Shantou (Swatow)   Tainan

Tengchong   *French influence*   Wuzhou   Guangzhou (Canton)

Mengzi   Nanning   Sanshui

Simao   Macao (Aomen)   HONG KONG

Longzhou   Kowloon

Beihai   Guangzhouwan *French Influence*

FRENCH INDO CHINA   Qiongzhou

SIAM   HAINAN

Sea of Japan

East China Sea

South China Sea

PHILIPPINES

N

0   250 mi

0   250 km

connections with China; others were inhabited almost exclusively by Chinese, because foreign traders found it much more comfortable to live with their Chinese servants, lovers, and business companions outside the limits of Western jurisdiction. The ones that really mattered were the large concessions in Shanghai, Tianjin, Guangzhou, and Wuhan, with the German- and Russian-leased areas of Qingdao and Harbin as special cases. The different zones in these cities, whether Chinese-controlled or foreign-controlled, did much to create modern China, economically, culturally, and politically. With their complex systems of governance and social interaction, they provided the spaces in which the hybridity and fluidity of contemporary Chinese society were born.

Shanghai's three sections—"international," French, and Chinese—provided the concession city par excellence, the place where much of Chinese modernity was created. Built around an already thriving port, new Shanghai became, by World War I, a city of 1.3 million people. While a few among the foreign population, which never counted more than 40,000 people in total, governed the International Settlement and the French concession, both parts were in reality Chinese cities, with around a third of all Shanghailanders in the former and a tenth in the latter. The trading significance of Shanghai had been obvious for centuries. It was located at the mouth of the Yangzi, on the central coast, and the main tea- and silk-producing areas were within easy reach. But from the late nineteenth century, what really distinguished the city was its role as the country's prime industrial center. It received more than half of all foreign investment into the country and became the place where the Chinese economy began to integrate and amalgamate foreign technologies, products, and tastes.

The first fifty years of concession life were bounded by foreign domination, but with Chinese providing the manpower that connected trade routes, provided supplies, and, increasingly, manned factories. While the Qing were struggling to break into the international system of independent, recognized states, and desperately trying to play the countries that harassed it off against each other, new kinds of societies emerged in some of the cities along China's coast and on the great rivers. These were societies in which ideas and practices developed fast and gradually spread to the rest of China, on matters as diverse as street lighting and company stocks, waterpipes and religious creeds, shipyards and schooling. In business, foreigners and Chinese were linked together from the beginning. In daily life, interactions and observations gradually created much that was new for everyone.

WHILE FOREIGNERS CARVED OUT their parts of China's cities, other newcomers to urban China were busy carving out theirs. From the mid-nineteenth to the early twentieth centuries, many Chinese cities doubled in size, as Qing restrictions on travel to and residence in the cities faded and more economic opportunities were created. The encounters between Chinese and foreign economies, products, and teachings were among the most important reasons for the urbanization of the late Qing era. But the decrease in official restrictions also played a role, especially for the growth in businesses, organizations, and learning that made the cities attractive. The young people who came to the cities, whether they settled in areas under Chinese or foreign jurisdiction, created new identities for themselves, as workers, traders, shopkeepers, or part of the intelligentsia, in ways that would not have been open to them had Qing power—with its skepticism toward unregulated cities—stayed intact.

The spectacle of change that met newcomers to Shanghai or Wuhan or Tianjin a hundred years ago would almost have been beyond their belief. It was not just the wide streets, trains and tramways, telegraph technology, movie houses, and dance halls that would have excited (and sometimes dismayed) them, it would be the way some people dressed—in skirts, blouses, and suits, rather than gowns—and how they lived—on their own, rather than with their families—that would have seemed odd and new. The presence of foreigners would of course titillate, as would the sights and smells of a new kind of city, in which production and transport were moving to the forefront of human consciousness. The new products for sale would also startle, from mirrors to soap, from bicycles to cameras, from corsets to flashlights. Sometimes they found their way into ancient cosmologies, as when mirrors were placed in hallways to ward off evil spirits. More often they were admired and, eventually, copied by local producers with twists that fitted local markets and tastes.

The role of the merchant had increased in urban China from the late fifteenth century on, but it took on a new significance in the late nineteenth century, when China was being drawn into an expanding world economy. The compradors (from the Portuguese word for "buyer")—Chinese who acted as bicultural middlemen in the trade with foreigners—stood at the center of economic change that was taking place, acting as negotiators, business assistants, or upcountry purchasers for Western companies. Ironically, while it was their cultural skills, primarily in language, that gave them their comparative advantage, the compradors became agents of a new kind of economic rationality in the cities, where the accumulation of capital and the possession of material wealth became the main symbol of status. The Confucian context, in which honor, sincerity, and social relationships were as important as economic gain, was gradually outflanked, as was the position of scholars and even imperial officials.[1]

The Chinese cities of the late nineteenth and early twentieth centuries were chaotic places, both for old and new inhabitants. As the Qing, who had, with some justification, prided themselves on their city planning, began to lose control, new forms of authority emerged, in some cases building on precedents that had been set long ago. One such form in urban China was the *huiguan* or *tongxianghui,* the native place associations, which represented and assisted workers who came to the city from a particular area, province, or region. In places like Shanghai, Tianjin, and Wuhan, they controlled areas of the Chinese city in which their adherents lived, where their dialect was spoken, and where their sort of food was served. Crucially, they also provided contacts with countrymen abroad. But, while powerful, the native place associations always competed for allegiance with trade and labor organizations and with secret societies of various kinds, from anti-Qing agitators to criminal gangs and those somewhere on the scale in between. The new urban China was unruly territory, with complex links across time and geographical space, hard to control because it was so hard to define.[2]

In 1832, a Scottish ship doctor, William Jardine, who had an extra income from dealing in opium, and his countryman James Matheson, set up what would become the premier foreign company, or *hong*, in nineteenth-century China. Jardine, Matheson & co. was primarily based in Hong Kong and Shanghai, with extensions through all the major trading routes within China, between China, Japan, and Southeast Asia, and between East Asia and Europe. It was in many ways China's first multinational corporation, with a hybrid structure that was replicated in most other foreign-led *hongs*. Its board and directors were all foreigners, but the company was linked to Chinese compradors who served as conduits to the major Chinese producers and retailers and who in reality provided much of the capital on which the company's business was based. Jardine's had agents—mostly Europeans—in all major ports on the coast and along the main rivers, and these agents had their own network of Chinese merchants whom they depended upon to get business done. A company like Jardine's of course existed mainly to provide the maximum profit for its foreign investors, symbolized by its involvement in the opium trade. But its structure became as much Chinese as European, and its business would have been impossible without the involvement of thousands of Chinese who led the way into markets and trade routes established long before any Scotsman had set foot in China.

One such area in which the European-led trading houses fitted into preexisting Chinese networks was in trade with and within Southeast Asia. In many cases the foreign companies simply slotted into trading structures that the Chinese diaspora had been building for many generations. The newcomers provided additional capital and stronger links with Europe. But while the Europeans were busy colonizing Southeast Asia between 1850 and 1914, the Chinese supplied the small traders and low-level administrators that glued the colonial possessions together. Singapore became the hub of the regional trade, and therefore a Chinese city in Southeast Asia, although under British administration. In Batavia (Jakarta) and Saigon (Ho Chi Minh City), Chinese traders provided key services for the Dutch and French colonialists, for foreign companies that settled in the area, and for companies operating out of China. Although both Southeast Asian elites and Europeans were fearful of Chinese influence and competition, they came to depend on the expanding markets that the Chinese helped set up. In British Malaya, for instance, Yu Ren Sheng—a company that began trading in Chinese medicine in the 1870s—came to link the peninsula to southern China on most things from banking services to food and contract labor.

The new Western-type banks, based in Shanghai and Hong Kong, also fitted into older Chinese patterns of credit and investment, forming great chains of finance. The links between various kinds of institutions were very close, with loans and securities moving from big banks to small banks to new-type Chinese banks to old-type Chinese banks. The number of Chinese who were—in one form or another—affected by the activities of banks grew rapidly in the nineteenth century, even outside the cities. The banks were also, of course, linked to the trading houses, big and small. Jardine's Fuzhou comprador sold, for instance, shares on behalf of the Hongkong and Shanghai Banking Corporation, the biggest of all the foreign-type institutions. HSBC had started operations from rented premises in Hong Kong in 1865, with a capital of five million Hong Kong dollars. By the 1880s, it was the biggest bank in China, with offices and agents all over the country. It was banker to the Hong Kong government for British government accounts in China, Japan, Malaya, and Singapore. It issued banknotes in Hong Kong and in Thailand. And most notably it was the banker to the Chinese government, managing most of its public loans between 1874 and the 1920s, making a substantial profit for its shareholders in the process.

Throughout the long period of wars and revolutions in China in the twentieth century, big foreign-run banks such as HSBC remained the preferred bankers for Chinese who gained from the capitalist expansion. While all foreign banks in China became more susceptible to risk after the collapse of the Qing empire in 1911, the romance between Western banking methods and Chinese capital continued to be strong. Ewen Cameron, the manager of HSBC's Shanghai headquarters, in 1890 boasted that "for the last 25 years the Bank has been doing a very large business with the Chinese in Shanghai amounting, I should say, to hundreds of millions of *taels* [Chinese dollars], and we have never met with a defaulting Chinaman."[3]

It was only in the early twentieth century that foreign involvement in Chinese industry started to catch up with foreign involvement in trade. One reason was that until the 1890s foreigners were not allowed to invest in production on Chinese soil. Another was Chinese resistance to the introduction of Western commercial law; it took up to 1904 before the concept of limited liability for corporations was accepted.[4] The first Chinese industrial enterprises had developed out of existing companies, mostly in handicrafts. During the 1870s the Qing state and its provincial governments had begun forging links with private companies under the slogan *guandu shangban* (official supervision, merchant management) as part of the Self-strengthening Movement. Many of the enterprises that were created as part of such schemes—such as the China Merchant Steamship Navigation Company (founded in 1872), the Jiangnan Arsenal (1865), the Shanghai Cotton Cloth Mill (1878), and the Kaiping Mines (1877)—were based on Western technologies. But even though some of these new companies carried out quite amazing feats of reverse engineering to understand and produce foreign machinery, they found it hard to compete against Western-owned shipping and imports. From the turn of the century, foreign investment expanded rapidly, beginning in the mining industry, then in foodstuffs, energy, and textiles, with Shanghai the biggest center of production. Many of these businesses grew quickly and were highly profitable.

There was always a surplus of peasants wanting to work in the cities, but conditions for those who labored in the nascent industries were often poor, whether they were employed by foreigners or Chinese. Hours were long, living conditions filthy, and wages low compared to the cost of living in the cities. Sick or pregnant workers were fired, and children were hired to do the most dirty or dangerous jobs. Women workers, who came to the cities in increasing numbers from the turn of the century on, especially to work in the textile industry, were vulnerable to sexual exploitation by their bosses and often felt that they had to send the greater amount of their wages back to their parents in their home village. Although many Chinese became workers not of their own free will, but because their families or clans decided that they had to, others were drawn to the cities by the freedom from family control that they offered. As in other countries at the dawn of industrialization, factory life in China was hard and hazardous, but the foreignness of the cities broke the monotony of farming and held out the hope of rich rewards to those who most eagerly broke the set moral guidelines of the past.

MANY CHINESE FIRST ENCOUNTERED foreigners as missionaries. As the empire was forced to open its doors in the mid-1800s, Christian missions sprung up in the treaty ports and itinerant missionaries began traveling to most parts of the country. In spite of both official and popular Chinese resentment, much cultural and educational interaction took place through Christian missions. Education and science, not religion, became the most significant fields of missionary enterprise. Still, the Christian faith came to have a deep impact on some parts of Chinese society, as did the many religious amalgams and cultural translations that came out of these contacts.

While the social and economic dislocation in China in the nineteenth century provided fertile ground for the entry of a new transcendental faith, the association of Christianity with foreign aggression
diminished the effectiveness of the missionaries' message. Although
many were impressed with the personal courage and sacrifice shown by
foreign and Chinese Christians, many more were disgusted with the
demands foreign governments made to pave the way for Christian proselytizing. When France declared itself a protector of all Catholic missionaries in China, or when the British or Germans exacted revenge for
attacks against Christians, much of the goodwill on which Christianity
could expand was destroyed. The sense that Christians were one of many
Western groups out to smash the existing order in China also damaged
their cause. In village after village, disputes, often violent, broke out
when Christians refused to contribute to popular festivals or the upkeep
of the village temple. In some areas reports of churches being vandalized
were followed by news of temples or sacred images being destroyed.
The attitude of Confucian officialdom toward Christians remained profoundly negative. A Christian man brought before a Shanxi magistrate
after a brawl over the man's refusal to help pay for the annual Chinese
opera performance was asked which country he was from. When he answered that he was a man of the Qing, the magistrate exploded:

> If you are a person of the Qing dynasty then why are you following
> the foreign devils and their seditious religion? You didn't pay your
> opera money when requested by the village and you were beaten.
> But how can you dare to bring a suit? You certainly ought to pay
> the opera subscription. If you don't you won't be allowed to live in
> the land of the Qing. You will have to leave for a foreign country.[5]

Two constituencies among which Christian missionaries made
some early inroads—as would the Communists later—were women
and ethnic minorities. Even though their position could be strong in
some regions and clans, especially in the south, women were the largest

oppressed group in nineteenth-century China. They lacked the rights of men and were under the command of their fathers, brothers, husbands, and even sons. For some of the most exploited women, Christianity, with its emphasis on choice and personal salvation, proved a way out, but often at the cost of breaking with their families or even their community. Some ethnic minorities, such as the Miao people in southern China or the Taiwan aboriginals, also had relatively high numbers of converts. After the end of the Taiping movement, groups among the Hakka joined with local missions—such as the Swiss-German Basel Mission—in order to defend against revenge from non-Hakka neighbors. The Deng clan—from among whom one of the key leaders of Communist China, Deng Xiaoping, would later emerge—was one such group of Hakka.

China's encounter with Christianity from the sixteenth century on had primarily happened through European Catholics, but most of the nineteenth-century missionaries were British or American Protestants. They were young men and women inspired by the Great Awakening in the United States and evangelical revivals in Britain. Some of the most influential of these missionaries were interested more in propagating Western educational ideals than in saving souls. Robert Morrison, sent by the London Missionary Society, started publishing books in Chinese in the 1830s. Elijah Bridgeman, sent by the American Board of Commissioners for Foreign Missions, published magazines in English and Chinese in Guangzhou. Unlike most foreign military officers, diplomats, and traders, the missionaries often learned Chinese, and so they became translators and interpreters of China to the West and the West to China. Some of them retired to fill the first positions for the study of China in Western universities. James Legge started as a Scottish missionary in Hong Kong, became the first professor of Chinese at Oxford, and made celebrated translations of the Confucian Classics.

Few societies have ever put more emphasis on the value of education in its various forms than did Qing China. Basic literacy rates were reasonably high compared to the rest of the world. Between a third and a half of men and up to ten percent of women could read. There were many schools in major cities, but competition for entry was fierce. Most Chinese knew that the path to success was literacy, knowledge of the classics, and taking some form of examination. Families whose members included officials and scholars had an advantage, but in each generation a few poorer families were able to put one of their sons through the imperial examination system and gain a status their forebears could only have dreamed of. No wonder whole clans pooled resources to educate their young in schools serving their area or lineage, or in order to put someone of special talent through a private, public, or official institute or even an imperial academy.[6]

What changed in the late nineteenth century was not the prominence of education but its content and organization. In addition to the kinds of schools that had existed since at least the Song dynasty, China now also got schools run by missionary societies and as well as secular schools, often run by Chinese, that concentrated on science in addition to the classics. Schools for women also began to spread, especially after 1900. A central tenet of the Self-strengthening Movement, launched by Zeng Guofan, Li Hongzhang, and others in the 1860s, was that the ideal person was someone who could combine an essence of Chinese learning with an outer form of Western science and technology. Throughout the 1870s and 1880s academies that taught Western Studies appeared, often in or around the new shipyards or arsenals that delivered the weapons the Qing needed for their protection. Well into the twentieth century, however, most Chinese continued to go to schools where Western science, geography, or languages made only occasional and fleeting appearances, and where the purpose was the improvement of one's character through study of Confucian texts. But some of the students who early on did receive training outside the Confucian curriculum were going to become crucial to China's future as bridge builders between two very different visions of human existence.

By the 1870s more and more Chinese were going abroad for their formal education. Building on the knowledge transmitted by pioneers who had left earlier—people like Rong Hong (known in the West as Yung Wing), who had graduated from Yale in 1854 as the first Chinese with a US college degree—both the government and individual families began sending young people to America and Europe, and, as we shall see, a bit later also to Japan. Zeng Guofan was behind one key government effort, the Chinese Educational Mission, which sent 120 young men to study in the United States from 1872 on. Similar expeditions were set up for Germany, Britain, and France. As happened with the next big wave of Chinese students going abroad, over a century later, in the 1980s and 1990s, some of the those who went away stayed away, while others returned to China, giving good service to their country as doctors, teachers, shipbuilders, officers, and railway and mining engineers.

The most prominent example of a foreign-trained student from the late nineteenth century, Sun Yat-sen, became the first president of the Chinese republic in 1911. A southerner like most of the others who went overseas, Sun left Guangzhou as a thirteen-year-old in 1879 for Hawaii, where his elder brother was a successful merchant. Sun was educated in Honolulu, attending the same school from which Barack Obama would graduate a hundred years later. Sun then went on to study medicine in Hong Kong, becoming one of the first graduates from its new medical college.

One example of the further career of the boys who were sent to study in America in the 1870s was Tang Shaoyi, who attended Columbia College in New York. Tang became a leading Qing-era communications' expert, diplomat, and provincial governor. After the collapse of the dynasty he served as prime minister and minister of finance and was a key adviser to Sun Yat-sen and Chiang Kai-shek. He was assassinated in 1938 when attempting to negotiate with the Japanese. Another was Rong Shangqian, who attended Hartford Public High School, joined the Qing military, fought as a captain, and was wounded both in the

Sino-French war and in the Sino-Japanese war. Rong later became a railway administrator and died a very old man in Shanghai in 1954. Tang, Rong, and the other pioneers of Chinese education abroad came to have a strong influence on China, often serving under three different governments in their homeland.

By the early twentieth century, education in China provided a fertile ground for encounters between natives and foreigners. The number of translations from other languages increased, expanding the influence of non-Chinese learning. The schools and universities inside the foreign settlements received more and more Chinese students, as did the foreign-run universities in the Chinese cities, such as Yanjing University in Beijing, a precursor to today's Peking University, and Guangzhou Christian College, which became Lingnan University in 1916. Qinghua University was established in Beijing in 1911, primarily as a preparatory school for students who would later study in US universities on state scholarships. New groups of students were particularly eager to avail themselves of these opportunities; by 1905 there were 10,000 Chinese young women in Protestant missionary schools.[7] The meeting of different cultures through schools and universities formed twentieth-century China by the impact it had on the minds of those who came to lead the country. By 1905, when the Qing abolished imperial examinations because of "the strenuous difficulties of the times," Chinese education was already on its way to becoming the hybrid of Confucian didactic values and empirical study that we see today.[8] The topics for the last countrywide exams (an emergency session held in Kaifeng in 1902) symbolize this fusion:

SECTION 1:
The military policies of Guanzi (725–645 BC)
The policies of Han Wendi (179–156 BC) toward southern Vietnam
Imperial use of laws
Evaluation procedures for officials

*The proposals of Liu Guangzu (1142–1222) for stabilizing the
    Southern Song dynasty*

SECTION 2:
The Western stress on travel as a part of studying
The Japanese use of Western models for educational institutions
The banking policies of various countries
The police and laws
The industrial basis of wealth and power[9]

During the nineteenth century, Chinese views of nature and of the human body began slowly to change under the influence of Western science and medicine. While in no sense a one-way exchange, foreign concepts had, by 1900, permeated the Chinese view of the universe and the human place in it in an unprecedented manner. There are perhaps no fields of contact between China and the world that are more important than these. China has its own millennia-old traditions of science and medicine. As the country's interaction with the West grew, its doctors and scientists began embracing new forms of knowledge in areas from gynecology to astronomy that transformed their understanding of life and its physical conditions. By the early twentieth century China's intelligentsia had joined the same mesmeric search for scientific truth as had Europeans, Americans, and other Asians, using the same measures and standards.

Because many of the crucial breakthroughs in knowledge around the world happened just as China's contact with the West expanded, the growth of science as a unitary field of investigation saw Chinese involved almost from the beginning. One good example is public hygiene. When British troops occupied Tianjin in 1860, they filled in the ditches near their camp because of fear of the "miasma" generated by stagnant water. In the process, they accidentally cut the city's drainage system, causing massive flooding and disease.[10] But some young British doctors with the troops began wondering whether the Chinese method for keeping cities clean might not be the best weapon against epidemics. The benefits of sanitation were discovered at about the same time in Europe and in China, and it was the combined work of European and Chinese doctors that removed some of the most immediate health risks from the growing Chinese cities.

As with other forms of knowledge, missionaries were key to transmitting Western medicine and science to a Chinese audience. In 1838 the American Peter Parker organized the Medical Missionary Society in Guangzhou, which instructed its Chinese students in the latest Western medical treatments. The British missionary Benjamin Hobson published in Chinese translation major Western works on science. Working with Chinese translators, including the mathematician Li Shanlan, Hobson put out books on astronomy (1849), physiology (1851), surgery (1857), and internal medicine (1858). While eager for new knowledge, Chinese doctors and scientists were understandably reluctant to throw out the old, keeping a healthy skepticism against parts of Western surgery and pharmacology well into the twentieth century. The gifted Wuxi optician and chemist Xu Shou, who had begun experiments inspired by Western chemistry in the 1850s, often called for the integration of Chinese and Western medicine. But as the number of Chinese trained in Western institutions—whether in China or abroad—increased, the dominance of Western approaches to science began to be established.

Only a small number of Chinese had access to translations or compendia of foreign knowledge, so changes in perceptions happened much more slowly in the general population. Some foreigners and Chinese in the last third of the nineteenth century began to publish popular magazines on science, by far the most important being by the remarkable Anglican missionary John Fryer. Fryer worked at the Jiangnan Arsenal and established the Shanghai Polytechnic in the mid-1870s. His *Gezhi huibian* (called the *Chinese Scientific and Technical Magazine* in English) reached well beyond the scientific community.[11] Its letters to the editor show the increasing awareness of new forms of interpretation; one reader from Qingzhou pointed out in 1880 that "Chinese books say that the rainbow . . . is the improper *qi* of Heaven and Earth, [caused by] the prolonged intercourse of sun and rain: it is the intercourse of those who ought not to engage in intercourse. . . . How do scientists explain it?"[12] Even in teaching, old habits died hard. The writer Guo Moruo tells of one of his science teachers around the turn of the century who misread the second character of the expresssion *tianran jingxiang* (natural conditions) as *tianlong jingxiang* (the appearance of heavenly dragons), and so interspersed his science lecture with manifestations of celestial creatures cruising the skies.[13]

THROUGHOUT THEIR HISTORY, the Chinese have traveled as much as any other group, but the past 200 years have seen more travel, to more places, by more people than ever before. The breakthrough for this new round of travel was in the nineteenth century, when the combination of foreign influences, new forms of conveyance, and state weakness combined to create a climate particularly favorable for venturing abroad. From the majority of those who made use of these opportunities—traders, workers, and emigrants of all sorts—we have very few written accounts of their experiences. But even the Chinese elite travelers who did report back have generally been overlooked, at least compared with the plentiful Western reports from travel in China that remain in print. The Chinese eye saw Europe, the Americas, Western Asia, and Africa with as much exoticism, cultural bias, guesswork, and misunderstanding as foreigners saw China. Traveling without doubt increased knowledge, both through personal experience and through writing, but in China as elsewhere it was and is knowledge delivered within a particular cultural context through which the traveling eye interprets the impressions it receives.

One of the first great Chinese travel writers was Wang Tao. Born near Suzhou in 1828, this learned scholar got into trouble with the

Qing during the Taiping rebellion and fled to Hong Kong. There he met James Legge, the eccentric Scottish missionary who was already engaged in the first translation of Chinese classics into English. In 1867 Legge invited Wang to join him in Scotland, and Wang set out on the long journey to Europe, traveling through Singapore, Sri Lanka, Penang, Aden, and Cairo before reaching Marseille. He then spent several weeks in Paris and London before arriving in the aptly named Scottish town of Dollar, where he settled down for two years amid the rush of industrialization, working with Legge on the translation of *The Book of Songs*, *Yi Jing*, and *The Book of Rites*. Wang, who also visited Japan after his return from Europe, wrote extensive notes about his travels, which he published after the Qing accepted his return to China.

The first Chinese travelers to North America were even more puzzled by what they saw than voyagers to Europe. Those who had seen both were perhaps even more perplexed. "The English and the Americans are closely related, they have much in common, but they also differ widely, and in nothing is the difference more conspicuous than in their conduct," observed Wu Tingfang, one of China's first ambassadors to Washington.[14] The democratic politics in the United States puzzled those who came: How could there be, many asked, collective decision making on administrative matters, when there was such extreme individualism in economic matters? The many tongues spoken, the grime and confusion of the industrializing northern cities, and the confrontations over ethnic, racial, social, and political issues in mid-nineteenth-century America made many Chinese visitors prescribe the need for harmony and stability. But at the same time the technological advances fascinated them endlessly, especially the railroads and steamboats. "The train," observed the Manchu visitor Zhigang in 1868, "is light, steady, and faster than Liezi [a legendary Daoist sage] riding the wind. It is constructed like a wooden house. . . . On both sides are rows of windows with three layers of glass, cloth curtains, and wooden shutters for protection against wind, rain, light, and dark."[15] Riding the "fire-wheeled vehicle" made Zhigang want to study it more closely, and he sent back to China a detailed description of how railroads were built.

Many Chinese travelers initially viewed the West as a form of anti-China, where Chinese values and mores were turned upside down. A few visitors wrote that this could not be otherwise, since Europe and America, after all, were on the other side of the world from China. Others sought explanations for what they saw in the West in the Chinese past, attempting to find periods in Chinese history that would be similar in organization and outlook to what they observed abroad, and speculating whether the foreigners had taken their inspiration from one or another epoch in China's long development. The matter that preoccupied Chinese more than anything else was the absence of filial piety and the lack of a moral rather than a material justification for actions taken. "It is not that our emperors or prime ministers of each dynasty were less intelligent than the Westerners," Liu Xihong exclaimed when visiting London in 1876, "but none among them strove to open up the skies or dig up the earth to compete with nature for enriching themselves. Our far-seeing ancestors also cared for the future, but not in the same ways as the English who always run at full speed to gain the advantage."[16]

Besides the puzzlement over foreign languages, food, customs, and hygiene, Chinese travelers wondered constantly about the preference of people in the Western empires for material progress over moral self-betterment. Chinese travelers to the West reported—in bewilderment more than shock—on foreign political systems, on the role of women, and on racial hierarchies. And they worried about China's survival in the encounter with countries as different and as powerful as those in the West. Observing the ongoing industrialization of the United States and some of the countries in Western Europe, Chinese travelers often commented on the destructive elements of the new technologies. The pollution, the changes in landscapes, and the impermanence of manners, methods, and lifestyles all shocked the visitors, even as Western products attracted them and the power and productivity of Western industry awed them. Many of those who came to visit chose to stay, either because they felt that foreign countries could provide a better life for them and their families than China could, because they despaired over the fate of China in its encounter with the West, or because they opposed the Qing regime. But even in the stories of most of those who returned, China and the West had changed their worldview—instead of one China as the center of the world and the adjudicator of morals, habits, and taste, the world had become a much bigger and more equal place, a place in which more choices would have to be made and where Chinese could be of many persuasions, political views, and state allegiances.

THE SINO-CENTRIC WORLD ORDER in East Asia took a long time to die. By the 1870s the new imperialist order was clearly visible, even to those who objected the most to the new shape of things. Having observed the changes within China and the weakness of the Qing, sometimes at close range through their missions to the imperial capital, or—in the case of Southeast Asia—to Guangzhou, the tributary states gradually reoriented themselves to a world in which the Western powers were dominant. Even the countries that were culturally and geographically closest to China—Vietnam, the Ryukyu islands, and Korea—realized a new era in their international affairs had arrived. For those further away, such as Burma and Thailand, the formal end of their relationship with the Qing state was almost an afterthought, coming well after the tribute missions had ended. The Qing world order ended in the same haphazard manner as it had begun, in spite of Chinese attempts at interpreting the new developments within the formal framework of ritual and precedent.

As we shall see in the next chapter, Korea's was by far the most dramatic and destructive case of a country's departure from the Sino-centric system. The Ryukyu (or, in Chinese, Liuqiu) islands—the long, sickle-shaped archipelago stretching from the southern tip of Kyushu toward Taiwan—set another example. For almost 300 years the Ryukyu kings had both been tributaries of the Qing and subject to the rulers of the southern Japanese domain of Satsuma. By the 1870s China's position on the islands was slipping and with it the chance of upholding Ryukyu's de facto independence. While continuing negotiations on the issue with China throughout the decade, Japan declared its single sovereignty over the islands in 1872, stationed troops there in 1875, and in 1879 annexed all of Ryukyu, abolished its monarchy, and transformed it into the Japanese prefecture of Okinawa. China's attempts at appealing to US and British mediators failed. Ryukyu's loss of independence was a harbinger of things to come.

In faraway Thailand, the leaders were also realizing that China's paramount place in eastern Asia was disappearing fast. When the Thai tributary mission arrived in Guangzhou in 1853, it is likely that very few Thais or Chinese suspected that it was the last formal recognition of the Thai monarchy's subservient position to the Qing. The Thai king's minister for Chinese relations—typically, a man who himself was of Chinese descent—explained Bangkok's view of what followed in an apologetic letter to the governor-general at Guangzhou in the mid-1860s:

> Siam and Peking have long been friendly, and each time tribute was due, Siam always remembered to send it, so as to not harm the friendship that had so long been maintained. However, [in 1853]. . . , Siam['s envoys] . . . were attacked by bandits who forcefully took away all of the emperor's gifts given in return to the court of Siam. . . . When it came to the monsoon season of the Year of the Hare [1856]. . . , which was when tribute to China was due, it was learned that the rebels were causing even more trouble than before, and therefore the tribute was waived. Then [in 1860]. . . , it was again time to send tribute to China. This time it was learnt that the city of Canton was at war with England, and that the Governor-General himself was not residing there. If Siam were to send envoys, no one would receive them. Then [in 1862]. . . , it was learnt that England and France were penetrating as far as Beijing and that Beijing was in the midst of a great war.[17]

By the 1870s the Thais knew that the old times would not return. They began reorganizing their Chinese tribute trade, which was always more trade than tribute, within the maritime routes now controlled by Britain and France. Only in 1882, did Bangkok unilaterally declare the official end of its subservient relationship to the Qing.

Given the way in which the imperialist powers had used the concept of international law to justify their subjugation of the Qing state, there was little reason for Chinese to believe that any state of theirs would be fully accepted within the Western-based system of major countries. Still, Chinese leaders showed a remarkable interest in understanding international law almost from the time of the very first Western attack. Parts of key texts, such as Emerich Vattel's 1758 *Law of Nations*, had been translated by the 1840s, in the wake of the First Sino-British War. But after the foreign invasion in the late 1850s it became obvious that China needed to learn the principles on which the Western powers claimed to base their foreign relations. William Martin, a Presbyterian missionary, translated the American diplomat Henry Wheaton's 1836 treatise *Elements of International Law* into Chinese in 1864. In spite of Wheaton's parochial belief—different from Vattel's universalism—that international law was solely an artifact of Christian civilization, the Qing grand council found it useful. They appealed to the emperor:

> we, your ministers, have compared this book on foreign laws and found that it does not completely correspond to the Chinese system. But in it there are occasional passages that are useful. . . . We, your ministers, have guarded against making use of such books and following them, have told [Martin] that China has her own laws and institutions and that it would not be appropriate to refer to foreign books. Martin, however, has pointed out that although the Collected Laws of the Qing Dynasty have been translated in foreign countries, China has never attempted to coerce these foreign countries to follow them. It cannot be that just because a foreign book [has been translated into Chinese] China will be forced to follow its customs.[18]

By the 1890s some Chinese leaders had come to see international law as a possible protector of the interests of their empire. As Li Hongzhang, who had participated in many international negotiations on behalf of the Qing (and were to conduct more after the 1895 war with Japan), argued, "International law belongs to all the nations of the globe. If they observe it, they may dwell in quiet; if they neglect it, they are sure to have trouble."[19] Some scholars claimed that international law was similar to the principles developed during the Spring and Autumn period (722–481 BC) or the Warring States period (403–221 BC), epochs in which China had been divided into several states and on which Confucius' teachings offer much commentary. But these comparisons did not prepare Chinese diplomats for dealing with their country's interests. Neither did the language in which these early translations were couched, which often used the terms of Chinese ethics dealing with interpersonal relationships, thereby missing the fluidity of law and its subservience to power.

Despite its venerable system of sending envoys to foreign countries and its considerable reservoir of knowledge about neighboring states, Qing China had not sought to have permanent representatives abroad. Unlike Europe since the seventeenth century, the Qing empire did not recognize other countries (even in theory) as equals with which almost permanent negotiations were necessary. It therefore had had no need for diplomats in the European sense of the term. After the Western interventions and the great rebellions of the mid-nineteenth century, the Qing had to adapt to the European tradition, although with regret. Prince Gong, the sixth son of the Daoguang emperor and a central player in the Empress Dowager Cixi's rise to power in the 1860s, impressed on the Court the importance of sending envoys abroad:

> I believe that in recent years, foreign countries have come to understand China very well, whereas China's knowledge of the outside world remains scant. The discrepancy is attributable to foreign diplomatic envoys being stationed in China, and the complete ab-

sence of Chinese missions abroad. This has led to the situation where foreign diplomats in China flout our rules and act inappropriately, and all we can do is try to mollify them. As we are unable to censor their conduct, we must try another approach. This situation is a cause of constant worry and unease to me.[20]

The competent but often dissolute Prince Gong was also one of the main forces behind the establishment, in 1861, of China's first foreign ministry, the Office of the Affairs of All Countries, the Zongli Geguo Shiwu Yamen, or Zongli Yamen. Although at the start regarded as a temporary, second-tier office in the imperial bureaucracy, the Zongli Yamen soon became a central mediator between the Qing Court, the provinces, the military, and foreigners. It also established the College for Interpretation (Tongwenguan), a school that trained future diplomats in foreign languages and Western learning and that became one of the centers for translation and publishing of foreign texts on everything from physics to international affairs.

Like the Zongli Yamen, the Imperial Maritime Customs Service was a locus for Sino-Western cooperative contacts. It was foreign-staffed and was often used by the foreign powers to collect reparations from China after wars and skirmishes. But it also made translations, conducted social and statistical investigations, and helped found the Chinese post office. During the late Qing era, it went from being seen as a foreign imposition to becoming an important source of government income and a training ground for Chinese officials. The transformation in the Chinese view of the Customs was mostly due to the work of Robert Hart, its Irish-born Inspector-General, who served from 1861 to 1907. During his long tenure, the young man from Portadown in Northern Ireland grew into the chief foreign confidant of the Beijing Court. While his officials, men from more than twenty countries, drew Chinese ire by policing the harbors of the foreign concessions (and often also the main rivers and coastal areas), Hart was a symbol of a foreigner who was, above all, a servant of the Qing.

By 1900 the Qing had begun setting up a viable network of foreign missions. Its first embassies were established in London, Berlin, and Tokyo in 1877, followed by ones in Washington and Moscow in 1878. They were staffed by trained diplomats from the Tongwenguan and other imperial officials. Some Chinese embassies proved themselves equal to their tasks, while others became little more than drags on Beijing's coffers. Amid its many rages about money misspent and information lost in transit, the Qing realized that it had among its ambassadors some people of outstanding talent, such as Guo Songtao, the first ambassador to London and a major Qing politician in his own right, who had helped organize the Qing response to the Taiping Rebellion. Zeng Jize, son of the Qing leader Zeng Guofan, the man who dominated Chinese politics in the wake of the great rebellions, replaced Guo in London and later served in Paris and Moscow. Zeng also acted as China's chief diplomatic troubleshooter in the early 1880s, negotiating the Treaty of St. Petersburg with Russia. Diplomats such as Zeng were influential in Beijing because they not only reported realistically on the power of the West but also stressed a Confucian approach to world affairs. Looking at London, Zeng confided to his diary:

> Just like one may imagine ancient China by looking at the West today, one may imagine the future of the West by looking at China today. A day will certainly arrive when one will return to the original state of things and when one will seek neither ingeniousness nor complexity, but only simplicity. Because material resources are limited and are not sufficient for the needs of all countries in the world.[21]

DURING THE LATE NINETEENTH CENTURY, the central areas of China gradually incorporated a new foreign presence as Western traders, missionaries, and officials began settling in the country. The Qing state wavered between accommodating the newcomers and the states that supported them, and resisting the foreign presence. At the local levels, Chinese and foreigners interacted, sometimes cooperatively,

sometimes in conflict, but always in puzzlement over each others' habits
and views. By 1900 the Sino-Western amalgams in taste and technologies that were emerging in the cities had further divided China into two
parts: a vast countryside in which the foreign presence was negligible
or nonexistent and an archipelago of urban islets where a new society
was developing. This new China was international, with outposts in
Southeast Asia and the Americas, and with people inside the country
who straddled Chinese and Western customs. But it was unsure of itself,
caught between being a creation of Western imperialism and a sometimes sincere hope of rescuing the nation through foreign methods,
money, and machines. As the twentieth century began, it was the tensions between the new and the old, and between the urban and the
rural—both of which had been exacerbated by the foreign presence—
that threatened to split China apart.

The foreign presence weakened the Qing state by reducing its autonomy, but it also helped preserve it by favoring it against its enemies
in the late nineteenth century. To many observers it seemed the perfect
exploitative relationship: The Western powers made use of the Qing's
weakness to extract privileges from it, but supported it so that it did
not collapse entirely, only then to exploit it a little bit more. The reality
was quite a bit more complex. The Qing became quite adept at maneu-
vering between foreign powers for advantage and never consciously became a tool of foreign interests. The leaders at Court were hoping and
waiting for a day when China would be strong enough to confront the
outsiders. At the same time, elite Chinese themselves became good at
exploiting the Qing state for their own purposes, presenting private
gain as public business. It was a climate of intense political and economic competition, in which foreigners had most of the advantages,
but by no means all of them.

Meanwhile foreign concepts and ideas washed in over China, buoy-
ing those minds that were looking for a way out for their country and
for themselves. As happened in the West, revolutionary thought often

centered on the relationship between science and society, feeding on the belief that Charles Darwin's theories of development also had a significance for human affairs. Mai Menghua, born in 1875, echoed the views of European and American social Darwinists:

> Consider the development of all civilizations on earth. There is not one of these that is not based on struggle. China has never existed in a time of struggle and its people have never had a mind to struggle. Therefore, it is no wonder that China has not been able to develop. Today, however, [the Chinese people] are struggling with others. The twentieth century is unquestionably the Chinese age of opportunity for development and the time when this ancient civilization may be restored.[22]

CHAPTER 3

JAPAN

N O OTHER ISSUE DEFINED China's foreign relations in the early twentieth century as much as the relationship to Japan. Japan is a small country in comparison to China, which has twenty-five times its land area. It is roughly the same ratio, in fact, as that of the earth and the moon. And the two countries have analogies to earth and moon in their interactions. Japan has always had to deal with the gravitational pull of its giant neighbor. Although its islands never belonged to China's direct sphere of control, Chinese culture, ideas, script, and religion have influenced Japan for more than a thousand years. The seventeenth-century Japanese neo-Confucian Kumazawa Banzan called China "the realm of the central fluorescence" and "the parent to the children, who were the eastern, southern, western, and northern barbarians, as the mountain was parent to the river's children."[1] But China has also been affected by its cultural satellite.

Starting in the mid-nineteenth century, China saw Japan as an inspiration and a possible ally in the encounter with the West. From the mid-1880s on, however, the Qing leadership began to consider its eastern island neighbor a rival and a threat. In 1894–1895 the two countries fought a bloody and destructive war over influence in East Asia, resulting in Qing China's first-ever military loss to another regional power. Korea and Taiwan became Japanese protectorates (and eventual colonies), and

China stood humiliated in the region. With the collapse of the Qing, many Japanese viewed China as chaotic and unstable. They thought of their giant neighbor as a magnet for more Western influence, and therefore tried to expand Japan's power for reasons of trade, security, and ideology. Japan, in the eyes of its elite, had a civilizing mission in China, just as the European great powers thought they had in Africa and South Asia.

D URING THE TOKUGAWA PERIOD IN JAPAN, from 1603 to 1868, the country limited its contacts with the outside world, but trade with China never fully ended. Many of the leading intellectuals of the period, both at the shogun's court in Edo (Tokyo) and at the imperial court in Kyoto, revered China as the center of an East Asian Confucian universe in a manner not much different from those of their counterparts in Korea or Vietnam. But from the late eighteenth century on, Japanese thinking slowly began to move in a more nativist direction, contrasting the naturalness, thrift, and industry of its own country's inhabitants to the perversions, indolence, and artifice of the Chinese. After the Qing's losses to the West and the great rebellions of the mid-nineteenth century, this new and more negative attitude turned into a flood of Japanese criticism of China. Having gone from being the center of the world to a country among countries, China was now represented as an horrid example of what Japan itself did not want to become: a divided, debased country, "an empire in name only," an outcast. More and more Japanese observed that because they and the Chinese looked alike, the travails of their neighbors across the ocean diminished them too. Rescuing China from its filth and denigration became a racial task for the Japanese of the first part of the twentieth century.

Chinese views of Japan also varied widely during the period up to the 1920s. From a view of the Japanese as eastern barbarians who had voluntarily cut themselves off from proper interaction with the imperial center, and who therefore were foolish or knavish or both, the sense of what Japan represented began to change rapidly in the middle part of the nineteenth century. Now, Chinese visitors commented on the willingness of Japanese elites to make use of Western knowledge and technologies during the Meiji era. Some Chinese saw the Japanese as deserters from a correct, Confucian worldview; many commented on a society gone mad, with factories and shipyards emerging as dark blots on Japan's pristine landscape. Others, and first and foremost those eager to see more Westernizing reform in China itself, saw Japan as an example, *the* example, of an Asian society transforming itself into something stronger and better. While all over China the concern about Japan's growing power increased through war and conflicts, the admiration for their eastern neighbor's achievements filled some Chinese with hope about what they themselves could do. It was this duality in the relationship that defined Sino-Japanese links in the late nineteenth and early twentieth centuries, and that gradually made a complex association one of enmity and hatred.

In the late nineteenth century, China and Japan both went through a set of political changes that became known as restorations. The one in Japan, the Meiji Restoration, was really a revolution that changed the country's economic, social, and political makeup forever. Under the Tokugawa regime, which, like the Qing, had ruled since the seventeenth century, Japan was an isolated society oriented toward self-sufficiency. But from the 1860s on, it commenced a profound transformation that would, within a generation, take it from international irrelevancy to the position of major regional power. The changes in Japan took place under the cloak of a restoration of direct imperial rule by Emperor Meiji, but the group of strongmen who held power after the Tokugawa collapse in 1868 wanted to take the country in new directions in response to the growing threat from the West and the unrest within Japanese society. Unlike the Tongzhi Restoration in China, which faced many of the same problems, the Meiji Restoration was headed by leaders who wanted a deliberate break with the past in order to save Japan. Frightened by the prospect of foreign control and growing instability at home, the Meiji elite set out to create a new Japan: outward-looking, industrial, militarized, and security-oriented.

It is hard to exaggerate the depth of change in Japan in the 1860s and 1870s and therefore difficult to fault the Chinese leaders for missing the possible consequences it might have for them. Through government initiatives and public enthusiasm, the look of the country was made new: from haircuts and clothing to books, transport, land ownership, education, and military affairs. Then, in the early 1880s, the country moved toward a new constitution and a parliamentary political system. In foreign affairs, Japan's main aim in the Meiji era was to abolish the unequal treaties that Western countries had imposed on it in the decade before the Restoration. But the Meiji leaders thought that in order to do so, Japan had to engage itself more fully on the Asian mainland, showing that it could conduct new forms of diplomacy with its neighbors. While building its new, centralized, and Western-trained army and navy, the Meiji oligarchs began collecting information on how they could rearrange international affairs in East Asia to strengthen Japan in its bid for autonomy vis-à-vis the Western powers.

While the Meiji Restoration revitalized Japan, the Qing's Tongzhi Restoration was a mirage. The Tongzhi group of statesmen (and women; the Empress-Dowager Cixi was a key figure) was aware of the dangers their regime faced, and had showed their survival skills through defeating the Taiping and other rebellions and by beginning the rebuilding of the Chinese state. While they were too split politically, too suspicious of each other, and too cautious in terms of reform to achieve a full restoration of Qing power, much was—as we have already seen—achieved in terms of finding Sino-Western amalgams. There was a sense in the 1870s—both among leading Chinese and foreigners—that China would find a way forward that was uniquely its own, that it was too big and too set in its ways to fail. The leading men of the Tongzhi era, such as Prince Gong and Li Hongzhang, believed that neo-Confucian self-strengthening would save China. The term implied making use of Western technology to protect and preserve Confucian China. The catchphrase for modernizers became "Chinese essence, Western form."

The Confucian core of Chinese learning remained valid. As the Confucian scholar Feng Guifen argued, "What we then have to learn from the barbarians is only one thing: solid ships and effective guns."[2]

Li Hongzhang, the foremost Chinese political and diplomatic leader between 1870 and the end of the century, agreed with Feng Guifen about ships and guns. Without military modernization, he argued, China would always be a victim of foreign powers. Born in 1823 in rural Anhui, Li was a classically trained scholar who had passed the central imperial exams in 1847 and made his mark fighting the Taiping and Nian rebellions. After he became governor-general of Hebei and Henan, including the capital Beijing, he headed an ambitious program of steering the imperial court toward importing Western technology and expertise in order to build arsenals and shipyards. As with Chiang Kai-shek in the twentieth century, Li's main hope was that China could keep war at bay until it was strong enough to defend itself.

Japan was the first foreign affairs problem Li Hongzhang faced as he consolidated his power at the imperial court. In spite of themselves having been forced to accept unequal treaties with the West, Meiji leaders quickly attempted to impose the same injustices on China. Instead, the Qing offered draft treaties that were reciprocal in terms of extraterritoriality. As negotiations got underway in 1870, Li Hongzhang noted

> Japan, which was not a dependency of China, was totally different from Korea, Ryukyu, and Annam [Vietnam]. That she had come to request trade without first seeking support from any Western power showed her independence and good will. If China refused her this time, her friendship would be lost and she might even seek Western intervention on her behalf, in which case it would be difficult for China to refuse again. An antagonized Japan could be an even greater source of trouble than the Western nations because of her geographical proximity. It was therefore in China's interest to treat Japan on a friendly and equal basis and send commissioners

to Japan who could look after the Chinese there, watch the movements of the Japanese government, and cultivate harmonious relations between the two states.[3]

But treaties to regulate intercourse between the two countries were
not enough for Japan. Its leaders felt that Western powers were seizing
the rest of East Asia in order to isolate the island country. The next
Japanese mission to China, headed by one of the young Meiji leaders,
Soejima Taneomi, in 1873, tried to widen Japan's position along the
Chinese coast by proclaiming Japan's right to send troops to punish
people on Taiwan for their attacks on Japanese shipping. The Zongli
Yamen, unwisely, chose to fudge the issue, by claiming that the islands
of Taiwan had both outer barbarians and inner barbarians and that
only the latter were under Chinese jurisdiction. China, in other words,
was not responsible for the actions of the coastal outer barbarians, the
ones who had attacked Japanese ships. The Japanese response was full
of the fear that would poison relations with China for two generations
to come:

> If foreign powers occupied the aboriginal territories under the pre-
> text of a massacre the aborigines had committed, and if these abo-
> riginal territories became like the French territories in Vietnam,
> Macao, Hong Kong, and Russia's expanding sphere of influence
> from the Amur river basin to our northern frontier, we would be
> confronted with a menace on our southern shores, which would
> threaten the islands in that area.[4]

In 1874 Japan used the unclear Chinese sovereignty statements
to send a punitive expedition to Taiwan, the first time the new Japanese army and navy had been deployed overseas. The expedition itself
was a fiasco—ten times more Japanese troops died from disease on
the island than the number of Taiwanese killed—and was soon withdrawn. But it emphasized an important point: If Japan wanted, it

could project its power all along China's coast without much chance for the Chinese state to intervene. This lesson was an ominous one for decades to come.

T HE CHINESE AND JAPANESE STATES saw each other as enemies throughout the twentieth century. But before conflict there was cooperation, admiration, and transmission. Some of these contacts remained in spite of the enmity of the states, even at times of war and occupation. Up to the end of World War I, many reform-minded Chinese believed that Japanese learning on matters of technology, science, politics, and international affairs was better suited to instruct China than what arrived directly from the West. In some cases these "Japanese lessons" were the result of misunderstandings: Chinese observers assumed that a certain form of knowledge was Japanese in origin simply because it was imported to China from Japan and its Japanese transmitters insisted on ownership (whereas in reality the Japanese had borrowed it from, say, a German magazine published a couple of years earlier). In other cases, Chinese wanted to believe that new things were Japanese in origin because it was easier to convince others of their appropriateness when they had already been adopted in a Confucian society. But often the transmission from Japan was genuine in the sense that laws, institutions, and technologies that had their origins in the West came to China after they had been adapted to Japanese purposes.

Japan in the Meiji and Taisho (1912–1926) eras was a great workshop of ideas. Visitors from all over the world were struck by the energy of the place, talking about how Tokyo bustled with debates and controversy, and how the government ruthlessly carried out reform even against the most long-established rules. The image of Japan, not least among other Asians, was that of a great laboratory of reform, from which their own countries could draw inspiration or apprehension, depending on the direction you wanted to go. For some Chinese, Japan's rapid transformation was part of a course they too wanted to follow, and a positive alternative to what they saw as the sluggish march toward change in Qing China. Chinese traders—operating in Japan's coastal cities under the protection of Western-imposed extraterritoriality—visitors, students, and an increasing group of political refugees, all reported back to their home country on the speed and success of Japan's transformation.

Most of the ideas that reached China from Japan were connected to science. The transmission happened almost on an assembly-line basis. Japanese books, tracts, pamphlets, magazines, and journal articles were translated into Chinese and used alongside texts that had been translated from Western languages or, increasingly, that had been written in Chinese by those who had studied abroad or with foreigners in China. The Japanese texts were particularly valuable for late Qing scientists, because like their counterparts on the other side of the East Sea, they were looking for practical implementations of the new knowledge of chemistry, physics, biology, and medicine. But other ideas also traveled: Concepts of citizenship and individual rights were part of the Meiji discourse and found their way into Chinese debates through Japanese writings. Jean-Jacques Rousseau was first translated into Chinese in Japan in the late 1870s,[5] and a great number of other translations followed, including of the work of some German nineteenth-century philosophers, among them Karl Marx. As we shall see later, political ideas transmitted through Japan would have a decisive influence on China in the twentieth century.

One field in which Japanese learning loomed large was in China's understanding of its own place in the world through international law. Both Japanese and Western scholars working on East Asia concluded that China was not a possible partner in international affairs because of its lack of a reliable legal system. Some members of the Chinese elite agreed, and the government engaged in several large projects on translating texts in international public and private law. Almost all of the main Chinese texts on the latter came from the pen of Yamada Saburo, the chair of the Law Faculty at Tokyo University, who, during his long life, also served as president of Keijo University in Seoul during the Japanese occupation. Yamada's terms became the Chinese terminology that is still in use. In field after field, Japanese concepts found their way into Chinese, irrespective of the diplomatic relations between the two countries. In strange ways, the closeness created by interstate conflict made Japanese society and culture even more attractive to many Chinese. As we shall see later, it was after the war between the two countries in 1894–1895 that the Chinese discovery of modern Japan really began. Liang Qichao, one of China's key reformers around the turn of the century, even managed to meet his 1898 political exile in Japan with enthusiasm:

> I have been in Japan . . . under these grievous circumstances for a number of months now, learning the Japanese language . . . and reading Japanese books. Books like I have never seen before dazzle my eyes. Ideas such as I have never encountered before baffle my brain. It is like seeing the sun after being confined to a dark room, or like a parched throat getting wine. So sated am I with happiness I dare not keep it bottled up, and so I let out with a shout and say to my fellow countrymen: Those of you yearning for new knowledge, join me in learning Japanese.[6]

But how was the rest of Asia going to deal with the shift in power to Japan? Culturally, politically, and organizationally, Korea had been the key state in the Sino-centric international system in the region. In terms of self-identification, it was closer to China than was any other independent country. Its Confucian scholars helped create a joint intellectual agenda. They wrote in Chinese and thought of their country as closely connected to the Chinese empire, but still distinct from it. Korean elites had for a very long time served as a bridge between China and Japan, across which ideas had traveled freely and often. Chinese script had arrived in Japan from Korea in the fourth century AD, Buddhism had come the same way two centuries later, and paper and printing, silk- and porcelain-making followed. As the world changed in the mid-nineteenth century and the flow of ideas started to be reversed, Koreans were reluctant to give up their perspective, which put China at the center. Large numbers of Confucian scholars appealed to the government not to violate set practice by accepting Japan as China's equal. One such petition, from 1881, sets out their view of Korea's traditional position and the dangers of changing it:

> We are a tributary state in our relations with China. For two hundred years we have sent tributes . . . and maintained our faith as a dependent state. If we are to accept official communications from Japan in which such honorifics as "the emperor" or "imperial" are used, suppose China questions our acquiescence. How are we to explain?[7]

From 1864 Korea was ruled by Prince Yi Haeung, termed the Daewongun (the Prince of the Great Court), on behalf of his son King Gojong, who was a minor. Prince Yi believed that Korea was coming under increasing threat from Western powers and Japan, and attempted to centralize power to be better equipped to resist. He fought a French landing in 1866 and an American one in 1871 but was removed from power in 1873 by his son, who had reached maturity. King Gojong wanted to negotiate with the foreigners, and he was encouraged to do so by Beijing, which hoped to maneuver between being seen as a facilitator in the opening of Korea to foreign trade and keeping its formal position of suzerainty intact. The scenario was not entirely dissimilar to Chinese–North Korean relations today.

The Meiji elite in Japan had different ideas. From the very beginning of the political changes in Tokyo, the leaders feared that Western domination of Korea would strangle the new Japanese experiment. They were particularly anxious when they learned about Russian advances on Korea's northern border. Regime hotheads, such as Saigo Takamori (who would later rebel against the Meiji order and suffer the consequences), suggested in 1873 that Japan should invade and occupy Korea, thereby seeing off foreign competition and revenge Korea's insults against the emperor, while providing gainful employment for thousands of unemployed samurai. Saigo's proposal was rejected, but Japan increased its push to gain access to Korea's resources and markets. In September 1875 the Japanese warship *Unyo* sailed to the Korean island of Ganghwa at the entrance to the Han river, which leads to Seoul, the capital. The Koreans shelled the ship, and, as retribution, Japanese marines landed and destroyed all they could find on the island, killing a number of Koreans in the process. In the aftermath of this first use of the new imperial navy, the Japanese government insisted on signing a Western-style treaty with Korea, patterned on the treaties Japan and China had been forced to sign with the Western powers. While the 1876 Treaty of Ganghwa did not give the Japanese extraterritoriality, it did open Korea to trade. Most importantly, it treated Korea as an independent state and ignored its tributary relations with China.

As in China and Japan, the 1880s was a turbulent decade in Korean politics. While the traditional elite tried to keep its rule intact and preserve at least some links with China, a new group of reformers emerged who, like their counterparts in China, were inspired by Japan's example. For the opponents of fundamental change, Japan was now the enemy. "It is obvious," one of them wrote, "that the Japanese and the Westerners are one and the same. How can one believe them when they say they are Japanese and not Westerners?" But for the reformers—among them the charismatic young nationalist Kim Ok-gyun who had traveled twice to Tokyo—Japan was a necessary ally in the battle for a strong and independent Korea. Two years after China had reasserted itself by sending troops to Seoul, the reformers tried to mount a coup d'état. Hoping that China would be too distracted by its war with France to intervene in Korea, Kim received promises from the Japanese ambassador for help. But the plan to assassinate leading members of the government failed, and Chinese forces and loyalist Korean troops confronted the rebels, who, after three days of fighting, fled to the port city of Inchon and boarded a Japanese ship bound for Yokohama. For the moment, the Sino-Korean alliance seemed secure.[8]

Given their difficulties with the Western powers further south, the Chinese Court had no intention of antagonizing the Japanese unnecessarily over Korea. Beijing followed a two-pronged strategy. Building on the victory of the traditionalists and the Chinese forces over the rebels, it increased the number of Chinese troops in Seoul and sent one of its most talented commanders, Yuan Shikai, to be the imperial resident there. The feisty twenty-six-year-old Henanese officer, who twice had failed in the imperial examinations and therefore had chosen an army career, became a sort of Chinese viceroy in Korea, moving into the royal palace and at times sleeping in the room next to King Gojong's chamber. For Yuan, his twelve years in Korea would launch a career that would make him China's president and, almost, its emperor. But his task in Seoul was not just to look after China's interests and prop up the tottering Korean monarchy. It was also to make sure that the Koreans settled their affairs with the Japanese properly in the wake of the failed coup, so that a future internationalization of Korean politics could be avoided.

Yuan Shikai did not succeed in creating a more stable situation in Korea. Even though Seoul and Tokyo in 1885 negotiated a protocol in which the Korean king apologized for the damage to Japanese property during the fighting the year before and allowed the stationing of a small unit of Japanese troops in the Korean capital, the direct negotiations between China and Japan over the situation on the peninsula undermined most of Yuan's work. The text of the Tianjin Convention between the two countries aimed at a non-interventionist policy with regard to Korea by sharply limiting the number of troops each country could have there. In effect, the convention undermined China's role as suzerain, while providing little incentive for the Koreans to attempt to work with both of its powerful neighbors. Over the next ten years, while Korean politics became increasingly factional and the model of Japan became more and more an inspiration for reformers, the role of the Chinese representatives in Seoul became more and more difficult.

By the early 1890s Korean society was fragmenting. In the south, a new syncretic religion called Tonghak (Eastern Learning) was challenging the authorities. The Tonghaks called upon the Korean people to rise up against foreign influence in the wake of the disasters that had befallen the country. "The people are the root of the nation," one of their pamphlets read. "If the root withers, the nation will be enfeebled. . . . We cannot sit by and watch our nation perish."⁹ By defining Koreans as constituting a separate and defined nation, the Tonghaks—mostly peasants from some of the poorest areas of the country—linked up with a new trend in Seoul in which some officials wanted not only to reform the state but also to emphasize Korean identity against the two other countries in the region. This new Korean nationalism was seen as a threat both by the Chinese and the Japanese, and by traditionalists at the Court in Seoul. When the Tonghaks marched on the capital in 1894, King Gojong asked for Chinese help in putting down what he viewed as a rebellion. Li Hongzhang, in charge of China's foreign relations in Beijing, obliged, after notifying Tokyo in accordance with the Tianjin Protocol. The Japanese responded by sending in their own troops, ostensibly for the protection of their citizens. By June 1894 the scene was set for a Sino-Japanese war.

At first, both Tokyo and Beijing attempted to avoid an all-out conflict. After landing 7,000 troops, the Japanese tried to get China engaged in setting up a joint commission for the reform of the Korean government. Beijing refused. Many leading Qing officials felt that China had done enough to appease Japan over Korea. They believed that China, after two decades of self-strengthening, was strong enough to defeat the "eastern barbarians." The belligerent attitude was supported by the rise at Court in the late 1880s and early 1890s of a faction that claimed that China's own reform had gone far enough, and that the Chinese essence was about to be lost. The Qingliu Dang, or purist party, as these officials were called, thought that compromise with foreign powers on internal or tributary matters was linked to China giving up its civilization through exchanging propriety and righteousness for barbarian habits. The Qingliu Dang often appealed to the Empress Dowager, Cixi, to quash plans put forward by Li Hongzhang and other moderate reformers. For her part, Cixi, who feared that the young Emperor Guangxu could be convinced to back radical reform in order to push her from power, more often than not concurred with the conservatives, including, in 1894, on the key issue of war or peace.

Li Hongzhang's dilemma was that he could not get direct backing from the Western powers, while the Beijing purists were pressing for war, and Japan was using its troop presence to take control of Seoul. When King Gojong rejected Japanese plans for government reform in late July, Japanese troops broke into the royal palace, kidnapped the queen and her children, and used their new leverage to bring the old Daewongun back into power. The Daewongun then declared Korean independence and war on China. When Li attempted to land Chinese reinforcements in Korea by ship, the *Gaosheng*, a chartered British steamer, was sunk by the Japanese navy on 25 July 1894 and 950 Chinese soldiers drowned. War could no longer be avoided.

The Sino-Japanese War of 1894–95 was the first war China fought with its new Western-type army and navy. It was also the first conflict between China and Japan in three hundred years, and the beginning of an enmity that was to define China's foreign relations for a century to come.[10] But in a curious way the war itself and the two decades that followed stand astride these two distinct periods in the Sino-Japanese relationship: China and Japan may have engaged in a bloody and terrible war, but the admiration that many Chinese felt for Japan's successes in building a new type of state and army was not diminished by China's losses. On the contrary, the sacrifices that China had to make were often blamed on the Qing dynasty and its inability to follow the examples set by Japan. To some Chinese, the Japanese model was in a perverse way validated by its victory: What should not happen and therefore could not happen in a Confucian world—that a younger brother beat and denigrated his older brother—had happened nonetheless. It was visible proof of China's decline and decadence. For people from Korea to Burma, the war redefined power in their region and turned the known order of the world upside down.

At the outset, Japan's victory was in no way assured. Chinese forces were well placed in Korea, and China's navy was about twice the size of Japan's. Both the civilian and military leaders in Tokyo were worried about the outcome, and much of their strategy was defined by the need to deliver decisive blows to the Qing military and thereby force it to accede to Japan's war aims, which was to remove Chinese influence from Korea. A long war, they feared, would be to China's advantage, since it would drain Japan's resources and manpower. The first engagement on land, in southern Korea, went Japan's way, but its leaders worried about what would happen in the north, where Chinese forces were stronger. And what they were most concerned about was what would happen at sea.

In September 1894 the Japanese forces landed at Inchon, the port city of Korea's capital Seoul, just as US General Douglas MacArthur's soldiers would do fifty-six years later. And, just as during that later Korean War, the Chinese forces concentrated on the defense of the north, assembling the majority of their troops around Pyongyang, a city 120 miles north of the capital. The Chinese forces were superior in numbers and consisted of some of the empire's best-supplied and best-trained Western-style troops, augmented by traditional Manchu cavalry, fighting with swords and lances. But when the battle started on 15 November, the Chinese could not match their enemies in terms of organization, logistics, and firepower. The Chinese defense was poorly coordinated and began to run out of ammunition, not least because of the lack of weapons' standardization among Chinese units. The Manchu horsemen attacked in wave after wave but were cut down by Japanese artillery, whose officers—in the midst of the slaughter—commented on the immense bravery of the old-style Qing army. With the city surrounded and the heavy Japanese guns trained on the main part of the imperial forces, the Chinese officers surrendered. Two thousand Qing troops fell in battle, against 700 Japanese, and the Meiji army continued its offensive toward the north.

The following day China's northern fleet engaged Japan's warships just off the mouth of the Yalu river, which marks the border between China and Korea. Again, on paper, the Chinese force was stronger than the Japanese. The Qing navy—and especially its northern fleet—was the modern pride of the empire. The Qing Court had spent immense sums buying ships from abroad and developing Chinese shipyards to serve them. The largest vessels in the northern fleet, the German-built battleships *Ding Yuan* and *Zhen Yuan*, were among the most powerful ships in existence (at 7,500 tons they were larger than the largest US battleship, the *USS Maine*). But China's sailors and marines, compared to Japan's, were poorly trained, and their officers—including the Western officers who served on them—did not understand naval tactics as well as their Japanese counterparts did. When the two fleets clashed, their training and tactics lost the clash for China. Tellingly, during the heat of battle the commanding Chinese admiral, Ding Ruchang—a former Taiping rebel turned Qing admiral—was seriously injured by a shell from his own ship that hit the bridge where he was standing. At the end of the four-hour engagement, four Chinese ships were sunk and all the others seriously damaged. With its army in retreat and the northern fleet destroyed, the Qing began to look for a way out of the war.

In Tokyo, leaders discussed whether to settle or continue the war. The proponents of continuing the war won hands down, since they could convincingly argue that Japan had been handed a golden opportunity to create a defensive environment that would secure their country against future Western encroachments, especially by Russia. Japanese forces now entered Manchuria by sea and land, and they landed on Shandong peninsula, and on Taiwan. The remnants of the Chinese northern fleet surrendered in February 1895, and Admiral Ding committed suicide. The following month armistice negotiations started, during which the Qing were advised by the former US secretary of state John W. Foster (the grandfather of John Foster Dulles, who would play a major role in China's next war in Korea). In the Treaty of Shimonoseki, Beijing had to recognize Korea's independence (under Japan's tutelage), it had to pay the equivalent of $133 million (more than a hundred times that amount in today's money) in indemnities, cede Taiwan, the Penghu islands, and the Manchurian Liaodong peninsula to Japan, open more treaty ports along the Yangzi river, and allow Japanese to run factories in China. If it had not been for a failed assassination attempt by a Japanese on the Chinese delegation leader, old Li Hongzhang, which embarrassed the Tokyo government, the resulting settlement would have been far worse for China. Even after a diplomatic intervention by Russia, supported by France and Germany, forced Japan to hand Liaodong back, the war stood as damning testament to the decline of the Chinese empire.

The defeat in the war against Japan led to a deep sense of crisis within the Chinese elite. But while there was much agreement about the problem—China's weakness—there was little consensus in terms of remedy. For the Empress Dowager and most of the Court, China had given up too much of its Confucian essence already, and it was only through regaining this spiritual core that the empire could retake its place in the world. The correct response to the wrongdoing of people inside and outside the empire was to appeal to justice and to reason, and thereby help them understand the natural order of things. If China held fast to its Confucian principles, then matters would correct themselves over time. Chu Chengbo, a censor in the imperial government, told the Court that "our trouble is not that we lack good institutions but that we lack upright minds."[11]

But for many Chinese who had witnessed their country's humiliation, an appeal to traditional principles was meaningless. Across the empire, demands for thorough reform of the government system emerged. Younger members of the elite felt that China could not survive if its society and its state were not profoundly changed. The candidates for the imperial examination, who were gathered in Beijing as news of the Chinese defeat came through, in a unique step broke with the very purpose that had brought them to the capital—the promulgation of Confucian knowledge—and took the lead in appealing for reform. One of them, Kang Youwei, a thirty-seven-year-old Guandong native from a prominent scholar-official family, organized most of his fellow candidates to sign a petition protesting the Shimonoseki Treaty and calling for fundamental reform of the Chinese government. It was an intellectual mass rebellion of the younger members of the elite that the Qing could simply not ignore, especially as the reform movement began to set up associations and discussion clubs both in and outside the capital, and the government—fearful of the consequences—did not dare suppress them.

While seeing himself very much as a reformer in the Confucian tradition, Kang looked abroad—and first and foremost to Japan—for models of how China through innovation and conscious adaptation could find a place as a respected state within an international system of states. "A survey of all states in the world," Kang wrote in a 1898 memorial to the throne, "will show that those states that undertook reforms became strong while those states that clung to the past perished. . . .

Our present trouble lies in our clinging to old institutions without knowing how to change. In an age of competition among states, to put into effect methods appropriate to an era of universal unification and laissez-faire is like wearing heavy furs in summer or riding a high carriage across a river. This can only result in having a fever or getting oneself drowned. . . . I beg Your Majesty to adopt the purpose of Peter the Great of Russia as our purpose and to take the

Meiji Reform of Japan as the model for our reform. The time and place of Japan's reform are not remote and her religion and customs are somewhat similar to ours. Her success is manifest; her example easy to follow.[12]

The young Guangxu emperor, so long under the thumb of the Empress Dowager and her Court officials, listened to the reformers, and acted on Kang's recommendations in the summer of 1898. During an intense period of change, Kang, with the emperor's blessing, not only remodeled the central government but set up new structures controlling the military, developing Western-style education, and improving government finance. The emperor himself had a long conversation with Ito Hirobumi, who had been prime minister of Japan during the war. For a brief moment China seemed to move toward fundamental reform of the Petrine or Meiji kind. Guangxu seemed a man in a hurry. One of his edicts read:

> Our scholars are now without solid and practical education; our artisans are without scientific instructors; when compared with other countries we soon see how weak we are. Does anyone think that our troops are as well drilled or as well led as those of the foreign armies? Or that we can successfully stand against them? Changes must be made to accord with the necessities of the times. . . . Keeping in mind the morals of the sages and wise men, we must make them the basis on which to build newer and better structures. We must substitute modern arms and western organization for our old regime; we must select our military officers according to western methods of military education; we must establish elementary and high schools, colleges and universities, in accordance with those of foreign countries; we must abolish the *wenchang* (literary essay) and obtain a knowledge of ancient and modern world-history, a right conception of the present-day state of affairs, with special reference to the governments and institutions of the countries of the five great continents; and we must understand their arts and sciences.[13]

But Kang's proposals for a constitution and a national assembly went too far for the conservatives to accept. Feeling that she alone stood between the empire and chaos, Cixi carried out a coup d'état in September 1898, ending the hundred days of reform. Her repression was intense: With the Guangxu emperor isolated on a small island in a lake inside the Forbidden City (not far, by the way, from where China's president Liu Shaoqi was to be kept under house arrest during the Cultural Revolution), the empress dowager not only overturned the reforms but also executed a number of reformers, including Kang Youwei's younger brother. For Cixi and the traditionalists, 1898 was about defending their personal power and defending China from an attack from within that could be more dangerous than any attack from without. In their view, reforms would do the empire no good if by adopting them it lost its Confucian soul.

To the surprise of everyone, including himself, Kang Youwei escaped the wrath of the Empress Dowager and fled to Hong Kong with the help of British officials. His main collaborator, Liang Qichao, made it to Tokyo on board a Japanese gunboat. Meeting up in Japan, they formed organizations that advocated fundamental reforms in their homeland. Kang and Liang also began translating into Chinese a large number of Western books that had already been translated or summarized in Japanese. Over the next decade they were joined in this effort by other exiles and by students who came to Japan to study at institutions set up for the purpose by the Japanese government. The largest of these, Kobun Gakuin (The Academy of Vast Learning), trained more than 7,000 Chinese in a broad Western curriculum during the 1900s, including Lu Xun, who would become a major writer, and Chen Duxiu, who would cofound the Chinese Communist Party (CCP). In 1905 alone there were more than 8,000 Chinese students in Japan, and some of them studied at the best new Japanese universities. At Hosei University, a special program trained them in law and administration. Others studied science, technology, agriculture, or—as did Chiang Kai-shek, who would later fight a seven-year long war against Japan—military affairs and strategy. The Chinese and Japanese worlds of concepts and terms were being more and more closely woven together; thousands of words for new basic terms, from *science* (*kexue*) and *law* (*falu*) to *republic* (*gonghe*) and *socialism* (*shehuizhuyi*) came to Chinese through Japanese (a language which of course is, to a large part, written in characters originally borrowed from China).

The two key concepts that Chinese in Japan and elsewhere discussed in the first decade of the new century were nationalism and republicanism. Unfamiliar and uncomfortable with the Western concept of nation, most Chinese preferred to believe that they lived in an empire ruled according to ancient principles and sustained by a common culture. Even Kang Youwei did not think of the Chinese as a nation; he wanted a constitution and representation, but he wanted to keep the empire in place. But the Japanese example jarred with this interpretation. Did not the Japanese emphasis on their uniqueness as a nation and on the bonds of blood and heritage that united them help make Japan an efficient and motivated modern country? Did not the Europeans and their new thinkers stress the universal applicability of the nation state in international relations? Younger Chinese scholars such as Zhang Binglin openly argued for the overthrow of the Qing and the establishment of a Chinese national state:

> Today five million Manchus rule over more than four hundred million Han only because rotten traditions make the Han stupid and ignorant. If the Han people should one day wake up, then the Manchus would be totally unable to rest peacefully here, like the Austrians in Hungary or the Turks in the former Eastern Roman Empire. It is human nature to love one's own race and to seek gain for oneself.[14]

Unlike Japan, where the reigning dynasty could be portrayed as holding the nation together, China had a dynasty that the nationalists saw as part of the problem. But if the Qing were to be overthrown, who should replace them? Few descendants of the last Chinese dynasty, the Ming, were still around, and the Ming had of course itself failed in the seventeenth century by letting the Manchus come to power.

Chinese republicanism—intimately connected to a new debate about democracy and representation—developed in exile, first and foremost in Japan, though one of its earliest advocates was Sun Yat-sen, who spent most of his first period of exile elsewhere. Like many ideas that entered into the hothouse of debate and contention around the turn of the century, Chinese concepts of democracy were mostly amalgams of Western models and earlier Chinese thought, first and foremost about people's rights and about representation at Court. And some of the first concrete proposals for a Chinese republic were inspired by Japanese intellectuals who argued for China to adopt the political system that they wanted, but did not dare ask for, in Japan. In Tokyo in 1905, several Chinese revolutionary groups founded the Tongmenghui, the League of Common Alliance. In its manifesto, written by Hu Hanmin, one of Sun's disciples, Hu emphasized Sun's version of republicanism:

> That absolute monarchy is unsuitable to the present age requires no argument. It is but natural therefore that those who propose new forms of government in the twentieth century should aim at the rooting out the elements of absolutism. Revolutions broke out in China one after another in the past, but because the political system was not reformed, no good results ensued. Thus, the Mongol dynasty was overthrown by the Ming, but within three hundred years the Chinese nation was again on the decline. For although foreign rule was overthrown and a Chinese regime was installed in its place, the autocratic form of government remained unchanged, to the disappointment of the people. We can overthrow the Manchus and establish our state because Chinese nationalism and democratic thought are [now] well developed.[15]

While the small group of revolutionaries was right that China was heading into unchartered waters in terms of its politics, they could not have been more wrong on Chinese nationalism and democracy. The Tongmenghui manifesto, with its echoes of Herbert Spencer and John Stuart Mill (via their Japanese messengers Nakamura Keiu and Fukuzawa Yukichi), was for China's future, not its present. The ideas about nation and governance that Chinese picked up in Japan would play only a small part in the death throes of the Qing empire, especially since the empire itself—though weakened—still had a decent arsenal of both ideological and material weapons with which to defend itself.

Japan's 1895 victory in the war with China meant that China was no longer the center of international affairs in East Asia. It did not, however, mean that Japan had replaced it. As the Meiji leaders had feared, the European powers and the United States were intent on preventing domination of a region by one power, and an Asian power at that. Just as most Europeans had failed to understand the ramifications of the remarkable rise of Japan, the Japanese had not grasped that all Western powers could come together against it. And since the Europeans had already taken control of most of the rest of the world, Japan needed to consolidate its predominance within its own region. As Tokutomi Soho, one of the many Japanese liberals who had influenced the Chinese in Japan, wrote in 1896,

> The countries of the Far East falling prey to the great powers of Europe is something that our nation will not stand for. East Asia becoming a mire of disorder is something that our nation will not tolerate. We have a duty to radiate the bright light of civilization beyond our shores and bring the benefits of civilization to our neighbors. We have the duty to guide backward countries to the point of being able to govern themselves. We have the duty to maintain peace in East Asia for this purpose. As a man has his calling, so too does a nation have its mission.[16]

A S THE TWENTIETH CENTURY PROCEEDED, Japan eliminated more and more of the liberal and constitutional principles that so many Asians were first inspired to follow in Tokyo. The Chinese who admired Japan also worried about its increasing subjugation of Korea and the occupation of Taiwan. But with the European powers pushing harder than ever for the expansion of their zones of control inside China, Japan was less of a concern to the Chinese at the beginning of the century. In spite of the war and the Chinese losses, Japan had after all withdrawn from the areas it had occupied inside China. Tellingly, the same ports from which the Japanese had moved out—Lüshun (Port Arthur) and Dalian in Liaodong, Qingdao and Weihaiwei in Shandong—were taken over by the Europeans (the first two by Russia, and the latter two by Germany and Britain respectively). The Russian expansion was of particular worry to the Qing government, since all of Manchuria seemed set for Russian control, with railway lines and commercial settlements spreading out from foreign strongholds in Harbin and Shenyang (Mukden) toward the coast. To the Qing imperial clan this was of course not about just any territory; it was about the defense of a region it considered its ancestral land.

Though their own claim to influence in Manchuria was only a decade old, the Japanese leaders were as enraged by the Russian expansion as were the Qing. But while the Qing was powerless (mostly) to resist, Tokyo had both the will and the means to react. Seeking to balance Russian power in East Asia, the Japanese leaders signed an alliance treaty with Russia's European rival Britain, and engaged in a massive military buildup. Since Japan's main concern was the security of Korea, and not Manchuria itself, it offered Russia an agreement in which the two countries were to respect each other's zones of influence. The government of Tsar Nicholas II turned the Japanese emissaries down. Describing them as "monkeys" and their army as "infantile," the tsar wanted war.[17] On 8 February 1904 Japan attacked, and before the declaration of war had been received in Saint Petersburg, the Japanese navy had badly

damaged the Russian Far Eastern Fleet at Lüshun. After landing reinforcements in Korea, the Japanese army moved north toward Manchuria.
While the Russians were still waiting for reinforcements from Europe,
Tokyo in reality had already won the war by gaining naval superiority
and pushing the Russian army ever further inland. After having taken
Lüshun, Japan in early 1905 forced the Russians out of Shenyang after
a major battle and in May destroyed the Russian Baltic Fleet, which
had just completed a journey of 18,000 miles to reach the front, in the
battle of Tsushima. In the latter engagement the Russians lost eight
battleships and more than 5,000 sailors. The Japanese losses were 116
men. Russia sued for peace.

For China, the outcome of the Russo-Japanese war was twofold.
Russia's advance into China had been stopped, while Japan's had been
accelerated. Some of the advisers at Court (and quite a few of their revolutionary opponents) thought the result was the better of two evils: It
would be easier to dislodge the Japanese than it would have been the
Russians. But the outcome of the war should be balanced by the dispir-
iting fact that a major war—sometimes referred to with slight hyperbole
as "World War 0"—had been fought on Chinese territory without any
participation by a Chinese state. When a peace conference was convened
in Portsmouth, New Hampshire, under the aegis of Theodore Roosevelt's administration, China was not even invited to attend. The
Portsmouth Treaty transferred Russia's possessions in Manchuria to
Japan, along with the southern part of Sakhalin island. Sovereignty over
its territory was to remain with the Qing empire, but the outcome of
the war was clear: Japan had become the main power in northern and
northeastern China. The Portsmouth Treaty, by the way, won the bel-
licose Rough Rider Roosevelt the Nobel Peace Prize for 1906, the most
unlikely peace laureate until Henry Kissinger in 1973.

In a sign of what was to come, public dissatisfaction with the
Portsmouth Treaty was strong in all three countries. In Japan, the sense
that its territorial gain was not commensurate with its military victory

fueled nationalist riots in Tokyo and other cities, which forced the resignation of the government. In Russia, its loss gave rise to the 1905 revolution, which forced the Tsar to give up his claim to unlimited power. And in China the seeming powerlessness of the Qing to defend national territory led to a public outcry that forced the regime to agree to a constitution and a national assembly. Just as after World War I in Europe, the governments of the region saw that nationalism could be a double-edged sword, which could be turned against them by those who saw revolution as the remedy for their country's ills. In China, the Qing for the first time began to fear that the main threat to their rule was not foreign powers, but their own people.

The Japanese occupation of Taiwan was a key cause for protest among Chinese nationalists. The Qing had claimed sovereignty over the island since the late seventeenth century, but the people of Taiwan had never been fully integrated into the Chinese empire before the island was ceded to Japan in 1895. In many ways it was a typical Qing border region, where local and central jurisdictions competed, and where the few officials who were sent to the island soon realized they had better work with local powerholders and local concepts of justice and order if some form of peace and stability was to be maintained. In the late nineteenth century, the population of 2.5 million was mainly Chinese whose ancestors had emigrated from the mainland, but most of these were concentrated in towns along the western coast, leaving most of the inland and the mountainous east coast to Taiwanese aboriginals. After the first and inglorious Japanese landing on the island in 1874, the Chinese government had tried to beef up its claim of controlling the island by building roads and a railway line, setting up schools, and promoting trade as well as agriculture. When the island was ceded to Japan in 1895 there was enough local elite resistance to help form a rebel Republic of Taiwan—the first Chinese republic anywhere and indeed the first republic of any kind in East Asia—which aimed at keeping the island Chinese through appealing to principles of popular sovereignty. But overwhelmed by Japanese power and ignored by the world's governments, the republic died after a few months.

After being the first republic, Taiwan became Japan's first colony. The Japanese leaders were keenly aware of how the Western great powers were watching their every move. The great question was whether a new non-European state could establish a modern colony and run it successfully. In Japan, as in the United States, which got its first subject territories (including the Philippines) at about the same time, opinion was divided. Some advocated full assimilation, making the Taiwanese Japanese linguistically, culturally, and eventually also politically, while others believed that the ethnic divides were too great to be bridged and that the island had to be ruled as separate from Japan, with its own laws and political system. The latter form of thinking held the upper hand in the first phase of the colonization. Colonial administrators viewed Taiwan as an exotic and disorderly territory, the population of which consisted of three main groups: Chinese who would go back to mainland China, Chinese who would become loyal to Tokyo, and aboriginals, who could be contained and kept in a permanently weakened condition, much as the United States had done with the Native Americans.

Most Chinese in Taiwan soon began working within the new colonial system. For some, the Japanese takeover meant new business opportunities or improved conditions for agriculture. For almost all, new programs for education, public health, and local administration meant a substantial improvement in the standard of living, so that a significant number of Taiwanese welcomed the new policies of integration and assimilation that came out of the liberal political leadership in Japan after World War I. The Taiwanese elite increasingly got its education at Japanese universities, started wearing Japanese clothes, and began making use of Japanese law to protect their business holdings (including on the Chinese mainland, where they could make use of Japanese rights of extraterritoriality). From the 1920s on, a rapidly expanding elite became more and more bilingual, as shown in the development of a distinct

Taiwanese literature, written in Chinese or Japanese, which helped form a sense of identity. The business opportunities and the social and political stability of the island ended up attracting people from the mainland as well; in 1936, the year before the next Sino-Japanese war broke out, more than 60,000 Chinese came to Taiwan to work or to settle.[18]

When China and Japan again went to war in 1937, many Taiwanese were caught in a horrible dilemma between the two lineages of their identity. The 1920s and 1930s had seen an increasingly self-confident Chinese leadership on the island. But it was divided between those who sought greater autonomy for Taiwan under Japan and those who hoped for reunification with the mainland. More than 200,000 Taiwanese volunteered for the Japanese armed forces, while many of their countrymen chafed under Tokyo's attempts at forced assimilation during the war, including ill-conceived ideas such as transplanting the Shinto religion onto Taiwan and requiring Chinese to adopt Japanese names.[19] As a colonial project, Taiwan, like Hong Kong, made it possible for people to create a new identity, but they also ran the risk of seeing that identity blown to pieces when the forces of history changed. Without forgetting their Chinese origins, the Taiwanese became both the beneficiaries and the victims of the rise of Japan.

THE RELATIONSHIP TO JAPAN was crucial in the final reformist phase of the Qing empire and during the period of instability and search for a new political system that replaced the empire in 1912. The rise of Japanese power meant that Tokyo was seen as a model and a source of support for Chinese leaders of all political hues. The constitutionalists around Kang Youwei wanted to see China take Meiji Japan as its political inspiration. The revolutionaries around Sun Yat-sen admired Japan's military and economic strength and sought Japanese funds for their missions. Chinese dissident organizations subscribing to these views—and all possible ones in between—were usually headquartered in Tokyo, where they benefited from many freedoms they encountered there and from Japanese largesse. Meanwhile, the new policy of administrative reform announced by the Qing in 1901 was also patterned on Japanese practices. Around 1910 one finds Qing loyalists and their opponents battering each other over the head with slogans adopted from the Meiji experience a generation earlier. When the former shouted, "Reform the state and revere the emperor," the latter countered, "Only the foreign can save China."

In 1910, frightened by an increasing Western predominance in East Asia, Tokyo had decided to annex Korea fully and make it a Japanese province. With Korean nationalism on the rise, the decision could not have come at a worse moment for the relationship between the two peoples. Even those Koreans who admired Japan refused to cooperate with the new authorities, at least at first. Tokyo's own gaze now quickly shifted from Seoul to Beijing, where the same form of chaos and dissolution that had made Korea a target for foreigners seemed to be threatening China. Intent not to lose out, Japan entered World War I as a British ally in order to try to seize the German possessions in China. In November 1914, when the German forces capitulated to the Japanese navy, Tokyo gained a strategic foothold on the Shandong peninsula. But Japan's leaders worried that it would lose out to Western powers when the war ended, as had happened in 1895 and 1905. And so, in January 1915, Japan issued a set of demands that intended to mark China out as an area for its own special influence.

Japan's Twenty-One Demands, as they became known, were a classic case of diplomatic overreach. The Japanese cabinet piled point upon point to satisfy the desires of each of its members and ended up with a text that, if accepted, would have made China a virtual Japanese protectorate. Not only would Tokyo gain full control of Shandong; it would also solidify its power in Manchuria and extend its position of primacy in Fujian, the coastal province across from Japanese-held Taiwan. Sections of the Chinese military and police would come under Japanese control. China would also pledge not to allow any other power to gain further concessions along its coast and would grant Japan permission to build railways in its southern provinces. The other allied powers, including Japan's old ally Britain, protested when the terms became known, because of their content and because Tokyo had tried to carry out the negotiations in secret. In the end, the Japanese had to beat a humiliating retreat, securing very little beyond what they had already got. Even that they could obtain only by threatening the weak Chinese government with war.

The Twenty-One Demands became a watershed in Sino-Japanese relations. To many Chinese they symbolized an aggressive Japan that had become the main threat to China's independence and that treated the country just as it had treated Korea before annexation. All over the country students protested Japanese pressure, and Japanese goods were boycotted. Both Yuan Shikai's government and the opposition were weakened as a result: Yuan because he had offered to cooperate with the Japanese, the opposition because it was badly split on the issue. Sun Yat-sen, in one of his less popular moves, had attempted to outbid Yuan's Beijing regime by offering to let Tokyo veto any diplomatic agreement China would make if he got back into the presidency. The result was widespread disillusionment among younger Chinese with an elite—whatever its political orientation—that was much too acquiescent to Japan.

The changing view of Japan, both in the West and in China, was an important reason why Beijing was allowed to join in World War I as an allied power in August 1917, after the United States had given up its neutrality. By then large numbers of Chinese laborers had been recruited to work for the allies on the fronts in Europe. It was by far the biggest and most concentrated mass transport of Chinese workers ever to go to another continent. It would have major consequences in terms of spreading information about Europe into even the remotest parts of China. And many of those who participated came back fired up by new ideas and new knowledge. China's diplomatic reward for having joined the war on the winning side was small, however: Article 156 of the 1919 Versailles Treaty confirmed Japan's control of the former German-held territory in China. The decision caused large demonstrations in China and provided the background for the May Fourth Movement, the attempt to create a new national consciousness, which would help transform China's approach to the world in the interwar years.

FOR CENTURIES THE MANCHU RULERS of China had tried to set off the northeastern part of the country, Manchuria, as their own preserve by preventing Chinese migrants from settling there. Manchuria is a beautiful land, in spite of its harsh winters. Its lakes, forests, and abundant natural resources have long been a draw for the more adventurous Chinese, a kind of inner frontier that beckoned with the promise of a better life on the other side. As the Qing came under siege from its foreign and domestic enemies in the nineteenth century, many Chinese moved to Manchuria and settled its rich farmlands. But it was not only the Chinese who coveted the northeastern provinces. Russia, first, and then Japan had moved in too, cultivating the fiction that the territory belonged to no one, and that they could therefore colonize it. In the 1850s Russia had wrested the eastern coast of Manchuria away from China, to become the Russian Pacific Maritime Provinces, where the city they named Vladivostok (Conqueror of the East) is today. After 1905, Japan controlled the southern part of Manchuria, while the Russians still, tenuously, held onto the north. The two powers signed a number of secret agreements, setting out demarcation lines for their influence both in Manchuria and in Mongolia, a Qing territory of which the northern part had declared its independence in 1912 under Russian tutelage, while the southeastern part was coming increasingly under Japanese influence. Manchuria and its neighboring dominions seemed lost to China.

After the revolution of 1911/12, the fate of Manchuria became a rallying point for Chinese nationalists and for leaders who themselves hailed from the region. To many Chinese the gradual exclusion of China's interests from the area was worse than the foreign occupations that had taken place elsewhere in the country. The European coastal concessions, most people thought, were reversible and therefore temporary. But the penetration of the northeastern provinces could become irreversible, because the foreign countries that operated there were China's neighbors. They aimed to take Manchuria permanently away from China. All over the country, the recovery of "Chinese Manchuria" became a rallying cry for those who wanted to define what Chinese nationalism meant. Some writers claimed that the test of a person's Chineseness was whether he or she was willing to shed blood in order to get back the Northeast and make China whole again.

When the Bolsheviks overthrew the Russian regime in 1917 and began building a socialist state, they unilaterally declared that they would withdraw all Russian forces from Chinese territory and abolish all unequal treaties. These promises, which were largely kept, had a massive effect in China, turning many young Chinese toward Soviet Communism. Inside Manchuria, however, the situation went from bad to worse after 1917. Japan attacked the new Soviet state together with the Western powers and thereby expanded its military influence all over the region, including in China. During the 1920s, Japan came to dominate all parts of Manchuria in an uneasy alliance with Zhang Zuolin, a flamboyant Chinese regional leader with national ambitions.

The initial phase of Japanese control of the three northeastern provinces was first and foremost economic. Exploiting the region's enormous agricultural potential (in part by forcing Chinese farmers off their land), Japan set up an export-oriented farming sector, producing processed and unprocessed agricultural goods. Japanese companies also developed small but increasingly influential industries centered on textiles and household goods. By 1928, thirty-two percent of all of China's exports came from Manchuria,[20] and the whole region's economy was increasingly linked with Japan's both domestically and internationally. That year Japan began a process of breaking even the formal ties that bound the northeastern provinces to the rest of China. Believing that Zhang Zuolin stood in the way of this process, local officers of the imperial army placed a bomb under his Japanese-made railway carriage and blew their former ally sky-high, demonstrating to all how far some Japanese were willing to go to fasten their country's grip on Manchuria. While Tokyo was increasingly losing full control of its army's actions abroad, the Japanese government feared the rise in Chinese nationalism and the vigorous new regime of Chiang Kai-shek. It also feared the effects of the global depression on Japan and its development aims. Japan's response was to do as much as it could to preserve Manchuria as its exclusive zone of influence, even if that meant fighting future wars over it.

WITHIN A GENERATION CHINA's Japan had gone from being the foremost inspiration in creating a new state and society to being the main threat to China's existence. In the 1920s and 1930s there were still people around on both sides who called for the relationship to be less confrontational and more cooperative. Sun Yat-sen, in one of his last speeches in 1924, claimed that the two countries were still connected by common blood and common interests:

> What problem does Pan-Asianism attempt to solve? The problem is how to terminate the sufferings of the Asiatic peoples and how to resist the aggression of the powerful European countries. In a word, Pan-Asianism represents the cause of the oppressed Asiatic peoples. . . . [W]e advocate the avenging of the wrong done to those in revolt against the civilization of the rule of Might, with the aim of seeking a civilization of peace and equality and the emancipation of all races. Japan to-day has become acquainted with the Western civilization of the rule of Might, but retains the characteristics of the Oriental civilization of the rule of Right. Now the question remains whether Japan will be the hawk of the Western civilization of the rule of Might, or the tower of strength of the Orient. This is the choice which lies before the people of Japan.[21]

But as imperial Japan moved to secure its role as a great power at China's expense, the voices of cooperation became fewer and increasingly reviled by their compatriots. Much of Chinese nationalism, as it was formed in the interwar years, became ingrained with a vision of Japan as China's deadly enemy, a vision that persists among many Chinese today. Instead of a new East Asia in which China and Japan were partners, as so many had dreamed about in the nineteenth century, the region in the next century became a nightmare of conflict, a nightmare that by the 1930s seemed to have no end.

There were several main reasons for this sorry outcome. As both countries broke out of their systems of beliefs and traditions in the late nineteenth century, they soon found that they had less and less in common. Japan's Confucianism, originating from China, but developing independently during the 250-year Tokugawa period, became less of a tie as old ideas and concepts came under pressure. After the 1890s, Chinese society became a permanent warning to many Japanese, in the form of what some today would call a failed state: an ungovernable region from which lawlessness, disease, and terrorism emanated. That Japanese and Chinese seemed closely related in a racial sense (at least under the Western gaze) made matters worse: Japan had to become everything China was not, almost to the degree that Chinese society by the 1920s was constituted as a kind of anti-Japan. It was dirty, when Japan was clean and hygienic. It was backward, when Japan was progressive. It was weak, when Japan was strong. It was wayward, when Japan was purposeful.

Both Japanese and Chinese nationalisms took part of their core purpose from ideas adopted from the West. But even so they were very different in character. Japan developed a form of ethnic nationalism, in some ways similar to the new nationalisms found in Germany and Italy, or in parts of Eastern Europe. Defining all Japanese as one *ethnie*, the state constructed a religion (Shintoism), an educational system, and an army that taught the new message: All Japanese were one, bound together by bloodline and territory (what the Germans called *Blut und Boden*) into one national state. In China such an ethnic nationalism was difficult to imagine. China had been everything, not just a group of people tied together by some form of inheritance. China was a culture as well as an empire, and it took a long time—really up to today—before Chinese fully began seeing themselves as one group, defined by where they live and what they look like. Still, the Chinese nationalism of the early twentieth century—centered on the state—was enough of a challenge to others, and especially to Japan, whose incursions into China were predicated on the absence of a viable Chinese state.

For Japan, the relationship to China was closely connected to the fear of foreign domination. As Japan's power grew in the early twentieth century, some Japanese elites came to believe that their country's survival depended on having an empire of its own, as the leading Western states had, and on not becoming isolated. To this form of Japanese thinking, which developed into the militarism of the 1930s, China was an object of conquest and subordination. But there were also Japanese who sincerely believed in East Asian cooperation as a barrier against the West, and who believed that Japan could help China protect itself and build a new state in close cooperation with its eastern neighbor. To both groups, however, Japan could not stay away from China: Either by conquest or by example, Japan had to prevent the country from becoming a Western dominion directed against Japan.

In China, the sense of enduring weakness that set in among some elites in the early twentieth century was projected onto the relationship with Japan. From being a model that could help China out of its despair, some Chinese came to see Japan as a root cause of their country's problems. China was weak because Japan was strong. Tokyo was not just exploiting China's condition but held it in place and extended it. Expanding on traditional stereotypes, some Chinese felt that it was only through destroying China that Japan could replace it as the dominant power in East Asia. The attempts by the Japanese to create an empire in China's place was so perverse, so against the natural order of things, that it was in its essence the worst problem China faced. Whatever existed otherwise and elsewhere, there was no room for two powers within the region. This attitude toward Japan is one that some Chinese have kept, even after their rival's spectacular collapse in World War II.

CHAPTER 4

REPUBLIC

IN THE EARLY TWENTIETH CENTURY, China went through a series of political convulsions that would shape all of its future foreign affairs. In 1900, large groups of ordinary Chinese organized violent protests against the foreign presence in what became known in the West as the Boxer Rebellion (but which should rather be known as the Boxer Revolution). In 1911, regional elites all over the country rose up against the Qing, and an army mutiny forced the mother of the last emperor, the four-year-old Puyi, to issue his abdication. By imperial decree, China became a republic, though very few people knew what a republic meant (the new Chinese word for it, *minguo*, means "people's country" or "people and country"). Did the new order mean elections and a representative government? Or did it mean the rule of the best-qualified experts? Was China ripe for republicanism, or would old patterns of patronage and deference reassert themselves? Did a republic mean every man for himself, the dissolution of central power, the end of Confucianism, and, eventually, the breakup of China? Or could the new authorities fashion a new country, one that kept its Chineseness while becoming one with the rest of the world?

Between 1900 and the late 1920s, China saw many different regimes, foreign interventions, and provincial centers of power. The Qing empire was replaced by a succession of weak central governments, which slowly ceased exerting full authority in most matters outside a section of northern China, around the capital, Beijing. Foreign powers, and especially Japan, were becoming more powerful within China than they had ever been during the Qing (though the political chaos made China less interesting for foreign investment than it might otherwise have been). Regional powerholders, some of them representing national minorities, became key political figures, often with effective control of both politics and commerce within their regions. It was a period of tremendous change, both in people's daily lives and, not least, in how the Chinese viewed themselves and their country.

Understanding China's foreign relations in this tumultuous period requires grasping two realities. Throughout the period and in spite of all challenges—domestic and foreign—China as a state retained enough cohesion to keep in place the semblance of a central government with a mandate to conduct foreign affairs. This mattered, because it would have been much easier for other countries to have shaved outlying provinces off China if there had not been a government of sorts claiming to represent the country as a whole. The remarkable fact that China's borders today are almost identical to those of the Qing empire in its waning years is testimony to the significance of the idea of one integrated state, even when the republic was at its weakest. But it is also important to understand that no foreign great power wanted the complete dismemberment of China. Even Japan, which was moving ever closer to full control over Manchuria, did not want to see China south of the Great Wall carved up into zones of foreign occupation, because Tokyo (quite sensibly) believed that such a division would privilege Western states over Japan. And the Western powers—including the Russians/Soviets—were happy to work through local powerholders, factions, or political parties: Always watching each other for advantage, they were perfectly willing to work through those Chinese authorities that gave them the best deal, while preferring a weak central government over its abolition. Western businessmen felt that a little Chinese disunity was good for business, but full dismemberment would unleash inner and outer power struggles that could do nothing but harm the prospects for the China trade.

The other main reality in the early twentieth century was the growth in Chinese capabilities in all sectors of society. After having been overwhelmed and numbed by the encounter with the West for almost two generations, China swung into action in ways that it had followed so often before: adapting Chinese means to foreign constructs, implementing foreign technologies (and amalgamating them with Chinese methods), learning through studies of the non-native, and inventing new forms of authority and concepts of self. By 1937 China had developed a Western-style sector of its economy that was open to the rest of the world. Industry, mining, transportation, communications, finance, and banking became increasingly international in technology, management, and ownership. Although this sector was only a small part (as low as ten percent, by some estimates) of a Chinese economy still dominated by agriculture, its visible manifestations became increasingly significant. Arsenals and shipyards, factories and railways, bore testimony to something new and strange being born. And new products, manners, and methods spread all over the country, including to regions far away from where a Chinese modernity was coming to life.[1]

By the early twentieth century, almost all Chinese were aware that the world they lived in was changing, but they had, of course, very different perspectives on this change. For some—many officials and intellectuals, for instance—the change was a collapse, pure and simple; a world that had been well-ordered and correct, with the Qing empire and China's traditions at its center, was overturned. For others, the new world opened up new opportunities, new ways of leading their lives, chances to travel or to read in ways that had never existed before. For most Chinese, however, illiterate and bound to the earth by convention or by contract, what changed was not their personal position, but the constellations of power in their village, the origins of people who traveled through, or the armies they were asked to support. It was a changing world, and one where the changes helped split people apart, sometimes by their own will and sometimes against it.

IN OCTOBER 1898 a small group of peasants began a movement that would open a violent new phase in China's confrontation with the West. They were inspired by martial arts and the secret societies that had long existed in their region of eastern Shandong, and they called themselves *Yihequan* or Fists of United Righteousness. Foreigners called them the Boxers. The group had long been involved in a conflict over rights to a local temple claimed both by Christians and non-Christians in the community. For the Boxers, the troubles of their region—Western incursions, Christian proselytizing, floods, and droughts—all seemed to have one cause: the willingness of Chinese to be overwhelmed by the foreign, and especially by foreign religion, without resistance. They dreamed of creating a China cleansed of the injustice of foreign ways, and they set out to free their region and their country from its humiliation by blood and fire.

The Boxers were a strange sight to Chinese and foreigners alike. Their red turbans and leather boots, their belief in magic, their invocations, shouts, and songs made them stand out even in a restless society where sects and secret societies were popping up all over—mad monks in Sichuan, sisters of Jesus in Guangdong, Ming descendants in Fujian, and Buddhists in Shanxi who believed in a nirvana on earth created by repeating mantras and smoking lots of opium. The Qing had their hands full catching and executing those who went too far in stirring up trouble or challenging authority. But the Boxers were different. In spite of their outlandish and often brutal behavior, they seemed to speak directly to China's ills and offer the chance for young lower-class Chinese men to show themselves as patriotic and brave. In Shandong, Germans were a growing presence, and they mixed support for missionaries with brutality toward the native people. And so, Cixi and the Qing conservatives at Court hesitated in suppressing the Boxers, at least as long as they professed their loyalty to the state.

The Boxer movement's attacks on foreigners, Westernized Chinese, and especially on Chinese Christians broke society wide open and unleashed a war that removed the last vestiges of international respectability from the Qing regime. In many parts of China, especially the north, news about the Boxers fed into ongoing conflicts between Chinese with links to the outside world and those who resisted such links. The result was violent confrontations. Western accounts focus on the killing of foreign missionaries and Chinese Christians. But during the three years of the Boxer Rebellion, only about a quarter of the total death toll of more than 120,000 were Christians; 250 were foreigners. The rest were non-Christian Chinese killed by foreign troops or by Chinese troops who joined them. One's point of view is usually determined by one's place of view: When in 2000 the Vatican canonized 116 Catholics who were killed by the Boxers, the Chinese Foreign Ministry referred to the very same people as "evil-doing sinners who raped, looted and worked as agents of Western imperialism."[2] For some, the Christians killed in China were saints; for others they were sinners against the natural order of things—then as now.[3]

The first Boxer groups began entering Beijing in the spring of 1900. The Qing state had already shown signs of fragmenting on the Boxer issue, just as it had fragmented over reform issues two years earlier. In some regions, officials and military commanders were hunting down Boxer bands or at least trying to keep the peace between Christians and anti-Christians, while helping foreigners evacuate. In other parts, however, commanders and officials were joining with the Boxers, either because they believed in the anti-Christian message or out of fear of the consequences if they confronted a popular movement. By early June, Qing soldiers and militia members in Beijing had joined in attacks against churches, foreign-style schools and hospitals, and the homes of foreign residents. At Court, Cixi was increasingly pro-Boxer, although she did not support the movement publicly until after foreign navy ships had attacked Chinese forts in an attempt to land forces in Tianjin, where the foreign community was also under attack by the Boxers. Cixi issued an edict on 21 June, in the name of the powerless Emperor Guangxu: "Our ancestors have come to Our aid, and the Gods have answered Our call, and never has there been so universal a manifestation of loyalty and patriotism. With tears We have announced the war in the ancestral shrines."[4]

With China at war, the Court ordered all of its forces to join with the militias and armed groups, including the Boxers, to defend the empire. Many commanders and regional leaders disobeyed. In the south, most promised to protect resident foreigners if foreign forces did not attack. Other long-time Qing advisers, disgusted with the Boxers, withdrew from public life. Most of the core of the army in the north did follow orders, however, and by late June the diplomatic community and other foreigners in Beijing were besieged in the legation quarter in the center of the city. The Cathedral of the Immmaculate Conception had been burned down on 13 June, with great loss of life; in the Northern Cathedral more than 3,000 people held out against sporadic attacks for more than eight weeks. The German ambassador, the arrogant and reckless Prussian officer Baron Clemens von Ketteler, set off to the Zongli Yamen, where he intended to deliver a formal protest, but he was shot and killed as he was carried in his sedan chair through the streets.

By early August 1900 there was fighting in Beijing. The neighborhoods around the legation quarter, including the great imperial library at the Hanlin academy, were burned to the ground. Eighteen thousand foreign troops were making their way from Tianjin to the capital, battling imperial troops and Boxers as they advanced. Towns and villages were torched and tens of thousands of civilians killed. To many of the newly arrived foreign troops, any Chinese, including women and children, could be a Boxer in disguise, and rumors about the horrible ways in which foreign missionaries and their families had been put to death fueled the bloodlust. For foreign leaders, China was the first "failed state," and the intervention in 1900 was the first "coalition of the willing," meaning, in this case, an alliance of the main Western countries and Japan directed against Chinese "barbarity" and against the Qing state's unwillingness to uphold "civilized" norms of government and public behavior.

The allied troops entered Beijing on 14 August with a vengeance. Cixi and the Court fled to Xi'an, and so it was the ordinary people of Beijing who felt the fury of the invasion. Russian and French soldiers massacred Chinese civilians. In one town near Beijing 500 young girls and women committed suicide because they had been raped by foreign soldiers or feared they would be. "There are things that I must not write, and that may not be printed in England, which would seem to show that this Western civilization of ours is merely a veneer over savagery," noted the British journalist George Lynch, who witnessed the occupation. The Chinese capital, including the imperial palaces, was thoroughly looted. The orders of the commanders of the foreign troops and the behavior of their soldiers caused a scandal in many of the countries that contributed to the allied operation. A major Japanese newspaper lamented that its country's army "purports to be an army that protects humanity and justice through a discourse of civilization. Our countrymen have been particularly proud of this honor since the war of 1894–95. . . . This looting . . . has resulted in the most outrageous disgrace to the military, the most appalling national disgrace to Japan."[5]

In spite of the criticism of foreign behavior in China, it was the Boxers and the Qing Court that almost all outsiders (and a fair number of urban Chinese) blamed for the disasters of the summer of 1900. More fully than any event before it, the Boxer war had placed China outside the Western-led international system, a pariah state, the center of a 1900 axis of evil that incorporated resistance against colonial domination everywhere, from Sudan to Afghanistan to Korea. The empress dowager, desperate to cling to power, recalled old Li Hongzhang, for his final bow, to negotiate the survival of the Qing state and her own return to Beijing. The foreign diktat imposed on China, the so-called Boxer Protocols, signed in September 1901, in effect made China a ward of the allied powers that had intervened against her: A strict weapons embargo was put in place, the leading pro-Boxer members of the government exiled or executed. Chinese forts guarding Beijing were razed and foreign troops stationed on the roads between the capital and the sea. All of China's state income was made to contribute toward paying a massive indemnity to the allied powers, totaling, over a forty-year amortization period, almost four times the Chinese state's annual income in 1900. The Qing had become hostage to the political and economic interests of the West and Japan.[6]

BESIDES JAPAN, the two main newcomers to the pattern of exploiting China were the United States and Germany. While having to operate within what was basically a British-constructed system, Washington and Berlin chose two distinct directions for their activities, directions that were to have implications for China well beyond the nineteenth century. In the United States, from the 1890s on, there was a strong suspicion that the imperial ambitions of others could bar American business interests from the Chinese market. The *Philadelphia Press* declared that "the future must not be put in peril. . . . China holds one-fourth the human race. Its free access to our trade and manufactures is vital to our future." In notes outlining the so-called Open Door Policy, sent in 1899 to all the great powers, US Secretary of State John Hay urged "the various powers claiming 'spheres of interest' that they shall enjoy perfect equality of treatment for their commerce and navigation within such 'spheres.'"[7] The United States sought to secure access for US products and capital to Chinese markets even though it was unwilling to establish its own areas of control and domination. Germany, united in 1871 into one strong imperial state, chose the more traditional route of requiring territorial concessions from China, but with specific aims of modernization along German lines in mind, as well as trade. After two German missionaries were murdered at Juye in Shandong province, the German navy took control of the port of Qingdao in 1897 and by the early twentieth century it had extended its power over much of the Shandong peninsula, aiming to make it into a model colony run from Berlin.

After the Spanish-American war of 1898, the United States was establishing its own overseas empire, which now included Cuba and the Philippines. But it refrained from trying to carve out regions of influence in China. Part of the reason was ideological; most Americans retained a solid portion of aversion against colonialism (and the entanglements with nonwhite peoples that it could lead to). Another part was based on perceptions of weakness: The United States would lose out to Britain and the other imperial powers that had already established themselves in China. Much better, then, for the Americans to claim lofty principles of free trade as the cornerstones of their policy. The Open Door notes demanded the right for trade from all countries to operate freely within the spheres of influence and even within the concessions granted to foreign powers in China. The US government also demanded that the great powers support China's "territorial and administrative integrity." But even if the other powers were happy to pay lip service to the US position, their policies in China were mostly unaffected by the Open Door principles. As Hay explained to President William McKinley, "The inherent weakness of our position is this: we do not want to rob China ourselves, and our public opinion will not permit us to interfere, with an army, to prevent others from robbing her. Besides, we have no army. The talk of the papers about 'our preeminent moral position giving us the authority to dictate to the world' is mere flap-doodle."[8]

The US interest in the China market faded, but never disappeared. The part of the Open Door Policy that stayed intact through the wars and revolution of the early twentieth century was the US determination not to be pushed out of China by other powers. As Japan's power grew, this resolve meant an increasing degree of conflict between the two countries. It was a conflict that diplomacy could not overcome. In spite of the understandings signed between the two countries in 1917 (the Lansing-Ishii agreement) and during the 1921–22 Washington Naval Conference (the Nine-Power Treaty), the Open Door remained more ideology than reality. US insistence on the right to trade and commercial operations in Manchuria, for instance, and its willingness to support the new Guomindang government in China after 1928, meant that Tokyo came to see Washington as a main enemy of its positions on the Asian mainland.

For Americans with an interest in the outside world, China also became a prime object of the American desire for reform and modernization. A powerful movement for reform at home took hold in the 1890s. Missionaries, health workers, economists, engineers, and businessmen went to China with lessons drawn from the American experiment. After China became a republic in 1912, some Americans believed that the US republican heritage would be of particular significance to the Chinese. But first the emphasis on improvement had to sink in in China itself. A part of the US portion of the Boxer indemnity was converted into scholarships for Chinese students to study in the United States. Another portion was used to establish an American college in Beijing, which later became Qinghua University (several Chinese Communist leaders, including President Hu Jintao, are Qinghua graduates). Other educational initiatives, mostly missionary-based, flourished as well. Yanjing University in Beijing was headed by John Leighton Stuart, who later became the US ambassador. Yanjing acquired the former imperial gardens between the old and new summer palaces, and set up a modern college that is now part of Peking University, the country's premier teaching institution. American missionaries and educators also helped establish Nanjing University, St. John's University in Shanghai, and Lingnan University in Guangzhou.[9]

Many Chinese had a love-hate relationship with the United States. The attraction was for American ideals and aid, the aversion because of America's racism and consequent immigration restrictions. Ordinary Chinese could not understand why European colonialists, having taken control of whole continents, would not even admit Chinese immigrants into these territories. In 1905 Chinese in China and abroad launched a boycott of American goods to change US policies and force the Qing authorities to stand firm in their opposition to the exclusion of Chinese immigrants from the United States. The boycott did not change Washington's approach or Beijing's willingness to accede to it. But it did alert many to US racism and Qing powerlessness. They realized that the Open Door opened only one way. China was open to US capital, but the United States was closed to the Chinese people. Their realization led to a disenchantment with America that would echo for generations to come.

Germany, the other latecomer to foreign influence in China, attempted to copy what Britain and France were already doing. The German enterprise in Shandong, however, was different from them in important ways. It stressed improvement and modernization of China. In this respect it had much in common with American idealism. For Germany the penetration by missionaries and imperial expansion went hand in hand. The government in Berlin had had its eyes on Qingdao as a naval base for several years, and the German Christian missions—whose existence in Shandong gave rise to the Boxer movement—were planned with imperial expansion in mind. The colony they set up was also intended to be a model colony, better in every way than what the other European powers could do. The German governor in Shandong reported to Berlin in 1905 that the "tasks that we Germans are facing in this colony within the most important area of the cultural life of modern peoples, education . . . [must] to a significant degree influence its spirit and character and be a tool for infusing the whole province . . . with German knowledge and German spirit."[10]

From its beginning to its end at the hands of Britain's Japanese allies in 1914, the concession in Qingdao and the surrounding Jiaozhou bay area was run by the German navy. It aimed at protecting Berlin's interests in East Asia and solidifying Germany's hold on the region through large-scale projects, constructing educational institutions, medical services, and missionary stations. As in most colonies, the German projects in Shandong both attracted and repelled the native population. Elite Chinese were impressed by German efficiency and organization, but wanted to conquer these virtues, and what they had achieved in the province, for China. The first president of the republic, Sun Yat-sen, visited in 1912 and admonished the Chinese students in German institutions there to learn from Germany:

> The students should take Germany as a model for the new China. . . . China in spite of its thousands of years old culture has not achieved anything that can be compared to what Germany has created [here] in the course of twelve years. Streets, buildings, ports, sanitation, all bear witness to diligence and ambition. What the students see here should spur them towards emulation, and it must become their aim to spread this model to all of China and put their homeland in the same state of perfection.[11]

While Germany's possessions in China ended in World War I, the interest in Germany as a possible ally of Chinese republicans continued right up to the outbreak of the next world war. German advisers, among them Max Bauer, one of the leaders of a failed right-wing coup attempt in Germany in 1920, helped reshape the finances and the army of the renewed Guomindang movement as it moved to take control of the country in the late 1920s. Under Chiang Kai-shek, in the 1930s, German advisors moved to the first rank among those supporting the new leadership. Hans von Seeckt, the former general commander of the German army, devised the training of China's army elite. All military academies and most army units had German officers attached to them. Germany supplied experts and loans for China's railway construction, German-Chinese trade expanded massively, and Germany became China's largest supplier of government credit. When Alexander von Falkenhausen, the last of the German chief military advisors, left China in 1938 after Germany had allied itself with Japan, Chiang Kai-shek continued to believe in Germany as a possible model for China's future.[12]

C HINA IN THE EARLY TWENTIETH CENTURY had to decide not only who its allies would be, but what form of government it would have. The development of a Western-style republic was not a sure thing. During the century's first decade, the Qing empire tried to defend itself against its enemies, foreign and domestic, and many observers expected it to succeed, as it had done so often before. The *Times* of London commented in 1909 that "nothing is more surprising than the respectful humility with which the representatives of the foreign Powers submit to indignity at the hands of . . . the Chinese Foreign Office. It would seem as if the old time exclusiveness of the Throne which forbade audience with foreign representatives on any footing of equality had been revived. . . ."[13] The Qing knew that foreigners depended on them to achieve anything in China and hoped to turn that dependence to the dynasty's advantage. But they also wanted their people to see that the government was able to enforce obedience from the populace, undertake necessary reform, and demand respect from other powers, all as part of the process of modernization. By 1910 both foreigners and revolutionaries alike had started to fear that the Qing of the future would be similar to the Qing of the past, only better organized and better armed.

Cixi, the empress dowager, died on 15 November 1908. Her nephew, the Guangxu emperor, had passed away the day before—poisoned, it was said, by those who wanted to prevent him ever becoming ruler in his own right again. The empress dowager had dominated the Court for forty-seven years. Her aim in the last few years of her life, she said, was to prepare the dynasty for another domestic battle for power, as happened with the great rebellions of the mid-nineteenth century. She agreed to the principle of a constitution and to limited forms of representative government in the provinces, measures that the Qing elite hoped would strengthen the dynasty's claim to power at the center. Cixi also abolished the imperial examination system and began a series of administrative reforms, based on reports by officials who had visited the United States, Europe, and Japan. Already in 1901, after the Boxer disaster, Cixi had set out a new course of gradual reform:

> The weakness of China is caused by the strength of convention and the rigid network of regulations. We have many mediocre officials but few men of talent and courage. The regulations are used by mediocre men as the means of their self-protection, and taken advantage of by government clerks as sources of profit. The government officials exchange numerous documents but they never touch reality. The appointment of capable men is restricted by regulations so rigid that even men of exceptional talent are missed. What misleads the country can be expressed in one word, selfishness, and what suffocates all under heaven is precedent.[14]

An early feature of the reform was a new office of foreign affairs. Waiwubu, created in 1901 after much foreign pressure, replaced the Zongli Yamen. In many ways the Waiwubu became a model for how the other new ministries were supposed to work. While the old Zongli Yamen dealt with all foreign matters—everything from cheese to railways—the new ministry dealt exclusively with the foreign relations of the Chinese government. It set about attempting to reverse the effects of the treaties that had been imposed on China. But it was also on the lookout for whatever would serve the dynasty's interests, especially access to credit, technology, and military equipment. In some ways, the pattern of interaction abroad that the Qing New Policy (*xinzheng*) aimed at was not so different from the Four Modernizations of the Chinese Communist Party after its self-inflicted disasters of the 1960s and 1970s.

The 1906 administrative and constitutional reform was an attempt to make the empire look like a Westernized state to its foreign rivals. It was also a concession to those who wanted more democracy at home. The fact-finding reports that the new arrangement was built on came from two "constitutional expeditions." Both groups went to Japan, the United States, and Europe. One focused on Germany, the other on Britain and France, meeting local politicians and experts—the group visiting London was addressed by Percy Ashley, a young history lecturer at the London School of Economics, on the different branches of the British government.[15] In the end the Japanese model won out. In August 1908 the Qing promised its people that it would introduce constitutional rule over the course of nine years, but with an emphasis on the powers of the executive branch, meaning the Qing dynasty itself. All reform had to be gradual, the Court and its supporters believed, or the empire would lose the essence that distinguished it from other countries. And, needless to say, the Qing would lose power in China.

After Cixi's death, the imperial family, the Court, and the higher echelons of Qing officialdom concentrated on survival. Their main worries were not the revolutionary opposition, by then mostly in exile or dead. The real threat was that provincial and regional strongmen, in league with foreigners, would break China apart. The Qing strategy was to weaken the provincial leaders and strengthen the central government by whatever means available. The Qing instituted local assemblies to compete for influence in the provinces as part of this strategy. It used foreign loans to take control of all of the railway network, some of which was controlled by foreign companies or by the provinces. The Qing was hoping to buy time for their kind of reform but was also preparing for a showdown.

THE SHOWDOWN CAME IN OCTOBER 1911. On 9 October, a group of revolutionaries who had infiltrated the army in the central city of Wuhan accidentally blew up the butcher shop in the city's Russian concession, where they were preparing explosives for use against the Qing. The police arrested two of the conspirators and found their detailed plans for an insurrection.[16] The following evening the leaders of the conspiracy acted to save themselves. Knowing that the Qing would be merciless in their pursuit, the young officers took control of a main armory, attacked the governor's office, and declared their allegiance to a republic of China. After a few days of sporadic fighting, all of Wuhan city was in their hands. They sent telegrams to other provinces to join in defeating the Qing and creating a republic. By late November it was clear that the Qing was in serious trouble. Most provincial strongmen south of the Yangzi had thrown in their lot with the revolutionaries, and power seemed to ebb away from Beijing.

The international situation was of crucial significance for the outcome of the Chinese revolution. While many Chinese, including the Qing themselves, had expected the great powers to assist the Qing in defeating their enemies, as had happened in the 1860s and in the 1890s, this time around each of them was too preoccupied with other affairs to pay much attention to China. The United States had its eyes firmly fixed on the Mexican revolution next door. France and Germany were dealing with their rivalries over North Africa. The Russian prime minister had just been assassinated. And Britain was dealing with a hung parliament and a constitutional crisis over home rule for Ireland. Only Japan was leaning toward intervention, but the Japanese elites could not make their minds up about whom to support. They liked the idea of monarchical constitutional government (as in Japan itself), but they knew that supporting various regional strongmen could help Japan further its influence within China. In the end, Britain acted on its need for a Chinese government that could give its business interests enough stability to operate. It would support whoever could hold the country together, if only in the short term. And, as usual, Britain's approach was the dominant one.

By the end of 1911, the British settled on the best candidate for keeping China united: the Qing general Yuan Shikai, the hero of the

Sino-Japanese war and later viceroy of Zhili, the region around Beijing. Yuan had been purged by the Qing Court in 1909, who feared that he might become too powerful. Now he was made prime minister and head of the Qing army. By December, his forces had pushed their way into Wuhan, forcing the revolutionaries to negotiate. Yuan knew that the conflict was moving toward a stalemate. He was able to take Wuhan but not to reconquer southern China. And he was eager to avoid blame for more Chinese blood to be spilled over a dynasty in which cause he no longer believed. By early 1912, Yuan was in close contact with the heads of the new republic, now headquartered downriver in Nanjing.

Yuan seemed to be the man to protect Western interests, but it was the revolutionaries who studied Western political ideas and put them into practice. In the southern cities, all sorts of political concepts were propagated openly, from anarchism to constitutional monarchism. Many of the most vocal revolutionaries grounded themselves in a form of nationalism that had developed during the previous decade. They blamed the Qing, now lambasted as "Manchus," for China's ills. Hu Hanmin, a key supporter of Sun Yat-sen, had written in 1906, "The Manchu government is evil because it is the evil race which usurped our government, and their evils are not confined to a few political measures but are rooted in the nature of the race and can neither be eliminated nor reformed."[17] Zou Rong, a young revolutionary hero who had died in prison in 1905, struck the same notes in a text that was widely distributed in 1911. Invoking both the legendary founder of China and the father of the American nation, he wrote:

> Sweep away millennia of despotism in all its forms, throw off millennia of slavishness, annihilate the five million and more of the furry and horned Manchu race, cleanse ourselves of 260 years of harsh and unremitting pain, so that the soil of the Chinese subcontinent is made immaculate, and the descendants of the Yellow Emperor will all become Washingtons. Then they will return from the dead to life again, they will emerge from the Eighteen Levels of Hell

and rise to the Thirty Three mansions of Heaven, in all their magnificence and richness to arrive at their zenith, the unique and incomparable of goals—revolution. How sublime is revolution, how majestic![18]

Not surprisingly, Qing officials of non-Han origin were often targeted by the populace after the revolution. In Wuhan, 10,000 were killed. By the 1920s, very few Chinese admitted to having been Qing supporters or members of the Qing nobility.[19]

Republican principles now replaced monarchical ones. But the various political groups defined them quite differently. Sun Yat-sen and his Revolutionary Alliance (Tongmenghui) argued for a presidential republic, with an elected executive controlling most state activities. Many of the revolutionaries from central and southern China preferred a federal republic, with a strong position for the provinces. The merchants in the cities argued for a parliamentary republic, in which different social and political constituencies could be represented. What united most groups was the sense of unlimited potential that the revolution had opened up. They felt that China could do what Japan had done, but on a grander scale, and that the new political system must make China rich and strong. The foreign examples that were used were often well beside Chinese realities; as one scholar puts it: "No characteristic of Chinese intellectual life in the decade or so before 1911 is more prominent than foreign influence."[20] While the revolutionaries debated constitutions, Qing officers and officials were preparing for life without the empire.

The Chinese who dominated society in the last half-generation of Qing rule were a mixture of high-level officials and capitalists. The combination often happened in one and the same person. As in China at the end of the Maoist era or the Soviet Union at the end of Communism, many officials got rich by exploiting contacts within the empire and with foreigners. Yuan Shikai was one of them; he was involved in several enterprises in northern China.[21] Huaxin Spinning and Weaving Mill in Shanghai, a legendary firm in the Chinese textile industry, was run by sons of the provincial governor. The commercial interests of these entrepreneurial officials were increasingly tied to limiting Qing power. They feared that a resurgent Court would punish them as corrupt and self-serving. As production, commerce, and trade became more important, the ties that bound China's elites to the monarchy were worn increasingly thin.

The Chinese diaspora was crucial to the success of the revolution. News of the extraordinary events in Wuhan found Sun Yat-sen six thousand miles away, in Denver, Colorado, where he was raising money for the cause from local Chinese. It was the culmination of Sun's travels, which had taken him all over the world on behalf of the Chinese revolution. In a sign of how important the international role was, instead of hurrying straight back to China in October 1911, Sun first went to London and Paris, to negotiate loans for the new republic. He got nothing, but he did return to his homeland armed with the crucial news that neither London nor Paris would likely intervene on behalf of the Qing. Accompanied by his American chief military adviser Homer Lea, a four-foot-eleven-inch hunchbacked "general" and geostrategist, Sun finally made it back to China on Christmas Day 1911. On arrival, he was elected provisional president of the Republic of China, a republic without territory, weapons, or much money besides what overseas Chinese supporters had provided.[22]

The rest of the story of the founding of the Chinese republic is easily told. Yuan Shikai betrayed his Qing masters, telling the empress dowager Longyu in February that the only way to save the lives of the imperial family was to issue a proclamation in support of a republican system of government. After long debates at Court and with guarantees being offered for their personal security, she issued a remarkable imperial edict on behalf of the six-year-old emperor on 12 February 1912:

> As a consequence of the uprising of the Republican Army . . . the Empire seethed like a boiling cauldron and the people were plunged into utter misery. . . . It is now evident that the hearts of the majority

of the people are in favor of a republican form of government: the provinces of the South were the first to support the cause, and the generals of the North have pledged their support. From the preference of the people's hearts, the will of heaven can be discerned. How could We bear to oppose the will of millions for the glory of one family? Therefore . . . We and His Majesty the Emperor hereby vest sovereignty in the people and decide in favor of a republican form of constitutional government. Let Yuan Shikai organize with full powers a provisional republican government and confer with the Republican Army as to the methods of union, thus assuring peace to the people and tranquility to the empire, and forming to one Great Republic of China by union heretofore, of the five peoples, namely Manchus, Chinese, Mongols, Mohammedans, and Tibetans together with their territory in its integrity.[23]

Having been made president with Qing consent, while keeping the loyalty of the northern army and getting increasing support from foreign governments, Yuan now held most of the cards in the game for power. Sun Yat-sen resigned his provisional presidency the day after the Qing abdication. Yuan took control of the governments both in Beijing and Nanjing as the new president of the Republic of China. Two hundred and sixty years of Qing rule had come to an end with a whimper, and China's international role was more undefined than at any other point in its history.

CHINA'S FIRST EXPERIMENT WITH a Western-style republic was not a happy one. After a hectic period of contestation and constitution-making, Yuan Shikai tried to return to the earlier system, with himself as emperor. He failed dismally, and died in 1916, a broken man. Yuan's biggest problem was that he could never define clearly to others—or even to himself—what China was supposed to be. Was it an empire aspiring to be a nation-state? Was it a coalition of different peoples, which because of a long historical tradition had become one country? Yuan, like his successors in what Chinese refer to as the Warlord Era (1916–1928), was caught between different concepts of China and its political future. His foreign advisors—of whom there were many, especially Americans—supported Yuan's somewhat self-fulfilling prophecy that China was not ready for democracy in any form. One of them, the later president of Johns Hopkins University Frank Goodnow, who was Yuan's chief legal adviser, opined that

> China has never really known any sort of government but personal government in accordance with immemorial custom. The Chinese people . . . are at present incapable of any large measure of social cooperation. . . . Under these conditions all in the nature of political reform which can be accomplished at present is to place by the side of a powerful executive a body which shall more or less adequately represent the classes of the people conscious of common interests. . . . It is extremely doubtful whether real progress in the direction of constitutional government in China will be made by a too violent departure from past traditions, by the attempt . . . to establish a form of government, which, while suited to other countries, does not take into account the peculiar history of China and the social and economic conditions of the country.[24]

A number of Chinese, especially those who had been opposing the Qing for decades and hoping for a democratic revolution, disagreed. As they were pushed aside by local strongmen and army leaders, they remained dedicated to democracy. Song Jiaoren, Sun Yat-sen's chief assistant, who was assassinated by Yuan's men in 1913, told his leader as he lay dying, "the foundation of the nation is not yet strong, and the lot of the people is not yet improved. I die with deep regret. I humbly hope that your excellency will champion honesty, propagate justice, and promote democracy, so that the parliament can produce an everlasting constitution."[25] Ironically, the new party that Song helped create, the Guomindang, the National People's Party, would play a key role in promoting China's unity and strength, although honesty, justice, and democracy would remain in short supply.

For the foreign powers, the main issues after 1912 were to keep a semblance of central power in place in China, while working with whoever held power locally to protect and advance their commercial interests. International loan consortia kept the Beijing governments afloat; by far the most important was a British-dominated consortium that made several big loans, including lending £25 million to Yuan's regime in 1913. In return, the bankers and their home countries insisted that all Chinese income from customs and fees be deposited in foreign-controlled banks in Shanghai and used first to pay interest on the international loans and existing war indemnities from the Qing era. This trick not only deprived the central government of a main part of its remaining fiscal autonomy, but also made it possible for foreign financiers to influence Chinese politics by making parts of China's own income available to whomever they favored. As one Chinese observer put it, it was like letting much of China's national revenue go into a massive foreign-controlled financial system, from which only a tiny fraction emerged to be spent in the country itself. Many Third World governments that suffered from the debt crisis of the 1980s would recognize the phenomenon.

Up to 1928, power in Beijing was in the hands of a confusing succession of northern politicians and warlords. They fought each other in several wars to seize central power. But such power meant less and less. While China retained a government recognized by other nations, real power increasingly went to the provinces or coalitions of provinces that were independent in all but name. Key provinces such as Hunan, Guangdong, and Sichuan were outside any form of control by the Beijing government. Some provincials felt that the central authorities had failed so dismally that provincial independence was the only viable alternative. China, they argued, was too big to be reformed—it was an empire rather than a normal state, and power could only be made accountable to the people if the political units were smaller, more integrated, and more culturally and linguistically coherent, as had happened in Europe. A young Hunanese, Mao Zedong, joined in the search for autonomy. "Our Hunan," he wrote in September 1920, "must wake up."

> Hunanese have but one alternative: that is Hunanese self-determination and self-government; that is for Hunanese to build, on the territory of Hunan, a "Hunan Republic." Moreover, I sincerely think that to save Hunan, to save China, and to look towards cooperation with other liberated people of the whole world, we can do no other. If Hunanese people lack the determination and bravery to build Hunan independently into a country, then there is no hope for Hunan.[26]

During the early republican era, while the concern about China's political future was great, Chinese had more freedom to explore the world than ever before. A quarter million young men and women left their villages each year to work in the cities. There they encountered a teeming and transnational world, dominated by foreign money, Chinese enterprise, and eclectic mores and fashions. Students and workers traveled abroad despite draconian travel restrictions imposed by foreign governments. Many of them would return with new ideas about China's future. For Chinese whose main concern was with the state and its competition with other states, the period after the fall of the Qing was one of dissolution and extreme danger. But for those who relished the hybridities that lack of effective state control permitted, it was an exciting time.

THE COLLAPSE OF THE QING EMPIRE immediately opened up the question of the makeup of a future China. For areas that had been conquered by the Qing—Mongolia, Tibet, and large parts of Central Asia—the question was especially acute. But it was also central to many regions in the south and the northeast which the Qing had Sinified and

further integrated within the empire. Some activists, infected by a nationalism similar to that of the Chinese revolutionaries, wanted immediate independence. Others wanted autonomy and special rights within
a Chinese federal state. In most regions adventurers or strongmen tried
to exploit local nationalisms, foreign interests, and Beijing's attempts
to reassert itself. All along the edges of the former empire, groups that
the Qing had forcefully incorporated into China were trying to define
their own politics and identities.

But defining China has never been an easy task, and it was certainly
not easy after the Qing collapse. Even as it had been fighting off foreign
incursions and rebellions at the center, the Qing had continued to reassert themselves along the borders of the empire. Indeed, to many late
Qing leaders the need to defend frontiers, crush nativist unrest, and insist on one inclusive identity for all was a crucial mission: Their China
would be doomed without it, even if they were to be able to defend
themselves successfully against other dangers. In 1908 the Qing sent
troops to take direct control of Tibet's capital, Lhasa. A few years earlier
the authorities—in a complete reversal of previous policy—had started
encouraging Chinese settlers to move into the Mongolian grasslands.
In the far western province of Xinjiang, the central authorities had been
able to overcome massive unrest and keep strict control on local Muslim
activism. The Qing wanted to show that even if it had been wounded
by the West and Japan, it was still a force to be reckoned with for anyone who had irredentist or secessionist claims.

In 1912, with the Qing gone, those who saw their future as not laying within a united China had their chance. Their work was made easier
by the support of foreign powers which, for their own strategic reasons,
want to see outlying provinces break free of the authorities in Beijing.
In some cases these powers made the success of breakaway provinces a
precondition for recognizing the new republican government. The Russians insisted on full independence for northern, or Outer, Mongolia,
the British on autonomy for Tibet, and the Japanese—less successfully,

as we have seen—on self-government for parts of the Northeast. Only the Russian demand succeeded fully, however, and that was less because of Russian power than because of the determination of the Mongolian separatist leaders, who in December 1911 issued their independence proclamation:

> At present we often hear that in the southernland the Manchus and Chinese are creating disturbances and are about to precipitate the fall of the Manchu dynasty. Because our Mongolia was originally an independent nation, we have now decided . . . to establish a new independent nation, based on our old tradition, without the interference of others in our own rights. We should not be ruled by the Manchu-Chinese officials. After taking away their rights and powers, an ultimatum for their extradition has finally put an end to their power, although by sending them back we do not intend that ordinary Chinese traders who stay at the Chinese trading towns should suffer. . . . All of you should live peacefully and harmoniously together without suspicion. Hereby we have issued this proclamation.[27]

The new leader was enthroned as the Bogd Khan in northern Mongolia. He was a religious figure, who appealed for Mongolian unity based on a shared reverence for Buddhism. His argument for independence from 1912 on was straightforward: A Chinese republic did not, could not, inherit the Qing's empire. All peoples within the territory that the Qing had conquered now had an equal right to form their own states. And although it protested the principle, Yuan Shikai's government after much wrangling succumbed to Russian pressure and, in 1913, agreed to autonomy for the northern part of Mongolia, although the territory was still to be "under the suzerainty of China."[28] For Chinese nationalists, the agreement with Russia on Mongolia was another sign of their republic's weakness, just as Japan's demands had been. For Mongolian nationalists, the agreement effectively divided their country, keeping the southern half of the nation under direct

Chinese control, while still not providing independence in name. Moscow was the main victor. It gained a vast zone of influence in Central Asia, while stopping further Japanese expansion into the region.

In Tibet, where Buddhism was also the great unifying force, the situation in 1911 was similar to that in Mongolia. The difference was that Britain played Russia's role. The Qing occupation of Lhasa had driven the main Tibetan religious and political leader, the Thirteenth Dalai Lama, into exile in British India, from where he attempted to get London's support for Tibetan independence. Following an uprising in Lhasa as the Qing collapsed, the Dalai Lama returned and issued what in effect was a declaration of independence:

The Manchu empire collapsed. The Tibetans were encouraged to expel the Chinese from central Tibet. I, too, returned safely to my rightful and sacred country, and I am now in the course of driving out the remnants of Chinese troops from DoKham in Eastern Tibet. Now, the Chinese intention of colonizing Tibet under the patron-priest relationship has faded like a rainbow in the sky. Having once again achieved for ourselves a period of happiness and peace, I have now allotted to all of you the following duties to be carried out without negligence: Peace and happiness in this world can only be maintained by preserving the faith of Buddhism. . . . Tibet is a country with rich natural resources; but it is not scientifically advanced like other lands. We are a small, religious, and independent nation. To keep up with the rest of the world, we must defend our country. In view of past invasions by foreigners, our people may have to face certain difficulties, which they must disregard. To safeguard and maintain the independence of our country, one and all should voluntarily work hard. Our subject citizens residing near the borders should be alert and keep the government informed by special messenger of any suspicious developments. Our subjects must not create major clashes between two nations because of minor incidents.[29]

Like the Bogd Khan in Mongolia, the Dalai Lama was only partly successful in his aims. The British forced Yuan's regime to participate in a convention at the British summer capital in India, Simla, to discuss the status of Tibet, but the Beijing representatives refused to give ground. They drew on the Qing view of relations within the former empire: "Tibet forms an integral part of the territory of the Republic of China, that no attempts shall be made by Tibet or by Great Britain to interrupt the continuity of this territorial integrity, and that China's rights of every description which have existed in consequence of this territorial integrity shall be respected by Tibet and recognized by Great Britain."[30]

In the end, the Chinese refused to sign any agreement that gave autonomy to Tibet. Part of the reason was that both the Tibetans and the British overreached with regard to borders. Defining Tibet was (and is) even more difficult than defining Mongolia. Based on historical precedents, a government in Lhasa could lay claim to large areas of what are now the Chinese provinces of Sichuan and Qinghai, which some Tibetans define as Eastern Tibet or Inner Tibet. It was the Dalai Lama's insistence on incorporating Inner Tibet into the new autonomous nation that killed the deal. Instead, London constructed a British legal fiction, in which it signed a note with the representatives of the Dalai Lama, whose regime it recognized as autonomous and which recognized the incorporation into British India of a large swath of land—what is today Arunachal Pradesh.

After the 1911 revolution, the region that the republicans in China feared most for was Xinjiang. In the eighteenth century, the Qing had conquered this vast northwest territory, and it had been reconquered, at great cost, only a few years before the 1911 revolution. The new leaders in Beijing knew that both campaigns had been difficult and that the Muslim groups in the region were likely to rebel, with support from Russia. Yuan Shikai was therefore only too pleased when events in the far-off province took a turn nobody had expected. Yang Zengxin, a Qing official posted to Xinjiang from the southwestern province of Yunnan, took power in the provincial capital of Urumqi with the help of Qing troops. Yang introduced a personal dictatorship built on terror. At an official banquet he once had two suspected rivals decapitated at the table. Muslims and Chinese in the province were terrified of Yang and he himself guarded his power carefully against the Russians while expressing at least token obedience to the Chinese central government. Many in Beijing thought that they had got as good a deal as they could expect to get at the far western border.

But Yang Zengxin had not solved the Xinjiang problem for the Chinese government. Encouraged by pan-Turkish ideas and modern forms of Muslim thinking coming in from India and the Middle East, an increasing number of young Uighurs and Kazakhs started thinking of themselves as inhabiting a Muslim Turkestan, half of which had been occupied by Russia and the other half held by the Chinese. After the Russian Revolution, independence movements blossomed on both sides of the frontier, and the Soviets—having crushed the Muslim rebels on their side—were only too happy to give cautious support to rebels real and potential in Xinjiang. All the way up to the Communist revolution in China, Xinjiang continued to be governed by local Chinese regimes, even though the last one—that of the Manchurian general Sheng Shicai—increasingly favored the Soviet Union.[31] Still, even in a newly conquered zone 2,000 miles from Beijing, the borders of the former empire stayed intact.

If the Chinese republic had been an experiment in civic government based on some form of popular representation, matters of identity, culture, and religion might have been possible to work out politically over time within a common framework. But even then the concept of a unified state based on the borders of the old empire would have been difficult to find support for on the periphery, since the central premise for the change of government in 1912 was Chinese nationalism, a nationalism that in the popular perception increasingly linked Chineseness to one's ethnic origin. If the rebellion of 1911–12 was necessary because of the Qing oppression of the Chinese majority, then it also follows that Chinese oppression of Mongols, Tibetans, and Muslims should cease through the construction of political entities for these nationalities.

This, after all, is what happened after the collapse of the Ottoman and Austro-Hungarian empires. But in China the transition from empire to republic—even a republic as unattractive as that of Yuan Shikai and his successors—happened without most non-Han areas being able to break away. And meanwhile the Chinese majority was far too busy defining and redefining their own identity to give much thought to the broader implications of their revolution.

WHAT IS CHINA? For people who had come of age during the transformations at the end of the Qing era and the beginning of the republic, the answers were complex, stirring, and threatening. Was China its ethnic majority, now free of Manchu domination? Was it one's home province and people who hailed from that province? Or was it, as the Republic pretended, all of the peoples who had lived within the former empire, from Manchuria to Central Asia and down to the tropical border with Burma? Was China first and foremost an idea or a culture, more than a state or even a society? And, if it was a culture, was that culture now dying under the impact of the West, and would China die with it? The efforts at defining what China was stood at the center of a cultural and political revival after World War I. This period in Chinese history is often called the May Fourth era, after the student rallies against foreign humiliations of China that began on that day in 1919. It was the beginning of a new period in China's relations with the outside world, through the creation of expressly hybrid cultures, political movements, and state formations. Beginning as an act of desperate protest, May Fourth came to show a way out for those who believed that they had witnessed the death of "Old China."

The Beijing government thought that when the world war ended it would be rewarded for having been on the Allied side. It believed that some of the preferences foreign powers had taken for themselves inside China would be removed. They and millions of other Chinese put their trust in the US president, Woodrow Wilson, whose Fourteen Points had convinced many that the war had been fought for self-determination and equality among nations. Chen Duxiu, a writer who later became one of the founders of the Chinese Communist Party, called Wilson "the number one good man in the world" and the augur of a new era in which "might is no longer reliable, justice and reason can no longer be denied."[32] A leaflet written by Chinese students in America begged for US support:

> Four hundred million people are facing a life-or-death sentence at Paris; and upon this sentence the fate of the permanent peace of the world is going to depend. China pleads for nothing but fair play and sound judgment. For the interest of world peace and for the interest of four hundred million people a death sentence should not be tolerated by the enlightened powers, particularly the United States of America, in whom China has deepest confidence and by whom the upright plan for the League of Nations was originated.[33]

But at the Versailles conference the Chinese not only failed in having the former German concessions returned to them but—even more importantly—did not get general acceptance for removing the regulations that gave foreigners extraterritorial rights within China itself. The principle of self-determination was apparently not applicable for Chinese or other nonwhite peoples, except the Japanese, who had adopted the instruments of the West. When the former Chinese concessions in Shandong were awarded to Japan in May 1919, Chinese cities saw massive protests, and the burning down of the house of one of the ministers who had signed the 1915 agreement with Tokyo. The government seemed weak when confronted with the fury of the population, with university students in Beijing and Shanghai taking the lead in opposing what they saw as China's international helplessness and humiliation.[34]

The May Fourth Movement came in the midst of a period in which many Chinese intellectuals were trying to redefine China and its position in the world. It was the writings of these intellectuals that inspired the students during the 1919 protests, even though their cultural and political direction was very varied. For some, like Chen Duxiu, it was China's political direction that had to be corrected: The state had to be made responsible to its citizens. For others, such as the writer Lu Xun, the real revolution was a cultural revolution: Without throwing overboard useless knowledge, empty forms and phrases, deference to tradition, China could not be reconstituted as a modern, effective, and just society. Some wanted to ditch the classical written Chinese language itself, always mastered only by an elite. Increasingly, men like Chen and Lu chose to write in the vernacular, inventing new Chinese terms for things foreign. Their starting point was not an optimistic one. To Chen, "the majority of our people are lethargic and do not know that not only our morality, politics and technology but even common commodities for daily use are all unfit for struggle and are going to be eliminated in the process of nat-ural selection."[35] Lu Xun lampooned the Westernized Chinese bour-geoisie and its ineffectuality in his short story "A Happy Family":

> The family naturally consists of a husband and wife—the master and mistress—who married for love. Their marriage contract con-tains over forty terms going into great detail, so that they have ex-traordinary equality and absolute freedom. Moreover they have both had a higher education and belong to the cultured élite. . . . Japanese-returned students are no longer the fashion, so let them be Western-returned students. The master of the house always wears a foreign suit, his collar is always snowy white. His wife's hair is al-ways curled up like a sparrow's nest in front, her pearly white teeth are always peeping out, but she wears Chinese dress.[36]

The response to pessimism that the actions of the students and oth-ers who protested in 1919 created was a call for a new form of Chinese culture and for a new, strong, united, and righteous state. The old rev-olutionary Liang Qichao asked: "What is our duty?" His answer: "It is to develop our civilization with that of the West and to supplement

Western civilization with ours so as to synthesize and transform them to make a new civilization."[37] And in politics new and radical trends emerged, which stressed the need to make China rich and strong within the borders of the former empire. The Russian Revolution and the democratic changes in Germany provided inspiration, as did anticolonial movements elsewhere in Asia. Socialism seemed to be the future, and some Chinese wanted to be part of it. Li Dazhao, who together with Chen Duxiu helped form the Chinese Communist Party (CCP) in 1921, wanted to "look at China's position among the nations. While the others have already advanced from free competition to socialist collective society, we are about to make our own start, meaning to follow in the footsteps of the others. Under these circumstances, if we wish to adapt ourselves and co-exist with the others, we must cut short the process by leaping to a socialist economy in order to ensure a measure of success."[38] Because of the May Fourth Movement, China to some seemed to have gone from despair to boundless opportunity.

AMONG THOSE SENSING the new opportunities in 1919 was the old warhorse Sun Yat-sen, who had spent the time since his resignation as president of the republic in 1912 retracing the steps from his revolutionary youth. He had lived in Japan for almost four years and—to the consternation of many of his supporters—had continued to receive money from Tokyo even as its pressure on China increased. Sun himself was uninterested in where his support came from; he needed funds to build a new revolutionary organization. His links with the United States increased further when he married the twenty-two-year-old Song Qingling, educated at Wesleyan College and the daughter of one of the richest men in Shanghai (her father, Charlie Soong, had arrived in Boston as a stowaway on an American ship in 1879 and made his money from publishing cheap translations). But it was neither Japan nor the United States that in the end inspired Sun to undertake another attempt at conquering China. It was the Bolshevik revolution in Russia, the same event that had convinced men like Chen Duxiu and Li Dazhao that socialism was the future. Though never a Communist, Sun began admiring the Soviets for their efficiency, their ruthless focus, and their promise of making a backward country rich and strong. He also liked the social message of Soviet-style Communism, though mainly as a means to strengthen the state. In 1920 Sun and the reconstituted Guomindang were back in Guangzhou with a new movement and with a tenuous grip on the city and its immediate surroundings.

The new Guomindang, which Sun Yat-sen headed, was a much more centralized organization than it had been before, and a more militarized one. Sun was recognized by his followers as the leader-for-life of the party and as the provisional president of China—the title he had held for a couple of months in 1912. The party's ideology was built on what Sun called the Three Principles of the People: nationalism, democracy, and "people's livelihood." But, while his ideas showed some influence from the Chinese Left and the Soviets, the Guomindang leader recognized that China needed foreign capital and trade in order to develop. Sun planned to lead a reunification campaign to the north. After it succeeded, the new China would request massive foreign loans in order to build communications, promote industry, and settle virgin territories in Mongolia, Xinjiang, and Tibet. In his book *The International Development of China,* Sun wrote,

> In my International Development Scheme, I propose that the profits of this industrial development should go first to pay the interest and principal of foreign capital invested in it; second to give high wages to labor; and third to improve or extend the machinery of production. Besides these provisions the rest of the profit should go to the public in the form of reduced prices in all commodities and public services. Thus, all will enjoy, in the same degree, the fruits of modern civilization. . . . In a nutshell, it is my idea to make capitalism create socialism in China so that these two economic forces of human evolution will work side by side in future civilization.[39]

Sun's main problem in the early 1920s was that while he had plenty of ideas, some of them similar to the Chinese reform programs of our own time, he had no solid power base. His ability to pick quarrels with those he depended on for support did not help. In 1922–1923 he was temporarily thrown out of Guangzhou by the local strongman Chen Jiongming, a military leader with an anarchist background who believed in provincial autonomy, not conquest by the force of arms. Sun tried to negotiate with other regional leaders, but they all found that supporting the Guomindang would mean a reduction of their own power and of their ability to work individually with foreign states, so they politely declined his offer of becoming their president. His negotiations with Japan and the Western powers fared no better: While they sometimes gave limited funds to Sun, they were unwilling to support his re-unification plans or recognize him as China's president. With his eyes set on a military campaign in the north to begin as soon as possible, Sun appealed to the powers to at least not oppose his aims. The coming war, Sun told them, is "no war between the North and South of China, but a struggle between militarism and democracy, between treason and patriotism. That the people in the North are sympathetic to the purposes and aims of the South has been demonstrated by the fact that they have spontaneously organized demonstrations and boycotts for the same purposes and aims."[40]

While Sun's appeals to the great powers for assistance in undoing their own positions in China may sound naïve, his point about the popular backing that the aims of the Guomindang were getting elsewhere in China was perceptive and right. The change from hopelessness to calls for action that the May Fourth Movement had led to benefited Sun's plans in regions that he knew little about and where his party had no presence. Peasant associations, often led by students who had been to the city, sometimes included support for Sun Yat-sen and nationalism among their demands. Striking railway workers in the north praised the patriotic policies of the Guomindang and condemned their own bosses for profiteering and treachery. Organizations in the cities—often a blend of new-type political groups and trade unions with more traditional guilds, native-place organizations, and gangs—appealed for a united China and the abolition of foreign privileges. The big strikes of 1922–1923 in the main cities from Hong Kong to Tianjin had specific nationalist demands. Chinese newspapers, teachers, and student unions advocated a new, activist patriotism, in which mass organizations became the custodians of the nation's conscience. By the mid-1920s the mood in many parts of China had changed enough to make the Guomindang a force to be reckoned with both by Chinese and by foreigners. In a rather alarmist fashion, the British Foreign Office reported that the GMD

> has long possessed a world-wide organization having branches and affiliated societies distributed throughout the globe. . . . The platform of the society has always been extremely democratic, and in its manifestos the society has declared itself in favor of Socialism. Sun Yat-Sen . . . coquetted at various times with every shade of revolutionary sentiment, with the result that an extreme revolutionary section rapidly sprang up [in the GMD]. . . , and has now attained such numbers and influence that it has virtually captured the control of the party machine. The society is in close touch with the Communist party in the Dutch East Indies and with Indian revolutionaries, with the result that it has to some extent assumed the aspect of a pan-Asiatic movement with the primary object of the destruction of Britain as the great despotic Power tryannising [sic] over Asia and therefore the chief obstacle in the way of world democracy. The danger of these activities has been aggravated by the close liaison which has been established during the last few years between the society and the Soviet. The [GMD] receives large contributions from Moscow, and the extreme section is infected with Bolshevik ideas and sentiment.[41]

By the early 1920s the new GMD had a popular cause and powerful backers in the Soviet Union. The Russian revolution had changed the landscape of politics in East Asia, as it had in Europe. The Soviets stood for national self-determination and social justice. Moscow was not just the center of a new state. It symbolized a set of causes that were international: anticolonialism, proletarian power, and radical culture among them. In China, Bolshevism fed into the ideas of the May Fourth Movement, and young Chinese intellectuals were infatuated with the appearance of a Western state that was righteous and could serve as a model of development that promised both modernity and equality. The declaration of Lev Karakhan, the Bolshevik deputy commissar for foreign affairs, in July 1919, sent shock waves through Chinese politics: "The government of the workers and peasants has then declared null and void all secret treaties concluded with Japan, China and the ex-Allies, the treaties which were to enable the Russian government and the Tsar and his Allies to enslave the peoples of the East and principally the people of China by intimidating or bribing them for the sole interests of capitalists, financiers and the Russian generals."[42] It is no surprise that some Chinese believed that Russia was setting the pattern for the future.

For a few young men and women, the Bolshevik revolution held the promise of a new world. They wanted to become part of the international movement that Soviet Communism represented. Inspired by Chinese socialists such as Chen Duxiu and Li Dazhao, who became their leaders, these young people formed urban radical groups and were gradually drawn into a more centralized organization, which, at a congress in the French concession in Shanghai in 1921 became the Chinese Communist Party. The money and organizational know-how for the new party were supplied by agents of Comintern—the Communist International, the Moscow center set up by Lenin in 1919 to guide Communist movements outside Russia—but Chinese Communism remained rooted in a variety of Chinese dreams and aspirations. Their expression for Communism—borrowed from Japanese—was *gonghe*, common property, but how that aim was to be achieved through Marxist doctrine was uncertain. Throughout its early years the CCP remained a small, often divided, group, and its main aim was assisting Sun Yat-sen with his revolution. "The great cause of revolution is no easy matter, even less so in China, a country under the twofold pressure of the foreign powers and the militarists," wrote Mao Zedong, a young Hunanese porter at Beijing University Library who was among the founders of the CCP. "The only solution is to call upon the merchants, the workers, the peasants, the students, and the teachers of the whole country, as well as all the others who constitute our nation and who suffer under a common oppression, and to establish a closely knit united front. It is only then that this revolution will succeed."[43]

The Soviets saw their main task in China as building the military and organizational strength of Sun Yat-sen's movement, with the Communists as a small but active part within it. The reasons were both ideological and practical: Lenin and his successors believed that China needed a nationalist bourgeois revolution before socialism could be put on the agenda. And the Guomindang seemed to fit the bill for leaders of such a revolution, given its political views and Sun's national prestige. In spite of Sun's exhilaration at getting Soviet support, he always kept his political distance from the Soviets and the Communists. But he was more than willing to accept Soviet aid in setting up a military academy, the Huangpu Academy, in Guangzhou, in which one of Sun's favorites, young Chiang Kai-shek, was commander. There Soviet military advisers taught alongside GMD leaders including Wang Jingwei, who later became Japan's chief Quisling in China, and Chinese Communists such as Zhou Enlai, the later premier, and Ye Jianying, a CCP officer who fifty years later would destroy the Communist left. The reorganization of the Guomindang forces was led by Vasilii Bliukher, a Soviet Red Army officer. And the preparations for a political reorganization of the party was strongly influenced by Mikhail Gruzenberg, who called himself Borodin, a veteran Comintern agent. By 1925 Soviet support had made the Guomindang into a very different and much stronger party than it had ever been.

Lenin's main successors in Moscow, Trotsky and Stalin, worked with the GMD but also kept the option of approaching the Beijing government or individual local strongmen who might serve Soviet security interests. Against Karakhan, who had promised to return the Russian-controlled Chinese Eastern Railway to China without receiving compensation, Trotsky wrote that he does "not understand why it is that rejecting imperialism presupposes renouncing our property rights . . . [and] why the Chinese peasant should have the railway at the expense of the Russian peasant. . . . Russia is also very poor and is absolutely unable to pay with material sacrifices for the sympathies of colonial or semicolonial peoples."[44] After Trotsky was outmaneuvered by Stalin in the Soviet power game, the emphasis on adjusting the aims of the Chinese revolution to Soviet interest and doctrine became even more pronounced. Stalin first wanted the Chinese Communists to ally themselves with the left within the Guomindang, in order to increase their influence within the movement. Then, when non-Communists in the GMD started attacking the CCP for what they considered factional behavior, the Soviet leader insisted that the only political future for Communists in China was within the Guomindang. Stalin's policy provided vital assistance for the Chinese nationalist alliance, but exposed the small band of CCP members to the jealousy and distrust of their allies.

Sun Yat-sen's first attempts at a military campaign to reunify China ended in failure. By late 1924, however, Sun, many of his advisers, and most foreign observers believed that the GMD's moment had come. The regional leaders in the north were increasingly at odds over who of them was to lead the republic. Soviet support had massively increased the military capacity of the GMD. And, crucially, some local strongmen in the south had concluded that the Guomindang might now be so strong that it was better to cooperate with it than to oppose it. To Sun, the political situation seemed to be in flux, and, true to style, he used the occasion to change his mind one more time. So he left Guangzhou for the north and for yet another attempt at getting the northern leaders to accept his supremacy without having to fight. On the way he stopped in Japan, in Kobe, where he gave one of his most pro-Japanese speeches ever, showing that he was in no way under the thumb of the Soviets. On arrival in Tianjin, Sun fell ill. He died in Beijing on 12 March 1925, with his closest disciple Wang Jingwei and his main Soviet adviser Borodin at his side. He was fifty-eight. On his deathbed he admonished his followers to unite, wrote a pro-Soviet final letter, and reaffirmed his belief in Christianity.

But those who thought that the Guomindang project was finished with the disappearance of this brilliant if inconsistent man had a big surprise waiting for them. In the spring of 1925 most of eastern China was engulfed in a series of anti-imperialist demonstrations that, for the first time, seemed to rock the stability of the system foreign powers had set up to manage China after 1911. In the international concession in Shanghai, on 30 May, nine student demonstrators were killed by British police. In other cities, foreign police also had to open fire on demonstrating students and workers who threatened to invade the key institutions of foreign power. Strikes and blockades spread, most of them spontaneously, but some organized by GMD sympathizers or Communists. The Beijing government, deeply divided and challenged by its northern rivals, with whom it had just fought a brief but bloody civil war, was powerless. And to all of the demonstrators in what became known as the May Thirtieth Movement, Sun Yat-sen was a martyr for the nationalist cause and a harbinger of a new, powerful, and united China.[45] The poet Wen Yiduo—an experimenter in hyperbolism—gave voice to the parts of China under foreign control and their longing to become again part of the motherland:

> *Do you know that "Macau" has never been my real name?*
> *I have been away from you for too long, Mother.*
> *They have captured my body*
> *But my soul is always yours.*

Oh, Mother, I have remembered you for three hundred years.
Call me by my baby name; call for me by the name "Aomen."
Mother! I want to come home, Mother!

In Guangzhou, the younger leaders of Guomindang and their Communist allies started understanding that the combination of Sun's martyrdom, Soviet support, northern political chaos, and the May Thirtieth Movement had created the best of opportunity ever for a march toward Beijing. Chiang Kai-shek, the powerful commander of the Huangpu Academy, urged an early start to the expedition north. Chiang believed that the GMD's time had come. He also insisted on action in order to honor the dead Sun Yat-sen, whom he had revered, and because of his revulsion at the killing of Chinese civilians in Shanghai, Wuhan, and elsewhere by foreign forces. Chiang saw himself as the natural choice to lead the military campaign; though still a young man at thirty-eight, he believed in an almost mystical way that his life and the cause of ridding China of foreign domination were one and the same.

Chiang Kai-shek was born in 1887 near Ningbo, a treaty port in Zhejiang province, just south of Shanghai. He received military training in Japan and served in the Japanese army for two years. Returning to China after the 1911 revolution, Chiang became one of Sun Yat-sen's trusted lieutenants, traveling between Shanghai and Japan in the service of his mentor. After Sun moved to Guangzhou, Chiang became one of his chiefs of military affairs and increasingly the man the president relied on for his personal safety. Chiang's vision of China was simple, but strongly held. He wanted a country that was united, orderly, and militarily powerful—all values that had been instilled in him during his strict Confucian upbringing and his military training in Japan. Sun's death was a profound shock for Chiang, and he imagined himself taking the dead leader's place and fulfilling Sun's dream of a new China.

The Northern Expedition, which began in July 1926, quickly became a stunning political and military success. Guomindang and Communist organizers, and local nationalists without any party links, helped set up underground committees and prepare the arrival of the revolutionary army through strikes and nationalist demonstrations. The military strategy that Chiang, Bliukher, and other GMD military leaders worked out was remarkably successful: Moving north fast, spread out in three main armies, the Northern Expedition overwhelmed their enemies one by one, with many local leaders finding it much smarter to submit than to fight. Propaganda played an increasingly important part. In spite of their differing social and political aims, everyone within the Guomindang spread a simple message of patriotism and national renewal. Their slogans were simple: "Chinese to rule China." "Long live Sun Yat-sen. Long live the People's Three Principles. Long live the national revolution." As the revolutionary armies approached the main cities in central China, the fighting intensified. The poet Guo Moruo, who fought with the revolutionary army outside Wuhan, saw fallen soldiers "strewn on both sides of the route of the railway. . . . In the lakes nearby . . . countless corpses floated—some with faces turned up, some with faces turned down, some on their sides."[46]

Wuhan fell to the GMD forces in October 1926 and a new national government was set up under Wang Jingwei. Nationalist celebrations were intense. Guo Moruo saw "the streaming of group, party, and national flags; the chorused singing of the 'International,' the 'Song of the Vanguard,' and the 'Song of the Revolution'; the shouting of slogans and of *wansui* [long live], the speeches to the multitude."[47] But the new left-wing Wuhan government did not have the loyalty of Chiang Kai-shek. As his troops approached Shanghai, Chiang was becoming increasingly skeptical of the aims of his Communist allies. Already in Guangzhou there had been bad blood between them. Chiang believed that the Communists were planning to have him killed. But it was the sudden success of the march north that drove the alliance apart. The CCP and the Soviets saw Chiang as a potential military dictator, a Napoleon. Chiang, on his side, was becoming increasingly worried that after the liberation of China from Western influence, the CCP and the left wing of the Guomindang would put the country under Soviet control. In his diary, Chiang was increasingly critical of his Soviet advisors: "I treat them with sincerity, but they reciprocate with deceit."[48] The Communists were criticizing Chiang in public and preparing to take control of Shanghai from within before his troops arrived. The clock was ticking for a confrontation.

Chiang Kai-shek struck first. The left-wing Wuhan government had ordered his arrest, but were without power to carry it out. Chiang's soldiers responded by putting Shanghai under martial law as soon as they entered the city. Chiang then acted on a plan, almost certainly prepared months in advance, to destroy the CCP and curtail the influence of the GMD left wing. Within days his agents and members of various organizations loyal to Chiang (including some criminal gangs in the coastal cities) had seized or killed almost the entire CCP leadership and tens of thousands of ordinary party members and leftist sympathizers. Even though a few party leaders (such as Mao Zedong, who fled to the mountains in southern China) survived the massacre, the CCP as an organization was destroyed for years to come. In Moscow, Stalin loudly demanded a revolutionary response in China. The Soviet leader was eager to hide that it was his insistence on preserving the CCP-GMD alliance that had led the Chinese Communists to their slaughter.

The Wuhan government gradually capitulated. By the spring of 1928 Chiang Kai-shek was the undisputed leader of the Guomindang. During 1928 the last of the main regional strongmen pledged allegiance to the new regime, giving the GMD at least nominal control of all of China except Manchuria. Sun's Northern Expedition, laughed off by many three years before as the pipedream of a soft-headed adventurer, had succeeded beyond the wildest imagination of its initiator.

The success of the Northern Expedition and the rise of Chinese nationalism were profound shocks to foreign observers. The spectacle of local strongmen, who had built their positions on promoting regionalism, now won over to the message of one united China, free of foreign domination (or at least too frightened to oppose that message) forced a revised view of the future. Britain, which in many ways had the most to lose, feared the combination of Chinese manpower and Soviet organization. "We are virtually at war with Russia," wrote the Permanent Under-Secretary at the Foreign Office, Sir William Tyrrell, in December 1926.[49] The possible loss of Shanghai was of particular concern. As the British foreign secretary told the cabinet, "Owing to the magnitude of our interests there, its loss would have lasting disastrous consequences on our position in Asia, and would have most serious reactions in India and on Japan."[50] Some Western observers conjured up images of the Boxer Rebellion and foresaw the slaughter of foreigners, except Russians. The British sent 15,000 troops to defend the concessions in Shanghai— for London this was a battle for civilization against rebellious Chinese and their insidious Russian masters.

NEITHER LONDON NOR OTHER FOREIGN CAPITALS understood how much Chiang Kai-shek and his Guomindang wanted to be masters in their own house. The destruction of the CCP was but one missed signal. By the end of 1928 all local strongmen had been forced to declare their allegiance to Chiang's government, even though the GMD's control in the provinces closest to the edges of the former empire was and would remain tenuous up to the outbreak of the Sino-Japanese war in 1937. During its ten years of governing from Nanjing, the GMD constructed what we today would call a national development state, which—in spite of corruption and poor administration—became the most effective government China had had since the mid-nineteenth century. Patterned politically on the authoritarian regimes in the Soviet Union and Italy (and later in Germany), Chiang's state tried to learn from the Western and Japanese development experiences without taking over their ideologies. In spite of the adverse international economic climate in the late twenties and thirties, the GMD government managed to oversee impressive growth in the urban sectors of the economy. Some claim that this growth happened at least as much in spite of the GMD's policies as because of them. But it is clear that without the relative stability the new government provided, it would have been unlikely for some parts of the Chinese economy to develop as fast as they did during the so-called Nanjing Decade.

Chiang's foreign policy aimed at regaining China's full sovereignty as soon as possible. He saw two main strategies as essential to this goal: reintegrating all outlying provinces back into China and abolishing all foreign extraterritorial rights. In carrying out these strategies, Chiang saw some successes, but mostly failures, mainly because of continuous and increasing pressure from Japan. Chiang started by informing the concession powers that he intended to unilaterally abrogate all unequal extraterritorial rights for foreigners in China by 1 January 1930. But confronted with the West's unwillingness to negotiate and weakened by the looming threat of war with Japan, he was in no position to follow up on his threat. The intransigence of the Western powers and their narrow focus on their rights and privileges prevented them from helping to fortify China as a counterbalance to Japan in East Asia. It was a shortsighted and narrow-minded policy, based on the fear that the Guomindang after all could end up in the clutches of the Soviets. To the British, the path was clear. "I have no hesitation," wrote Tyrrell, "in stating that our policy should be based upon the assumption that Russia is the enemy and not Japan. The most we have to dread from the latter is commercial rivalry."[51]

Just as after the collapse of the second Sino-Soviet alliance in the 1960s, it took the Western powers a lot of time before they realized that the GMD-Soviet break in 1927 was permanent and real. They did not see Chiang's determination to recover China's rights from the Soviets nor his conviction that the Chinese Communists had to be eradicated by all means possible, because they formed a Soviet fifth column within China. When Stalin refused to negotiate over ceding control of the Chinese Eastern Railway in Manchuria to China in 1929, Chiang tried to seize it by force, causing a brief border war with the Soviets. Commanded by Bliukher, who had been the GMD's chief military adviser in Guangzhou, the Red Army won decisive victories in northern Manchuria in November 1929. The USSR kept control of the railway until 1931, when they lost it to the Japanese. But Stalin's policy was as much a failure as that of the Western powers, since it indirectly strengthened Japan and made a direct confrontation between the two countries more likely in the future. The Soviet leader's attempts at mobilizing Chinese Communist support for his aims in Manchuria—including an abortive set of CCP attacks on cities in the south—destroyed any chance the Communists might have had to ally with the GMD left and helped impress on Chiang more than ever the CCP's perfidy and treason.

While the Soviets were a threat to Guomindang China, Japan was a deadly danger. As the only foreign country Chiang Kai-shek knew and respected, Japan had seemed to him—as it had to his teacher Sun Yat-sen—to be the ideal ally. Together they could form a pan-Asian development partnership that would drive out Western dominance. But the Japanese military gave him no chance to test out his desires for an understanding. As GMD forces moved northward in the final part of their unification of China, Tokyo sent troop reinforcements to Shandong to protect its positions there. After fighting broke out in the provincial capital Jinan in April 1928, imperial army units attacked Chiang's troops, with Chinese losses of more than 1,500 men. In Manchuria, Japan feared the rise in Chinese nationalism, which saw the local strongman, Zhang Xueliang, declare his adherence to the Nanjing government. That Japanese officers had assassinated his father, Zhang Zuolin, a few years before undoubtedly strengthened Zhang's determination to switch sides. Japanese leaders, and commanding officers in Korea and Manchuria, also felt that the Soviet Union was getting too strong and that it and the GMD stood as the forces of chaos in Northeast Asia.

For Chiang Kai-shek, Manchuria was an inalienable part of China. He had no plans to give it up. But he needed to bide his time. China could not confront Japan unless it was united and militarily prepared. In the early 1930s Chiang still had much domestic trouble. Dissatisfied GMD leaders and local strongmen rebelled in serious challenges to his power, and the CCP, although much reduced, still operated from hideouts in southern China. The Chinese armies were neither well-trained nor well-equipped, but a massive armaments and training program—headed in part by Chiang's German advisers—was starting to show results. With tension on the boil in Manchuria, Japanese army officers stationed in Shenyang planted a bomb near the South Manchurian Railway in September 1931, blamed Zhang Xueliang's troops, and attacked the Chinese garrison in the city. Against clear orders from Tokyo, the Japanese army in Manchuria fanned out from its barracks along the railway line and, within weeks, occupied most major cities in the region. With the Soviets eager to stay well clear of a conflict with Japan and with the Tokyo government reluctantly accepting its military's conquest of Manchuria, Chiang Kai-shek faced a hopeless situation. He was lambasted by many of his countrymen for deciding not to launch an all-out war against Japan in 1931, but—given the lack of outside support—China in reality had no other choice. War with Japan would come, Chiang told his closest associates. But China's survival depended on postponing that war as long as possible.

IN 1912, FEW INFORMED CHINESE or foreigners had given the new republic much of a chance for survival. It was seen as an anomaly: a government based on democratic principles in a country where eighty percent of the population was illiterate, a constitutional regime in a country that through its long history had known only autocracy. But the republic did survive, although in a very different form from what its founders had imagined. Through its survival it brought China closer to the world at large. It gave the country a form of government that was internationally recognizable (in spite of its various peculiarities). It continued a move toward a more open society, in which individuals and groups could make their own choices on trade, travel, and relations of friendship. And it gave China the possibility of making advances in the dissemination of ideas and practices, and in the building of educational networks, that would be of crucial importance during the dark decades that followed.

There are two main reasons why the Republic of China survived, and both of them connect to the international. It was saved by Chinese nationalism, which broke through in its modern form in the 1910s and 1920s. This nationalism put the need for a strong state at its core, and its main protagonists were always willing to support those in power if they were seen as standing up for China's interests. And the new republic was also lucky with the international constellations of its time: World War I made the main Western imperialist countries focus on Europe, and the outcome of the war weakened them, at least temporarily. As during the Napoleonic wars and during the late Cold War, a weak Chinese state survived because the main international predators were preoccupied elsewhere. The troubles in the international system also opened up a chance for China to cooperate with other international outcasts, mainly the Soviet Union and Germany.

Within this international framework, Japan became the prime threat. By the early 1930s it was abundantly clear that Chinese nationalism and Japanese expansionism could not coexist, in spite of the many attempts from both sides to draw on a common cultural and racial heritage. But, ironically, Japan's march toward confrontation with the world also meant opportunities for China's republic. The nationalist reaction within China made the country more cohesive, even if there were strong disagreements on strategy. And Chiang Kai-shek's lifeline message from 1931 on—that Japan's "unnatural" ambitions would get it in trouble and create a grand coalition to defeat it—pointed to China's chance to become a founding member of a new postwar international society. China's leaders, in other words, had started to see themselves as part of a global system, which, even though they had not chosen to be part of it, could provide advantages for China.

By 1937, the year an all-out war against Japan began, China had become a part of the world in ways that its leaders at the turn of the century could never have imagined. Its legal system was modeled on that of the West. Foreign products found their way to the far reaches of the country. Education was mostly based on foreign concepts and ideas. In the younger generation, there had been a substantial change in how Chinese saw themselves. No longer a people apart, they wanted to be treated like other people elsewhere and have the same opportunities. But the 1930s was not a good time for a generation to come of age, in China or elsewhere. The decade saw a broadly shared sense of a lack of purpose, of determination, of a specific Chinese contribution to world affairs, and a sense of maltreatment in a world where dictatorships determinedly marched ahead. As Chinese nationalism formed itself under the pressure of Japanese aggression, those who had embraced the transnational networks in the cities became increasingly suspect. When the war came, even many of the educated young people in Shanghai, Tianjin, Beijing, and Guangzhou—those who went out in the evening wearing Western dress and listened to jazz—had become convinced that the only possible answer to China's ills could come from within China itself.

CHAPTER 5

FOREIGNERS

D URING THE FIRST HALF OF THE TWENTIETH CENTURY, China became internationalized. In 1900, both natives and foreigners saw
the Chinese empire as a thing apart, but by the late 1940s the country
had become integrated into a capitalist world of expanding markets and
movements of people and ideas. Foreigners in China played a significant role in this transformation. Coming from all parts of the world
and representing all kinds of backgrounds and professions, they helped
transform China (though not always in directions that most Chinese
appreciated). They were missionaries and businessmen, advisers and adventurers, revolutionaries and refugees. While some came for short-
term profit, many stayed in China and died there. In each single case
they influenced and were influenced by their Chinese contacts, often
in directions that would profoundly affect China and the world up
to today.

Until the mid-twentieth century, the relationship between Chinese
and foreigners within China was profoundly unequal. Most foreigners
had rights of extraterritoriality, meaning that their legal affairs in China
could only be handled by courts set up by their own country. Many
lived in concessions or settlements inside Chinese cities run by foreign-
dominated councils and administered by foreign officials. In a classic
colonial mode of interaction, Chinese were often critical of foreigners

and their habits in private, while in public they felt a need to express admiration for the foreigners. This unhealthy and sometimes racist form of interaction often stood in the way of close personal relations between Chinese and foreigners but did little to diminish the exchange of ideas and practices, especially over time.

The numbers of foreigners in China varied year by year according to conditions in the country and internationally, but it is likely that the average in the first half of the twentieth century was between 300,000 and half a million (maybe surprisingly, the figures in 2005 were about the same).[1] Of these, about half were Japanese subjects; the British, who long were the most influential, were never more than 15,000. Of the total, more than 100,000 came as refugees from troubles in Europe, including the Russian revolution and the Nazi persecution of Jews. Most lived in the cities though not always in the foreign concessions. Harbin and Shenyang had many Russians and later Japanese, and Shanghai had by far the largest number of foreigners, with 70,000 in 1932. But foreigners were also found in the countryside, usually as missionaries, teachers, or traders along the country's edges. To the Chinese, the foreign presence provided a cornucopia of impressions of the outside world and inspired many to seek out a closer connection with non-native ideas and knowledge.

Some parts of the country were a world apart. These were the regions where foreigners aspired to full control—British-held Hong Kong, Portuguese-held Macao, and Japanese-held Taiwan and Manchuria (especially after 1931). There different forms of hybridity that the colonial experience created blossomed in full, with concepts of what was Chinese and what was foreign starting to blur. Eminent Chinese in Hong Kong became British subjects and were educated at Oxford, Cambridge, or the London School of Economics (LSE). In Taiwan, the younger generation of Chinese adopted Japanese language and culture, and some moved between mainland China, Japan, and Taiwan. Japanese tastes and habits in everything from art to baseball came to the island to stay.

The world sometimes returned the seed of Chinese emigration: A number of highly trained overseas-born Chinese from all continents came to China throughout the twentieth century and some played leading roles in the country that their ancestors had left. In spite of war and continuous political change, the first part of the twentieth century was China's age of openness, an age in which foreigners delivered some of the key premises for the country's development.[2]

In the first half of the twentieth century, much of China's international trade was still in foreign hands. The main foreign powers set tariffs for goods imported into China, and the Chinese government was simply notified of the outcome. In 1917 there were ninety-two cities and towns open to direct foreign trade, of which about half had foreign concessions or settlements where foreigners had the right to reside, to trade, and to own property. Everyone who lived in such concessions was taxed by the foreign-led local administrations, not by the Chinese government, province, or city. The land on which the foreign concessions stood had been expropriated from its owners and leased in perpetuity to foreign powers, with subleases given by them to individuals or companies. As a rule, Chinese were not allowed to own land in the concessions, but some did so through proxy. Conveniently for subversives of all sorts—aspiring capitalists, revolutionaries, and religious fanatics—they too could make use of the extraterritoriality given to the foreign concessions. There, Chinese could be arrested by Chinese authorities only with the permission of the foreign consul in charge of the territory. Thus, the CCP held most of its founding congress in a former missionary school in the French concession in Shanghai, rather than in Chinese-governed areas.

Of the concessions, Shanghai was the biggest, but others were equally cosmopolitan and complex. The main northern port of Tianjin had seven foreign national administrations, with three British municipal districts. Wuhan on the Yangzi river originally had four concessions, which looked like miniature European cities: Orthodox churches,

British customs houses, German breweries, and French restaurants. It is, wrote a foreign visitor in the 1920s, "a bustling city, wholly Western in its architecture and layout, even though completely surrounded by China, among buildings looming high into the air, with several theaters, even though they offered only American movies, with automobiles dashing their imperious way up and down the river-front Bund."[3] The concessions, all on the rivers or at the coast, were defended by foreign naval ships, which patrolled day and night. Even though the foreign military presence was limited, it could be deadly. Gunboat diplomacy sometimes involved shelling of Chinese cities until the foreign power had got its way. For its China Station, the British navy developed the Insect Class of ships, small maneuverable vessels with six-inch guns. Small contingents of foreign troops were stationed in the main concessions and settlements. Then, of course, there were the Japanese troops on Taiwan and in Manchuria, the British in Hong Kong, and the French in Indochina. The foreign possessions in China could be well defended.

The main foreign concessions were reasonably self-contained. Foreigners often prided themselves on how little they had to do with ordinary Chinese in their businesses, a task better left to their Chinese middlemen. Even so, a surprising number of foreigners who lived in China learned the language well enough to communicate in it. Many also developed an appreciation for Chinese food (not surprising, since the most available foreign fare was English) and for Chinese art and esthetics. Personal relationships of all kinds flourished in spite of the restrictions that the colonial setting tried to impose: Chinese and foreigners met each other as friends, teachers, or lovers. Sir Sidney Barton, the British consul-general at Shanghai, was a fluent Chinese speaker and knew the business and government communities in his city like nobody else. Silas Hardoon, Shanghai's richest property tycoon (who was born Salih Harun to a Jewish family in Baghdad) married a Chinese woman, Luo Jialing, and became a chief benefactor for Buddhist causes in the metropolis. Increasingly—even as they tried to keep apart—the mores and attractions of the modern city brought Chinese and foreigners together, at the race track, the dance halls, and the cinemas.

But not all foreigners in China were wealthy citizens of the world. Some came as settlers, especially Japanese and Koreans who moved into Manchuria or Taiwan, or Russians who had come before the 1917 Bolshevik revolution. Some came as refugees, Russians after 1917 and German Jews after 1933, and some as servants of empires: Indians and Malays to Shanghai and Hong Kong, North Africans and Indochinese to the French concessions and to Guangzhouwan, the French-leased territory in Guangdong province. With the South Manchurian Railway zone, Liaodong peninsula, and all of south Manchuria open to Japanese settlement and investment, and preference for Japanese as advisors to the Chinese local government throughout the region, it is no surprise that half the foreign population in China were subjects of the Japanese Empire. Well before Tokyo's puppet state in Manchuria, Manzhouguo, came into existence in 1932, the South Manchurian Railway Company operated a Japanese pseudo-state within northeast China, running factories and mines, shipping lines and warehouses, and setting up schools, hospitals, and public utilities. A very large number of those who staffed these operations were Koreans.

For the many Chinese who came to the foreign concessions to work as servants, street-sweepers, or factory workers—and even more for those who just happened to be passing through—the allure of the foreigners' world competed with the horror at its values and ways of behavior. The greed, the exploitation, and the status that money brought rankled Confucians and radicals alike. In Beijing, where the foreign section—the Legation Quarter—had been set up only a few steps from the entrance to the old imperial palace at Tian'anmen, many Chinese were insulted that the quarter's banks, shops, hospitals, churches, and hotels were for foreign use only. And even if the existence of a sign denying access to dogs and Chinese in Shanghai parks is an urban myth, Chinese were de facto barred from many clubs, parks, and sports grounds in the foreign settlements at least up to the late 1920s. The essayist Yang Yibo saw Shanghai as "a seething cauldron. . . . I hope to utterly destroy this old Shanghai, to smash asunder this oriental bastion of imperialist domination, to inter forever those golden dreams of bloodsucking vampires."[4] To Yang and to most Chinese the foreign concessions produced a lasting impression of foreigners' unceasing pressure for unique material advantage to themselves and their country at China's expense.

CHINA IS VAST, and change came to its various regions with varying intensity. A traveler who visited the Chinese interior in the 1930s, following the great trade routes into Central Asia or moving along the edges of the northern plains from Shanxi to the mountain passes into Sichuan, would have reported on a country in which little had changed since the Western incursions began. But if the same traveler went along the main rivers or the coast or visited cities all over the country or smaller towns in the south, along the Yangzi delta, in Shandong or Manchuria, a very different story would emerge. It would be a story of change that had taken hold and was being indigenized, of a transformation of people's dress, dwellings, and social interaction, of objects and technologies that had been integrated into Chinese life with an ease many visitors found astonishing, and not least of people's embrace of change. Even revolutionaries, who wanted to use the tools of this new world to defeat its masters, dressed in Western-style clothes, read foreign texts, and adhered to political theories imported from abroad.

Things travel alongside ideas, and sometimes the material travels faster than the idea it came from. In China in the early twentieth century, products from the industrial revolutions in Europe and North America reached the far corners of the country, handed down from imports to middlemen to county fairs, traveling merchants, or the town store. Bicycles, batteries, glass, telephones, lights, cotton, leather shoes, perfumes, wristwatches, photography, and radios—all things foreign and therefore modern created a sense of excitement in China just as they had done when they had been introduced a few decades earlier on the continents where they were created. Almost immediately the Chinese started to integrate such products into their own lifestyles and esthetics, and very soon the most advantageous of them were produced in China, for domestic consumption and then for export. Nobody who has studied the introduction of foreign products into China in the early twentieth century will be surprised at the speed with which the country was to become an export dynamo three generations later, when the political pendulum swung back toward enterprise values and interaction with the world. Although the willingness to adapt to rapid change also created resistance, the ability to find ways to integrate the Chinese with the foreign baffled many observers and made urban China seem well poised for being on the cusp of modernity.

The houses in which people lived and worked also went through a series of modern adaptations. By the 1930s most towns and even some villages had examples of new types of buildings, contemporary and utilitarian, with large glass windows and electric light and heating, designed according to standards developed by architects in Chicago, Paris, or London. The cities were of course the vanguard, and especially Shanghai, where tall buildings were rising up at the waterfront. The 1908 Palace Hotel, by the British architect Walter Scott, incorporated the first use of elevators in China. Across the street the Cathay Hotel, thirteen stories with the Baghdad-born financier Sir Victor Sassoon's private apartment on top, was the most impressive building in China when it opened in 1929. By the 1930s, Shanghai had become a center for modern architecture, with the world's top architects and designers competing for commissions. But styles changed elsewhere in China, too. In Beijing new public buildings were mostly in the Western style from the early part of the century, exemplified by the German architect Curt Rothkegel's republican provisional parliament building.[5] By the 1910s Chinese architects began designing new kinds of buildings in China, which like those of their Western counterparts closely followed international trends in architectural style. While some architects, foreign and Chinese, experimented with incorporating elements of classical Chinese style into their new buildings, most clients were happy enough with moving into constructions that they felt served their purpose better than what the old-style houses had done.

As with buildings, styles of dress were also changing quickly. In the 1880s most elite Chinese wore their Western clothing on special occasions, but thirty years later it would dominate the way people looked in the cities and sometimes in village China, too. But it did so in ways that were often surprising to the beholder: Chinese elements woven into Western styles, Chinese modifications of imported fashions, appropriations of dress across class, nation, and sometimes gender. According to the Shanghai magazine *Shenbao* in 1912, "Chinese are wearing foreign clothes, while foreigners wear Chinese clothes; men are adorned like women and women like men; prostitutes imitate girl students, and girl students look like prostitutes." The explosion in Chinese production of cotton cloth in the 1920s and the arrival of the sewing machine and talented Russian and German tailors spurred the revolution in fashion. Picture magazines and advertising spread the message of new fashion all over the country. People in China changed their clothing style for all kinds of reasons, as do people all over the world, but looking good often came with some form of message. In China this message was "New Nation."[6]

Two examples of New Nation fashion stand out. The *qipao*, the long, sleeveless dress for women that became popular after 1910, and the *Zhongshan* two-piece suit, which, reincarnated in a cheap form as the Mao suit, was to clothe China's men and women after the Communist victory. The qipao was a Westernized version of Manchu upper-class dress from the nineteenth century. It became popular because it was *both* Chinese and Western, because it could be made cheaply or expensively with all kinds of cloth, and because it could be as revealing or strict as the circumstances warranted. The Zhongshan suit had a similar purpose. It was adapted from German military-style school uniforms that Sun Yat-sen saw in Japan, and was named after Sun's honorific name Zhongshan, Central Mountain.[7] Sun himself began to wear this simple form of suit in 1920, and it represented the need for regimentation and militarization of China to achieve the nationalist revolution. By the 1930s it had become de rigeur for nationalists and Communist alike, at least when a political point needed to be made. The status of the person who wore it was recognized by the cut or the quality of the fountain pen worn in the left breast pocket.

Chinese material culture in the twentieth century was increasingly eclectic, as was the case in most countries. The foreign blended with the domestic to such an extent that it quickly became impossible to say which was which. Sometimes, as with the qipao or the Zhongshan suit, quite a few Chinese started believing that recent imports were originally Chinese and ancient, and sometimes used that belief to attack those who wished to dress differently. But mostly the eclecticism of Chinese dress or building styles or consumer patterns were accepted in a society that most people realized was in flux. The encounter with the foreign in China happened within a context of intense social change, in which a mixing of traditions and patterns was common. In this sense, Chinese material culture changed in patterns similar to other parts of the world where change came quickly and, for most people, unexpectedly. There was not much difference between the experiences of peasants in France, Italy, or those who worked the land in the western parts of the United States, and those of their Chinese counterparts. A few decades of divergence in timing often obscure processes that were remarkably similar in content. Even less of a difference was there in the cities, where the concepts of what was modern were created. By mid-century, Chinese urban life was taking on most of the characteristics of cities everywhere, from Paris and Berlin to New York and Tokyo. And first among the modern Chinese cities stood Shanghai.

CHINESE MODERNITY WAS CREATED in Shanghai. In technology and organization, in taste and style, the great city at the mouth of the Yangzi river shaped the hybrid patterns that gave meaning to modern China. Shanghai modernity was always contested. Some Chinese abhorred it because of its foreign cravings and moral perturbations, and its ability to rattle their concepts of the native, national, or original. In the imagination of leaders from the Empress Dowager to Mao Zedong, Shanghai was unclean, the great whore whom everyone moved in and out of but who belonged to no one. It was chaotic, uncontrollable, and un-Chinese. In 1949 Mao and the Communists seriously contemplated abolishing the city and driving all its inhabitants out into the countryside, Pol Pot–like. But for most Chinese who saw the city, who lived in it or who dreamed about it, Shanghai symbolized the kind of existence they wanted for themselves and their children—cleaner and more well-ordered than the actual city, perhaps, but with the dynamism, fun, and riches that was contained within it as nowhere else in China.

In 1936, Shanghai, with its three and a half million inhabitants, was one of the world's largest cities. Much of the central city fell within the International Settlement (made up of the original British and American zones), with its eight square miles roughly twice the size of the French Settlement to the south. Most of the population lived in the old Chinese city outside the settlements or in the vast industrial zones to the east or in shantytowns that grew up on the city's edges. All who could afford it had the right of residence in the foreign settlements. But only foreign residents who owned land of a certain value, around ten percent of the total foreign population by the early 1920s, could vote in elections for the Shanghai Municipal Council (SMC), the governing body of the International Settlement. The SMC appropriated power from the foreign consuls during the early part of the century, and its own adminstration also grew in importance. Mostly British or British Indian in composition, the SMC civil service handled policing, public utilities, roads, and, increasingly, schools and hospitals. Up to 1927, civil or criminal court cases in the Settlement, even those that only involved Chinese, were decided by a so-called Mixed Court, in which a foreign assessor sat with a Chinese judge and generally dominated proceedings. Shanghai, with all its extensions, was a hybrid city, where its perhaps 70,000 foreign citizens, often joined by parts of the Chinese elite, became increasingly determined to exclude the Chinese state from any influence in their affairs (an attitude, by the way, which foreign consuls looked upon with a great deal of suspicion).

Foreigners who arrived in Shanghai found ways of sticking together. They could join clubs for modern, Western activities like ballroom dancing or playing bridge, which long excluded Chinese. Even if they could not participate at the same tables or on the same dance floors, foreign activities and tastes influenced natives as well. Mao Zedong always liked to dance to Western music, and the last position Deng Xiaoping ever held, in the 1990s, was chairman of the Chinese Bridge Players' Association. Other associations had a broader purpose. The YMCA, established in China in the 1890s, reached its peak in the 1920s, when it ran large public education programs, including public health education, vocational training, sports events, and English classes. From being an exclusively foreign organization, the Y became increasingly Chinese, and a number of China's late twentieth-century radical leaders confessed that they had benefited from their association with the Y.

Not least because of the protection that the foreign settlements provided, modern journalism in China was also born in Shanghai. English-language newspapers, such as the *North-China Daily News*, established in the 1850s, and the more sensationalist *Shanghai Evening Post and Mercury*, established in 1920, inspired Chinese papers like *Shenbao* (from 1871), *Dianshizhai* (the first pictorial, from the 1880s), and tabloids such as the *Libao* (from 1935), published by the newspaper magnate Cheng Shewo, with a circulation of more than 200,000.[8] By the 1930s Shanghai had a flourishing newsmarket, with papers published in Chinese and English, and in German, Russian, Japanese,

French, Polish, and Yiddish. Its book publishing houses were the most important in China, often co-owned by foreign and Chinese interests, but managed by Chinese editors.

Pre-1949 Shanghai is often dubbed Sin City, and with some right, even though sin is often defined by those who object to what they see as cultural or even racial miscegenation. The main sin, in the eyes of many Chinese, was gross inequality and the flaunting of wealth, which was blamed on the foreign presence. For foreigners, and especially the English, sin was often about sex, usually in situations where one of the partners was Chinese. Many new histories of Shanghai attempt to break the focus on nightlife and entertainment, shopping and gambling. But "Shanghai beyond the neon lights" is not an easy construct, since the neon lights were, quite literally, visible from all over the city.[9] If they were not blocked by racial discrimination, everyone who could afford it participated in some of the entertainment that the city offered. They could go to one of thirty-seven cinemas, the horse and dog race tracks, or the great leisure centers, such as the Da Shijie, Great World, on Edward VII Avenue, with its restaurants, dance floors, theaters, circus, and casinos. Or they went shopping or window shopping along Nanking Road, where the two great department stores, the Wing On and the Sincere, faced each other across Asia's busiest street. People who were not appropriately dressed or seemed "the wrong sort" were thrown out, just as they would be in Shanghai's mega-malls today. But that did not prevent them from coming back, even if in the meantime they had joined a revolutionary society to oppose the depravity and oppression of Shanghai.

The owners of the two great Shanghai department stores had all learned their initial lessons in commerce abroad. The brothers who started Wing On, Guo Yue and Guo Quan, had lived in Australia, where they converted to Christianity and began working as green-grocers. When they returned to China around 1900, they settled in Hong Kong and spread their commercial empire from there, with the key branch soon being in Shanghai. Sincere Department Store developed the same way, also started by two brothers, Ma Yingbiao and Ma Yong-can, who had lived in Australia and then settled in Hong Kong. The Guos and the Mas came from adjacent villages close to Macao in Guangdong province. They even married sisters from the same family, one of whom, Huo Qingtang, became one of the founders of the YWCA in China. Chinese merchants such as the Guos and the Mas in the twentieth century drew on their own traditions, on their new freedom to travel, and on their ability to associate with foreigners to enrich themselves and promote their quest for a modern China. They learned from the foreign companies they worked with, and they helped build business enterprises in China that were neither entirely foreign nor entirely Chinese.

The big foreign companies in China were also transformed in the early twentieth century. Through working closely with Chinese middlemen, Jardine Matheson had become a conglomerate, which—in addition to trade—was running wharves, warehouses, and cotton mills, developed mining and engineering companies, and had its own railways and steamship companies. It became a limited company, with considerable Chinese capital invested in it, in 1907 and moved its headquarters to Shanghai in 1912. Jardine's filled a series of functions, most of them connected to transport in the broadest sense. It linked British India, Malaya, Singapore, and Australia with China and Japan through shipping and related services. Across the river from Shanghai, Jardine's wharves in Pudong (where the city's new financial center now is) became the central point in one of the world's great trade networks. All Chinese towns of any significance had a Jardine's agent, who could handle transport, insurance, and often banking. Crucially, Jardine's developed a Chinese web of business that went far beyond the compradors who worked directly with the company. In many parts of the country— and in Hong Kong not least—small Chinese-run companies grew through their links with Jardine's or similar companies, which provided the services they needed for their expansion.

China remained a favored country for foreign investment up to the beginning of the 1930s. Companies saw opportunity there in spite of China's domestic political turbulence. They also appreciated the absence of a strong central power that could limit their activities. As late as 1932, roughly five percent of all French investment abroad, for instance, went to China (which is about ten times the rate of such investment in the 2000s[10]). Most of the profits these companies made in China never reached the Chinese. But the knowledge that major international players—Standard Oil, Shell, Singer Sewing Machines, British-American Tobacco—brought with them led to a major transformation of Chinese business, particularly with regard to business models and management. Gone were the days when members of the Chinese elite felt caught between Confucianism and business acumen. By the 1920s most believed that the Confucian emphasis on family, hierarchy, personal obligation, and thrift could be easily wed to foreign management principles. The mostly American prophets of "scientific management" from the interwar years were keenly studied in China (more so, in fact, than they were in Europe or Japan). Most Chinese business leaders realized that rationalization and reorganization were crucial if they were to compete with foreign companies. In some cases, workers were treated more harshly by their Chinese bosses than they were by foreigners, which fueled resentment against the foreign system of capitalism. As workers flocked to Shanghai or other big cities to find work in factories, some of them began to dream of another world in which they themselves owned the means of production.

A crucial capitalist principle that took a long time to get established in China was that of the limited liability company. Chinese preferred private ownership, with a family in charge, and most companies kept a very narrow circle of shareholders comprising family members and long-term associates. The limited availability of credit from banks and the cumbersome nature of the capital structure of private partnership restricted the availability of working capital up to the outbreak of the Sino-Japanese war in 1937.

Only gradually did Chinese entrepreneurs learn how to expand without giving up control of their companies, or, if they wanted to, to give up control to maximize profit. Businessmen learned how to look after their shareholders after the company had gone public. In a country where legal protection was weak, such an application of Confucian principles was both necessary and profitable. A master of the process was Liu Hongsheng, who started his business career in a Sino-British mining company, and went on to form successful cement and matchstick companies of his own. His Hong Song Match Company became the main producer through a series of mergers and takeovers. In 1936 he set up the China National Match Manufacturers' Production and Sales Union, which was in effect a cartel that, with government blessing, controlled prices and production. In the 1930s, as today, business in China worked best when it could work with the government.

In terms of transport, railways were by the 1930s becoming almost as important for business as waterways. Some of the railways were developed by foreign companies or states, others by Chinese-foreign consortia, which often involved, on the Chinese side, private and provincial interests. The governments in China, both before and after 1927, were eager to stimulate railway development, and foreign interests were equally eager to buy the bonds or issue the loans that were needed. In spite of the Chinese government defaulting on its debts both in 1920 and 1929, and coming close in 1935, foreign banks and investors kept supplying credit. The flow of money continued because of high interest rates and because there were few other good options in a turbulent time for the world economy. There was also the hope that building infrastructure would stimulate the Chinese market, which stood at the center of foreign economic desires. It was the expectation that Chinese consumers in the future would start buying foreign products that was behind much of the extraordinary interest foreign capital showed for the country before World War II.

The largest foreign company in China before 1945 was the Japanese-owned Mantetsu, the South Manchuria Railway Company. Under its founding president, Goto Shimpei, the former governor of Taiwan, the company set out to be the core element in the transformation of Northeast China under Japanese influence. Mantetsu was a private business concern with partial government ownership and strong connections to the Japanese state. It rebuilt the region's railways using US-made equipment and then branched out into running coal mines, harbors, hotels, and warehouses. From the 1910s on, it built schools, libraries, hospitals, and public utilities to encourage Japanese and Korean settlement. Its academic wing made up the largest modern research enterprise ever undertaken in China, concentrating on agricultural research for industrial-scale farming. By the 1930s, Mantetsu was almost a separate state within Manchuria. Its subsidiaries produced steel, ceramics and glass, flour and cooking oil, electricity and chemical products. It had become not only the largest company in China, but also in Japan. Mantetsu is rightly seen as part of Japan's colonization effort in China. But it was also Tokyo's most important card in proving to the Western states that Japan, and Japanese business, contributed to the modernization of China that they all sought.

In the early 1900s, foreign merchants and companies transmitted knowledge about capitalism, markets, and management to the Chinese. But the form of development they stood for was always controversial. To many who lauded the virtues of Old China, merchants, investors, and business managers were suspect because they were driven by company profit rather than personal virtue. To young radicals, capitalism was a particular evil because it symbolized the form of exploitation that foreigners were trying to introduce into China. But first and foremost the role of business was problematic because so little of the products it traded in reached the peasant majority, except in the form of wares that many wanted but few could afford. It symbolized a new market economy that favored cities over countryside, and deepened the social dividing lines in rural areas as its elites moved to the urban centers. For many Chinese, foreign merchants and the merchandise they promoted became divided symbols of a modernity they aspired to and a social organization they resented. But there was no denying the importance of foreigners and their products. Few peasants knew who Sun Yat-sen was, but most had heard of the British-American Tobacco Company through the cigarettes they produced.[11]

With the new economy came a new banking system. Banks have existed in China at least since the Song dynasty (960–1279), but from the late nineteenth century on, powerful Western-led banks became China's main financial institutions. The Hongkong and Shanghai Banking Company was set up in Hong Kong in 1865. HSBC operated under a British charter with the intention of serving as a British bank in East Asia. But the Bank, as it became known in China, was much more than a British bank. In the subsequent decades it turned into the main banker for the Chinese government, for Chinese and foreign businesses in China, and for transactions among trading partners from Tokyo to Bangkok. It issued its own currency, introduced new banking and accounting practices, and trained bankers with knowledge of China, who later worked in Asia and around the world. Its founders had intended the HSBC as a tool for the exploitation of China, through organizing Chinese government loans that would go toward paying war reparations to the Western powers. But its mandate broadened, as it became an instrument for the industrialization of the country and the creation of a new financial sector.

From its inception, the British directors of the Hongkong Bank looked for new ways to maximize profits. To benefit from the country's commercial development, they realized they would also have to lend through traditional Chinese banks. Despite the growing presence of the Bank, through branch offices in different parts of China, the native banks continued to serve as middlemen up to the mid-twentieth century, becoming a transmission line for knowledge going in both directions of the banking sector. Although the senior staff remained exclusively European, an increasing number of Chinese served the Bank at different levels, enjoying the benefits of extraterritoriality (for their business, if not always for their person) that came with working for a foreign institution. The need to remain under British jurisdiction kept the Bank's headquarters in Hong Kong, even if the main part of its business was linked to Shanghai after 1912.

By the first decade of the twentieth century, China was getting its own banks and finance institutions. They were, however, still mostly led by foreigners—including the central bank, known from 1912 as the Bank of China. The banks generally adopted the regulations of HSBC, and they grew very quickly, into all regions of the country. In spite of the absence of effective banking regulations (or, for that matter, the effective rule of law), the Chinese Western-style banks carved out territory for themselves well beyond what most observers had expected. Working closely with Chinese companies, they were often able to defend themselves against predatory government practices. By the 1930s the GMD government had realized that these banks served a crucial role in China's development. They provided credit when foreign banks would not lend. They served as key intermediaries for China's public finance as it tottered from crisis to crisis during the decade. The government and the elite classes might not have liked Western-style financial institutions, but by 1937 they had come to depend on them for many of their most cherished activities.

The trouble with capitalist finance in China may be seen best through its continous problems with private accounting practices. Up to the late nineteenth century, internal accounting in China had been based on a system of single bookkeeping with ample room for nonmonetary forms of value, including the value of friendship or the cooperation of local officials. Confucian ideals made documenting profit undesirable, and fear of government malfeasance made disclosing the books to anyone beside the owners almost inconceivable. After the first general accounting provision was introduced in 1918, most Chinese privately owned companies and native banks preferred their earlier methods over

Western-style double-entry bookkeeping, thereby creating a buffer that insulated them from capitalist methods of expansion. Even in Hong Kong and Singapore professional accounting only broke through in the 1960s, while in most of China the links between accounting and accountability are still vague and weak even today.

RELIGION IN CHINA has rarely been much of an official preoccupation, except in cases when the government has wanted to regulate it or harness its power. Rather, it has been a means of survival for the poor and disposessed, giving meaning to their lives and hope for an afterlife. Buddhism, a Chinese import from India, served this role for centuries. Christianity, another foreign import, became a major religion in China in the nineteenth century. Until the renewed interest in religion over the past twenty years, the period between 1900 and the late 1920s stood out as China's Christian decades. During that time two to three million Chinese converted to this foreign religion, which evolved from a missionary enterprise into a locally led phenomenon. But missionaries continued to have an impact in China, most notably through the schools and universities they set up. These institutions may not have produced a large number of Chinese Christians, as the missionaries had fervently hoped. But studying in such institutions influenced many of those who transformed China in the late twentieth century, even though in directions their missionary teachers would hardly recognize.

Traces of Christianity dating to the seventh century have been found in China. Jesuit missionaries tried to establish themselves in the sixteenth and seventeenth centuries, mostly from Macao and Japan. After the double disasters of the nineteenth century—the Christian-inspired Taiping movement and the anti-Christian Boxers—Catholicism in China began a careful rebuilding of its structure. In some areas Christian communities had survived from early evangelization, in a few cases from the early seventeenth century on. In others Catholic missionaries began a painstaking work of proselytizing, mostly led by Lazarist and

Jesuit priests. Many Catholic missionaries concentrated on working in the cities, setting up educational institutions, hospitals, and orphanages, such as the St. Ignatius School in Shanghai, and a number of superb European Catholic intellectuals spent many years in China; Pierre Teilhard de Chardin, the philosopher, paleontologist, and geologist, spent twenty years there. Still, Catholicism as a religious practice spread mostly in the countryside, and in areas where there were established Chinese Catholic communities and Chinese as well as foreign priests. These centers of Chinese Catholicism, most of which exist and are in some cases expanding today, can be found all over the country, with a particular influence among minority peoples in the south, in Fujian, Zhejiang, and parts of Hebei and the Northeast.

The form of Christianity that expanded most rapidly in the early twentieth century was Protestantism. Sun Yat-sen was a Christian, baptized by American Congregationalist missionaries when he was in his teens. Chiang Kai-shek converted to Christianity in 1930, and his Methodism remained a matter of great importance to him for the rest of his life (in spite of his critics sneering at yet another "Christian warlord"). The muscularity of Chiang's Christianity was not in the least in conflict with how the Gospel was presented by many Protestant missionaries. One such was C. T. Studd, one of the Cambridge Seven, a group of Cambridge University graduates who spent their lives as missionaries in China. Christian life had to be a life of battle, Studd claimed. "Some want to live within the sound of church or chapel bell; I want to run a rescue shop within a yard of hell."[12] Like their nineteenth-century predecessors, Studd and his colleagues combined their Christian missions with a dedication to advancing knowledge in China. Henry W. Luce, the father of the founder of *Time* magazine, was a Presbytarian missionary. He spent three decades in China, mostly at Qilu University in Jinan, the capital of Shandong. With funding from the Rockefeller Foundation, Luce helped build Qilu into one of China's premier universities. Its medical school, established in 1911, provided full medical training for Chinese men and women. The most remarkable medical school in China was also a missionary enterprise: the Hackett Medical College for Women in Guangzhou, founded in 1901. Its graduates would influence the course of medicine in China right up to the present. Little wonder that some young Chinese women regarded Christianity as a way of breaking out of the confines of a patriarchical society.

Of the missionary universities one had a particular status, because it would develop into present-day China's most famous institution of higher learning. Yanjing University, founded in 1919 through a merger of five Christian colleges in Beijing, was a liberal, high-level academic institution. It was led for much of its existence by a second-generation American Presbyterian missionary in China, John Leighton Stuart, born in Hangzhou in 1876. With help from American foundations and donors Stuart bought an old Qing pleasure garden north of Beijing, which he equipped as a modern university. Today it is the central campus of Peking University. Many of its graduates from the 1920s and 1930s became leading political figures in China, not least on the Communist side. When Leighton Stuart, in his tragic tenure as US ambassador to China, tried to negotiate with the Communists in 1949, he sat across from a former Yanjing student, Huang Hua, who had become a key CCP foreign affairs specialist and promoter of anti-US slogans.[13]

Just as the early part of the twentieth century was a high point for Christianity in China, it was also a high point of the indigenization of Christianity. Across the whole roster of religious movements Chinese priests and ministers were gradually replacing foreigners or working alongside them. Nothing contributed more to this trend than the Shandong revival of the late 1920s, in which existing Christian communities were exhorted to follow the Holy Spirit to an emotional and direct experience of God. The catalyst for this movement was the quasi-Pentecostalist Norwegian missionary Marie Monsen, but it soon branched out into new Chinese Christian communities, some of which began to incorporate transcendental themes from other Chinese religions, such as Buddhism and Daoism. Among the Christian sects—with names such as The True Jesus Church, The Jesus Family, and The Little Flock—a remarkable group of native preachers emerged, some of whom had influence both inside and outside China. Ni Tuosheng (dubbed Watchman Nee), the founder of The Little Flock, became a revivalist leader in Asia and Europe. The communalist and nationalist strains of the "new" churches became a challenge to Chinese Christians and non-Christians alike. Preachers such as Ni were preoccupied with making Christianity native, because for them China was key to Christ's second coming. Others had to respond to that message, whether they liked it or not.[14]

The relationship between Christianity and nationalism in the mid-twentieth-century China was a complicated one. At the peak of nationalist agitation in the mid-1920s, many radical Chinese began to believe that Christianity was a tool of Western imperialism and that it was a narrow and intolerant faith. They argued that most Christian teachings—just like those of Islam, Buddhism, and Daoism—had been rendered obsolete by science and that modern men needed no such superstitions. But at the same time others saw an indigenized form of Christianity as part of China's rebirth: Why should the religion not serve the same purposes in China as it had in the West, where it had given purpose and meaning to unsettled lives, and steadiness through unsettled times, for almost two thousand years? For China's Christians it was not difficult to see themselves as part of their country's rescue, even if their opponents objected to it.

A LL CHINESE GOVERNMENTS in the twentieth century, with the brief exceptions of the Qing's Boxer adventure and Mao's Cultural Revolution madness, have employed foreign advisers. Some of these have served their masters faithfully, to the great benefit of the regime they represented. Others have been at least as corrupt and neglectful as the majority of Chinese civil servants. But without the labors of these foreign advisers, much of China's infrastructure and government organization would have looked very different throughout this period. Its income would also have been much reduced—even if foreigners who collected taxes and fees did so in part so the Chinese government of the day could repay its loans to foreign institutions, what the state kept constituted a major part of its income. The Salt Administration, which collected the salt tax that the state levied on both producers and importers, in the 1920s provided close to twenty percent of the state income. But even more importantly these advisers influenced the Chinese they worked with and opened up new avenues for civilian administration in China, some of which remain up to today.

Just as in other countries that came under pressure by European states during the nineteenth century, China's main foreign advisers concentrated on diplomacy, law, and military affairs. Later they became attached to various Chinese government departments, from infrastructure to health, education, language reform, and propaganda. In late Qing and the early Republic, most were Japanese, and during early Communist rule, most were Soviets. Ariga Nagao, one of Japan's foremost scholars of international law, served in Yuan Shikai's government. He was born in Osaka in 1860 and trained in law in Germany and Austria. Ariga saw sovereignty as the key element of statehood and was convinced that China needed centralization in order to protect its sovereignty. Concerned that Japan's appetite for expansion in Asia was leading it away from the internatonal and domestic norms he wanted it to adhere to, Ariga counseled Yuan Shikai to use force to bring the provinces under control. He also interceded with the Japanese government over its Twenty-One Demands in 1915, urging it not to attempt to coerce China, advice for which he almost paid with his life at the hands of Japanese ultranationalist terrorists.[15]

Sir Robert Hart's successors as inspectors-general of the Chinese Maritime Customs Service were always among the closest foreign advisers of various Chinese governments. The service had been set up to control China's customs income for Western purposes, but in the

twentieth century it became an integral part of the Chinese central administration. The career of the last foreign inspector general, Lester
Knox Little, symbolizes this development. Little was born in Rhode
Island in 1892 and spent forty years in China, first as a clerk in the Customs Service, then head of the customs administration, a foreign affairs
adviser to the Chinese government, and finally (after World War II) as
inspector general, in which capacity he fled with Chiang Kai-shek to
Taiwan in 1949. He had hundreds of colleagues with similar careers.
The Italian Luigi de Luca became China's foremost trade and tariff negotiator. The Frenchman Théophile Piry developed the Chinese postal
service. The Norwegian Johan Munthe worked as a customs official,
military adviser, and banker. They spent all of their careers in China, did
well for themselves there, and contributed much to China in return.

The other main foreign-led administration in Republican China,
the Salt Inspectorate, was almost as important as the Maritime Customs.
Its founding director, the former head of excise in the Indian civil service, Sir Richard Dane, created in the 1910s an administration that
worked for the Chinese government but was independent of other departments. Staffed by Chinese and foreigners, the inspectorate offered
good salaries, clear lines of authority and promotion, and even a pension
plan, and through its efforts on its employees' behalf earned their loyalty. Principles of staff rotation and expulsion of those found guilty of
nepotism or corruption served the service well. But as important were
the positive values through which organizational ideals were translated
into concrete administrative strategies. The experiences of the Salt Inspectorate were also drawn on by another major foreign adviser, the
Frenchman Jean Monnet. Monnet worked in China from 1934 to
1936. He was chairman of the Chinese government's committee to facilitate the availability of credit to Chinese companies and foreign companies that wanted to invest in China. The cosmopolitan Frenchman
helped set up the Development Finance Corporation, made up of the
main Chinese banks and government agencies to fund promising ven-

tures. Monnet went on to become one of the main founders of the European Union.[16]

Foreign advisers were part of China's weakness and part of China's strength. Some Chinese resented their presence, because they felt that it belittled their own country and made it seem that China depended on foreigners. They also suspected that in reality these foreign advisers would always be working for their own governments first and foremost; when push came to shove they would be little more than foreign intelligence agents or agents otherwise carrying out the will of their home countries. But other Chinese lauded those among the foreign advisers who were incorrupt and hardworking, and who made a contribution to building state institutions while introducing new forms of administrative and economic skills. The new nationalist government in China under the Guomindang and Chiang Kai-shek knew that it needed models for how to build the modern state it wished for. It needed a new state. And it needed protection against its enemies.

For the GMD government in place after 1927, a modern army was essential. Chiang Kai-shek was himself a military man, and he wanted China to have armed forces similar to those found in Japan, the United States, and Europe. The purpose of such an army was not just to protect the country and his regime. It was also to embody a form of modernity that Chiang believed in—a well-regulated state, a hierarchical system of command, purposeful training, and regimentation of people's lives. He wanted to see the army as the key element in the new state, not just because everyone depended on it for their protection, but because it could symbolize in a smaller form the kind of society that Chiang and many of his contemporaries believed could deliver a modern China. And the way to arrive at this kind of army was through the best possible training, led by foreign instructors.

By far the most important influence on military affairs in Guomindang China came from Germany. The Nazi regime continued the

cooperation that had been built in the 1920s, and in 1934 Hitler sent
Hans von Seeckt, who had been chief of the German army staff during
the Weimar Republic, to China. There, von Seeckt headed a German
Advisory Commission, which provided assistance on economic planning and military affairs. Alexander von Falkenhausen, who succeeded
von Seeckt in 1935, concentrated on planning and training for the
Chinese army. One of the best German military strategists of his generation, von Falkenhausen immediately saw that China did not stand
a chance in massive battles against Japan. He advised Chiang Kai-shek
to throw everything into planning for the coming war and develop a
strategy of attrition, in which the Japanese would have to fight for all
of the territory they wanted to conquer. The Germans promised to train
twenty Chinese infantry divisions by 1938 and help China build a navy
by the early 1940s. Germany also gave China access to advanced
weapons and military technology, which Chinese could not obtain elsewhere. From the German perspective, arming the Guomindang showed
Nazi Germany as a world power and gave it access to China's strategic
raw materials.

Germany's Nazi dictatorship was a kind of modernity that appealed
to Chiang. Although he was never a fascist, he certainly admired order.
He also believed that Germany and China were a near perfect fit. Both
had been outcast nations and were now reemerging. The German chief
instructor for Chiang's bodyguards, Walter Stennes, was among those
who convinced the Chinese leader about this affinity. Stennes's own
background was in the Nazi movement, but he had broken with Hitler
in 1931, because he believed in a more radical social revolution in Germany. For understandable reasons Stennes kept his distance from the
official German advisers in China, but he had a strong influence on Chiang and on the GMD head of police, Dai Li. Stennes stayed in China
to 1949, even after Hitler's alliance with Japan had forced von Falkenhausen out, reluctantly, by mid-1938. Chiang Wei-kuo, Chiang's son,
who was receiving military training in Germany, stayed on in Berlin

until right before the invasion of Poland in 1939. (Chiang's older son, Chiang Ching-kuo—a child of another era, quite literally—had been educated in the Soviet Union, where he stayed until 1937).[17]

For his air force needs, which the Germans were not able to fill, Chiang turned to the United States. By 1934 the Americans were supplying substantial numbers of military aircraft to China, and Colonel John Jouett, who had been in charge of training in the US Army Air Corps (as the US Air Force was called at the time), became the chief instructor for the new Chinese air force. By 1937, when Claire Chennault took over from Jouett, China had 645 military aircraft in twelve tactical squadrons, several aircraft factories and aviation training schools, and more than 250 airports. Captain Chennault, who had had a checkered career in the US Army Air Corps, directed the Chinese air force during most of the war against Japan, both when the United States was a supposed neutral and after the attack on Pearl Harbor in 1941.[18] Meanwhile much of the regular police training in China was also undertaken by US advisors, led by A. S. Woods. Woods had worked under the legendary police chief, August Vollmer in Berkeley, California, who is considered "the father of modern law enforcement." Chiang Kai-shek considered US policing methods the wave of the future, even though (or maybe especially because) he was skeptical of what he saw as the moral laxity of American society.

As Japan's pressure on China increased, Chiang Kai-shek also turned to an old adversary for help. To get access to military supplies, he restored relations with the Soviets in 1932. Stalin realized that giving aid to the Chinese government, in spite of their clash with the Chinese Communists, was the only way Moscow could buy added security against Japan. After China's war with Japan broke out in the summer of 1937, the Soviets began a large-scale support program for Chiang's armies. Soviet advisers and technical personnel replaced the departing Germans. Stalin sent several of his top people to China, including Pavel Rybalko, who would become the key tank-warfare strategist of World

War II; Pavel Zhigarev, who later commanded the Soviet air force; and Vasilii Chuikov, who was to conquer Berlin in 1945. Chuikov, who had studied Chinese and been part of the support team for the GMD during its first Soviet alliance, in the early 1920s, made a very strong impression on the Chinese commanders, who saw him as embodying the will to win. Chuikov believed that the Chinese were capable not just of resisting Japan but of creating modern armies on a vast scale, the like of which, as he wrote in his memoirs, the world had never seen.[19]

General Chuikov was in many ways a link between the first foreign Communist involvement in China, in the early 1920s, and the second, at the outset of the war against Japan in 1937. Chuikov had served as a young military adviser to the Guomindang's Northern Expedition in 1926, along with many other Soviet officers who had helped build and equip the armies of the Chinese nationalists and their then Communist allies. From the 1920s to the 1940s, China was a focus point for left-wing revolutionaries from all over the world, most of whom were connected to the Communist International. The Chinese Communist Party was founded and formed by the advice of foreign radicals, who influenced a whole host of Chinese organizations, societies, and intellectual trends. They were the link between the Russian Revolution and China, and between European and North American Marxists and like-minded Chinese. They were without doubt among the most important foreigners in terms of China's future development.

The creation of the Chinese Communist Party in 1921 was largely due to the 1917 Bolshevik Revolution. At the CCP founding congress, the Dutch Comintern official Hendricus Sneevliet (in China known as Maring) had a strong influence on questions of doctrine and strategy. Most importantly, he insisted that the new party should ally itself with the Guomindang in a united front. Sneevliet, who had lived in Indonesia (then a Dutch colony), had represented the Indonesian Communist Party at the founding congress for the Comintern in Moscow, and had been hand-picked by Lenin to help set up a Communist party in China.

His successor as Comintern representative, the Soviet Mikhail Borodin, designed how the united front would function and how Soviet aid to the Guomindang would be organized. Borodin, an old Bolshevik and an experienced Comintern agent, had proven his skills as an organizer in the United States, Mexico, and Britain before coming to China. He believed in a long-term alliance between the GMD and the much smaller CCP, during which the CCP would help the nationalist revolution while recruiting members and gaining influence.

For Comintern agents and foreign radical supporters of Communism in China, Chiang Kai-shek's eradication of most of the CCP in the late 1920s was a disaster. Stalin chose the facile explanation that China was simply not ready for socialism, but many of the adherents of an international socialist strategy within the Comintern hoped to resurrect the CCP. The main Comintern agent in China in the early 1930s was Manfred Stern, who would go on to command the international brigade in the Spanish Civil War under the nom de guerre Emilio Kléber. Stern's task was to make alliances between the CCP and the left-wing GMD opposition, while designing a strategy for the Chinese Communists to find their way back into the cities from their scattered rural redoubts. The strategy failed. It fell to his successor, the German Otto Braun, a veteran Communist, to help the CCP escape the offensives of the GMD army. Ironically, during the CCP's Long March to the north in 1934–1936, both the Communists and their pursuers were aided by German advisers, Braun on the CCP side and Alexander von Falkenhausen on the GMD side. Mao Zedong is said to have commented later that the GMD had the best Germans.[20]

Some foreign radicals came to China on their own rather than being sent by the Comintern. The American journalist Anna Louise Strong, who came to the country to cover the Chinese revolution from the inside, is a good example, especially because she settled in China and died there in 1970. The daughter of a Nebraska minister, Strong had traveled to the Soviet Union in the 1920s. "Will Moscow," she wrote in 1935, "become the center also for hundreds of millions—the yellow and brown races to the south and east of Asia, unlike, and yet so like their brother peasants of the Soviet Union?" Strong married a Russian and became a leading propagandist for the Soviet system—her most notorious book is *The New Soviet Constitution: A Study in Socialist Democracy*, published as Stalin's purges were reaching their peak in 1937.[21] She believed that only a socialist revolution, and an alliance with the Soviet Union, could save China from collapse and give hope to the millions of poor people she encountered on her travels in the country.

Revolutionaries from other Asian countries were also drawn to China in the early part of the twentieth century. The Vietnamese leader Ho Chi Minh (then known as Nguyễn Ái Quốc), born in 1890 in north-central Vietnam, had studied Chinese as part of his Confucian upbringing. Spending most of the 1910s in Europe and America, Ho became a founding member of the French Communist Party and was sent to China by the Comintern in 1924. While there, he taught at the Huangpu military academy in Guangzhou, where Chiang Kai-shek was commander and Zhou Enlai political commissar. He married a Chinese woman and lived in the same house as Borodin. Expelled from China after Chiang's 1927 coup, Ho secretly returned in 1929, working for the CCP in Shanghai and Hong Kong. He spent the years 1938–1945 with CCP units in southern China, except for a period in 1942–1943, when he was in a GMD prison. Ho remained very close to the Chinese Communist leaders for the rest of his life.

Kim Il-sung, who after 1945 became the leader of North Korea, had an even closer relationship with China. Born in 1912, he grew up in a Christian Korean family in Manchuria and studied in Jilin City, where he started his activities against the Japanese occupation of Korea. Kim joined the CCP in 1931, when he was nineteen years old, was imprisoned briefly by the Japanese, and became part of a Chinese Communist guerrilla unit. By the late 1930s he commanded a Communist group of around a hundred, mostly Koreans, in southern and eastern

Manchuria with occasional symbolic forays into Korea. In 1940, after the Japanese pressure against them increased, the leaders of Kim's group were evacuated to the Soviet Union, where he trained as a Red Army officer, before returning to Korea in 1945 as the president the Soviets had selected for the country. Kim was formed as a leader through growing up in China, and his understanding of Korea's neighbor helped him navigate through the international affairs of the Cold War.[22]

THROUGHOUT THE TWENTIETH CENTURY, massive amounts of foreign texts were translated into Chinese, and some of these translations had a profound impact in China. The first concentrated on science, religion, government, politics, and society. As we have seen already, the texts on science had a particular influence in China: Within a generation the scientific worldview of the Chinese elite was transformed, paving the way for the further development of knowledge and for the import of technology. Books on law and social theory were almost as influential as those on science. John Dewey, the American philosopher and educator, taught in China between 1919 and 1921, and his translated work became very influential. Much of the Western philosophical tradition was introduced to China through translations of Dewey's works. By the 1910s China also had its first translations of Karl Marx and Friedrich Engels, most of it retranslated from Japanese.[23]

By the 1920s, translations from foreign languages had become big business in China. The main publishing houses produced large compendia, often in hundreds of volumes, of the Western canon, which all Chinese bourgeois families aspired to own. As can be imagined, some translations were less than authentic, and some downright disastrous. In some cases translators changed the storyline of foreign fiction, so that it would (in their or their publisher's opinion) fit a Chinese audience. In spite of such attempted embellishments, foreign fiction became increasingly popular in China. The great Russian writers of the nineteenth century—Leo Tolstoy, Fyodor Dostoyevsky, Ivan Turgenev—

were particularly popular, but so was later Soviet literature and Western authors who discussed problems of society, such as Henrik Ibsen or George Bernard Shaw. But it was crime and entertainment literature that were the surest winners: In terms of copies sold the most popular Western writer in prewar China was Sir Arthur Conan Doyle. His Sherlock Holmes stories inspired Chinese variations, notably Cheng Xiaoqing's tales of the Shanghai master detective Huo Sang and his faithful sidekick Bao Lang. While more preoccupied with social issues than the originals, Huo and Bao are in no way their inferiors in detection as they cut through the Chinese underworld of the 1920s.[24]

Film was the universal art form of the twentieth century, and no less so in China than elsewhere. From 1898, films were shown in China, and the first movie house opened in Shanghai in 1908. By the 1920s there were cinemas all over the main Chinese cities and towns, including in working-class neighborhoods. The movies were mostly American, and films were the medium through which the United States was introduced to most Chinese. Their movie heroes were American stars, and many elements of style and fashion were taken over from Hollywood. The early Chinese film industry often remade American movies, done in Chinese and with Chinese actors, and one of the stars of such films was Jiang Qing, who married Mao Zedong. There was even a film made, in 1922, about a (fictitious) visit by Charlie Chaplin to China. By 1933 the major US movie companies had distribution offices in the country. In remote villages where most residents were illiterate and never traveled outside their county, movies were shown by itinerant projectionists. People would walk for days to witness such events. For many Chinese I met in the late 1970s, memories of the pre-Communist period were linked to seeing an American movie projected on a wall in the village square.

Like film, other forms of art were influenced by the foreign presence in China. Chinese artists had known about foreign techniques and styles for centuries, but by the late nineteenth century this knowledge infused all forms of art, and a number of hybrid styles appeared. Chinese painters and sculptors became masters of mixing Western and Chinese motifs and styles, just as Chinese porcelain artists had been doing for generations for the export market. Meanwhile, in the West in the late Victorian era, collecting classical Chinese porcelain—especially from the Ming dynasty (1368–1644)—became all the rage. The collecting was followed by research and an improved foreign understanding of Chinese art. In the West, modernism in both art and literature was inspired by East Asian examples; in painting, artists from Claude Monet to Picasso and Matisse drew from Chinese sources, and Ezra Pound and other poets wrote in Chinese styles. The influence in music also went in both directions. Western classical music was performed in Chinese cities as one of the hallmarks of modernity, and Western tonal systems influenced music written for Chinese instruments. In Europe, several modern composers—Stravinsky and Mahler first among them—used elements of Chinese music in their works. But during the 1930s no type of music linked East and West more closely than jazz. Shanghai became a center for jazz, with foreign, mostly American, and Chinese bands competing and mixing in a place for which jazz seemed a perfect expression.[25]

The first Chinese world exposition in 1929 was intended to show Chinese and foreigners the modern China. Over four months the beautiful city of Hangzhou on West Lake became a focus for demonstrating what China now could produce and how new technologies could further help Chinese businesses expand. The exhibition had eight main halls, showing among other things the plans of the new government, Chinese traditional art and modern design, agricultural products and technology, textiles, pharmaceuticals, and ninety-six other branches of industry. The organizers hoped that the exposition would raise the awareness of domestic products and stimulate strategies for exports. But because it coincided with the onset on the great depression, it also attracted a fair number of foreign companies that hoped to expand their share of the Chinese market. Although small if compared with the Paris and Chicago world fairs, the West Lake expo helped show Chinese who were eager for a view of the outside world a tightly managed version of what it contained.[26]

MUCH OF THE TWENTIETH-CENTURY transformation of China happened because of international influences on education, advanced training, and research. As we have seen, Christian institutions played a key role in this transformation, but there were a host of other key contributors as well: universities, foreign teachers and experts, and transnational networks of scholars and scientists, some Chinese and some non-Chinese. For radicals in China, the goal was to create a modern nation, through foreign ideas and foreign assistance if needed. Chen Duxiu, who became the first general secretary of the CCP, in 1919 made the point with Mr. Democracy and Mr. Science:

> In support of Mr. Democracy, we must oppose Confucian teaching and rites, the value of chastity, old ethics and old politics. In support of Mr. Science, we must oppose old arts and old religions. In support of both Mr D and Mr S, we must oppose the "national essence" and old literature. . . . How many upheavals occurred and how much blood was shed in the West in support of Mr D and Mr S, before these two gentlemen gradually led Westerners out of darkness into the bright world? We firmly believe that only they can resuscitate China and bring it out of all the present darkness of its politics, morality, *scholarship* and thought.[27]

By the 1930s China had its first modern unified school system. It had compulsory six-year primary education, with centralized curriculum management, roughly following the US model. In reality, of course, access to primary education varied from region to region. It was underfunded, and there was massive corruption at the provincial level and in school boards. The Guomindang's attempts at controlling foreign-run education institutions also did not help the advance of China's educational system. Despite these problems, a new generation, born around 1920, grew up with educational opportunities that earlier generations had not had. And they made good use of them.[28]

Universities were more quickly transformed through foreign influence than any other aspect of Chinese education. We have seen the roles of Christian universities and of missionaries in secular institutions. Along with these, government-run universities were rapidly expanding. Peking University (PKU), which in 1952 was merged with Leighton Stuart's Yanjing University, was the largest and most prestigious. It had two remarkable leaders in Cai Yuanpei, who was chancellor from 1917 to 1927, and Jiang Menglin, who served from 1930 to 1937. Cai was a classically trained scholar who went to Germany to study in 1907 and later became China's best-known educator. Jiang received a PhD from Columbia University in 1917 and championed the integration of foreign and Chinese approaches to learning. He wrote of his goals:

> On the stem of the Confucian system of knowledge, which starts with the investigation of things, or nature, and leads to human relationships, we shall graft the Western system of scientific knowledge, which starts with the same investigation of things or nature but leads the other way round to their interrelationships. As in the West, the moral universe will co-exist in China with the intellectual, one for stability and the other for progress.[29]

The most remarkable advances in learning in modern China took place in physics, chemistry, and biology. The preconditions for these were a combination of translations of Western texts, foreign teachers, good basic training programs, and the opportunity to study abroad. Some historians of science also argue that China was well placed to benefit from the latest advances in science because it had no traditional approaches that stood in the way of new ideas. As soon as Western science was adopted, it was all fresh and new. The acceptance of relativity in physics is a good example of this: When Albert Einstein visited China in 1922 at Cai Yuanpei's invitation, his principles were already accepted by most Chinese. The leading Chinese physicist of the next generation, Wu Dayou, who was also at PKU, trained a whole string of Chinese scientists who would go on to global recognition, including Li Zhengdao and Yang Zhenning, who won the Nobel Prize in 1957 for their discoveries regarding elementary particles. In less than fifty years, Chinese science had gone through a remarkable transformation.

Advances in learning were in no way limited to science. During the early twentieth century the Chinese language itself went through a fundamental change, inspired by foreign models. Classical Chinese, a written language for the elite with no spoken equivalent, was gradually replaced by *baihua*, plain speech, a vernacular based on Beijing dialect. Although there had been some vernacular writing around for at least two centuries, it was the Bible translations of the late nineteenth century that popularized the practice. In many ways the defeat of classical Chinese was the last great clash between opponents and supporters of foreign influence. The opponents of the reform argued that China would lose its culture by adopting a new type of language. The proponents, who gradually won in the 1920s, based their positions on a new form of Chinese nationalism, as set forth by Hu Shi during his studies at Cornell in 1916:

> What we need today is a readable, audible, singable, speakable, dictatable language which we can read aloud without the need to translate into the spoken language, with the help of which we can take notes without the need to translate into the literary language, which we can use at the speaker's desk as well as on the stage, and which even village grannies, women and children can understand if we read it to them. Any language that does not meet these requirements is not a living language and can under no circumstances become the national language of our country.[30]

The debate over language is characteristic of the debates that surrounded Chinese learning in the early part of the twentieth century.

Different groups wanted to move in very different directions, often under the influence of different foreign ideas. Some scholars suggested abolishing Chinese altogether and replacing it with English as a national language. Meanwhile, in Moscow, Qu Qiubai was making a phonetic alphabet, based on Soviet inventions for its Asian republics, which eventually became today's romanized version of Chinese. Of course, China was not unique in having to deal with a classical heritage under modern circumstances—Greece and the Arab world also come to mind. But the solution imposed in China was typical of its approach to modernity: replacing its written language with the transcribed speech of the capital, thereby making learning both more difficult and more accessible at the same time.

Contact with the rest of the world also changed forever the roles of Chinese women and the family. Though their relative position had differed from region to region and between different social groups, women in Qing China were subservient within a patriarchal system that favored fathers, husbands, and first-born sons. Usually denied education outside the household, they were limited to reproduction and housekeeping, often under the supervision of a depreciating mother-in-law or a husband they had not chosen. Even if China was ruled by a woman for forty years—the Empress Dowager Cixi—there was no recognition during her time that the overall position of women should be changed. The conservative Cixi, it was said, willingly took on the role of everyone's least favorite mother-in-law. By the late nineteenth century, however, Chinese were learning about women's emancipation in the West. Young elite female nationalists, often educated in missionary schools, began insisting on new roles for themselves in society and politics. For many traditionally minded Chinese, female emancipation was the most disastrous part of foreign influence; it destroyed the family, and would, they believed, therefore also destroy China.

Much of the early agitation in China for women's rights was connected to *political* rights. Both male and female activists believed that the position of women would improve if they were given an opportunity to participate in creating a new state based on the nationalist agenda. Qiu Jin, an anti-Qing cross-dressing, sword-wielding revolutionary who was executed in 1907, symbolized this trend. She thought that after the Qing was overthrown, women would gain their rightful role in society. Later feminists—female or male—were not so optimistic. In the May Fourth era, Chinese *society* was seen as the root of the problem, irrespective of the state that ruled it. Institutions such as arranged marriages and patriarchal control came under attack, inspired by foreign ideas. In a famous essay on Henrik Ibsen's *A Doll's House,* Lu Xun pondered where Nora went after she left home and concluded that the economic independence of women was the key to change in society. Mao Zedong, who himself had been in an unhappy arranged marriage, attacked all such pacts. In 1919, he wrote about a young girl who had killed herself before her wedding: "In the Western family organization, father and mother recognize the free will of their sons and daughters. Not so in China. . . . The parents of Miss Zhao very clearly forced her to love someone she did not want to love. . . ; that is a form of rape. . . . Chinese parents all indirectly rape their sons and daughters."[31]

Relationships between Chinese and foreigners also put pressure on the family system. In the nineteenth century, some Chinese women in the cities became the lovers of foreign men, only to be left by them when the men returned home. Typical of colonial presences, these relationships were profoundly unequal, but still in many cases provided women with knowledge and wealth that they otherwise would not have had access to. In the twentieth century, many more such affairs became lasting marriages, even though negative Western attitudes toward interracial marriage persisted. In 1927 the British Commissioner of Police in Shanghai declared that "mixed marriages are not in the interest of the force."[32] But still such unions took place, and both Chinese and foreigners were forced to accept them. Some Chinese wives of foreign citizens became cultural interlocutors. Anna Chennault, who was born

Chen Xiangmei in 1925 and married US General Claire Chennault, has influenced Sino-American relations for fifty years. Chiang Kai-shek's son Chiang Ching-kuo married a Soviet citizen during his long exile in Russia: Faina Vakhreva, known as Jiang Fangliang, became the first lady of the Republic of China on Taiwan.

For more ordinary Chinese and Westerners, love across national and cultural borders was difficult, but increasingly common. Foreign soldiers in China married Chinese girls: 9,000 Chinese wives went with their American husbands back to the United States after World War II. A number had married at a time when US immigration laws still forbade them from ever living in their husband's country. Some foreign wives lived with Chinese husbands in China, not only in the cities, but also in the countryside, especially in villages in Guangdong and Fujian. Mary Yue, née Ferguson, a Scottish-born New Zealander, in 1890 traveled with her children to her husband's village in Taishan, where the children grew up. Her family was essentially transnational, part of the global China that we will discuss in the next chapter. But it was also local: The presence of foreign wives changed the villages in which they lived more than many locals would admit.[33] Sometimes the cross-cultural strains became too much. Esther Cheo Ying, the daughter of a Chinese student at the London School of Economics and his Cockney wife, sympathized with both her parents:

> It could not have been easy for my working-class mother to under-stand what marrying a Chinese Mandarin's son entailed. She was too young to understand and too ignorant of the different cultures of East and West to try to conform even a little to the customs of Chinese life. My father's family ostracized him for marrying a "for-eign devil." The odds were too great for either of these two young people to try to make the marriage work.[34]

In spite of the cross-cultural tensions, love between Chinese and foreigners influenced the international history of the region and the world. Equally important was the debate in China about new forms of relationships between men and women and between generations. For some people the foreign was a threat, for others it was about freedom and opportunity. In China, these perceptions fluctuated throughout the century and up to today. Mao Zedong, whose hatred for arranged marriages helped transform the role of women in China, also attempted to cut off much of China's interaction with the rest of the world, leaving many transnational Chinese families stranded or divided. But even Mao's regime was unable to completely cut China's international family ties, or reduce the worth of Chinese families. In the end family love was more important than concepts of nation, nationalism, or ideology.

THERE ARE MANY, often contradictory, ways of interpreting the role of foreigners in China before 1949. Some observers focus on the exploitive colonial aspect of the relationship, which did so much to undo China's first period of interaction with capitalist modernity. In this negative version China often is seen as regaining its autonomy and its nationhood only through the expulsion of foreigners after 1949. Others find in the hundred years between 1850 and 1950 more that is positive than negative in Chinese interaction with foreigners, and tend to emphasize that foreign interactions helped produce modern China. The discussion is not helped by the Chinese Communist government having written most foreigners (except their favorite few) out of Chinese history; my students today often do not know the degree to which China was an open country before 1949 or the key role foreigners played in China's development. On the other hand, though, foreigners often do not understand the sense of humiliation today's Chinese feel when they look back on the past, at least in the version they get presented: The concessions, the extraterritoriality, the financial reparations, and the haughty behavior of foreigners in China would be a bad example of international interaction for any country, but they particularly rile a generation grown up on spoonfuls of government-sanctioned nationalism.

In reality, foreigners in China played as many roles as the Chinese did. Some came there out of enthusiasm for China and its people. Some came to win souls for Christ or for commercial advantage. Some became Chinese (as some Chinese became foreign). Some came for love and some came for the need to punish and destroy. Their lives bear witness to these roles, and to how they were often combined in one person. Think, for instance, of Silas Hardoon, a Baghdadi Jew who lived in Shanghai for six decades, made his fortune in real estate development and cotton, and died the richest man in the city. A British subject (though he had never been to Britain), married to a Chinese woman (though he barely spoke her language), he was buried according to Jewish *and* Buddhist rites. Hardoon stood for everything that made empires suspicious and nationalists mad. Neither Iraqi nor Chinese nor British, he had a massive impact on China. Any nationalist attempt at writing him or other "foreigners" out of Chinese history will diminish its complex reality.

The relationship between the "Chinese" and the "foreign" in the twentieth century is also about understanding historical change, in politics as well as terminology. China did not retrieve its full sovereignty only in 1949, as is often claimed, but step by faltering step between 1925 and 1946, under a Guomindang government. It was during this period—well before the Communists took over—that customs autonomy and foreign concessions reverted to China. Its new government wanted to plan the country's future according to nationalist principles, and resented the "chaos" that allowed foreigners and Chinese to regulate their own lives. The war against Japan and the Communist victory only put the final nails in the coffin of China's "foreign century."

CHAPTER 6

ABROAD

I N SPITE OF OFFICIAL DISAPPROVAL, Chinese traveled, sojourned, and settled abroad in increasing numbers at the end of the Qing era. An eighteenth-century trickle turned into a nineteenth-century flood, with Southeast Asia being the main destination. Of the twenty million or so Chinese who went overseas to stay before 1949, around half in the mid-nineteenth century and more than ninety percent in the 1920s went to the countries to China's south. The British-ruled states on the Malayan peninsula received 6 to 7 million, the Dutch East Indies 4 to 5 million, and French Indochina 2 to 4 million. Three and a half million went to Thailand and a million to the Philippines. The rest of the world, including the Americas, saw a Chinese immigration of two and a half million.

The numbers for Chinese emigration are significant, but small compared to the scale of European outward migration. While the Europeans took over and settled three continents, mostly exterminating the local population in the process, Chinese migration was limited to following commercial advantages as they arose, mostly along the trade routes set up by European empires. As a result, more than 350 million people of European origin live outside Europe today, while only 40 million people of Chinese descent live outside China. Even if one counts Chinese settlement of China's border zones (Manchuria, Xinjiang, Inner Mongolia, Yunnan, and Tibet) the number of migrants and their offspring is substantially lower than that for Europeans abroad. The significance of what became the Chinese diaspora is therefore not in numbers, except in parts of Southeast Asia, but in the impact these Chinese had on the countries where they came to live and, especially, in the impact they were to have on China itself.

As from Europe, there were many different types of Chinese emigration. Push factors included poverty, wars, natural disasters; pull factors were commercial opportunities, education, land. Most Chinese who went abroad had to battle attempts to drive them out from where they wanted to be, and almost all arrived poor. The Chinese taught themselves to follow the edges of empires, where it was easier to be let in and where economic opportunities were likely to arise. The story of Chinese settlement abroad is therefore to a great extent the story of European maritime trade routes along the South China Sea and across the Pacific. A new stage began when the Suez Canal opened in 1869, connecting Europe and Asia more closely. Still, travel across these vast distances was more often organized by Chinese than by any foreign agencies. Chinese migration, from the beginning, was first and foremost a Chinese affair.

Just as elsewhere, emigration from China was often a two-stage process. People moved to the cities to find work, and then went abroad. Most emigration was voluntary, to the extent that emigrants made a conscious decision about going abroad, although labor recruiters were known to trick or even abduct laborers to fill their recruitment quotas. Most emigrants went to work the fields or factories of others; they grew cotton or sugar, dug mines or tunnels, or made ammunition or foodstuffs. Some sewed, cooked, or laundered. Their employment was as varied as that of European migrants. Most stayed poor, and a larger percentage than among European migrants eventually went back to live in their hometowns. Some got very rich, especially in Southeast Asia, or, in a few cases, in the Americas in the late twentieth century. But the number of rich Chinese was always far smaller than many in their host nations believed.

There were waves in the pattern of Chinese emigration, even though the numbers overall show a steady increase until hit by economic depressions or immigration restrictions. Emigration doubled in the late 1870s, with further peaks right after the 1911 revolution and in the 1920s. The number of women emigrants increased sharply from the 1920s on, meaning there were more settled Chinese families abroad. In some cases, though, Chinese male emigrants who could afford it had families both abroad and in China, through various forms of concubinage. Degrees of integration among Chinese who chose or were allowed to stay vary from country to country, but are not dissimilar to first- and second-generation European migrants; they soon begin counting themselves as locals (but with a significant part of their Chinese identity intact).

The great majority of Chinese migrants came from the south and especially from the coastal provinces of Guangdong and Fujian. Though leaving from the same ports, these southern Chinese went to very different destinations. More than thirty percent of the original emigration to Southeast Asia was from Fujian, while more than half of those who settled in the Americas were from Guangdong. As in China, the emigrants always joined brotherhoods or companies, which protected them and gave them some form of collective say in the new country. The first to be established were usually the *gongsuo*, which can loosely be translated as guilds or commercial associations. Since merchants and traders were more powerful than others, they were usually the first to organize. These were followed by *huiguan* or *tongxianghui*, different forms of native place organizations, which helped look after Chinese from one region, village, or clan. *Bang* (societies) and *hui* (associations) then followed. The latter were often mutual-help groups or political gatherings (such as of the Guomindang), but in some cases criminal organizations, later known as underground societies or triads. The abilities Chinese had to organize and stick together made life easier abroad but could lead to exploitation within the communities themselves.

The most significant role of Chinese emigration was as a conveyor of ideas and technologies between China and the rest of the world. Chinese who had lived abroad came home with new thoughts and goals; they stimulated others to travel and set up new businesses and organizations. Along with foreigners living in China, they introduced new products and tastes, and new concepts of how people should live their lives. They organized visits for others to their places of residence abroad, set up Chinese schools, and formed business networks. By the late twentieth century transnational Chinese families often thrived in several places at once—in Hong Kong, California, and Singapore, for example, or in London, Taiwan, and Shanghai. The origins of China's resurrection as an economic great power after 1980 would be impossible to explain without the framework that such families provide. They were, and are, the glue that holds China's relations with the world together, in good times and bad.

NANYANG, THE SOUTH SEA, became the main destination for Chinese emigration in the eighteenth century and has remained so ever since. The Chinese concept of Nanyang encompasses all of what we today would call Southeast Asia, with extensions as far away as Australia and the east coast of India. Trade and limited degrees of settlement by Chinese in parts of the region go back centuries. There are a thirteenth-century tomb of a Chinese envoy in Brunei and a fifteenth-century tombstone of a Brunei sultan in Nanjing. For centuries commercial motives drove the interaction; as we have already seen, the Chinese concept of paying of tribute to the emperor in Beijing often went hand in hand with commerce. By the late eighteenth century, groups of Chinese began to settle in Southeast Asia as European colonial control expanded, and in the nineteenth century, this trickle became a constant stream of people moving back and forth between China and Southeast Asia. In no other part of the world has Chinese immigration been so significant for the region and for China itself.

A very large group of Chinese settlers in Southeast Asia came from Fujian province. Today their descendants make up roughly half of all Chinese in Indonesia and Malaysia. This coastal province could serve as a microcosm of Chinese emigration. Its population, 36 million today, is made up of several dialect and population groups and is very diverse in terms of social conditions; there are rich merchants in cities on the coast and a very poor upland group where survival has always been tough. About a quarter of the population is Hakka, a distinct Chinese ethnic group that settled in the province in the fourteenth century. From the eighteenth century Fujianese colonized Taiwan, where they today form around 70 percent of the population. The combination of seafaring skills and products to sell (notably tea: the English word for the product comes from Fujianese, *te*) made for lengthy expeditions to surrounding countries and paved the way for labor migration. Today every village in Fujian has families with relatives overseas, and many residents in these villages have spent time overseas.

Most Chinese who traveled to Southeast Asia went as laborers, and even if some brought commercial skills from home, most remained poor. Compared with life in their home provinces in the late nineteenth and twentieth centuries, Chinese who migrated to Southeast Asia still counted themselves lucky. For a long time, they benefited from political stability and economic opportunities and relished their relative autonomy and ability to send remittances home. As a result, their numbers grew. Today around thirty percent (7.5 million) of the population in Malaysia is of Chinese descent. In Indonesia the figures are three percent (6 million), in Thailand ten percent (6.5 million), and in the Philippines two percent (2 million). In Brunei, twenty-five percent of its 400,000 people are of Chinese descent. Elsewhere in the region, from Indochina to Burma, elites of Chinese origin are well represented in business and industry. By the late twentieth century, Chinese immigrants had contributed significantly to Southeast Asia's modern transformation.

The Nanyang Chinese have had a profound effect on China. Even during the Japanese occupation or during Mao Zedong's campaigns, it was impossible to completely cut ties between Chinese in Southeast Asia and the homeland. Money, letters, and sometimes people found their way in. In the worst of times, the most daring went upriver from Hong Kong or across from Taiwan without asking for visas or other documents. Since the reform period started in the late 1970s old links to Southeast Asia were renewed. Instead of Marx and Mao on the wall, many villages in Guangdong and Fujian now have pictures of their overseas benefactors. Investment in those provinces has flourished, mostly through Hong Kong. The Thai company Charoen Pokphand, among the largest foreign conglomerates in China, was founded in 1921, when Xie Yichu and his brothers, originally from Chenghai in Guangdong, started the Chia Tai seed shop in Bangkok's Chinatown. They imported seeds and vegetables from China and exported pigs and eggs to Hong Kong. Xie's son, who uses the Thai name Dhanin Chearavanont, is Thailand's richest man and has been close to all Chinese leaders since Deng Xiaoping.

As both Chinese and Southeast Asian nationalisms grew in the twentieth century, the Chinese presence in the region became more significant for China and more problematic locally. Nanyang Chinese early on became key supporters of the Guomindang, and after World War II some joined up with local Communist parties. The Chinese revolution of 1911–1912 and the GMD's conquest of power in the 1920s could not have happened without Southeast Asian assistance—Sun Yat-sen used to call the overseas Chinese "the mother of the revolution." The amount of money that came in from organizations in the region kept Sun's project alive through the lean years out of power, and fueled the GMD takeover in 1928. At the same time, Chinese nationalism in China gave some Chinese Southeast Asians a new identity they could take pride in. They were no longer just from their village or province but from a reawakened China. While the majority of Nanyang Chinese sought integration of a kind, some groups took pride in being outsiders.

When the colonial empires collapsed after World War II and new states, based on some form of national identity, emerged all over Southeast Asia, the situation for Chinese minorities became more problematic. A bit like the situation for European Jews in the first half of the century, overseas Chinese were criticised for being rich, even though few were. Or they were accused of being Communist agents, even though fewer still were. In Malaya, quite a number of ordinary Chinese ended up in the rebellion of the Malayan Communist Party, mostly out of fear of being marginalized in an independent Malay state. After the rebellion was crushed, the Chinese-Malaysians had to accept living in a country where they were excluded from political influence. In other places things got far worse. In Indonesia several thousand Chinese-Indonesians were murdered after the 1965 coup, even though they had not been involved in politics. But the worst atrocities against Nanyang Chinese happened in countries where Communist China had supported the very authorities that then turned on their Chinese populations. In Cambodia the CCP-supported Khmer Rouge killed half of the country's Chinese-Khmer population after 1975. In Vietnam after reunification Chinese-Vietnamese merchants and shopkeepers were hit by the Communist regime's antibourgeois campaigns, which developed into a racist campaign against people of Chinese origin. Half of Vietnam's Chinese population left; 60 to 70 percent of the refugees who left by boat from South Vietnam were of Chinese descent. In the north at least 200,000 fled across the border to China.

In other countries, integration has progressed well, at least on the surface. In the Philippines the Chinese have prospered without being politically excluded. Both the independence hero Emilio Aguinaldo and President Benigno Aquino Jr. are of partly Chinese descent. There are schools and newspapers using Chinese, while most younger Chinese are integrated into Filipino culture through the use of English or Tagalog or both. In Thailand, although there is resentment against Chinese influence, the main banks and much of the country's industry are run by people of Chinese descent. In the country at large, at least three Thai prime ministers have been of partly Chinese origin, including the controversial Shinawatras, whose great-grandfather came from Meizhou in Guangdong province. The great, mostly unspoken, fact in Bangkok is that the Thai royal family originates in part from a Guangdong immigrant in the eighteenth century. In Thailand, as in most of Southeast Asia, the Chinese presence is woven into the fabric of the countries themselves and cannot be easily extirpated by nationalists of any kind.

Nationalism has also led to problems for overseas Chinese who returned to China. In the 1930s and 1940s the Japanese occupiers regarded them as British or American spies. The Guomindang tried to draw those who had left the motherland back to it, to participate in Chiang Kai-shek's modernization efforts and denounced them as traitors if they did not. But the worst period for overseas Chinese in China was during the Communists' great campaigns, from the late 1950s to the mid-1970s, when any sign of foreign connections could mean a death sentence. Villagers on the coast had to fight Red Guards who wanted to attack their clansmen who had come back from abroad. Even though ties with relatives or friends abroad were never entirely cut, even in the depths of the Cultural Revolution, Chinese who had lived and worked abroad were met with suspicion in China. Ironically, they became victims of a nationalism that many of them, or their ancestors, had helped create by bringing foreign ideas to China in the early twentieth century.

Today most of the mental rejection within China of countrymen who have lived abroad is gone. There are still hurdles that people who travel between countries have to jump in order to be tolerated in China, but the idea that you can live abroad and still be Chinese is more or less accepted. For those who see themselves as partly Chinese, or have their primary identification as a link in a transnational network or family, things are still somewhat unsettled. Transnationalism as a concept does not sit easily with Chinese nationalists of any breed. But still there are whole regions along the south China coast that depend on family ties abroad for their economic development. These *qiaoxiang*, sojourner villages, have large numbers of foreign-born Chinese or people who have spent time abroad who now contribute decisively to the Chinese economy by transferring skills or starting companies. Moreover, they feed into the export-led economic growth by having relatives or contacts in Southeast Asia, or in Catalonia, or in Belfast. It is very hard even for the most rigid Chinese nationalist to beat this basic economic argument for *qiaoxiang* ties or transnational existences.

O NLY IN ONE PLACE OUTSIDE CHINA did Chinese become the majority population and predominant in politics and business. That was in Singapore, the colony the British set up at the tip of the Malayan peninsula in 1819 to serve as a business entrepôt and a strategic outpost, controlling the Strait of Malacca. When Singapore was created, there was already a substantial Chinese population in the region operating in close connection with Batavia (now Jakarta), Penang, and Malacca. By the 1840s, Singapore was already a predominantly Chinese town whose activities revolved around trading and transport. In the 1880s, it was the port of entry for Chinese laborers who came to work on the plantations and in the mines that the colonial authorities had set up on the Malayan peninsula and on the islands. The exploitation of newly arrived workingmen from China was so bad that the British established what they called Chinese Protectorates in the Straits Settlements, with William Pickering as the first Protector. Pickering, a veteran of the Chinese Maritime Customs Service who spoke both Mandarin and Fujianese, became a key figure in convincing local Chinese that they could benefit from the protection of the British empire.

And benefit they did, or at least some of them. By the early part of the twentieth century, Chinese owned rubber plantations and opium farms, banks and trading companies, shipping lines and machine factories. While the majority of Chinese remained as poor as other inhabitants, some used Singapore as a kind of double entrepôt, importing cheap Chinese labor, learning foreign skills, accessing capital, and following the trading opportunities that the British empire provided. It is not surprising that the Singapore Chinese bourgeoisie became almost manically loyal to the British throne. The inscription on the statue of the queen, which the Chinese organizations presented to Victoria at her Golden Jubilee in 1887, calls attention to "the loyal affection of Her Majesty's Chinese subjects and their gratitude for the benefit of her rule." Some were knighted for their services to the empire. The Cambridge-educated lawyer Sir Song Ong Siang (Song Wangxiang) founded schools and newspapers, and the Malaccan Sir Tan Cheng Lock (Chen Zhenlu) set up businesses and Chinese organizations.

But Sir Cheng Lock also symbolized the direction that many Southeast Asian Chinese were moving in. A firm supporter of the empire before World War II, he became an advocate of an independent Malayan union, with Singapore as part of it, after the war ended. Tan Kah Kee (Chen Jiageng) is another example of new forms of thinking. Born in Fujian, he went to Singapore in 1890 and built a vast fortune in the rubber industry, earning him the nickname "Malaya's Henry Ford." But by the late 1930s war relief work in China preoccupied him more and more, and in 1950, after the CCP victory in China, he moved to Beijing, where he died in 1961. The two directions—integration within a new Malay-dominated Malaysia and loyalty to Chinese nationalism— threatened to destroy the position of Singapore in the late 1940s and 1950s. But in 1965 after two unhappy years within the same federation, Singapore was thrown out of Malaysia because of its resistance to the government's taxation policies and preference for Malays in public office. The People's Action Party (PAP) has ruled the city state ever since, first under Lee Kuan Yew (Li Guangyao) and since 2004 under his son, Lee Hsien Loong (Li Xianlong).

PAP rule in Singapore stresses authoritarian government, social welfare, and multiracialism in a meritocratic setting. Though it is a democracy in theory, in practice Lee Kuan Yew wanted a regimented state that emphasized economic development over liberal politics. Originally a social-democratic party, the PAP began to veer toward free-market economics in the late 1970s. Watching Hong Kong's success, Lee concluded that "state welfare and subsidies blunted the individual's drive to succeed." "I watched with amazement," he wrote, "the ease with which Hong Kong workers adjusted their salaries upwards in boom times and downwards in recessions. I resolved to reverse course on the welfare policies which my party had inherited or copied from British Labour Party policies."[1] By the 2000s, Singapore, with 77 percent of its population ethnically Chinese, was rated top on the free-market index alongside Hong Kong, even though the government continues to control around 60 percent of the total GDP.

IN THE EAST, ACROSS THE OCEAN, the Chinese imagination saw mountains of gold as news of the California gold rush spread in 1848. Just as people in other parts of the world, Chinese wanted to be part of this accumulation of riches in the region they called *Jinshan,* Gold Mountain. Thousands came in the decade that followed to the US West Coast and western Canada. Even though there had been small numbers of Chinese in North America for almost a hundred years—some came with the Spanish from the Philippines and others followed the trade routes to both American coasts—it was 1848 that became the great dividing line. By 1880 there were more than 100,000 Chinese living in the United States, working in all kinds of trade: mining, railway construction, garment making, canning, farming, or in services such as laundering and cooking. An even larger number had sojourned in North America and later returned to China. In Southern China, which went through a bad time because of rebellions and famines, Gold Mountain began to be seen as a preferred destination for the most adventurous travelers, who hoped to settle permanently across the ocean.

The Chinese dream of being treated like other immigrants in North America was never realized. During the economic downturn in the 1870s, racist agitators blamed the Chinese for having taken jobs from white Americans, and began to argue for ending all immigration from China. Some West Coast labor leaders were particularly active: The Workingman's Party in California mobilized under the slogan "The Chinese Must Go." An 1879 pamphlet of theirs argued that Chinese exclusion was a matter of life or death—"Either we must drive out the Chinese slave, and humble the bloated aristocrat, or we shall soon be slaves ourselves."[2] Intellectuals of various kinds were also brought in evidence. The poet, travel writer, and translator of Goethe's *Faust,* Bayard Taylor, wrote:

> It is my deliberate opinion that the Chinese are, morally, the most debased people on the face of the earth. . . . Forms of vice, which in other countries are barely named, are in China so common that they excite no comment among the natives. They constitute the surface level and below them are deeps . . . of depravity so shocking and horrible that their character cannot even be hinted. There are some dark shadows in human nature which we naturally shrink from penetrating [and which] inspired me with a powerful aversion to the Chinese race. *Their touch is pollution,* and, harsh as the opinion may seem, *justice to our own race demands that they should not be allowed to settle on our soil.*[3]

The US government banned Chinese immigration in 1882. It is the only restriction Congress has ever enacted directed against all citizens of a specific country. The ban lasted up to 1943, when Chinese officials managed to sufficiently embarrass their wartime ally to have it withdrawn. Exclusion cut the growth in population, though it never succeeded in reducing the overall number of Chinese in the United States (or Canada, which restricted immigration from 1885 to 1947). Within Chinese communities, the racist agitation against them set off soul-searching and resistance in roughly equal amounts. Some Chinese felt that they were targeted because they were different in culture, customs, and language, and responded either by leaving or by attempting to assimilate fast. Others put up a fight. In the United States, as in China itself, Chinese protested an exclusion arrangement that was unfair and racist. When the traditional Chinese organizations in the United States failed to protest effectively, new organizations, such as the Chinese Equal Rights League in New York and the Chinese American Citizens' Alliance in San Francisco, emerged. While the new generation of American-born Chinese were able to progress socially in the early part of the twentieth century, the cutting of ties with the old country that exclusion represented created both economic and cultural problems for them, which they had to work hard to overcome.

Today Chinese represent one of the most successful groups of immigrants to the United States and Canada. More than half of those over twenty-five have earned a college degree (as against a quarter of the general population), and they have a higher-than-average family income. Even though discrimination still exists, the example of prosperous Chinese American entrepreneurs or scientists such as Jeffrey Yang (founder of Yahoo!) or Steve Chen (founder of YouTube) help the overall image of success to the point that some young Chinese in the United States are now afraid of being branded as geeks and nerds. Still, most of the population started their road to prosperity at the very bottom. Out of 3.5 million, more than two-thirds were born abroad, increasingly in the People's Republic of China. Most struggle to make a living after arriving in the States, often taking jobs that demand much fewer qualifications than they had when they entered. The bright future that all immigrants hope for has yet to arrive for most of those Chinese who have arrived since the 1980s.

One part of the United States where Chinese have faced less discrimination overall, and where they today make up a larger percentage of the population than in any other state, is Hawaii.[4] Chinese were already well established on the islands before the US annexation in 1898. Even though exclusion was attempted there too, fewer left as a result of discrimination, probably because of better employment opportunities and especially because of a largely missionary-run multiracial educational system that suited Chinese hopes for their children. Hawaii became an important staging ground for Chinese politics and enterprise, and a key link between the Chinese in Southeast Asia and those in the United States. It also saw a large number of intermarriages between Chinese and other ethnic groups much earlier than in the rest of the United States. Perhaps in Hawaii, almost halfway to Asia, Chinese and other Americans found it easier to begin a process of collaboration and of reaching out to other continents that would in the end enrich them all.

Because of the consistent European attempts to exclude them from the temperate zones of the world, some Chinese often first settled in the tropics. Thus, we find longtime Chinese communities in Southeast Asia, the Pacific, and the Caribbean. In a few countries, Chinese immigration was of great consequence, either as labor or in terms of trade networks. It also created links between China and faraway places that were often surprising and always enlightening, and which in some cases last up to today. When, for example, a Brazilian political leader of Chinese descent pays an official visit to China, it means something beyond the very small amount of background that guest and hosts share. For the Chinese it illuminates their country's centuries-long engagement with the rest of the world. For the visitor it reminds him of a heritage to be proud of. He will likely be given opportunities that would rarely come the way of other foreign visitors. Most importantly, such visits create ties that both sides will want to strengthen.

In South America, the largest numbers of Chinese can be found in Peru and Cuba. In Peru most came as contract laborers from the 1850s on, working under very brutal conditions on sugar plantations, in the guano mines, or in building the Andean railroad. Most felt they were treated little better than slaves; they were cheated out of their wages or flogged or starved for any infraction of the rules. Exclusively male, the immigrants became increasingly restless because of the horrible living conditions and racism they encountered. During the War of the Pacific of 1879–1883, which pitted Chile against Bolivia and Peru, any Chinese who could sided with the invading Chileans, whom they saw as liberators. Some served in the army of Admiral Patricio Lynch, who had picked up a smattering of Cantonese while serving with the British during the Opium Wars. Close to a thousand Chinese died, most of them killed by Afro-Peruvians who had borne the brunt of the Chilean attack.[5]

During the twentieth century, Chinese-Peruvians gradually gained respect and prosperity. Most married Peruvian women, and some settled in small towns in the Amazon, working as traders or farmers. Today Peruvians who have some Chinese background—about fifteen percent—see their ethnicity as an advantage. Some have spearheaded Peru's linking into international networks of trade and finance, while others have gone into politics. Two recent prime ministers— José Antonio Chang and Víctor Joy Way—are of Chinese descent.

The other Latin American country to which Chinese came in large numbers is Cuba. At least 125,000 arrived between 1847 and 1874, mostly to work on the sugar plantations. Treated almost as cruelly as those who went to Peru, the Chinese resisted their Spanish masters and appealed to the Chinese emperor:

> His Majesty's kindness is like a wide ocean, extending to all corners of the world. . . . We, as ordinary civilians, are humble and foolish laborers with misfortune. Youths trapped in a land faraway from home; adults wasting their lives in a foreign country. We regret that we are poor and sickly. We feel woeful that the harsh government here is making more cruel policies. That is why we dare to voice our grievance to you.[6]

When their appeals to the emperor went unanswered, the Chinese on Cuba joined others in rebellion. Two thousand fought in the Cuban forces in the first war of independence in the 1870s.[7] Some of the Chinese soldiers must have had battle experience, probably from the Taiping Rebellion, and they played a substantial role in the struggle for Cuban freedom up to 1902. A monument to the fallen Chinese in Havana has the following inscription: "There was not one Cuban Chinese deserter, not one Cuban Chinese traitor." But in spite of the gratitude of the new nation, the Cuban Chinese prospered only very gradually. Frustrated, many joined Fidel Castro's rebel forces in the 1950s. The best known, Armando Choy, Gustavo Chui, and Moisés Sío Wong, rose to become generals in the Cuban army, later fighting in Venezuela, Angola, and Nicaragua. The majority of the Chinese-Cubans did not see Castro's regime through rose-tinted glasses, though; there are now less than 7,000 left—the rest have fled the island for better opportunities in Florida or New York.

The English-speaking Caribbean received far fewer Chinese mi-grants than Peru or Cuba, but the commercial opportunities there turned out to be far greater. These countries have strong Chinese orga-nizations and many community and business leaders of Chinese origin. In Guyana, Arthur Chung was the first president of the country, from 1970 to 1980—and the first ethnic Chinese head of state of any country outside Asia. Most remarkably, there has been a significant remigration of highly educated Chinese Caribbeans back to China over the past generation. But even before then, a striking example of remigration took place: Eugene Chen, born in Trinidad in 1878, served as China's foreign minister several times in the 1920s and 1930s, though he spoke no Chinese. One of his sons, Percy Chen, became a committed Com-munist and one of the Comintern's key Chinese agents (under his Rus-sian name, Pertsei Ievgenovich Tschen). Even in and around China, the Caribbean stayed transnational.

In the Pacific islands, the first Chinese came on ships as sailors, cooks, and carpenters. In Fiji, Samoa, New Guinea, and Tahiti, workers were brought in from Guangdong province to labor on plantations or in construction. Today there are about 20,000 people of Chinese de-scent in the Pacific, and they have a significant and increasing influence both on business and politics. In Fiji, most hotels and restaurants are owned by Chinese from Fiji, from Southeast Asia, and from China. Sir Julius Chan was twice prime minister of Papua New Guinea. Anote Tong is the current president of Kiribati. Gaston Tong Sang is the president of French Polynesia. The ancestral homes of all three are within a small area of northeastern Guangdong.

Australia and New Zealand were favored destinations for Chinese sojourners or emigrants. But—as in the United States and Canada— the white authorities increasingly tried to exclude them. In New Zealand entry was restricted from the 1880s and almost impossible from the early 1900s—one law required all who entered to be able to read one hundred randomly chosen words in English. By the 1910s there were concerted efforts to force even naturalized citizens of Chinese descent out. In Australia the situation was similar. In the middle part of the nineteenth century, Chinese were attracted by opportunities for work and for learning skills; half a generation later the new state, based on a racist foundation, tried to throw them out. What was different in Australia was that in some parts of the labor movement anti-Chinese agitation did not really catch on, and some Chinese-Australian workers were able to organize and fight back against the government's systematic discrimination. The Australian-born journalist Vivian Chow (Zhou Chenggui), who became one of the key newspaper editors in China in the 1930s, was not surprised: "Send a Chinese to America and he tries to become a monopolist because of the ambitious example set before him; send him to British Singapore and he strives to become a contractor with designs on knighthood. . . . Send a Chinese to Australia, he becomes a labor leader and a booster 'for the working man's paradise.'"[8]

E VERYWHERE THEY WENT, Europeans dominated the world that the Chinese entered into. Through their colonial empires and their ethnic offshoots in the Americas, Australasia, and eastern Russia, people of European origin ruled the roost in terms of politics, the economy, and military affairs. Chinese mostly wanted to work or settle outside Europe—where there were more opportunities and easier access—but the European continent itself pulled them through a combination of fascination and abhorrence. Those who came were impressed, to the point of profound shock, by the might of European industry and weapons. They marveled at the products that were available to those who could afford them, and felt dizzy at the speed and intensity of changes in production and in landscape. But they also were dejected by what they saw as Europe's lack of universal moral rules and personal sincerity, and by the racism directed against them as Chinese. Europe was a conundrum, ever attractive and ever repellent.

Chinese had visited Europe for centuries and some had settled there. British ports, such as Liverpool, Bristol, and London, had a Chinese population in the eighteenth century, as had Paris, Moscow, and St. Petersburg. Most of the early settlers engaged in different forms of trade, and by the late nineteenth century they had been joined by other immigrants from their home areas in small Chinatowns in the main European cities. The first big influx of Chinese to Europe, however, was not workers but students, hundreds of whom arrived every year by the 1890s. In the first part of the twentieth century, the largest number of Chinese students went to Germany, followed by France and Britain. They mostly studied engineering or technical subjects, and some stayed, forming the first Chinese-European intelligentsias. Chinese from Hong Kong and Singapore went mostly to Britain, for obvious reasons. By 1960 the Chinese-British population was around 40,000 and it is ten times that today. Britain is by far the most favored European destination for Chinese immigrants.

After 1980, when China became more open to foreign contacts, travel to Europe started up again. Some came as tourists, with Britain and Italy the favorite destinations. Some chose to stay. The Italian city of Prato, in Tuscany, now has a population of more than 25,000 Chinese—about fifteen percent of the total population—who work in the garment industry. In Hungary, where there was a total of nine registered Chinese before Communism fell in 1989, there are now 27,000. As Europe's own population declines, more Chinese are likely to be attracted by good salaries and decent working conditions within the European Union. The cultural attraction may be waning, though. One Chinese tourist, who had saved a lifetime to visit France in 2007, was not impressed. According to an article in *Der Spiegel:*

> When she was a young girl, Liu learned to admire the French as a people worth emulating, because of their polish and elegance. But now, as she stands on the Champs-Élysées with her video camera, she sees them as nothing but ordinary, jostling city dwellers, many of them out of shape and poorly dressed. Bits of paper and plastic bags float around on the street. "My dream has been destroyed," she says.[9]

More than ninety percent of all Chinese who emigrated went to do simple forms of menial work. They cleared forests, dug mines, and laid railroad tracks. In some countries, as we have seen, they worked on plantations, growing sugar, cotton, or opium. Though the majority came of their own will, some were press-ganged into going abroad, and some went before they were old enough to properly consent to the fate that awaited them. A significant number—possibly as many as a third of the total Chinese emigration—were contracted out as labor gangs during their initial period abroad, often for seven to eight years or more. The majority of those who went abroad returned to China, though some left again later in life. Most never got rich, except in experiences and impressions that their clansmen and neighbors who stayed at home never got, except through those few who traveled.

As with other groups of migrants, Chinese often thought they were going abroad only for a time and would then return to China. These sojourners in a foreign country often turned into permanent emigrants and residents. They worked, got married, learned the local lifestyle, and got entangeled in a thousand bonds that made it difficult for them to leave the new country behind. What is remarkable is the number who insisted that their sojourn abroad was for limited time and did go back. A set of "reverse" push and pulls contributed: racism and exploitation abroad, attempts to push them out when their contracts finished, and the attraction of family, ancestors, and fields in the old country. For most uneducated Chinese emigrants, encounters with foreign customs and societies were a shock. They found attitudes and behavior (not to mention food) hard to stomach, and longed for home. One of them, arriving in New York around 1900, had been warned he would meet people who were

> Wild and fierce and wicked, and paid no regard to the moral precepts of Confucius and the Sages; neither did they worship their ancestors, but pretended to be wiser than their fathers and grandfathers. They loved to beat people and to rob and murder. In the streets of Hong Kong many of them could be seen reeling drunk. Their speech was a savage roar, like the voice of the tiger or buffalo. Their men and women lived together like animals, without any marriage or faithfulness, and even were shameless enough to walk the streets arm in arm in daylight.[10]

And still the immigrants kept coming. Just like those who went from their villages to work in factories in the Chinese cities, they often found their new environment repulsive, but it contained opportunities that their villages simply did not have. Funding for their travel was usually paid by clansmen who already lived abroad or through a credit-ticket system, in which migrants first borrowed to pay for their trip. The debt was then sold to employers in the new country, whom the workers had to repay through their labor. A number of middlemen, mostly Chinese, profited in the process, and diasporic networks were created around the trafficking of migrants. It often took long to repay the debt, but most workers learned skills in the process that they could later use abroad or at home.

Exploitation of Chinese migrant labor in their new countries was rampant. Some was considerably worse than that encountered by other immigrant groups. Causes included racism and the opportunity to exploit innocent villagers who knew nothing about the country or its laws. But there was also considerable exploitation of Chinese by other Chinese who had arrived before. Criminal gangs were ubiquitous in some Chinese communities abroad, and even established native place organizations or self-help societies exploited new arrivals for the profit of their elders through arranging work or housing at an added cost. Many new immigrants were entirely dependent on the advice of those who had arrived before them. Even though a surprising number of Chinese emigrant families did well in the second generation through their own labor, their fathers and mothers often struggled to learn a few basic truths about some of their countrymen. Just as in China itself, "Confucian values" or "common good" were fine phrases that could be used as covers for exploitation.

The immigrants' response to poor working conditions was often resistance and rebellion. The image of docile Chinese coolies abroad simply does not hold up to scrutiny. Not only did Chinese join the opposition against their oppressors, as we have seen in South America and Southeast Asia, but they also sometimes formed that opposition themselves. In places where it was difficult to join the established labor unions—because these very unions were campaigning against Chinese immigration—Chinese organized among other Chinese, often to confront foreign as well as Chinese employers.

Much of the conflict within Chinese immigrant communities—which local authorities often wrote down to family feuds or gang conflict—was class based. Many who returned to play key roles in Chinese revolutions first earned their spurs organizing Chinese workers in Europe. Zhu De, who had been a soldier in China, arrived in Berlin in 1922, and became an organizer of Chinese workers there even before he joined the Communist party. In 1928, after he had returned to China, he helped found the Communist People's Liberation Army.

Several of Zhu's fellow organizers of Chinese in Europe fought against Franco in the Spanish Civil War; about a hundred Chinese from all over Europe served in Spain.[11]

Chinese played a significant role in the wars that engulfed the world in the twentieth century, and not only in those that were fought in China. During World War I, large numbers participated in Europe, and during World War II Chinese and people of Chinese ancestry fought on all fronts. War destroyed and opened opportunities at the same time. For many Chinese Americans, World War II was the first time they felt they were treated as equals, not least because their skills were much needed in the war effort. "The war made a world of a difference to everyone. Not only to us, but mostly to us Chinese people. It was a lot of help," said Tommy Wong, a US-born Chinese who served as a navy mechanic in the Pacific.[12] War—especially a war in which the United States and China were fighting on the same side—became the great equalizer for a minority that felt under pressure. Unlike their Japanese fellow-citizens, Chinese Americans generally had a good World War II.

But it was the First World War that had introduced Chinese to foreign wars and foreign ways of killing. Some 150,000 Chinese were recruited to serve as laborers on the Western Front in Europe, and at least 50,000 served on the Eastern Front, in Russia. The recruitment happened as part of an elaborate Chinese government plan to buy favors with the Allied Powers, which they thought would win the war. The first Chinese workers arrived in France in August 1916, officially as employees of private companies, since China was still neutral in the war (it waited to declare war on Germany until August 1917). As Allied losses increased, the need for Chinese workers grew exponentially. By the time the war ended, the Chinese served not just with the French army, but with the Russian, British, and American armies, too. They dug trenches and airfields, worked in munitions factories, steel mills, and mines, and helped bury the dead. At least three thousand died on the Western Front or on their way there. How many died in the East we do not know.

The life of Chinese workers in Europe during World War I was tough. Many had been recruited among students and teachers eager to see Europe, and not from among the working class. The work was back-breaking, and carried out under military discipline, with little reward and many forms of punishment. The Chinese workers were supposed to return to guarded camps after work, though the camp system soon broke down. Many felt the harshness of European racism, being laughed at in the street or kicked by their commanders. The *Times* of London reported that though "a capable worker . . . the Chink, like the Kaffir, has to be kept under ward when he is not working. He gives little trouble if rightly managed, gambles a good deal, but does not get drunk or commit crimes of violence and is docile and obedient. But he must be restrained from contact with Europeans, and he has his own little tricks and dodges. . . . He is also taught to conform to British ideas of sanitation, cleanliness and discipline."[13] No wonder many Chinese felt their stay in Europe to be one long sorrow, undertaken for China's sake. A song, often sung in the camps, showed their sadness:

Thick mist now hides the sun
And gentle dropping on pattering spots
Urges the dull day on[14]

But there were important exceptions to the general misery. By early 1917 evening classes were set up, and Chinese newspapers began to be published, at least on the Western Front, bringing news from home. The Chinese workers learned to organize, and the first strikes and protests took place against poor working conditions, low pay, and overt racism. Contacts with French and Belgian civilians increased. Some Chinese got local girlfriends, whom they later married. One worker, Zhang Changsong from Jiangsu province, married his French girlfriend in 1920; their marriage produced thirteen children and lasted sixty years. Many stayed long periods after the war, in part because of a lack of capacity to repatriate them to China, and often used the time to learn important skills. More than three thousand remained indefinitely in France, joining with the Chinese who arrived as students, and forming the first Chinese labor organizations in Europe.

There are a number of little-known international connections between China and World War I. One involves Chinese labor transports to the Western Front in Europe going through Canada. Canadian authorities made every effort to squelch defections and fraternization between ordinary Canadians and the transiting Chinese, but for the visitors these journeys meant the discovery of Canada, a country that over time would become a favorite for Chinese emigrants. Another unexplored story is that of Chinese workers on the Eastern Front. Most of them probably came from the eastern parts of the Russian empire, or from Russian-held areas of Manchuria and were sent to the western Russian borders beginning as early as 1915. Many joined the armies there, especially after the Russian Revolution, with most ending up fighting for the Bolsheviks in the Baltic region and along the Romanian front. Even though they made their careers with the Bolsheviks, the survivors suffered in Stalin's great purges because of their foreign origin, with at least 11,000 arrested and 8,000 internally deported back to the eastern areas.[15]

Besides workers, the other big group to go abroad from China was students. From the first students who were sent by the government in the late nineteenth century up to the explosion of Chinese brilliance in the world's top campuses in the twenty-first century, some of China's most vital links with the world have come through engaging with educational institutions abroad. As a group, students have been more mobile than any other part of the population—most have to travel to a new city in China, and some go abroad. Ideas travel with them, including new concepts of how to do things and of how things should be. While workers have populated China's immigrant communities, students have given them their edge. They, more than any other group, have come to represent China to the world and the world to China.

The explosion in numbers of Chinese going abroad to study started in the early twentieth century. Already by 1911 there were at least 10,000 students overseas, with the majority in Japan and the United States. Although the figure declined during the depression and the war with Japan, it is likely that by 1949 at least 150,000 Chinese had studied abroad. Of these roughly half returned to China. By 2010 the total number of those who have studied abroad exceeds 1.5 million, but during the first twenty-five years after China began to open up in 1978, only twenty-five percent of students abroad returned to their country.[16] As with laborers, many students trained abroad live their lives between China and other countries, setting up families that are Chinese and transnational at the same time. Except in the period from 1950 to 1980, most Chinese students have traveled abroad on their own accord, supported by their families rather than by the government. And most of them have done well, struggling through a foreign language and a foreign culture to end often near the top of their class.

Most Chinese students who went abroad were, or became, intensely nationalistic. One of them, writing to his fellow students in the United States in 1915, stressed the predicament of being a Chinese born in their generation:

> Most of us were born somewhere around the year 1894. Have you not been taught what a year 1894 was for China? It was the year of the Chino-Japanese war over the question of Korea. . . . All these humiliations of our country happened when we were just raising our first baby cries. Do you not realize that you were born in the time when your country was perishing? . . . Having realized that we are the people of a perishing nation, we instinctively want to know what we shall do to save China.[17]

The number of students born in the decade around 1894 who went abroad and came back to try to save China is very large. Among the top Communist leaders, Cai Hesen (born 1895), Zhou Enlai and Liu Shaoqi (both 1898), Li Lisan (1899), Wang Ming and Deng Xiaoping (both 1904) went abroad as students. Among their senior leaders from the first generation, Mao Zedong was in fact the only one who did *not* go abroad. He had no money and found foreign languages difficult.

Cai, Zhou, Li, and Deng were among 1,600 students who went to France between 1919 and 1921 as part of the work-study movement. Organized by radical educators in China, it furnished the contacts the students needed to get a job in French factories (which suffered a labor shortage after the war) in order to earn enough money to later enroll at a university. Zhou Enlai arrived in Marseilles in 1920, hoping to study at the University of Edinburgh, but ended up spending three years in Paris working in a Renault machinery plant and, from 1921, organizing for the Communists. Deng Xiaoping was only sixteen when he arrived in France in 1920. For five years he worked in factories around Paris, developing a taste for croissants, playing bridge, and reading. In 1926 he left for Moscow to join the world revolution.

After the Communists came to power in China, Moscow became the chief destination for Chinese students. The students who went to the Soviet Union in the 1950s were sent by the government and kept under strict political control. They mostly studied science and engineering and had in some cases already been assigned to the institutes or plants they were going to work with in China after graduation. Most felt that their time in the Soviet Union was a happy one. They were funded by Soviet government stipends, making many times more than what their Chinese salaries would be (or what their Soviet fellow-students received). They studied well, but also had time for play and for falling in love, in spite of their CCP minders' attempts at regimenting their lives. The problems came when the Chinese were about to go home to a much more restrictive society and political atmosphere. The CCP told them that "in regards to love you should restrain yourself, deal with it correctly; it's not permitted to marry during your time of study." Thousands of Chinese men had to leave their girlfriends behind and in most cases never saw them again. Maybe for that reason, as much as for the education they received, the Soviet Union influenced the students deeply, well beyond the period of Sino-Soviet alliance. As late as in 2002 a third of the members in the Communist party's ruling Politburo had studied in the Soviet Union and eastern bloc countries, and much of their approach to life and to politics remained distinctly Soviet.[18]

Since 1980, the number of Chinese students abroad has really taken off. During the 1980s the majority went to the United States, where many decided to stay, thereby enriching American academia and knowledge-based industry. Later other countries became popular, too, but the Anglophone countries still dominate in terms of where students want to go. In 2010, of those who intended to study abroad, 43 percent wanted to go to the United States, 19 percent to Britain, and 12 percent to Australia. Language obviously plays a role in the choices, but there are also strong indications that Chinese like the close contact between faculty and students that they get in the best American or British universities. Of those who wanted to go to Britain in 2010, business studies predominated; almost 70 percent wanted a business-related education, preferably at least at master's level.[19] Even after China's economic boom, which began in the 1990s, the majority would prefer to stay abroad, at least for a while, after graduating. As with those from other emerging economies, the nationalism that Chinese students abroad evince does not prevent them from taking their opportunities wherever they can find them.

CHINESE ABROAD HAVE HAD an immense influence on China's political fortunes in the twentieth century. In spite of the often repeated truism that all change in China comes from within, I can think of no other major country for which the diaspora and people in exile have played such a significant role in the reshaping of its fortunes. The opposition against Qing rule found its strength abroad, as did the Guomindang in the 1910s and 1920s. The Communists were not only foreign-inspired but foreign-funded and trained. The market revolutionaries from the 1980s and 1990s were linked to the diaspora. The opposition to the current regime mobilizes outside China, much like the opponents of the Qing did. For Chinese revolutionaries, abroad has always been the initial staging ground for their dreams and hopes.

Sun Yat-sen, the founding father of the Republic of China, spent more than twenty years abroad, in Hawaii, the United States, Canada, Japan, Europe, and Southeast Asia. He studied abroad, worked abroad, and collected money for the revolution abroad, especially from wealthy Chinese in Hawaii and Singapore. His brother, Sun Mei, became a prosperous rancher in Kula on Maui. Sun Yat-sen married a young woman from a prominent Chinese American family, Song Qingling, who had attended Wesleyan College in Macon, Georgia (her sister, Song Meiling, married Chiang Kai-shek). In 1896 Sun was kidnapped by the Chinese embassy in London and after his release (following a campaign by British newspapers) published the sensational book *Kidnapped in London!*, which made him a household name among Chinese intellectuals. Sun's revolution was almost entirely foreign made. As we have seen, he almost missed the real revolution in 1911 because he was raising money in Colorado. He reminded his American listeners of foreign involvement in their own revolution and tried to sell bonds that he promised would be redeemed ten-fold after he came to power in China:

> In order to make sure of our success, to facilitate our movement, to avoid unnecessary sacrifice and to prevent misunderstanding and intervention of foreign powers we must appeal to the people of the United States in particular for your sympathy and support, either moral or material, because you are pioneers of western civilization in Japan; because you are a Christian nation; because we intend to model our new government after yours; and above all because you

are the champion of liberty and democracy. We hope to find many Lafayettes among you.[20]

In the generations after Sun, the Soviet Union became the center for Chinese revolutionaries abroad. Many went there to study, and some became Soviet residents. Chiang Kai-shek's son Chiang Ching-kuo, who later became the great democratizing president on Taiwan, was one such. Chiang went to Moscow as a student in 1925 and spent twelve years there, working as an engineer in the Urals. Li Lisan, who had studied in France and became general-secretary of the CCP, went to Moscow in 1931 and stayed for fifteen years; he was later tortured to death in Mao's Cultural Revolution.[21] Wang Ming, who had been the Comintern's favorite and had opposed Mao's rise within the CCP, had the good sense to stay in Moscow after he went there for medical treatment in 1956; he spent the last twenty years of his life denouncing Mao's dictatorship.

As we will see later, the Chinese diaspora played a key role in the transformation of China after 1978. The first country Deng Xiaoping visited after he became China's paramount leader was Singapore. Lee Kuan Yew, the wily anticommunist leader of the island state, whose ancestors, like Deng's, were Hakka from Jiangxi province, was uncertain about what to expect. Lee recounts that at their first dinner together, Deng turned to him and congratulated him on having done "a good job in Singapore":

> I said, "Oh, how's that?" He said, "I came to Singapore on my way to Marseilles in 1920. It was a lousy place. You have made it a different place." I said, "Thank you. Whatever we can do, you can do better. We are the descendants of the landless peasants of south China. You have the mandarins, the writers, the thinkers and all the bright people. You can do better. . . ." Within weeks, the *People's Daily* switched lines, that Singapore is no longer a running dog of the Americans, it's a very nice city, a garden city, good public housing,

very clean place. They changed their line. And he changed to the "open door" policy. After a lifetime as a Communist, at the age of 74, he persuaded his Long March contemporaries to return to a market economy.[22]

After the crackdown on prodemocracy protesters in Tian'anmen Square in 1989, China got its fifth generation of revolutionaries abroad. Fang Lizhi, one of China's leading astrophysicists, became a symbol for the student movement when he published essays calling for the democratization of China. He now lives in exile in the United States. Han Dongfang, a railway worker from Shanxi who led the nascent independent labor movement, lives and organizes in Hong Kong, "in China, but not of it," as he once said to me. Wang Dan, who as an eighteen-year-old history student at Peking University was the brains behind the democracy protest in 1989, received a PhD from Harvard in 2008, where he went after spending seven years in Chinese prisons. Like their predecessors, they hope to return to China and change it into a better country. Their position often seems hopeless, but then that was the case for the young Sun Yat-sen and the young Deng Xiaoping also.

Many overseas Chinese, even those who have never set foot in China, hope one day to go to the country of their ancestors. Many Chinese who have gone abroad have returned to China and tried to settle there. Even though the relative numbers have been declining over the past two generations, there is reason to believe that China's economic upturn will tempt more to go back. The problem is of course that it is not easy to return to a country you think you know but whose reality turns out to be very different from what you imagine. Although many returnees have become successful in China, quite a few have gone there full of optimism and patriotism, only to find that their country spurned their advances and, in some cases, made their and their families' lives hell.

The generation that returned in the early twentieth century mostly did well in China, but toward the end of their lives they saw much of what they achieved destroyed by war and revolution. The Guos and the Mas, the sojourners in Australia who came back to found Wing On and Sincere department stores, survived into the 1940s and died under Japanese occupation in Hong Kong. Their businesses on the mainland were confiscated by the Communist government. Rong Yiren, who inherited one of China's largest textile companies with roots back to the late Qing era, saw his inheritance seized in the 1950s and became a target during the Cultural Revolution—he was beaten and forced to work for eight years as a janitor. In 1978 Deng rescued him and asked him to use his know-how to develop industry and corporations that would make China rich. Rong founded Citic as a state enterprise. His son Rong Zhijian is among the richest people in China.

But some returning Chinese did not bounce back from persecution. Zheng Nian, who married her husband when they both were students at the London School of Economics in the 1930s, went back to work for Shell in China and stayed on after the 1949 revolution. In the 1960s all they owned was confiscated, her daughter was murdered by the Red Guards, and Zheng herself was imprisoned and tortured for six years on the charge of being a British spy. When she tried to defend herself against the charge of having studied abroad by mentioning LSE's Fabian socialist background, her jailers laughed in her face: "Lenin denounced the Fabian socialists as reformers," one of them told her. "They were not true socialists because they did not advocate revolution by violence. Don't try to ingratiate yourself with us. . . . All the senior staff of foreign firms are spies."[23]

The Western-trained architects who returned to help build new socialist Beijing also suffered in the Cultural Revolution. French-born Hua Lanhong (Leon Hoa), a modernist who had worked with Le Corbusier in the 1930s, went to a China he had never seen to become deputy head of the city planning bureau in Beijing in 1949. Hua oversaw much of the destruction of Ming-dynasty city in the 1950s. He was later purged as a promoter of Westernization, and spent twenty years building outhouses for rural communes when he was not brought out to be publicly humiliated as a representative of "deviant architecture." Hua was finally able to go back to France in 1977. Ironically, his daughter, the French architect Hua Xinmin, has now emerged as a key defender of what is left of old Beijing after the ravages of the plan her father helped implement in the 1950s.[24]

Some returnees were protected by the Communist Party even during the darkest years of the Cultural Revolution. Qian Xuesen, the father of China's missile program, who had worked in the United States, and the German-trained nuclear physicist Wang Ganchang, who had also served as deputy director of the Soviet Bloc joint nuclear research institute at Dubna, were both spared public humiliation. Qian's deputy, however, the brilliant German-trained engineer Zhao Jiuzhang, was hounded to commit suicide by the Red Guards in 1968. Even some of the Cultural Revolution activists themselves had foreign background. Brooklyn-born Tang Wensheng (Nancy Tang), a third-generation American, went to China with her parents in the 1950s and became Mao's English-language interpreter. In the Foreign Ministry she became a leading Cultural Revolutionary. Together with Mao's niece, Wang Hairong, she helped set the tone for China's foreign policy in the early 1970s.

Today's returnees are less exposed to disaster than their predecessors, though even now they know to keep their options open. Many have American green cards or other forms of permanent residence permits abroad. Even those who have never lived outside China like to have the foreign option. Zong Qinghou, the founder of the leading beverage company in China, Wahaha, and reputedly the richest man in the country, has a green card. But even though some who return from overseas are viewed with suspicion by their countrymen, this is based more on envy than on politics. The half million or so overseas students who have returned home during the past thirty years generally do very well, and some of them have become rich and famous in their home country. The only field in which they are definitely underrepresented is in politics. The Communist party still distrusts those with foreign connections. China's former president Jiang Zemin received his engineering training at the Stalin Automobile Works and former premier Li Peng studied hydroelectric engineering at the Moscow Power Institute, but today's Harvard or Oxford MBAs rarely are let close to power in China.[25]

CHAPTER 7

WAR

T HE EIGHT-YEAR WAR with Japan is the founding event of modern China's international history. The country had not exactly been peaceful during the previous hundred years, but from 1937 to 1945, many Chinese felt that they were fighting an enemy intent on eliminating China from the map. From the 1830s to the 1930s, war against foreigners had been localized and sporadic, but in the resistance against Japanese occupation, war was everywhere. Peasants in the Shaanxi and Fujian countryside were affected by the war as much as city dwellers in Shanghai or Beijing. For the majority of Chinese, their first-ever encounter with a foreigner was in the form of a Japanese officer barking out orders in a language they could not understand. No wonder that China's initiation into world politics was an unhappy one, and that it created myths and dogmas that have lasted up to today.

The war with Japan came at a point when the slow development of Chinese nationalism, begun in the late nineteenth century, had reached a peak. Although China's government, under Chiang Kai-shek, would for strategic reasons have preferred to put off fighting Japan, Chinese public opinion gave it no choice but to fight back as soon as large-scale hostilities began. Forms of Chinese nationalism had been sharply on the rise since the mid-1920s, but it was the Japanese attack in Manchuria in 1931, and Tokyo's subsequent transformation of the region into a separate state under Japanese tutelage, Manzhouguo, that set Chinese hearts racing for a unified military response to Japan's aggression.[1] In this sense, many of Japan's policies up to 1937—and indeed after the outbreak of war—were based on a misunderstanding: The Tokyo government feared Chinese nationalism but did not realize that it was its own actions that more than anything else fueled a new sense of self in China. From its very beginning, Chinese nationalism as state policy was aimed at resisting Japan.

In this second Sino-Japanese war, begun in 1937, two very different images of China came into conflict. One, held by most Japanese, came out of the nineteenth century and saw China as less a state than a geographic region with different power holders: Rival governments, local strongmen, and foreign representatives combined in different ways to keep some semblance of order, while advanced powers, such as Japan, promoted development within China. It was the advent of a nationalist central government, in the form of the Guomindang, with the stated purpose of resisting Japanese policies, that imperiled the image of a quiescent, pragmatic Chinese approach to international affairs. And this resistance came at a time when many Japanese felt that they and their country were under pressure from the Western great powers (including the Soviet Union) and from the global economic crisis, which the Western world had unleashed. The other image of China was one held by increasing numbers of young urban Chinese and their offshoots in the Chinese countryside and abroad: China was the state representing the Chinese nation. Its natural and legitimate borders were those of the Qing empire. Its enemies were foreign countries that would not recognize this China as an equal, and especially Japan, which seemed intent on carving out ever larger chunks of Chinese territory for itself. China, in their view, had to unify to fight Japan.

When war came, it had disastrous effects for China. Large numbers of soldiers and civilians died, and much of the country's infrastructure was destroyed. China lost at least two million men in battle, and twelve million Chinese civilians died as a direct result of warfare. Others died from starvation, destruction of dams and dikes, and disease and mistreatment in the Chinese army. Japan lost 400,000 men fighting in China (and 1,500,000 more in the other wars that the war in China started). Japan also lost 1.2 million civilians in World War II, including 300,000 in prisoner of war camps after the war, mostly in Manchuria and in the USSR. In addition, 400,000 Chinese were killed fighting together with the Japanese army in China or elsewhere in Asia.[2] These are staggering figures. Their effects were to be felt in China and in Japan for two generations as a misery of loss, blame, and guilt.

Politically, China's first big foreign war on its territory since the Manchu conquest in the 1630s and 1640s changed the landscape forever. The war broke the back of the GMD, which had represented Chinese nationalism for thirty years. The damage was in part due to the fighting itself, of course. But it was also because of the civilian challenges of war, which the state the GMD had set up was barely able to handle. The CCP had the chance first to survive and then to expand, sheltered by the war the GMD had to fight against Japan. And the war meant dislocation on a grand scale within the country, both socially and politically, with the power of traditional elites broken, the power of the state questioned, and millions of people displaced. War, as often, became a catalyst for modernity, but not necessarily the form of modernity that most people had wanted to see.

AT THE BEGINNING OF THE 1930s Japan was an inherently unstable state. Its political system has been called "government by assassination." Prime Minister Hamaguchi Osachi was shot in 1931, and his successor Inukai Tsuyoshi a year later. Both were killed by young rightwingers who wanted a more autocratic regime at home and a more expansionist policy abroad. By 1936 right-wing terror had succeeded in totally immobilizing Japanese democracy. Part of the reason for this sharp turn to the right was the Great Depression, which hit the Japanese economy severely, causing the first deep crisis in the country's modern economy. Some politicians and intellectuals, and not least many officers, viewed the Depression as a deliberate attempt by the West to damage Japan's economic rise. Japan had agreed to many Western proposals for arms limitations, tariffs, and international institutions in the 1920s. Now its rivals were attempting to make use of Japan's self-imposed restrictions to sabotage its economy. Japan, the right believed, needed to throw off the political system it had taken over from the West, re-orient itself toward "Asian values," and expand its zone of control on its own continent.

The first step in this Japanese expansion was Manchuria. There, in September 1931, officers from Tokyo's imperial army made use of the political chaos in Japan to attack Chinese forces at Shenyang and then move swiftly to occupy the rest of the region. Neither the Japanese gov-ernment nor the high command of the army acted to stop this conquest by mutiny. Instead, Tokyo gradually gave way to the wishes of the rad-ical officers in its army in China, the so-called Guandong Army. In the war that followed the Japanese attack, Chinese forces in Manchuria were quickly put on the defensive, and within five months Japan had taken control of most of China's northeastern provinces. Unlike before, this time Tokyo did not give in to international pressure to withdraw. Instead, when the League of Nations defined its actions as aggression, Japan withdrew from the League in March 1933. Even before its break with the West, Japan had begun setting up a separate state in China's northeastern provinces, which it called Manzhouguo—Land of the Manchus. Most of the former Chinese power holders were forced out, and a new administration fully beholden to Japan was put in place, led by the hapless Puyi, the last Qing emperor, who now became the Kangde emperor in what he considered his ancestral homeland. The Man-zhouguo emperor's role in the East Asian system that Japan was putting in place was clear: At one point Puyi performed an elaborate quasi-

Japanese ritual from which he emerged as the younger half-brother of Hirohito, the Japanese emperor.[3]

The construction of Manzhouguo contributed to several key international developments of the 1930s. It pushed Japan's weak civilian governments toward accepting a new form of state organization dominated by the military and aimed at overseas expansion. It intensified Chinese nationalism and convinced a younger generation of Chinese that they had to aim for a unified and centralized state. And it destroyed all attempts at international cooperation in East Asia, making the new powers in the region, the United States and the Soviet Union, concentrate, each in its own way, on dealing with Japanese expansionism. In spite of Soviet unwillingness to stand up to Tokyo and US inability to do so without the backing of the European powers, it did not, by the mid-1930s, take prophetic gifts to understand that East Asia was heading for war. What held the shaping of an international coalition against Japan back was the focus that all main powers had on the situation in Europe and the rise of Nazi Germany. And Japan was watching closely what Germany was doing on its continent: creating hegemonic forms of integration that could help it resist great power attempts at keeping it down.

Manzhouguo therefore came to symbolize a new form for Japanese imperialism, in which economic development and public services stood at the forefront. Japan was well prepared for this effort. Already before the world crisis, eighty-five percent of Japanese foreign investment was in China, and of its Chinese investments, eighty percent was in Manchuria. Between 1932 and 1941 Japan, in relative terms, invested far more in Manchuria than any Western power did in their colonies. By 1945, its investment there was larger than the total of its investment in Korea, Taiwan, and the rest of China put together. Production, both in industry and agriculture, tripled, with machinery, tools, and consumer goods being the fastest-growing sectors. The Manzhouguo government, and its Japanese advisers, also invested heavily in transport, education, and public health, offering a completely new pattern of development to a population that had suffered decades of warfare and economic chaos. Not surprisingly, some, especially among the traditional elites, chose to work closely with the new state and its foreign backers.

By the early 1930s, Manchuria was roughly ninety percent Chinese in population, with smaller groups of Koreans, Manchus, Mongols, and Russians. This pattern changed little during the Manzhouguo period, except that the number of Koreans, who could enter freely from Japanese-controlled Korea, increased sharply. The vast majority of Chinese in Manchuria continued to believe that the territory they lived in was a part of China, and while only tiny groups were willing to take up arms to resist the new state, resentment and passive forms of resistance existed everywhere. The Japanese army responded with repression and violence, including forced land confiscations to benefit new forms of industrialized agriculture. Even though the Japanese preferred to define Manzhouguo as a multinational development state, in which all national identities could and should play a part, the Chinese felt that they were the ones who benefited the least from the new order.

The creation of Manzhouguo meant a new phase of Japan's expansion, and, to some extent, a new Japan. In its confrontation with the West, Tokyo's actions became more similar to US or Soviet forms of control over others than to the arrangements within British or French empires. The pan-Asian developmentalism that Japan was to put forward over the next twelve years through 1945 gave purpose to the lives, and, eventually, often the deaths, of many young Japanese. It also appealed to some Chinese, through its anti-Western stance and its successes at modernization. But, as in Hitler's Europe, in Japan's Asia there could only be one nation at the peak of the development ladder. For those living in the shadow of the Empire of the Sun, the only way to become fully modern was to become fully Japanese. And that was a next to impossible process, because it led away from the emerging nationalisms that other Asians increasingly identified with.

FROM THE 1920S ON, the Guomindang leader Chiang Kai-shek had regarded Japan as the foremost threat to China's unity and integrity. While admiring Japanese fighting skills and organizational abilities, Chiang realized that these very qualities could be turned against China if Tokyo so decided. From 1931 on, Chiang knew that a war was coming, and he wanted to postpone it for as long as possible, giving his regime time to complete the unification of China and gain foreign allies. Though much maligned then and now, Chiang's strategy made eminent sense: He knew better than anyone else just how weak China was compared with Japan, and that the only way in which his nationalist project could be saved was through buying time. Throughout the early 1930s, against considerable opposition from friends and foes alike within China, Chiang clung to his strategy. He would not fight a full-scale war against Japan until he absolutely had to, and then, he predicted, there would be a long war in which China's very survival would be at stake. It was a war China could not fight without unity, weapons, and foreign assistance.

In the early 1930s the GMD government led a country that was more united than it had been for two decades, but where significant parts of the country had forms of self-authorized autonomy. Besides Manchuria, where the Japanese installed themselves as overlords, Outer Mongolia had a Communist regime, which Chiang, rightly, saw as an extension of Soviet power. In Xinjiang, Chiang had to confront a Uighur rebellion and then forces allied with the Soviets. Having overcome both, he lost control of the province in 1937 to Sheng Shicai, a GMD official who preferred to throw his lot in with the Soviets as Chiang's government faced its final showdown with the Japanese. In Tibet, the regime acting on behalf of the boy Dalai Lama turned to the British in India to maintain its autonomy from China. And in the south, Yunnan was semiautonomous under the local strongman Long Yun and Guangxi under Bai Chongxi and Li Zongren. Chiang still had a long way to go to reunify China fully. And then there were the

Communists, his most intractable problem, who had survived the on-slaught against them in 1928 and were now making a limited comeback as a guerrilla force in Jiangxi/Fujian border areas.

For Chiang, the Communists were different from all his other chal-lengers for power in China. Supremely self-confident, the generalissimo believed that the ethnic separatists or regional strongmen would, in the end, submit to the power of the central government he was construct-ing. But the Communists would not, because their political ideology prevented them from doing so. They were, he rightly thought, governed by their political beliefs and their ties to the Soviet Union and would therefore resist if not destroyed militarily. In 1934 Chiang therefore made the CCP bases the primary objective of his military campaigns, forcing the main Communist armies out of the south and on a long flight toward the west and north, leaving the survivors, by late 1935, to set up a new base in a desolate part of Shaanxi province. The Com-munists had survived again, but barely.

It was the Long March, as they called their flight from the south, that became the founding myth of the renewed CCP during World War II. The retreat also gave the Communists their new leader, Mao Zedong, who would be in place from 1936 until his death forty years later. Mao led a main part of the CCP armies into Shaanxi, and the capital the Communists set up there, Yan'an, was increasingly domi-nated by Mao and his political thinking. Even though Mao was a war-rior who hoped to organize new armies in the north to take his revenge on Chiang, he was bound by Comintern discipline and by the orders given by Stalin—more difficult to ignore now that the CCP headquar-ters was in the north and closer to Soviet-held territory. And Stalin wanted the CCP to join Chiang in a new united front to fight Japan, the most dangerous enemy for the Soviets, too. Mao grumbled but had little choice but to comply, especially since he himself saw the propa-ganda advantages of calling for united resistance against Japan.

Then, in December 1936, matters came to a head. Chiang had gone to the army's northwestern headquarters in Xian in order to urge the troops there to renew their offensive against the CCP. As often before, Chiang thought that he was within a hair's breadth of wiping the Communists out. Instead, the local officers, headed by Zhang Xueliang, the strongman Tokyo had driven out of Manchuria, took the Generalissimo prisoner. They wanted to force Chiang to authorize combined action with the CCP and other Chinese autonomous armies against Japan. Chiang was outraged, but faced treason with his usual composure. He told his captors that he would rather be shot than offer them any concessions. Zhang soon realized that he was the one who was in big trouble. From all segments of Chinese society came requests for him to release Chiang. Most people did not believe that China could organize against Japan except under the Generalissimo's leadership. Even Stalin and the Soviets chimed in, since they believed that all alternative leaders to Chiang would be less likely to wage successful war against Japan. Zhou Enlai, Mao's second in command in the CCP, went to Xian to secure Chiang's release. While Mao must have been fuming at seeing his archenemy get away, he knew that Stalin was keeping an eye on his every action, and that there was no other way out. He may even, in his heart of hearts, have agreed with the majority of his countrymen: With Chiang there might be little hope of ever defeating the Japanese, but without him there was no hope at all.

CHIANG KAI-SHEK RETURNED to his capital, Nanjing, in the snow on Christmas Day 1936, accompanied by his captor, the "Young Marshal" Zhang Xueliang (who might have opted to stay behind if he knew he would remain the Generalissimo's favorite prisoner for many decades). Chiang had promised a ceasefire against the Communists and, in the vaguest possible terms, a united front against Japan. He told his closest advisers that he was furious that, in his view, a bunch of warlords and traitors had ruined his plan for buying time before fighting Japan. But Chiang had also recogized that he was running out of time. Even before the incident in Xian, he had confided in his diary that although he wanted another two years of preparation, "life" might not give him that much. If the choices were to lose control of his own country or go to war against Japan, Chiang obviously preferred the latter.

By the spring of 1937 some form of limited cooperation directed against Japan had been put in place. The Chinese central government and most of the regional power holders were beginning to work together. Since 1935 the CCP had been promoting a Chinese People's Anti-Japanese United Front, and now even some of Chiang's closest colleagues were using the term. The rhetoric against Japan contributed to strengthening Chiang's position in China even further, but—understandably—had very negative consequences in Tokyo and in Manzhouguo, where even moderate politicians and officers believed that Chinese nationalism was reaching fever pitch and that war was not far off. Japan was also feeling the sting of its international isolation. Not only were the United States and Britain indicating their support for a more hard-line Chinese position, but so were the Soviets, Japan's arch-enemy. Even Germany, technically Japan's ally, had not withdrawn its military advisers in China.

The Japanese government was inclined to reduce the pressure on Chiang's regime in order to avoid war, but tension was building in north China. The situation was especially volatile in Hebei province around Beijing, where Japanese forces of the Guandong army had been creating a buffer zone between Manzhouguo and the rest of China since the mid-1930s. On the evening of 7 July 1937, while Japanese forces were conducting an unannounced exercise southwest of Beijing, close to where the city's fifth ring road runs now, Chinese soldiers fired shots at them. Finding one of their numbers missing, the Japanese demanded access to a nearby fortress to look for him. When the Chinese officers hesitated, the Guandong army shelled the fortress and took control of the key bridge coming out of the city, the Lu Ditch Bridge, or the Marco Polo Bridge as it is known in English. Chinese forces reacted and by morning had retaken the bridge, but when the Japanese commanders demanded an apology, the Chinese refused to back down. Sporadic fighting continued up to 26 July, when the imperial army declared a ceasefire. Even after most of the fighting stopped, the Guomindang officers rejected the Japanese demands, which by then had widened to imply a full Chinese evacuation of the area.

Not long after the fighting in Hebei broke out, Chiang Kai-shek decided that this was it: The war that he had dreaded, and prepared for, had come. He could not order his troops to accept the Japanese demands. On 30 July he declared that "the only course open to us now is to lead the masses of the nation, under a single plan, to struggle to the last." Seeing the Japanese pour troops into North China, Chiang decided to strike back where his best troops were, in and around Shanghai. Egged on by the Shanghai commander, Zhang Zhizhong, who was communicating both with the CCP and the Soviets, the GMD air force on 14 August attacked the Japanese flagship, the aged battle cruiser *Izumo,* in Shanghai harbor. Although failing to hit the ship, the Chinese operation told Tokyo that a full-scale war was now on, and the Japanese fleet turned its guns on Chinese positions in the city. Addressing his countrymen by radio, Chiang said that "Japan's limitless expansion impels China, gives it no choice, but to act in self-defense [and] to resist by armed force from now on."[4] The battle for Shanghai raged back and forth for two months, with both armies attempting to stay away from the foreign concessions. By early November the Japanese had secured the city and were moving toward the Chinese capital, Nanjing.

Although the Japanese tried to portray the GMD government's actions as akin to the Qing government's during the Boxer War, Tokyo's international isolation only increased after the war broke out. By drawing on its putative alliance with Nazi Germany, Japan was able to get Chiang's German advisers recalled. But Britain, Japan's old ally, now viewed it as an aggressor. The United States was also edging closer to condemning Tokyo outright, though it still resisted any collective action. In a speech on 5 October 1937 clearly directed against Japan, President Franklin Roosevelt condemned "those violations of treaties and those ignorings of human instincts which today are creating a state of international anarchy and instability from which there is no escape through mere isolation or neutrality." Meanwhile, the Soviets, to forestall a two-front war against both Germany and Japan, began taking steps to confront the growing power of their eastern neighbor. Stalin not only agreed to arm the Chinese; he sent Soviet planes and pilots to combat the Japanese air force. During the first year of the war, the Soviets provided the Chinese government with 348 bombers, 542 fighters, 82 T-tanks, 2,118 vehicles, 1,140 artillery guns, 9,720 machine guns, and 50,000 rifles. In the summer of 1939, the Soviet Union and Japan fought a war for control of Mongolia around Nuomen Han, on the Manzhouguo-Mongolian border. The Japanese forces were soundly defeated by the Red Army under the command of General Georgii Zhukov. The Soviets lost 9,000 men; the Japanese at least twice that.[5]

By going to war against China in 1937 Japan had achieved exactly what many of its leaders had hoped to avoid: international isolation, distraction from fighting the Soviets, and a massive commitment of men and materiel for an uncertain purpose. Although the emperor's armies were advancing, the cost was great, and on the Chinese side Chiang Kai-shek had not only mobilized the country behind his leadership but also won the sympathy of the world. It gradually dawned on the Japanese government that Chiang was committed to fighting the war, holding on in the hope of international assistance. This war, Tokyo concluded in the winter of 1937–1938, would not be like its China wars of the past, in which the Chinese side agreed to negotiations after being defeated in initial engagements. It would be a long and bitter modern war. One Japanese soldier, after landing on the Chinese coast in 1937, noted in his diary:

> I was filled with a sense of fortune and gratitude for having landed safely on this land, taken by the blood and tears of the marines and forward land units. I offered a small prayer to the spirits of the war

dead and, facing towards the Emperor in the far, far East, while feeling how grateful I am for my country Japan, I was able to sense how horrible this thing called war really is.[6]

Some of the worst fighting of the Sino-Japanese war took place in the autumn of 1937, in the region between Shanghai and the GMD capital, Nanjing. The GMD's best troops defended Nanjing but were gradually decimated and pushed back. The Japanese army laid siege to the capital on 7 December, while Chiang vowed to defend it to the end. After a number of battles by the city's walls, the Japanese broke through on 13 December, and the Chinese defenders fled. The next six weeks saw the worst atrocities against civilians in a captured city during all of World War II. More than 200,000 inhabitants of the Nanjing region and prisoners of war were murdered by Japanese soldiers, often encouraged or even under orders by their superiors. Rape and torture were widespread. John Rabe, a German businessman and Nazi Party member who organized and headed the International Committee for the Nanjing Safety Zone, gave witness to the inferno:

> Two Japanese soldiers have climbed over the garden wall and are about to break into our house. When I appear they give the excuse that they saw two Chinese soldiers climb over the wall. When I show them my party badge, they return the same way. In one of the houses in the narrow street behind my garden wall, a woman was raped, and then wounded in the neck with a bayonet. I managed to get an ambulance so we can take her to Kulou Hospital. . . . Last night up to 1,000 women and girls are said to have been raped, about 100 girls at Ginling College for Girls alone. You hear nothing but rape. If husbands or brothers intervene, they are shot. What you hear and see on all sides is the brutality and bestiality of the Japanese soldiers.[7]

It is hard to explain the causes of these atrocities. Japanese soldiers were incensed that the Chinese army was fighting back after so many

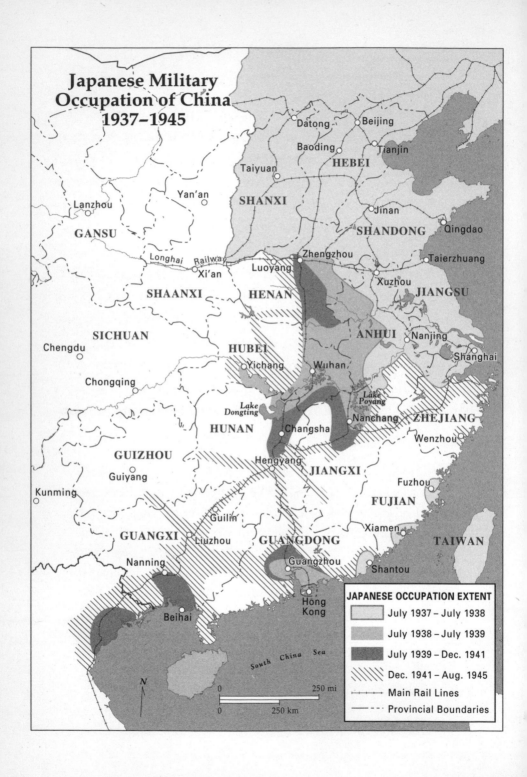

Japanese Military
Occupation of China
1937–1945

JAPANESE OCCUPATION EXTENT

July 1937 – July 1938

July 1938 – July 1939

July 1939 – Dec. 1941

Dec. 1941 – Aug. 1945

Main Rail Lines

Provincial Boundaries

years of accommodation. They regarded themselves as better than the Chinese, and seeing comrades killed by Chinese bullets gave rise to a lust for revenge and punishment. The ultimate responsibility lay with the officers who commanded the imperial army as it entered the city, especially Prince Asaka Yasuhiko, the emperor's uncle, who headed the troops.

The Rape of Nanjing, as the massacre became known, helped solidify Chinese resistance against the invaders. During 1938 and 1939, as the Japanese armies won victory after victory all over the country, the Chinese front held, and the foreign forces had to fight for most of the land they conquered. In October 1938 Wuhan, the biggest city in central China, and Guangzhou, the biggest city in the south, fell to the Japanese. By late 1939 the imperial army had taken control of nearly all of coastal China and was pushing into the interior in the south and west, already holding most of the north. Tokyo had expected Chiang Kai-shek to capitulate or at least seek urgent negotiations for a settlement. But this time there was no way back for Chiang. By putting himself at the head of Chinese nationalism at its moment of truth, Chiang had nailed his colors to the mast of China's resistance against Japan. Much as General Charles de Gaulle did in France, Chiang had come to believe that he *was* China, that in these fateful months the country only existed through him and the resistance he could offer against Japan. He gave Tokyo no choice but to give up on negotiations, try to destroy Chiang's government, and break China up into various regimes under Japan's tutelage.

This policy turned out to be hard for Japan to put into practice. It did, as we shall see, get collaborationist regimes set up in various parts of the country, but it was never able to inflict a decisive defeat on Chiang Kai-shek. Even though Chinese battlefield victories were few and far between, the continous resistance against the Japanese offensives inflicted significant losses on the imperial army and sapped its morale. The fluidity of the frontline as the defenders—both GMD and CCP—

turned to guerrilla warfare led to several cases of Japanese overextension, leaving supply lines and military outposts exposed. Leaders in Tokyo continued to believe that they could force an end to the war by military means, but this victory was projected further and further into the future, as the Chinese resistance destroyed hopes of a sudden overall triumph for Japan.

The costs for China of the first two years of war were enormous, however. Besides the battlefield losses, the civilian population was hit by both warfare and its consequences. In June 1938, thirty-six thousand square miles in Henan, Jiangsu, and Anhui provinces were flooded when Chiang's government decided to sabotage the dikes of the Yellow river to hinder the Japanese advance. At least half a million people died, and three million were made homeless. Many provinces in north and central China were hit by famine as a result of wartime dislocation. Desperate peasants fled their homes to avoid battles, reprisals, or enforced conscription. Instead of the order they had promised, the Japanese invaders created anarchy in parts of the countryside, as they competed with different Chinese armies for control. Still, the GMD regime survived in spite of the sacrifice they demanded of the population.

In 1939, Chiang Kai-shek and his increasingly exhausted men had two main reasons for a little hope or at least not total despair. The GMD had been able to transfer some of its personnel to a new wartime capital at Chongqing, away from the battlefronts in the western province of Sichuan, and had retained the allegiance of most local leaders in unoccupied parts of the west and south. And Japan was still obsessed with the USSR, to the extent that it kept some of its best troops in the north away from the battlefront against Chinese forces to hold them in reserve in case of a Soviet attack.

IN LATE SUMMER 1939, the external circumstances for China's war changed dramatically, and not for the better. At the end of August, the Soviet Union and Germany signed an agreement pledging cooperation on European matters, the so-called Molotov-Ribbentrop Pact. A few days later, Hitler invaded Poland and World War II began. While the Japanese initially were shocked at the marriage of ideological enemies, and at their German ally's failure to consult with them, the Soviet-German pact did remove the pressure from their northern flank and let them concentrate on the war in China. The GMD government also lost Soviet support for its war effort. For twenty-eight grueling months, China was left to fight the war against Japan alone, testing both the force of Chinese nationalism and the GMD state to the breaking point.

Left free to advance into China, in late 1939, the Japanese went on the offensive on several fronts. In central China they moved into Hunan province from several directions, and even though their attempt at conquering the capital, Changsha, failed, they strongly improved their strategic position. Toward the end of the year, the Japanese invaded Guangxi province in the south. Its capital, Nanning, fell in January 1940. Even worse for Chiang Kai-shek, some local strongmen in the north with long-standing links to his party, such as Yan Xishan in Shanxi, arranged separate ceasefires with the Japanese army. Internationally the war also went badly for the GMD. In July 1940 Britain, which was eyeing limited forms of cooperation with Japan after the Soviet-German pact had soured relations between Berlin and Tokyo, temporarily closed the roads through Burma that had brought vital supplies to the Chongqing regime. At the same time the French authorities in Vietnam, now loyal to the German-controlled Vichy regime in France, cut off supplies from the south. And in late September 1940 came another disaster: Japan and Germany joined in a military alliance, the Axis. Its purpose, according to the treaty text, was "to stand side by side and cooperate with one another in their efforts in the sphere of Greater East Asia and the regions of Europe respectively, wherein it is their prime purpose to establish and maintain a new order of things, intended to promote the mutual prosperity and welfare of the peoples concerned."[8]

Japan celebrated its new international breakthrough by a massive bombing offensive in China, similar to that of Germany against Britain. With the Chinese air force destroyed, Japan had full control of the air, and Chinese cities and their civilian populations were made to feel the consequences. With a new collaborationist regime in place in Nanjing, Tokyo believed that Chiang, finally, would be forced to agree to a cease-fire. But Chiang battled on, despite massive defections from the ranks in central China and increasing disobedience from his field commanders, including those of the CCP, with which the government had to fight several battles at the darkest moment of its war with Japan. What saved Chiang was, yet again, Japanese overextension. Japan's attempts at broad offensives left their front troops exposed, and territory gained sometimes had to be given up because of logistical problems. The battle of Shangao, in southern China, in the spring of 1941 is a good example. The imperial army reached all of its strategic objectives but was still forced back with heavy losses because it could not easily reinforce its frontline over long distances.

With the Soviet Union effectively out of the war in Asia, Chiang Kai-shek was looking for new allies. He knew from the time of the German victories in Europe that his only realistic hope lay with the United States, and he tried desperately to influence Washington to provide aid to China. By the autumn of 1940, the Americans were finally starting to listen, and in November Chiang received his first batch of US credit. In the spring of 1941, just as the GMD were fighting its most desperate battles in south and central China, the administration of Franklin Roosevelt extended the Lend-Lease Agreement, which had supplied Britain during its darkest days, to China. American volunteers began flying new Chinese fighter planes that had been delivered by the United States. Although Chiang knew the United States was not about to enter the war in China with its own forces, the increasingly strict US sanctions against Tokyo convinced him that Roosevelt saw Japan as a growing threat to US positions in the Pacific. When the Japanese leaders signed a neutrality pact with the Soviets in April 1941, Chiang concluded that Japan would move south and attempt to take control of Southeast Asia. It would get into a war with the Americans and with Britain, he predicted, in which Tokyo would "court its own destruction." China only had to hold out a bit longer and "the situation in the Pacific will change."[9]

After 1937, China, for the first time in its history, mobilized for all-out war as a country driven by ideas of nation and nationalism. Given the mighty odds that the GMD regime went up against, it did not do badly. Most importantly, it avoided a military collapse, which, seen through the prism of the first months of the war, had been a real possibility. Unlike in any international war China had fought since the 1840s, the morale of government troops did not break as soon as fighting began. Instead, in most areas, Chinese troops hung on, with massive losses, against armies that were far superior to their own in technology and training.

The German attack on the Soviet Union in June 1941 meant some nervous weeks for the Chinese leaders. They tried to determine whether this widening of the war in Europe would also mean a widening of the war in Asia. But the Japanese had no appetite for a war against the Soviets and soon concluded that Germany would not succeed in overcoming their new foes within anything like the time Berlin had anticipated. Inside China, the main consequence of Hitler's attack on the Soviet Union was a renewed alliance between the Chinese government and the Communists, who now were instructed by Moscow to join in an all-out war against the aggressors and their allies. Even though Chiang never succeeded in getting the CCP to play the military role he wanted against Japan, he now at least had it removed as a major troublemaker within nonoccupied China. But he also had to realize that the Soviet Union, now fighting for its own existence, was in no position to support China militarily.

In Tokyo, the Japanese leaders were becoming increasingly frustrated by China's ability to resist. By early autumn the military officers who wanted to attack the United States and Britain to crush what they saw as Western attempts at strangling Japan were getting the upper hand in a remarkably open policy debate. By conquering Southeast Asia, some Japanese planners believed that they would force China to surrender and get access to the resources they needed to fight a wider war. The imperial army's failure to make major gains in China in late 1941 helped push the argument that Japan could not win and preserve its honor without engaging its enemies on a broad front. Privately, many Japanese officers had started talking about a "China quagmire." Defeating the Western powers in Asia through the use of the navy would erase the memory of the army's humiliations on the Chinese front and let Japan be seen as the power that brought modernity to other Asians.

When an aide awakened him in the early morning of 8 December 1941, Chiang was in no way surprised at the news he received. More than anyone else in the Chinese leadership, the Generalissimo had been convinced that Japan, sooner or later, would move south. Learning of the full extent of the attack on Pearl Harbor, he sent a message to President Roosevelt: "To our new common battle we offer all we are and all we have, to stand with you until the Pacific and the world are free from the curse of brute force and endless perfidy."[10] Even the rapid Japanese advance into Southeast Asia did not rattle the Generalissimo, though the quick surrender of Singapore, on 15 February, came as something of a shock. Chiang had believed that the British would put up more of a fight. With two-thirds of the Japanese army still in China, Chiang could rightly pride himself on holding the main front against Tokyo's attempts at imposing a new order in the region.

Chiang's first fear was that the Japanese southern offensive would cut China's lifeline through Burma. He did not trust the fighting capacities of the British. When their commander of the Indian forces, Field Marshal Archibald Wavell, hesitated at receiving the divisions Chiang was willing to transfer to northern Burma in early 1942, the Generalissimo lashed out at him: "You and your people have no idea how to fight the Japanese. Resisting the Japanese is not like suppressing colonial rebellions, not like colonial wars. The Japanese are a serious great power. . . . Fighting against them for so many years, we Chinese are the ones who know how to do it. For this kind of job, you British are incompetent, and you should learn from the Chinese how to fight the Japanese."[11] In his meetings with the one-eyed British field marshal, Chiang must have considered how perceptions of power and alliance had changed since his own youth: China was no longer a despised outsider to the international system, and the British were no longer at the top of the world. Even when British forces retreated into India in May 1942, leaving the newly arrived Chinese divisions in the lurch and abandoning the Burma Road into China's southern Yunnan province, Chiang did not despair. He knew that the Chinese military presence in Burma had made his point about China being a great power and had scored points for him with the only military power that really could support China: the United States.

The Sino-American alliance developed rapidly after the Japanese attack on Pearl Harbor. Even after the Burma Road was closed, Allied planes brought US supplies, military equipment, and advisers in "over the Hump," the dangerous flight from northern India into China across the Himalayas. Without US backing there was much doubt whether the GMD regime would have survived the final three years of the war. Still, Chiang had reason to deplore Allied strategy with regard to China. Of US assistance to its allies, the portion that came to the GMD averaged around one percent up to 1945. The reason involved not only the difficulties of transport. The Allies had also decided on a Europe First strategy. Their main resources would initially be used in the war against Germany, and only be employed against Japan after victory in Europe. Chiang, understandably, deplored this strategy, as he did much of the military advice he got from his chief US adviser, General Joseph Stilwell. A curmudgeonly Yankee who disdained the Chinese war effort, Stilwell was about as much of a mismatch for the leading GMD generals as could be imagined. They accused him of holding back on supplies and US troops while promoting useless offensives. He accused them of corruption, waste, and incompetence. By 1944 Stilwell was in direct conflict with Chiang, whom he referred to as the Peanut. After a particularly brazen encounter the US general doggereled:

I have waited long for vengeance,
At last I've had my chance.
I've looked the Peanut in the eye
And kicked him in the pants.[12]

But the conflict between Chiang and Stilwell should not overshadow the close cooperation that developed between Chinese and US forces during the final years of World War II. The Americans trained and equipped Chiang's best troops, his intelligence services, and his administrators. In spite of his general dislike of American society and culture, Chiang knew in which direction world power was turning. And he saw great opportunities for China in it.

The main benefit China got from its first US alliance was its increase in international standing. At the Allied war summit in Cairo in November 1943, Chiang sat down at the table with the US president and the British prime minister as an equal, though he was kept away from their deliberations on Europe and the Soviet Union. He also got promises of continued US assistance for China after the war and a permanent alliance with the world's leading power. According to the State Department's offical records, "President Roosevelt proposed that, after the war, China and the United States should effect certain arrangements under which the two countries could come to each other's assistance in the event of foreign aggression and that the United States should maintain adequate military forces on various bases in the Pacific in order that it could effectively share the responsibility of preventing aggression."[13] In need of Chinese help to win the Pacific war, Roosevelt gave Chiang's

China status as one of the Big Four allies, with special influence over the occupation of Japan and the future of Korea and Southeast Asia. Well before the Cairo conference, in January 1943, the United States and Britain had relinquished their extraterritorial rights in China. The GMD proudly declared that they had returned China to its proper status: "We, the Chinese nation, after fifty years of sanguinary revolutions and five and a half years of sacrifice in the War of Resistance, have finally transformed the history of a hundred years of the Unequal Treaties of sorrow into a glorious record of the termination of the Unequal Treaties."[14]

A NY SOCIETY PUT UNDER the stress of massive warfare will suffer, not just at the time but for years to come. China was no exception. Everywhere the Japanese armies went, Chinese civilians suffered, through war-induced atrocities, starvation, or the humiliation of foreign control. But those who were drawn through the meat grinder of the defending power, the Guomindang, suffered too. It is likely that more GMD soldiers died from disease and starvation during the war than the number of those who fell on the battlefield. As the GMD armies ran out of supplies, they confiscated the scarce goods and produce of the peasants. And as the war wore on, more and more peasant communities in China cared less who was in control than how hunger and killing could be avoided in their villages. In many areas the Japanese were simply considered one outside power among many, and the population's anger was sometimes more intense at the behavior of Chinese troops than against the Japanese.

In economic terms, the war against Japan was a disaster for China. A significant part of what had been constructed in the first part of the twentieth century was destroyed: communications, industry, irrigation. It is often said that regions that depend on basic agricultural production suffer less during wartime than more complex economies, but this was not true for China in the mid-twentieth century. The war with Japan came as a climax of a century of rural deprivation, in which peasant room for survival had become increasingly narrow. Trade, which had always played a key role in the Chinese agricultural economy was impeded, and in some areas stopped. Access to fertilizers and water was limited. Henan province went through a large-scale famine in 1942–1943, in which drought and military procurements combined to kill off two to three million people and make another three million homeless. While peasants in the province starved, Chinese armies continued to requisition grain and conscript laborers. As the American journalist Theodore White described it,

> There were corpses on the road. A girl of no more than seventeen, slim and pretty, lay on the damp earth, her lips blue with death; her eyes were open and the rain fell on them. People chipped at bark, pounded it by the roadside for food; vendors sold leaves at a dollar a bundle. A dog digging at a mound was exposing a human body. Ghostlike men were skimming the stagnant pools to eat the green slime of the waters.[15]

The war made between 60 and 90 million Chinese into refugees. Some went to the cities to survive, creating new urban environments, both in the occupied zones and in GMD territory. Crime and exploitation thrived, and life for refugees and city dwellers alike became chaos.[16] Even those who tried to work with the authorities were stifled by what they saw as unreasonable demands by the state and by uncertainties about the future. Choices that were made today could be utterly nonsensical tomorrow, and behavior that was lauded in society one morning could bring about the death penalty by the following afternoon. For the bloated and terrorized cities, wartime was not so much about collaboration or resistance as it was about survival or death, or at least about possessions or penury. Abhorring the Japanese and feeling abandoned by the GMD government, most urban Chinese, rich and poor, exited the war disillusioned and downcast.

Despite its overall failure to deliver for the population, the GMD did succeed at increasing production and at organizing a sometimes unwilling populace for resistance. The government's problem was of course that two-thirds of production and almost all of its income went to fight the war. Like governments elsewhere, it attempted to compensate for this permanent crisis by becoming more centralized and efficient (which often meant brutal). It also benefited from the use of experts who returned to China for patriotic reasons and who mostly recommended increased state control. Some of the methods that the Communists later used to rule China were first tested out by the GMD during the war against Japan. Production quotas, price controls, and militarization of the population were cherished aims of the wartime GMD leaders (though most intended to relax these corporative arrangements after the war). But in spite of all of the regime's calls for unity and sacrifice, its biggest problem was handling its own finances. It was deprived of almost all of its prewar tax base, which was located in the productive and relatively prosperous eastern coastal regions, areas largely controlled by the Japanese. And so the GMD never achieved any kind of fiscal stability during the war. New taxes, especially the new land tax in kind from 1942 on, were seen as unfair and an attempt to shift the burden onto the peasantry in the government-held zones.

The war against Japan both made and unmade China.[17] On the one hand, it furthered ideas about centralization, effectivization, and a modern state that were to come to fruition in the late twentieth century, long after the war ended and under a new Communist government. On the other hand, it brought almost limitless destruction and dislocation to many parts of China, and influenced peoples' lives in ways that underlined abandonment and brutalization. For those who lived through it, there is little doubt that the war was more about destruction and loss than about renewal and modernization. It took China's suffering to a new level and made it, in the eyes of the Chinese, the country that the rest of the world had scorned and abandoned.

WITHIN CHINA, THE CCP turned out to be one of the main beneficiaries of the war. The Japanese threat helped the Communists survive the onslaught by the GMD. The war made it possible for the party to mobilize in its new bases in the northwest and behind the overextended Japanese lines, where the GMD state had collapsed. When the war began, the CCP was a small group, but in 1945—with 1.2 million members and 900,000 men and women under arms—it was a force to be reckoned with. Even more important than its numerical expansion, though, was the ability the party had gained to work with all segments of Chinese society through a system of centralized decision making. The war had made it possible for Mao Zedong and the group who had promoted his leadership to achieve two very different goals at the same time: Make all party members obey a secret and cloistered Mao-centered inner organization but present a moderate and cooperative outward image. It was a stunning transformation that would help the party gain from the war and succeed in Chinese politics after the war was over.

The CCP had been advocating a united front against Japan, but immediately after the war started, it was less than clear how the party should behave. The Comintern wanted the party to put military pressure on the Japanese, but Mao resisted appeals for large-scale warfare against the enemy, whether they came from Stalin or from Chiang. Instead, he emphasized guerrilla tactics, meaning—most often—a clandestine presence behind Japanese lines aimed at building the CCP as a party. From 1939 to 1945, the CCP mainly fought either to preserve its own territory or to avenge Japanese atrocities against the civilian population in rear areas where the Communists operated politically. The CCP killed many more Chinese—whether GMD, collaborators, or just local forces who got in the way—than Japanese. But Mao needed to maintain good relations with Moscow, so in late 1940 he embarked on the Hundred Regiments Campaign. It was a response not just to Stalin's repeated calls for action but also urging from his own CCP officers. The Hundred Regiments Campaign was a set of offensives against the Japanese in northern China, but it was poorly coordinated, and the results were near disastrous for the Communists. Four times as many CCP soldiers were killed as those from the imperial army. And after it was over, the Japanese took a terrible revenge on the local population.

By 1941 Mao's forces were fighting something close to a civil war against the GMD. The worst battles were in Anhui province, where Chiang was determined to stop CCP expansion and force the party to submit to his authority. But government victories were not solid enough to deter the Communists and took much-needed GMD forces away from the battles with the Japanese. Throughout the rest of the war, Mao stuck rhetorically to the Comintern's policies, calling for a continued united front and for a new coalition government, while concentrating on expanding CCP positions. Georgi Dimitrov, the Comintern head, told Mao in December 1943 that he considered the CCP policy "to wind down the struggle against China's foreign occupiers, along with the evident departure from a united national front policy" to be "politically mistaken," but Mao stuck with his policy of emphasizing the internal over the external and it brought great returns.[18]

While the united front policy toward the GMD was neglected, Mao put in place another form of united front within the areas controlled by the CCP. Instead of executing landlords and businessmen, dividing up land and confiscating savings, as had been done before, the Communists now proclaimed what they themselves called a moderate policy of rent reduction, collaborative farming, price caps, and credit schemes. In the name of national resistance, the CCP had a policy for everyone: peasants (who got a guarantee against starvation), landlords (who got money and stable prices), company owners (who got predictable taxes and property guarantees), and workers (who got a minimum wage). Instead of Marx and Lenin, the party began talking about a "reasonable tax burden." In the western Shandong borderlands, salt-producing locals had made use of the wartime receding of the state to avoid much-resented taxes and thereby achieve prosperity. In that region, the CCP became very popular with its promise of protecting local welfare and tax reduction. In other parts of the country, the party recruited members and soldiers, promising to maintain the stability that the CCP had brought to the area and to punish collaborators.[19] The war, in other words, provided a near perfect foil for the Communists to spread their influence.

While they built up the party, Mao and his followers carried out ruthless inner-party campaigns to destroy their old Communist rivals. And they worked to gain the undivided and unquestioning loyalty of those who had joined the party since 1937. These campaigns, known as *zheng feng* or rectification, criticized, arrested, and even executed those who would not accept the party's new tactics and the recentering of party literature and programs on Mao and his understanding of the CCP's historical mission. Instead of the internationalist Marxism that the party was born of, Mao and his supporters brought in writings that underlined the party's role as the redeemer of the Chinese people after a hundred years of denigration and weakness. Instead of Communist materialism, the CCP began preaching to anyone who cared to listen that they could achieve liberation by the force of will. China, Mao told his inner-party audience, was not weak and poor. It was strong, because the CCP brought it the revolutionary spirit that would set it free.

WHILE THE CCP UNITED, the GMD seemed to fragment. Many leaders questioned Chiang's authority. Wang Jingwei was one such. He had been one of Sun Yat-sen's closest associates and a key founder of Chinese nationalism. Jailed by the Qing authorities in 1910, he became a hero on his release after the 1911 revolution, and later served several times as prime minister during the republic. A left-winger within the Guomindang—much in the spirit of Sun himself—Wang stood for cooperation with the CCP and fervent anti-imperialism, even after Chiang Kai-shek had attacked the Communists in 1927. As a result, Wang became Chiang's main rival within the party, and the personal relationship between the two leaders went from bad to worse. In 1937, Wang at first joined the government in its flight to Sichuan, but upset many of his colleagues by insisting that Western imperialist powers were greater threats to China in the long run than Japan, which, after all, was a fellow Asian nation. By 1939, Wang was in Hanoi, where, after Chiang's agents had tried to kill him, he fully threw in his lot with the Japanese. In March 1940 he became head of what he called a reorganized Guomindang regime at Nanjing. In November, Wang signed a peace treay with Japan which recognized Manzhouguo and gave the Japanese special rights over the territory it claimed to control. In reality, Wang's regime was entirely dependent on Tokyo's support for the five years it existed.

But for all his reputation as a traitor, Wang Jingwei was no simple stooge of the Japanese. His political journey in the 1930s had taken him from a vague socialism to a position that emphasized Asian racial values and cooperation against the dominant Western powers. Wang believed that China was wasting its strength fighting Japan. Instead it should join in the Greater East Asian Co-Prosperity Sphere that Tokyo was about to create and build its power in Japan's image. In January 1943 Wang's regime declared war on the Allies, and it remained a quarrelsome ally of the Japanese empire until its capitulation in August 1945. But although the collaborationists managed to recruit soldiers to fight alongside the Japanese, there were never any doubts about who were calling the shots. Wang's legitimacy, even within his own regime, was entirely built on his ability to get the Japanese to do less harm in China than they otherwise would have done. The "reorganized" Guomindang were generally seen as traitors, but as traitors who could serve a useful purpose for some.

For most Chinese during the war years, the goal was survival, pure and simple. They needed an outcome for themselves and their families, and to avoid being harmed by the armies they encountered. In urban China, mostly occupied by Japan, this often meant finding some modus vivendi with the occupiers. Most tried to avoid Wang Jingwei's regime, not just because it was considered traitorous but also because it was considered inefficient. If one needed to deal with the new regime, many thought, better deal directly with the Japanese. Of course, all-out collaboration was as difficult in Japanese-occupied China as it was in German-occupied Europe. A central part of the occupiers' ideology was their own national or ethnic superiority, and even those who wanted to take over Japanese ideals could not become Japanese. In parts of China, especially those that had suffered the most during the social and political turbulence in the early part of the century, the desire to work with the newly arrived power was great. This was especially true among the elites, who saw the Japanese as a protection against unruly peasants and workers. But even those who tried to find an ideological position that allowed collaboration were often put off by Japanese brutality and fiats. As in German-occupied eastern Europe—Lithuania, Poland, Ukraine—to collaborate was not always easy or safe.

In the cities, the occupiers immediately tried to find ways of getting industrial production going again after the fighting ended. At first, the Japanese confiscated Chinese enterprises at will, running them through army units or Japanese business conglomerates, the *zaibatsu*. But output still dropped 50 percent from prewar levels, and Tokyo's dreams of using China's industrial capacity to make their armies in China self-sufficient and to help supply Japanese forces elsewhere turned out to be a chimera.[20] Overall output was down, probably as a result of supply difficulties and Chinese workers being less than enthusiastic. But Japanese production in China had also fallen from prewar levels. Before the war, half of all textile mills in Shanghai were Japanese-owned but many had been destroyed in the fighting. The *zaibatsu* were reluctant to invest in China; many found that they could not make a profit. As with all occupiers, the fall-back position was a mix of the carrot and the stick. Chinese owners were allowed to get their factories back if they would collaborate with the war effort. Many did. But in strategic areas of production—a term that widened and widened as the war went on—the Japanese army instituted direct control through corporatist companies that produced directly for the war. Neither approach was successful. The imperial army had confiscated most ships and trains for the war effort, so the market had little chance to work. And price setting did not stimulate production. All the way up to 1945, Japan faced the classic occupation dilemma: The occupiers wanted to increase production. Their collaborators wanted managers that were politically beholden to them. And the workers resented unskilled and collaborationist managers as well as the occupation itself. It was not a scenario for success.

In the countryside there were not many more options available than in the cities. Local elites often chose to collaborate, but their return for doing so was minimal. They resented the Wang Jingwei regime and got little from it. They sought stability, but the Japanese either could not or would not provide it. The situation in one county is illustrative. Neihuang in northern Henan province had suffered from various civil wars prior to the 1930s. But in the years before the Japanese attack, the GMD had gradually asserted control against bandits, Communists, and secret societies. When the Japanese approached in 1937, local GMD leaders fled south. Prisoners broke out of jail and public storage facilities were raided. Bandit groups begin to operate openly. On the very day in March 1938 that the imperial army prepared to take control of the county, two squads of bandits clashed near the Japanese advance. The invaders, believing they were coming under attack from a nearby village, arrested all the men they could find, stripped them naked, and put them in a house, which they torched with kerosene. Anyone trying to escape was shot. Eighty villagers died. Throughout the war, civilians in the county were preyed on by criminals, occupiers, and wannabe authorities. The GMD could offer no protection. No wonder that villagers in the region were eager to accept security from the CCP when it started to operate in the county in 1944.[21]

THE JAPANESE ARMY MADE little progress in 1942–1943. Many observers expected the China front to be relatively uneventful for the remainder of the war. But the Japanese High Command did not plan for status quo. It knew that if Japan should have any chance of winning the war, it would have to knock the GMD out of the fighting first. In 1944 it started the largest offensive yet on the Asian mainland, intending to break Chinese resistance and establish direct land links between north China and Southeast Asia. The Japanese planners almost succeeded. By early 1945 the GMD regime was in dire straits and may not have survived the war in spite of the Allied victories in the Pacific and Southeast Asia if it had not been for Japan's sudden capitulation.

As so often happened during the war, Japanese planners could not agree on what was the most important objective of what they called Operation Ichigo (Number One). Some emphasized supply lines, others destroying the GMD. As the offensive developed, they came much closer to the second objective than the first. The GMD regime in Chongqing was suffering from an acute economic and social crisis in 1944 that made determined resistance difficult. The government's attempts at collecting new taxes had mostly failed, leaving much ill will among the population. Supplies of all kinds were running out, and famine had begun in parts of GMD-held territory. Under such circumstances it is only natural that resistance against further conscription increased. Half of all desertions and anticonscription revolts happened in the last year of the war. The GMD's proudest achievement, the alliance with the United States, meant little to most people. Why, many were asking, did the United States not do more to help China? If Washington could send substantial forces of its own to guard Brazil against an Axis invasion, why could it not send a single regular soldier to fight in China? And the GMD's response to its funding crisis, to print more money, led to runaway inflation that impoverished almost everyone, including its own supporters. The combination of all these ills forced active support for the government to its lowest point in the war just when it needed it most.

Operation Ichigo began in April 1944. In less than a month it had driven the GMD's forces out of Henan province. It had also conquered the capital of Hunan, Changsha, where the Chinese had been resisting since 1939. The Japanese forces then drove south into Guangxi province, capturing Guilin in November and began moving toward the GMD's stronghold in Sichuan from the south and east. Ichigo's successes were in part due to poor planning by Chiang's US advisers. But it also exposed how the GMD's economic and political weakness was eroding its ability to resist. Even though the Japanese began running out of steam in the spring of 1945, when they had to redeploy their forces to the near Pacific, the GMD's counteroffensives were largely ineffective. Chiang was still seen as a hero by most Chinese, but his party's capacity to govern had taken a serious drubbing in the latter stage of the war.

Unlike the GMD, the CCP could make use of the war to expand. When Ichigo drove the GMD out of key parts of central China, the Communists could begin to build their own political institutions behind the overextended Japanese lines. They could also, where needed, attack the decimated government forces, as they did in the Shandong-Jiangsu border area. To their surprise, the CCP could also begin their first contacts with the Americans. Fed up with Chiang's cautious strategy, Washington attempted to mobilize other power holders, including the Communists, against Japan. Mao had been told by the Soviets that Stalin expected the Soviet-American alliance to continue after the war had ended, and the CCP chairman interpreted the US overtures as part of this new international framework. CCP contacts with the Americans would help push Chiang and other anti-Communists toward compromise in postwar China. CCP hopes were high when President Roosevelt's representative to China, the vain and utterly naïve Oklahoma lawyer Patrick Hurley, during a high-spirited visit with the Communists, put his name to a demand for a coalition government in China that Mao himself had written. Hurley also promised US supplies for the CCP, in preparation, Mao thought, for American landings on the coast.[22]

But it was not Hurley's visit to what he called "Indian territory" that harmed the standing of the GMD most. Nor was it the party's failure to offer effective government during wartime. It was rather the feeling that spread, especially among China's educated classes, that the international system that the GMD so desperately wanted to join had little to offer China. China's involvement with capitalism on a global scale had not been a happy one, and many people longed for a new economic strategy after the war that would benefit the Chinese people. Like war-weary peoples everywhere, the Chinese in 1945 wanted peace and a solution to problems at home. If Chiang Kai-shek was able to deliver that, people would follow him. If not, they would start looking for an alternative.

IN FEBRUARY 1945, Roosevelt, Churchill, and Stalin met at Yalta to map out the postwar future. Unlike in Cairo in 1943, Chiang was not invited and he was furious at the snub. He resented that China was being, yet again, used as a bargaining chip among great powers. Still, he found the outcome of Yalta useful. The Generalissimo recognized his regime's military weakness and feared that a Soviet entry into the war against Japan could have disastrous consequences for China's unity. Therefore he wanted the United States to regulate the Soviet role in East Asia, and US guarantees concerning Soviet behavior were what the secret Yalta protocol gave him. Chiang also wanted the war to end soon and believed, like Roosevelt, that a Soviet attack on Japan was the only way of effecting this. Chiang's condemnation of Yalta—similar to that of Charles de Gaulle, who also had not been invited—was therefore more about form than content. He wanted a deal with the Soviets, and he wanted it fast, but he needed the Americans to work out the framework.

The 11 February 1945 secret Yalta text on Japan, agreed to after Stalin had got much of what he wanted on Europe, speaks for itself:

> The leaders of the three great powers—the Soviet Union, the United States of America and Great Britain—have agreed that in two or

three months after Germany has surrendered and the war in Europe is terminated, the Soviet Union shall enter into war against Japan on the side of the Allies on condition that: The status quo in Outer Mongolia (the Mongolian People's Republic) shall be preserved. . . . The commercial port of Dairen [Dalian] shall be internationalized, the pre-eminent interests of the Soviet Union in this port being safeguarded, and the lease of Port Arthur as a naval base of the U.S.S.R. restored; the Chinese-Eastern Railroad and the South Manchurian Railroad, which provide an outlet to Dairen, shall be jointly operated by the establishment of a joint Soviet-Chinese company, it being understood that the pre-eminent interests of the Soviet Union shall be safeguarded and that China shall retain sovereignty in Manchuria. . . . It is understood that the agreement concerning Outer Mongolia and the ports and railroads referred to above will require concurrence of Generalissimo Chiang Kai-shek. The President will take measures in order to maintain this concurrence on advice from Marshal Stalin. The heads of the three great powers have agreed that these claims of the Soviet Union shall be unquestionably fulfilled after Japan has been defeated. For its part, the Soviet Union expresses its readiness to conclude with the National Government of China a pact of friendship and alliance between the U.S.S.R. and China in order to render assistance to China with its armed forces for the purpose of liberating China from the Japanese yoke.

After Germany surrendered in May 1945, the race was on for who would win the peace in East Asia. GMD representatives were in Moscow negotiating with the Soviets, but the talks seemed to be going nowhere. The United States was increasingly concerned over tensions with the Soviets in Europe, and Chiang tried to use this anxiety to win US support for only minimal concessions to Stalin. Meanwhile, the Soviet dictator's negotiators pushed for the widest possible control of postwar Manchuria. Unless they got their way, Chiang was told, the Soviets could easily choose to work with the CCP and/or postpone their offensive against Japan.

On 6 August the United States dropped an atomic bomb on Hiroshima, killing 80,000 people. Three days later it used another nuclear weapon against Nagasaki, killing 60,000. The same day the Soviet Union attacked Japanese forces in Manchuria. Stalin could not wait any longer if he were to get his slice of the Japanese empire. Chiang's negotiators signed a treaty with the Soviet Union giving Stalin what he had been promised at Yalta, but getting a promise that Moscow would cooperate only with the Chinese government. Japan capitulated unconditionally the following day, though Stalin, for good measure, continued Soviet operations for another two weeks, making sure that his troops occupied as much territory as possible.

Within a month in mid-1945, the international situation in East Asia had been turned upside down. Japan has ceased to exist as an independent power, though there were still 2.3 million Japanese soldiers and close to 1.5 million civilians in China, including Manzhouguo and Taiwan, after capitulation. The Soviet Union occupied Manchuria and the northern part of Korea, where more than 700,000 Red Army troops were stationed. The collaborationist regimes had collapsed. All over China, GMD forces were preparing to take over, helped by their US allies. The CCP seemed to have little access to the spoils of war. Though his party was exhausted and his army on its knees, Chiang was triumphant. He was now ready to build the unified and strong central state that had eluded him for twenty years. But first he had to repatriate the Japanese and deal with those Chinese he saw as traitors.

Though under strong pressure to exert draconian revenge, the Generalissimo wanted to be as lenient as possible with former enemies willing to accept the new GMD state. Around 25,000 collaborators were put on trial, less than 0.005 percent of the population. It is a remarkably small number if one thinks of the parallel figures for France (close to one percent) or Norway (more than three percent), both of which had seen much less warfare than China. Although much dislocation came out of confiscations and fines against industrialists and businessmen who had worked with the Japanese in the occupied cities—imposed, some people thought, as much in order to line the pockets of returning

GMD officials as for an official purposes, the sentences passed on leading collaborators were mild. Even the second in command of the Wang Jingwei regime, Zhou Fohai, was spared the death sentence (Wang himself had died in 1944). The collaborationist leaders among minorities mostly survived. Prince Demchugdongrub, the head of the much-feared Japanese-supported separatist regime in Inner Mongolia, lived out his life as a curator in a history museum in Hohhot. Puyi, the Manzhouguo emperor, and the last emperor of the Qing dynasty, worked as a gardener in Beijing after his release from Soviet captivity. Unless they much later became part of the Communists' show trials, top pro-Japanese traitors in China stood a better chance of survival than World War II collaborationists anywhere else.

W HEN CHINA'S WAR OF RESISTANCE against Japan ended, the international situation had already been transformed. Not only Japan, but also Britain, France, and Germany were gone as great powers in East Asia. The Soviet Union remained, now stronger than ever. And the United States had become the other main power, in control of Japan and with strategic interests in Southeast Asia, both in terms of resources and shipping routes. All Chinese political groups had to take this new international landscape into consideration when they made up their minds about the policies to pursue. As leaders everywhere else, those in China were uncertain whether some form of cooperaton between the United States and the USSR would continue after the war, or whether there would be conflict. The answer to this question, they knew, would determine how advantage could be had in foreign affairs.

Inside China, Chiang Kai-shek's prestige was at an all-time high. While many people resented the way the Guomindang had conducted the war—the unnecessary losses, the economic mismanagement, the lack of democracy—little of this clung to the Generalissimo himself. Chiang was seen, across the country, as a genuine national hero, who had known when to fight the war and had had the courage to persist against all odds. Of course Chiang's and China's international standing furthered his domestic prestige. The American president, Harry Truman, had accepted China as a great power, and given it one of the five permanent seats on the United Nations Security Council. The Soviet leader, Joseph Stalin, had formally recognized Chiang's regime as China's central government and publicly called on all other parties—including the Chinese Communists—to cooperate with it. In 1945, China seemed poised to regain its position as the main country in the region, and Chiang seemed set to create the fully unified China that he, and so many other Chinese, had dreamed about since their childhood. Nationalism, defiance, and international cooperation had made China strong, Chiang told his countrymen, and there were bright times ahead.

"It is my sincere belief," the Generalissimo said in his victory message, echoing the Confucian values that were so close to his heart, "that all men on earth—wherever they live, in the East or the West, and whatever the color of their skin may be—will some day be linked together in close fellowship like members of one family. World war is indivisible and world peace, too, is indivisible. It has encouraged international understanding and mutual trust which will serve as a powerful barrier against future wars."[23]

CHAPTER 8

COMMUNISM

CHINESE COMMUNISM WAS BORN in the fear of the future that many Chinese intellectuals felt around the time of the May Fourth Movement in 1919. If their country was to be rescued, they would need a model that could make China rich and strong, an example among nations, not a pariah. Those who lived through the May Fourth Movement and became Communists found such a model in the Soviet Union. To them, and they were a minority, Lenin and the Soviets had already constructed a new kind of country out of the ruins of the Russian empire, a new Soviet state that combined advanced modernity with social justice. To young Chinese like Mao Zedong, Soviet Communism was having your cake and eating it: The country, which had been an empire, remained, but reborn as a new state with equality and justice for all. The Confucian idea of rectitude married the modernity of organizational power and technology that the Soviets provided, a modernity that was even more advanced than that of the imperialist powers, which had humiliated China in the past. It was, for both means and purposes, a perfect instrument for those who came to believe in it.

It cannot be emphasized enough that what inspired the first Chinese Communists was Leninism rather than Marxism. It was the organizational ideals of the Soviet revolution rather than Marx's predictions about world capitalism that fired their minds. Marxism in China was always the preoccupation of a minority on the Left, rather than a faith that imbued the whole party. What preoccupied the generation that founded the party and their immediate successors—all the way up to the late 1980s and Deng Xiaoping—was building an organization and a state that would employ the tools that Lenin and Stalin had used to create a modern, powerful Soviet Union: party power, hierarchy, militarization, and strict regulation of the lives of party members and all citizens. Marxism was understood to mean the science of society that ensured that the Communists, not just in China but worldwide, were on the right side of history: Eventually all the world would move toward socialism. But the detailed understanding of capitalist modernity that Marx had attempted was not at the center of Chinese Communism. *Das Kapital*, Marx's main work, had not been fully translated into Chinese before the outbreak of the Sino-Japanese War in 1937.[1]

Part of the reason why Marxism was only of peripheral use to the Chinese Communists was that their party was forged in war. There was almost no time to stop fighting and study texts. After 1928, when Chiang Kai-shek nearly succeeded in wiping out the CCP, the remnants of the party took to the hills, only to have to fight successive expeditions that Chiang launched against them. Even though the party leadership stayed in contact with Moscow and the Comintern, the priority was always survival and reorganization, as the CCP was driven further and further toward the edges of China. The rise of Mao Zedong was, somewhat grudgingly, sanctioned by Moscow, but as recognition of the fact that his organizational genius had rescued the party from oblivion rather than his skills as a theoretician. There is no evidence that Mao ever seriously studied Marx beyond the basic texts that were translated into Chinese in his youth. Mao, and the leadership that he formed in the late 1930s, were warriors, first and foremost, survival artists who learned to extricate themselves from the most precarious of military crises.

The basic problem for the CCP before World War II was in numbers. At its first peak in 1928 the party had had around 40,000 members, a drop in the ocean of the Chinese population. By 1937, after its Long

March to the north, it had around the same number, although with another 40,000 nonmember soldiers and civilians working alongside it. Without a breakthrough in recruitment and territory, the party would never be able to challenge the Guomindang for power in China. That breakthrough, as we have seen, came with the Japanese attack on China in 1937. With GMD power knocked out in most of the country, and with Mao's decision (with Comintern blessing) to move the party's public profile toward the political center and emphasize the defense of the nation, CCP membership skyrocketed. In 1938 it had more than 200,000 members. By 1945 it had 1.2 million. It was ready to do battle with its domestic and foreign enemies.

As we have seen, the CCP's stance of moderation and its appeal to the nation were only one side of its wartime development. The other was an institutionalization and internalization of a specific line of thinking that later was called Maoism and Mao Zedong Thought. During harsh wartime conditions, new recruits to the party and senior members both had to go through intense ideological training in a political curriculum designed by the Chairman himself. The key parts of it were a mixture of the writings of Lenin, Stalin, and Mao, and the study of a Mao-centered version of the CCP's history. Through a tough rectification campaign, in which the new party leadership tried to stamp out all forms of independent thinking, Mao's canon and the Chairman himself increasingly took center stage. It became what historians, drawing on Western theology, have called a logocentric movement with strong sectarian and charismatic traits.[2] Mao's emphasis on self-sufficiency, courage, sacrifice, and the power of the human will replace some of the elements of Marxism in the CCP of the 1940s. Liu Shaoqi, Mao's trusted lieutenant, summed it up at the Seventh Party Congress in 1945, the first one in more than seventeen years: "Mao is not only the greatest revolutionary and statesman in Chinese history, but also the greatest theoretician in Chinese history." Ironically, as the party's public image became more moderate and popular, its internal line became increasingly esoteric and utopian, with immense consequences for China's relations to the rest of the world.

THE END OF THE WAR against Japan came suddenly in August 1945, with the US nuclear attacks of Hiroshima and Nagasaki and the Soviet entry into the war. At the beginning of the month the Japanese imperial army was advancing toward Chongqing, the GMD wartime capital in western Sichuan province, and the CCP, despite its political operations behind enemy lines, found it difficult to fulfill its strategic aims of moving into Manchuria and central China. At the end of August the situation was turned almost entirely upside down. Japan had capitulated. With US aid, Chiang Kai-shek's forces were moving fast to take over the cities, the railway lines, and the main towns and junctions in all parts of the country that had been in Japanese hands. US commanders instructed all Japanese forces to hold their positions until Chiang's representatives arrived. In Moscow, the GMD government had struck a deal with the Soviets that would deliver Manchuria into Chiang's hands in return for economic and military base concessions to the USSR. The Chinese Communists had been completely shut out of the peace settlement and were being pushed both by Moscow and by Washington to reach a negotiated settlement with the GMD.

August 1945 was probably the darkest moment in Mao Zedong's political life. All of the visions he had drawn up at the party's Seventh Congress had come to nothing. Mao had expected a continued expansion of CCP power, which would have enabled the Communists in the postwar era to achieve autonomy for the territory they controlled and the ability to compete politically with the GMD elsewhere. Instead he had to force the party to accept negotiating with the GMD from a position of weakness and to make concessions to Chiang just to avoid being attacked by GMD troops. The much-vaunted postwar era of Communist power was fast shrinking into about as much influence as the party had held in 1937, and with far fewer avenues of expansion. Mao believed that it was the international situation that was responsible for his setback and regretted the lack of emphasis the party had put on understanding international affairs. He saw the United States as responsible for his defeat. But he also viewed Stalin's role with skepticism and doubt.

Chiang Kai-shek had been enormously successful with his international alliances but always disliked his allies' attempts at influencing Chinese politics. He had no use for the mediation mission, led by former US chief of staff, General George C. Marshall, that President Harry Truman sent to China in December 1945. In spite of Marshall's best efforts, Chiang continued to put military pressure on the CCP whenever the negotiations between them were stalling. As the price of peace, the GMD wanted the full incorporation of all CCP forces into the government army and access for government officials to all CCP-held areas. When the Soviets tried to prolong their occupation of Manchuria in order to wrest further economic concessions from the GMD, Chiang used his alliance with the United States to pile diplomatic pressure on Moscow. Despite Marshall's genuine attempts at mediation, it was clear to Chiang that as Soviet-American tension increased elsewhere in the world, Washington saw his government as a key ally.

The summer of 1946, as the world was sliding toward a Soviet-American Cold War, was the time of decision in China. Under pressure from both the United States and Britain, Stalin had ordered a full Soviet withdrawal from Manchuria in late spring, arming CCP forces while leaving. With the Soviet troops gone and with Stalin no longer insisting on negotiations with the GMD, Mao ordered his troops to resist the government's advance into Manchuria and to fight for "every inch of territory." The CCP hoped that the Soviets would help supply and train the party's military forces so that they could hold their own against the numerically and technically superior GMD troops. But first and foremost, they hoped that the Communist military could survive the initial onslaught of the government army, prepared, equipped, and assisted by the United States.

THE CHINESE CIVIL WAR, which lasted from mid-1946 to the beginning of 1950, defined China's foreign relations for more than a decade. It cemented the alliance between the Chinese Communists and Soviet Union, an alliance in which Moscow increasingly became not only the CCP's main international supporter but also its concrete model for how a Communist state could be built. The war revealed to the United States the weakness of its position in China, in spite of all the assistance it had provided to the country and its government. And the war's outcome helped provoke an anti-Communist backlash inside the United States that would last for half a generation. But most importantly the civil war showed the weakness of the Chinese body politic and the desperate search of most ordinary Chinese for some order and stability in their lives, which they believed that only a strong, unified, and modern state could provide.

The military development of the war, and its international implications, are easy to present. In the beginning, in 1946 and 1947, the GMD went on the offensive, pushing the CCP out of almost all of its territory south of the Great Wall, including the Communist wartime capital Yan'an, which fell in March 1947. The CCP was battered, but survived. And then began an astonishing turnaround. In late 1947 the Communist armies, now called the Chinese People's Liberation Army (PLA), counterattacked in Manchuria and began reorganizing in north China. By autumn 1948, the GMD had lost Manchuria as well as its own best armies. In the spring of 1949 the PLA crossed the Yangzi river. Beijing fell in January, the capital, Nanjing, in April, and Shanghai in May. Guangzhou and the south were conquered by October. By December 1949 the GMD was defeated in Sichuan and kept fighting on the mainland only in limited zones in the far west and south. Xinjiang was conquered, with Soviet assistance, by April 1950. In October 1951 the PLA entered the Tibetan capital, Lhasa, and all of former Qing China—except Outer Mongolia, which had its own socialist regime, and Taiwan, where Chiang Kai-shek prepared his last stand—was in Communist hands.

Why did the Communists win the civil war, and what role did China's international affairs play in their victory? The Communists won because they made fewer military mistakes than the government, and because Chiang Kai-shek—in his search for a powerful, centralized post-war state—antagonized too many interest groups in the country. As a party, the GMD was weakened by the drubbing it had got during the war against Japan. Meanwhile, the Communists became masters of telling different groups of Chinese exactly what they wanted to hear and of cloaking themselves in Chinese nationalism. Only they themselves, they insisted, were the bearers of the fate of the nation. Chiang was lampooned as a stooge of imperialism. Internationally, the United States could have postponed GMD China's collapse by offering more aid, but they could not have prevented it. The gradual increase in Soviet assistance enabled the CCP to go on the offensive, but it did not determine the outcome of the civil war. General Marshall summed it up well in 1947 when he told the Chinese ambassador that Chiang "is faced with a unique problem of logistics. He is losing about 40 percent of his supplies to the enemy. If the percentage should reach 50 percent he will have to decide whether it is wise to supply his own troops."[3] While the United States gave the GMD government more than $1.9 billion in assistance between 1945 and 1950, equaling more than $40 billion in today's money, it could neither control its policies nor determine China's political trajectory.

On 1 October 1949, at Tian'anmen Square in Beijing, in his heavy Hunan accent, Mao Zedong proclaimed the establishment of the People's Republic of China. It was a cold and clear autumn day. The Chairman's voice was thin and shrill; he was ill and felt faint, and perhaps the significance of the occasion overcame him. Instead of a memorable inaugural-type speech, Mao simply listed his closest comrades and the positions they would hold in the new government. A week earlier, however, he had outlined the program for CCP rule in a speech to the People's Consultative Conference, a body with nonparty membership that the CCP kept on through Soviet insistence, even though Mao himself had wanted to get rid of it. The Chairman was triumphant: "We have defeated the reactionary GMD government backed by U.S. imperialism."

> Our work will go down in the history of mankind, demonstrating that the Chinese people, comprising one quarter of humanity, have now stood up. The Chinese have always been a great, courageous and industrious nation; it is only in modern times that they have fallen behind. And that was due entirely to oppression and exploitation by foreign imperialism and domestic reactionary governments. For over a century our forefathers never stopped waging unyielding struggles against domestic and foreign oppressors . . . now we are proclaiming the founding of the People's Republic of China. From now on our nation will belong to the community of the peace-loving and freedom-loving nations of the world and work courageously and industriously to foster its own civilization and well-being and at the same time to promote world peace and freedom. Ours will no longer be a nation subject to insult and humiliation. We have stood up.[4]

Nine weeks after setting up his new state, Mao left Beijing to meet with Stalin in Moscow. It was the Chairman's first-ever trip abroad. His delegation was well received by the Soviet leader. But Mao was horrified to find that Stalin did not plan for a comprehensive new agreement on bilateral relations with the PRC, preferring instead to work within the format of the treaty he had signed with the GMD government in 1945. Only significant pressure from the Chinese and from some of Stalin's own advisers brought the Soviet leader around. On 14 February 1950, after Mao had spent two months in Moscow and the Beijing leadership was becoming increasingly desperate, the two countries signed a Treaty of Friendship, Alliance, and Mutual Assistance, in which the Soviets pledged to defend China from attacks by "Japan and her allies" (meaning the United States) and provide military and civilian assistance. They also agreed to transfer to China, free of charge, their concessions in Manchuria obtained in 1945. In return the Chinese agreed to set up a number of joint stock companies, owned in halves by each country, on everything from food canning to aviation, to accept the independence of Outer Mongolia, and to prevent any country but the Soviet Union from operating in Manchuria and Xinjiang. Mao had got the treaty he desired, providing security and assistance. But his nationalist pride had suffered sharply in the process, as his wish to be dealt with as an equal by the Soviets had gone unfulfilled.

To the Communists, their almost miraculous victory in the civil war had confirmed their view of themselves as China's men of destiny. They had conquered the country and would now set out to cleanse it of its ills. They had a charismatic leader in Mao Zedong. The goodwill and prestige they enjoyed among most groups of Chinese at home and abroad were unlike anything enjoyed by any Chinese government after the fall of the Qing. Internationally, they had broken with Western imperialism and allied themselves with the Soviet Union, as they had always aimed to do. History was on their side, in spite of the uncertainties many of them had as to how to run a modern state. It would come together in the end, their leaders told them, as long as imperialist attacks could be avoided and the Soviet Union would continue its support.

THE CCP LEADERS, busy building their new state, could not have foreseen the trouble that would soon come from the empire's edges. Korea had been divided into a US and a Soviet occupation zone at the end of World War II, and the two parts of the country soon saw competing regimes. The new PRC had cordial, but not close, relations with the Korean Communists, who held power in the northern part of the country under Soviet tutelage. The Korean War was not a war of the new CCP regime's choosing, even though it in the end decided to fight. It was Stalin who in the spring of 1950 gave the go-ahead to the Korean Communist leader Kim Il-sung to reunify his country by force, just as Mao Zedong had done in China. The Soviets had kept the government in Beijing updated as the plans progressed, and Mao had given his blessing to the venture in May. But there were no plans for direct Chinese participation, even though Mao suspected that things might not work out quite as easily as Kim and his Soviet advisors were telling Stalin. The Soviets were aware of the CCP's hope for a period of peace for China, and Stalin may have picked the timing of the Korean War precisely as a way of testing the Chinese Communists' loyalty to him and to the Soviet Union as the leader of world Communism. In spite of the Moscow agreement, Stalin continued to see the CCP as a party of intellectuals and peasants, without the working-class component that would make it into a real Communist party.

The attack across the line that divided the two Korean regimes took place in the evening of 25 June 1950. Soldiers of the Korean Communist army rapidly moved south. With the Soviets boycotting the UN Security Council, President Truman immediately got a resolution through authorizing the use of force to support South Korea. But there was little that at first could be done to stop Kim Il-sung's offensive. By August the remaining Korean anti-Communist forces and their US advisers were hemmed into a small area around the southeastern coastal city of Pusan, with the rest of the country in Communist hands. But on 15 September, US amphibious landings at Seoul's port city of Inchon broke the Korean Communist offensive by splitting their forward divisions in two halves and then defeating them in the south before moving north into what had been the Soviet occupation zone. Pyongyang, the capital of Kim Il-sung's Democratic People's Republic of Korea (DPRK), fell to US and allied UN troops on 19 October. Mao's regime suddenly had a serious problem on its hands.

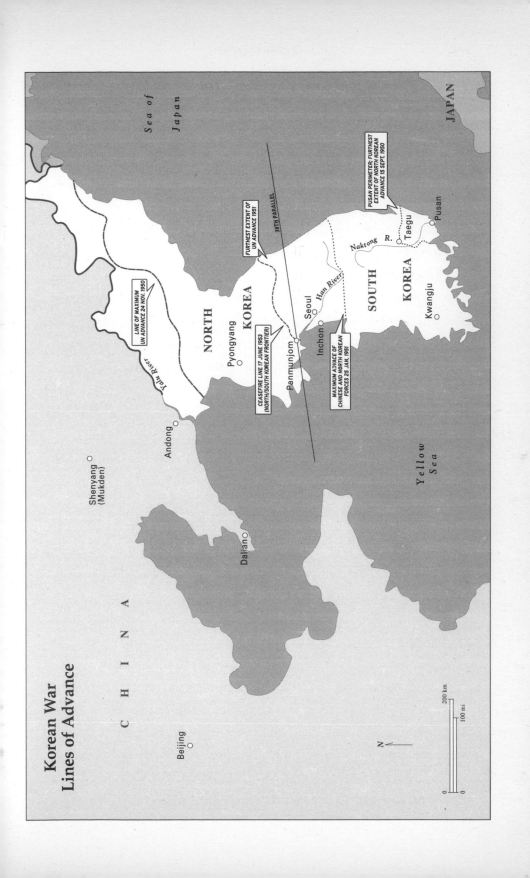

Korean War
Lines of Advance

CHINA

Beijing ○

Shenyang
(Mukden) ○

Dalian ○

Andong ○

Yalu River

Pyongyang ○

NORTH

KOREA

LINE OF MAXIMUM
UN ADVANCE 24 NOV. 1950

CEASEFIRE LINE 17 JUNE 1953
(NORTH/SOUTH KOREAN FRONTIER)

Panmunjom

FURTHEST EXTENT OF
UN ADVANCE 1951

38TH PARALLEL

Sea of
Japan

JAPAN

Pusan
Taegu

PUSAN PERIMETER: FURTHEST
EXTENT OF NORTH KOREAN
ADVANCE 15 SEPT. 1950

Naktong R.

SOUTH

KOREA

Kwangju ○

Seoul ○

Han River

Inchon ○

MAXIMUM ADVACE OF
CHINESE AND NORTH KOREAN
FORCES 25 JAN. 1951

Yellow
Sea

N

200 km

100 mi

0

Under intense pressure from the Soviets and the Korean Communists, the leadership of the CCP deliberated for more than a week about how to act. Chinese troops had already been moved to the border with Korea after the war broke out and were ready to intervene. But Mao had a political problem. Most Chinese wanted peace after almost fifteen years of war. Even the majority among Mao's colleagues on the ruling body of the Communist Party, the Politburo, were at first against intervention. Lin Biao, the civil war hero whom Mao had in mind to lead the Chinese troops, was so much against the prospect of another war, this time with the most powerful military machine in the world, that he refused to take up the post and and left Beijing. But Mao had made up his mind even before the US northward offensive began. As the US troops marched toward the Chinese border, the Chairman saw the situation in black and white: "We have to enter the war," he told his colleagues. "To enter the war will be very rewarding; not to enter the war will be extremely harmful."[5] Mao wanted to show solidarity with the Korean Communists and thereby solidify China's standing within the world movement. He also believed that it was important both for the domestic and regional policies of his new regime that China be seen as willing to fight its enemies. It was not the fear of a US attack on his own country that helped Mao convince his colleagues: He won the day in the Politburo in the name of international solidarity, national pride, and his own position as China's leader.

The Korean War at first went well for the PRC in military terms. With some of their troops already in position on the south bank of the Yalu river, they had a strategic advantage over the Americans. The UN soldiers were unprepared for the wave after wave of Chinese Communist troops who came against them and were soon driven back to the former demarcation line between the two Korean regimes. But inside China the domestic consequences of the war were dire. War-weary PLA soldiers— some of whom had walked all the way from Manchuria to South China—were transported back to the north to fight in an unpopular war abroad. The United States Navy, meanwhile, intervened as soon as the war broke out to shelter the remnants of the GMD regime on Taiwan, postponing indefinitely a reunification that most Chinese had thought was imminent. The country's economy was redirected toward war, and few of the benefits that people had expected to come from the end of domestic strife materialized. For the CCP the war meant that socialism in China was born in even more poverty than what the party had expected. But the results of the conflict in Korea—a messy stalemate that basically confirmed the status quo ante—brought distinct benefits for the Communists as well. They were able to show that new China could stand up to the mightiest country on earth and hold it to a draw, which was a boon for their nationalist credentials. They firmed up their alliance with the Soviets, in spite of occasional complaints about Moscow's limitations in its wartime assistance to the PRC and the DPRK. But most importantly the war against the United Nations forces helped the party leaders do something they had long craved: destroy that wish to be part of a wider world that many Chinese cherished.

WHEN IT CAME TO POWER, the CCP represented a form of government that China had never seen before. The party was disciplined, inward-looking, and directed by a charismatic leader. It did not allow for any reference points outside the party and feared and resented any outside influence on its policies, domestic or foreign. The party had constructed a pseudo-Marxist version of Chinese history in which everything in the past inevitably led to the assumption of power by the CCP: All that had happened in China and to China since the Qing's first trouble with foreigners in the 1830s was a preparation for Communist rule, and the new regime was the logical consequence of, as Chairman Mao put it, the Chinese people having stood up. The concept of liberation was (and is) central to this version of Chinese history: The Communists had liberated China from foreign rule and its domestic supporters. Of course, China had been ruled by a nationalist, and at times xenophobic, government under Chiang Kai-shek for more than twenty years and many Chinese wanted to be associated with foreign teachers, partners, or lovers. But the new regime set out to destroy China's links with the rest of the world in a comprehensive and deliberate manner, believing that its rule would never be safe as long as any major foreign influence, outside the party's Soviet links, remained in China.

The CCP's first step was to get rid of foreigners who remained in China. At first, this seemed an easy task for the party. So many had already left during the civil war. Those associated with business and trade would soon leave of their own accord, because the new government would not give them any chance to operate with a profit in new China. In terms of numbers the CCP turned out to be right: The vast majority of foreigners left China voluntarily or were easily deported in 1950–1951. The problem was usually with foreigners who had lived in China for most of their lives and were running hospitals or schools. In order to drive these out, the CCP had to resort to political pressure on their Chinese associates, colleagues, or friends, and have them publicly attack their foreign acquaintances as "running dogs of imperialism" or "bloodsuckers of the Chinese people." Even after such campaigns a minority of long-term foreign residents in China, mostly missionaries, chose to stay.

The second step was to attack the businesses or organizations with which foreigners were directly associated. The CCP government levied large fines on businesses that had part foreign ownership until the foreign ownership ended. In some cases foreign-owned enterprises were confiscated outright or accused of wartime collaboration with the Japanese and seized. Such accusations were particularly resented by foreigners who had spent years in Japanese prison camps and chose to remain in China after the war. Foreign-influenced aid organizations were more difficult to target. The YMCA, for instance, was kept on in light disguise as a state institution after the foreigners and Christians who were involved in running it were driven out. In other institutions, doctors, teachers, and missionaries were accused of financial irregularities, sexual deviation, or espionage to whip up campaigns against them so they could more easily be expelled. The CCP urged its cadre to try to alienate foreigners and the Chinese who worked with or associated with them, so that these Chinese, who often had important expertise, could more easily be brought to work for the government after the foreigners had been got rid of.[6]

The third step in Communist antiforeign campaigns involved attempts to limit access to foreign books, films, and products. This activity proved much more difficult than getting rid of the foreigners, to the point that party activists in several cities were close to despair even after the nationalist argument could be fully brought to bear during the Korean War. Purging unwanted foreign books from libraries and bookshops was not particularly difficult, although it had to be carried out at night to prevent curious onlookers. The problem was that texts the CCP wanted to get rid of had a tendency to reappear in bookstalls and secondhand shops. Living without American movies turned out to be hard, especially for city youngsters, who went to great lengths to save illegal copies and show them privately. Though some girls reveled in dressing in Mao uniforms as a symbol of joining the cause, those who had had access to imported stockings, perfume, or lipstick seemed to miss these products to the point of being willing to buy them from various smuggling operations. But with book imports censored, publishing houses, record companies, and film studios taken over by the government, and lipstick smugglers publicly executed, the CCP gradually got things under control.

The antiforeign campaign's fourth step was the use of terror and imprisonment. Some foreigners who refused to leave were arrested, and some spent years in labor camps. Chinese who refused to reform their behavior or views, or who thought that China's self-imposed isolation was idiotic or criminal, or who simply had foreign links or foreign education, were "struggled against" in public sessions, where they were accused by their fellow citizens, beaten up, and sent to prison or to the camps. The party wanted to set an example through such people, by forcing them to conduct self-criticisms and recant their foreign ways. In some cases, even with serial offenders, the party wanted to retrain them so that they would become good citizens of the PRC, serving the people. The worst offenders—for instance, a young man who read aloud in English from the American Declaration of Independence, or a young woman who wondered when the CCP would allow multiparty elections—were executed.

The reason why these antiforeign campaigns succeeded was not just the combination of terror, nationalism, and the burden of history. It was first and foremost because the new regime organized the lives of Chinese citizens in ways that had never been seen before. Through neighborhood committees and informants the state found its way into all parts of life, even inside families and close friendships. Regions of the country that had not seen much central state presence for a hundred years found themselves regimented along the same lines as everywhere else. And there is little doubt that the CCP was carried forward by the enthusiasm of the great majority of Chinese for the reconstitution of the state and for the social reforms that were carried out. The regime did much to improve the position of women, by abolishing arranged marriages and the economic or sexual exploitation of young girls. Factory workers got set working hours and increases in pay. Peasants could break free of generations of abuse by landlords. Campaigns against opium use and prostitution were widely hailed, also outside China, and the CCP's literacy campaigns, modeled on the Soviet experience, were the most successful the world had ever seen. It did not matter much, most people thought, that jazz records or jazz musicians disappeared, or that the regime—to better coordinate its campaigns—set all of the country on the same time zone (Beijing Time), forcing farmers in the far west to get out of bed at two a.m. to start their day. It was all to create a new China, modeled on the Soviet Union, of "cleaning house before entertaining guests," as Mao Zedong put it.

Soviet advisers who served in China during the 1950s have often described the PRC approach to Moscow as "schizophrenic," meaning, presumably, incoherent and delusional. Though this is a grossly exaggerated critique of an alliance that worked well for more than ten years, there is something to the Soviet criticism. The Chinese Communists wanted Soviet aid and wanted to copy Soviet models. But they were afraid of any Soviet influence within the Chinese Communist Party itself and therefore wanted to prevent, for instance, unsanctioned personal contacts between Soviets and Chinese in China. The CCP's problems with wanting to copy the Soviet Union while wanting to screen itself off from Soviet influence were compounded by the fact that the party was split on how direct and immediate the lessons from the Soviets could be. From the very beginning of the PRC, leaders like Liu Shaoqi (Mao's second in command in the party) and Zhou Enlai (the Chinese prime minister), as well as planners and specialists who had worked with the Soviets in Manchuria or been trained in Moscow, saw the Soviet Union as the China of tomorrow. Chairman Mao, on the other hand, and some of his old comrades in the military and in the party, wanted Soviet aid and Soviet examples but believed that they had to go through a process of vetting to fit the CCP's specific intentions. While Mao spoke often and dearly about the need to make foreign constructs serve Chinese purposes what he really was afraid of was Soviet control of his party's political processes.

In spite of the CCP leaders' dissonant views about their relations with the Soviet Union, there is no doubt that they wanted and needed Soviet aid. Nor is there any doubt about the genuine admiration the Chinese Communists showed for Soviet military achievements, political organization, and technology. The key was Soviet modernity. The cadre who visited or read about the Soviet Union saw in it a state that was modern and strong but not imperialist and therefore not inimical to

China. People who had criticized Western modernity in its capitalist form, as seen for instance in Shanghai, but who still found the technologies, products, and culture of advanced capitalism alluring, could in the Soviet experience find a modernity to be proud of. The terrible human cost of Stalin's socialism—the targeted hunger campaigns, the mass killings, the labor camps—members of the CCP wrote off as imperialist lies, or, at the worst, the necessary price to pay for human progress. By the late 1940s, to most members of the Chinese party, it was not the real Soviet Union that mattered as much as an idealized image of it, a kind of future China, prosperous, strong, and just.

By the late 1940s the CCP had two kinds of members. The leaders were hardened Communists of the 1920s, people who had fought for their party and seen friends die for it. They had internalized the Mao-centered loyalty, the deep sense of isolation and danger, and the willingness to purge dissent. They had been through the rectification campaign of 1942–1943, intended to weed out all opposition to Mao's leadership of the party. They had organized the first CCP labor camps for landlords, bourgeois elements, and political opponents during the civil war. They knew and approved of the methods Stalin had used to solidify Soviet power north of the border. The other group were recent recruits to the party, many of them young and from the cities. Some had left their bourgeois families to join the Communist cause. All had dedicated themselves to the party, but they had little experience of it. The party leaders needed them and their expertise but never trusted them fully and were afraid they could pollute the hard-won purity of the Communist Party. The process of practical learning from the Soviet Union, the CCP leaders believed, would create the means by which to integrate the newcomers and keep them gainfully employed.

The Sovietization of the CCP, which started in 1945 when party cadre began working directly with Soviet Communists in Manchuria and lasted for fifteen years, meant learning how to build a state and a ruling party. Mao and his followers had no intention of taking over and using the state the GMD had constructed. They wanted a new state, built on the pattern of the Soviet Union, a full break with China's earlier history *and* with the Chinese state that had come into being after the 1911 revolution. Even the leaders who were most dedicated to learning from the CCP's own history realized that it did not prepare them for building a modern state. By 1949 all of the plans for a socialist China were drafted based on Soviet models and with Soviet expert assistance. From city planning to agricultural reform, from cultural institutions to labor camps, from nationalities policies to foreign policy, the new socialist state that the CCP wanted to build was to be modeled on the Soviet experience. Its capital city, which the party in 1949 decided would be Beijing, was to be fully refashioned in Soviet style. The earliest Communist plans for the city simply superimposed the Great Stalin Plan for Moscow of 1935 on the already existing old Ming grid. The link to the Soviet Union was intended to be the largest transfer of foreign knowledge into China ever and to enable the new regime to break with China's troubled past in a quick and streamlined manner.

Some foreign observers in 1949 thought that the PRC faced a choice in terms of its foreign policy. Some Americans even believed that China might become an independent power rather than be close to the Soviet Union. They would have been rather shocked to find how total the orientation toward working with the Soviets was inside the CCP in the late 1940s. In foreign policy terms, the question was not whether to agree or not agree with Soviet positions, but how to find out enough about Soviet thinking to ensure a fast and full CCP compliance. There was the question of Yugoslavia, for example. There in the spring of 1948 Stalin very quickly moved from approval to condemnation, accusing the Yugoslav Communist leader Josip Broz Tito of resisting Soviet orders. CCP foreign affairs personnel were desperate to keep up with current thinking in Moscow, especially since Tito's party had been the only East European party the CCP had independent relations with. As soon as Stalin's castigation of Tito became fully known to the CCP,

Mao—out his temporary dwelling in the town of Xibaipo—issued a proclamation using the exact phrases the Soviet leader had used in his condemnation. When Yugoslavia recognized the PRC in 1949, the new Chinese foreign ministry was ordered to send the letter of recognition back. The Chinese Communists were in no mood to deviate from Stalin's point of view on any issue, domestic or diplomatic.

THE SINO-SOVIET ALLIANCE was to have a deeper impact on China than any other alliance in the country's modern history. So far it has taken other foreign influence more than thirty years, since the 1970s, to try to move China away from its Soviet heritage, but only with limited success. Education, defense, government, and party institutions, all seem very Soviet in style still, even after decades of so-called opening and reform.

Why did the Soviet experience fasten itself so deeply in China? One reason is the core value the Soviet project represented for the Chinese Communist Party. It was, after all, the basis on which the party had been founded. Another is the breadth and depth of the encounter with the Soviet experience. Not only did Soviet aid to China become, in relative terms, history's biggest foreign assistance program from one country to another, but it also came at a time of unprecedented expansion of the Chinese state: Tens of millions of Chinese who had limited experience with foreign models first encountered them through Soviet plans, Soviet experts, or Soviet education.

Stalin's ideologically based distrust of the CCP prevented the civilian assistance program for China from becoming fully functional, but his successor Nikita Khrushchev knew no such boundaries. On the contrary, Khrushchev made a deepening of the alliance with the PRC a cornerstone in his rise to power after Stalin's death in 1953. To Khrushchev China was an obvious ally: It was a large, neighboring country, led by a dedicated Communist party that wanted to emulate the Soviet experience. To the new leader, Stalin's hesitancy with regard to the CCP stood as an example of the old boss's increasing madness. No sane person, Khrushchev liked to stress to his colleagues, would forgo such an opportunity. Khrushchev's own first major foreign visit was to China, in 1954. To Mao as well as to ordinary Chinese it meant a lot that the new Soviet leader came to Beijing instead of the Chinese going to pay homage in Moscow. It showed the importance the new Kremlin leaders attached to China and the respect they had for their CCP counterparts. Even more importantly, Khrushchev promised much more Soviet assistance to China, both civilian and military, than Stalin had ever dreamed of giving. One-third of all projects under the first Chinese Five Year Plan were to be built and paid for by Soviet or East European assistance. By 1955, sixty percent of China's total trade was with the USSR.[7]

It is hard to overestimate the significance of total Soviet Bloc assistance to the Chinese Communists between 1946 and 1960. Without it, the first steps toward the modern China that the CCP envisaged would have been impossible. The total economic assistance, including loans, was about $3.4 billion (US) from 1946 to 1960 in 1960 value (which is about $25 billion today). This is, on average, a little bit less than one percent of the Soviet GDP year by year. In reality, the transfers for 1954 to 1959 were much higher than this, in value as well as percentage-wise. This sum does not include technology transfers, salaries for Soviet experts in China, or stipends for Chinese students in the USSR. Even if we subtract the roughly eighteen percent that came from Soviet allies and around fifteen percent that was, over time, paid back by the PRC, we are still dealing with a vast program of resource shifting with significant effects for both countries.[8]

By the mid-1950s, Soviet advisers were attached to all Chinese ministries, regional and provincial governments, and major industrial enterprises. Soviet experts advised on every aspect of life in new China—from working with youth and women, minorities, soldiers, teachers, and engineers, to education, science, mining, military training, and general fitness. The Soviet advisers generally worked well with their Chinese counterparts. To the Chinese, in spite of the CCP's attempts at preventing too enthusiastic fraternization, the Soviets were models for what they themselves wanted to become: educated, dedicated, and efficient. To the Soviets, the Chinese honored them and their experience by wanting to model their new state on the Soviet Union. There were plentiful conflicts over food, sex, hygiene, or status, the usual elements of cultural clashes. But the significance of what the advisers were doing usually overrode the problems that arose, despite attempts by propriety-obsessed party commissars from both parties to magnify any difficulty that arose. For most of the decade the Sino-Soviet alliance worked well and fulfilled the purpose that both countries aimed at: to create the most powerful anti-Western alliance the world had seen since the rise of the Ottoman empire.

THE MODERN NATION that the PRC aspired to be needed a modern defense force. After the end of World War II, with the Red Army in Manchuria and the Japanese empire in ruins, the CCP, for the first time in its history, began the building of a modern army. While the party's military experiences from the previous fifteen years obviously formed the backdrop for what in 1945 became the People's Liberation Army, the inspiration for its organization, as well as its strategy, were explicitly Soviet. Some 1,500 young Chinese officers got their training in Soviet military academies before the People's Republic was set up. Others were trained by Soviet instructors in Manchuria between 1947 and 1949. The likely figure for those trained in the Soviet Union from 1950 to 1960 is nine thousand. The number trained inside China must have been many times that. The result was a modern Chinese army that looked increasingly like the Soviet Red Army, that served the same purposes internally and fought wars more or less in the same way.

The organization of the new People's Liberation Army was consciously and directly fashioned on that of the Soviet army. The units, the ranks, the weaponry, the tactics, and even the uniforms were taken from Soviet textbooks or from advice given by Red Army instructors. The new force was the pride of the party leaders. They saw it as an impressive combination of battle skills learned in the war against Japan and the Chinese civil war, on the one hand, and Soviet teaching on the other. Even though some Chinese officers found it hard to give up the much more improvised and flexible approach to military affairs propagated prior to the final offensives of the civil war in 1948 and 1949, they too were easily won over by the increased status that their modern hardware and their bright new uniforms gave them. By 1955 this Sovietization of the PLA was more or less complete, with the concept of fourteen military ranks somewhat difficult for the egalitarian-minded Chinese soldiers to swallow.

The PLA became not just a defense force but something perhaps even more important. It became a school for socialism and the country's most effective instrument for mass education and social betterment. Only a small percent of the country's young men ended up drafted for two to three years of service in the new conscript force. There were exemptions for most things from study to farming. But the 800,000 who did serve each year were educated in the army, they traveled, and they learned about their country and about the new creeds of socialism and nationalism. The PRC spent a very high percentage of its annual budget—an average of 30 percent in the 1950s—on the military, but certainly the part that went into training officers and soldiery was paid back later, as many of these men came to play important roles in China's general progress and development.

This symbiosis of military and civilian matters has been particularly important for China's technological development. The patents, models, and training received from the Soviets in the military field in the 1950s were crucial to China for two decades to come. Much of Soviet technology was intentionally dual-purpose; it could be used in the military as well as in the civilian sector. While the Chinese navy and air force developed according to Soviet models, the technologies taught in China's military academies became crucial for China's capacity in other fields as well, such as in its nuclear programs, its aircraft industry, and much of its heavy machine building. The first Chinese-built aircraft in common use, the Y-5 (Yunshu-5, or Yun-5), was a copy of the Russian Antonov An-2 light cargo biplane designed in the 1940s. Although an extraordinarily slow plane, it was well suited to China's needs because of its versatility and low operating costs.

China's military, as it still exists, was formed on the Soviet model. It became a rather cumbersome edifice capable of flashes of strategic brilliance, which treated its conscript soldiers harshly while catering to their basic needs. While kept under civilian control up to the chaos of the Cultural Revolution, the PLA became a crucial part of the power equation within the PRC, the seemingly streamlined and purposeful part of a republic that became increasingly given to political excess.

THE IMPLEMENTATION OF THE SOVIET MODEL in education started in earnest in China after 1945. Even outside the CCP, there was much admiration for Soviet training and teaching methods going back as far as the May Fourth era. During the Second World War, the Chinese People's Anti-Japanese Military and Political University and Yan'an University introduced Soviet pedagogical methods on a large scale. During the civil war, the lessons of the Yan'an period were deepened by much more direct contact with Soviet educational and technical advisers, especially in the Northeast. The First National Higher Education Conference in June 1950, the first of the normative conferences on changes in education, advocated a complete rebuilding of the Chinese higher education system according to a Soviet model. All universities and colleges were to be placed directly under the Education Ministry, young teachers were to be sent to the Soviet Union or Soviet-staffed training colleges in China for instruction in pedagogical methods, and a massive program of translating Soviet textbooks was inaugurated. Simultaneously, the conference decreed the abolition of the system of individual teachers being responsible for training students. From now on there should be full-fledged departments that taught students collectively and were collectively responsible for the political content of their teaching.[9]

The purges of the early 1950s delayed the full implementation of the 1950 program for higher education until the academic year 1952/1953. At that point, all institutions were supposed to be fully restructured. In the capital, for instance, a new Peking University was created by adding departments from Yanjing University and Qinghua University. Most important of all was the creation of People's University in Beijing, a new institution that taught politics and social sciences, and prepared students for further study in the Soviet Union, just as two generations earlier nearby Qinghua University had been set up to prepare students for study in the United States.[10]

The wholesale importing of curricula and pedagogics led to much enthusiasm and not a little confusion. In some cases, newly translated Soviet textbooks replaced US or European ones that were better informed on the subject, and a whole generation of Chinese technicians paid the price. In others, students were trained for technologies that did not yet exist in China or that called for skills in subjects not taught in Chinese universities. The party's insistence that work skills were as important as study skills led to the entry of large numbers of unqualified students into the universities. The needs of the First Five Year Plan, introduced in 1953, put enormous pressure on universities and colleges to produce high numbers of personnel for industry, causing slippage in standards. There was a fair share of claims of unrealistic achievements, leading to a need to falsify results.[11]

No other area of cooperation attracted as many Soviet advisers as education. Generally, they were left unimpressed with what they saw as piecemeal Chinese attempts at reforming the educational system. Education in China was hopelessly backward, as they viewed it. By the mid-1950s, there was still far too much deference toward teachers and far too little emphasis on political education. Some of the Soviet advisers placed in the central bureaucracy advocated large-scale campaigns directed primarily against illiteracy in the countryside; they thought that too much in terms of resources was being spent in the cities and on higher education. The models, as they saw them, were the methods developed in Soviet Central Asia and in Mongolia in the 1930s. Progress in this area could be, and ought to be, faster than the First Five Year Plan envisaged.[12]

The year 1955 became the year of reckoning in Chinese education. On the one hand, there was more and more criticism of the universities for slipping standards and not providing personnel with the skills needed to fulfill the Plan. The programs for adult education—to turn workers into students, as the Soviets did in their *rabfaks*—were criticized for being unrealistic and expensive, and were in effect abolished at year's end. On the other hand, the party leaders (and probably Mao himself) were increasingly impatient with the educational sector, but for different reasons. Their sense was that reform in education was moving too slowly to catch up with the country's needs, and they attributed this inertia to a lack of political motivation. At the same time, there was an increasing sense, shared by the Soviets, that the countryside was being left behind. The so-called Little Leap, launched by the Chairman in the spring of 1956, was intended to correct these tendencies.[13]

The year 1956 saw the beginning of the divergence of approaches to education in China and the Soviet Union. These cannot simply be explained by the CCP's perceived need to Sinify or radicalize their policies. Soviet advisers criticized the Chinese planners of the early 1950s in a manner that shared much of the Chairman's concerns, especially with regard to incrementalism and lack of rural development. The Leap approach was as much a Soviet invention as a Chinese. When turning to more fundamental methods for forcing change, Mao and his associates looked as much to high Stalinism in the Soviet Union in the mid-1930s as to their own Yan'an experience. An April 1957 article in

Jiaoshibao traces the origins of the Little Leap to Stalin's methods in 1929/30.[14] The lessons given by Soviet advisers, in other words, were neither unitary nor extrinsic. Ideological elements happily crossed any national divide.

Besides land reform and education, perhaps the most important transformative policy of the new regime was in the field of urban planning. In spite of its Marxist origins, the CCP had grown up as a party deeply skeptical of life in the cities. Mao had famously refused at first to move into Beijing after the Communists had taken the city in the spring of 1949, preferring to stay with the troops on its periphery. Having had to conquer the cities from the outside, the Chinese Communists expected little support there, even from among the proletariat so important to Marx himself. The rurally oriented CCP generally regarded China's big cities as dens of vice and counterrevolution. In 1950 there had even been a heated debate in the Politburo on a proposal from the head of the Manchurian party, Gao Gang, one of the CCP's senior leaders, to demolish Shanghai and send all its pre-Revolution inhabitants for rectification in the countryside.[15]

In the early 1950s in China, the new regime and many non-Communist intellectuals agreed that the cities should be remade. The government wanted to regulate the urban centers to keep control. The intellectuals believed that urban planning could improve living conditions. Both sides distrusted all elements of what they liked to call Old China, including the urban environments in cities such as Beijing, Tianjin, and Wuhan. Their problem was whether these cities could be transformed quickly from a parasitic to a productive part of society. If they could, how to go about it? The CCP had inherited an urban crisis from the GMD. Refugees, unemployment, inflation, and the scarcity of goods contributed to the urgency. Output in the cities continued to fall during the first two years of Communist rule.[16]

As Chinese educators did with Soviet education theory, Chinese city planners turned to Soviet urban planning theory. That discipline was developed in the 1930s and embodied in its most complete form in the 1935 General Plan for Moscow. In the mid-1930s, Stalin had wanted to transform Moscow, to make it a fitting symbol of socialism, to make it more productive, and to make it more secure for the Communist elite. The city needed more central regulation and more immediate functionality. The wanton destruction of old Moscow that had taken place in the 1920s was no longer enough. There had to be a centralized *plan* for both destruction and construction, not the experimenting and individual or group-based architectural projects of the early Communist period.[17] The Style of the Plan, so to say, when transplanted onto China, was a celebratory, historicist version of Western development.

Paradoxically, it was Chinese non-Communist intellectuals who introduced CCP cadre to the specific Soviet ideas of urban planning. The intellectuals were preparing the cadre for receiving larger numbers of advisers from Moscow. The more the party faithful understood these principles, the more they liked them. For a leadership that distrusted their city populations, however much they lauded the virtues of the proletariat, the Soviet urban planning ideas were eminently practical, as well as theoretically correct. Broad avenues and big urban squares facilitated mobility of workers from home to factory and back, and they also could come in handy in case the PLA needed to enter the city center to crush a counterrevolutionary rebellion. But first and foremost, it seems, the Party leaders were convinced by the glory of it all. By transforming their cities in the Soviet image, China would for the first time have urban centers that were celebrations of the modern form—planned, functional, and productive, rather than haphazard, dysfunctional, and consumptive, as they believed the cities of Old China to have been.[18]

During the 1950s, Beijing—the Chinese city I know best—symbolized the development of the modern. Exceptional in many ways because it had been designated the capital in 1949, Beijing also became a showcase for Communist China's urban planning. When work on transforming the capital started—well before the People's Republic was declared in October 1949—the 1935 Moscow plan was immediately taken as the model. The first Soviet planning team that arrived in Beijing, in September 1949, helped this process along, even though there were disagreements within the joint teams set up to work toward a General Plan for Beijing.[19]

A major disagreement among the Chinese and Soviet planners concerned where to build the headquarters of the party and the new government. Some Chinese architects and planners, such as Liang Sicheng, the US-educated son of the famous Chinese reformer Liang Qichao, proposed erecting a completely new administrative center *outside* the old city, in the western parts of Beijing. Liang and his colleagues wanted to rescue the Ming and Qing areas from destruction by locating a new center away from the Forbidden City and the old imperial quarters. His notes from that time also indicate a desire to start the modern, architecturally modernist Beijing in a location away from the clutter and complications of the old city. His son remembers that Liang Sicheng "believed that the time had come for mapping out a real scientific, reasonable plan for the city, because under socialism all the urban land is owned by the country and all the architectural activities are brought under a unified management." Whatever Liang's own motives may have been, the planners close to the CCP leadership had another motive for their insistence on a new location: They argued that the Party leadership simply would not be secure enough in the center of a city that was still "unreconstructed" and where "old elements" were roaming freely.[20]

The Soviet advisers, on the other hand, asserted that relocation would indicate weakness. The Red government had to take possession of the capital and show, symbolically as well as functionally, that it was the master of the place. In order to remake Beijing as a Red City and China as a Red Country, the Communists had to be at the center of it, not hiding away on the outskirts. The Soviets were supported by most of those who were providing planning and architectural advice to the new regime, including the Japanese-educated Zhao Dongri, who later designed The Great Hall of the People, and the French-educated architect Hua Lanhong.

Mao agreed with the Soviets that the party and the government should be in the center of the city. Given the peregrinations of his thirty-year revolutionary career, he had by now had enough of hiding on the outskirts. "Apparently, emperors can live in Beijing, but I cannot," the Chairman is said to have exclaimed angrily as he rejected Liang Sicheng's plan. When it came to the transformation of China's cities, Mao and the Politburo realized that whatever their own preferences had been at first, they would have to lead from the inside. If the Soviet Union had created socialist cities, China could do so as well. And Beijing would be the key example. In the work toward the first draft of the General Plan for Beijing, finally published in spring 1953, the whole city was to be reconstructed on a grid system according to strict zoning principles, with the factory as the overall model. Crucial to the plan was that Beijing should become not just a capital but an industrial center to serve the whole country. The population should be relocated to live in new housing near their places of work. There should be complete equality of services among different groups of the population, and most of these services should be provided through their work units, with the city government being in charge of overall planning.[21]

It is tempting to blame the first CCP leaders and their Soviet advisers for the destruction of old Beijing. The story of what actually happened, however, is more variegated and complex. The old city could not survive the needs of a modern city that was to be superimposed on it. The extensive use of Soviet models, ill-suited as they were for a Chinese city, carried its part of the blame. But the main reason why the old city fell was the link between Western-trained modernizing intellectuals, who admired the Soviet version of city planning, and the rough balance between rapid development needs and long-term goals that the new government sought. While prerevolutionary Moscow was envisioned as the Third Rome (Constantinople being the Second), Beijing was going to be the Second Moscow, but even bigger and more modern.

I F CREATING THE SYMBOLIC and functional capital city was essential to the new Chinese government, so was coordinating a vast country of countless nationalities. And once again the Soviet experience was invaluable. Minorities' or nationalities' policy was probably the field of social engineering in which Chinese approaches were most closely modeled on those of the Soviets. There were many reasons for this. Soviet nationalities' policy was regarded as highly successful, not just by the Chinese but by most of the rest of the world. Besides, the Chinese knew that minorities' policy was a particular area of interest for Joseph Stalin himself. Georgian by birth, he had served as commissar for nationalities in the early 1920s and written extensively on the topic.[22] Also, Old China, like old Russia, had been an imperial state with many different ethnic groups, and the Soviet solutions could therefore provide a practical blueprint for new China.

In the first conversations with the Soviets that the CCP had after coming to power, the nationalities issue loomed large. Much of the reason for this concern may be found in the rediscovery of China's ethnic minorities that the party had gone through during the civil war, when it had come into contact with a far larger segment of the country's ethnic minority population than ever before. The CCP rank-and-file observed the oppression and terrible social conditions many of these groups lived under and sympathized with their predicament. They also noticed how difficult it was to develop real alliances within these groups, because centuries of suspicion against Han Chinese stood in the way. Liberating the minorities was therefore an urgent task, and it could only be done by convincing them that the new China, unlike governments of the past, truly represented *all* those who lived within the state. It was to be a new type of central government.[23]

While improving the conditions for national minorities, the CCP leaders insisted that the new China was to be a unitary, not a federal state. Their entire political genesis dictated that aim: The CCP had been born as a reaction against imperialist designs to break up China. The party leaders firmly believed that with the right kind of policy everyone who lived within Chinese territory could be made to feel and think Chinese, as part of a Chinese socialist state. The resistance and distrust the party was met with as it tried to penetrate regions that in effect had been self-governing for more than two generations—Tibet, Qinghai, Xinjiang, and parts of the Southwest—convinced CCP leaders even further that Soviet advice was urgently needed. The Chinese party had to get the theory right, and found—rightly to some extent—that Marxism possessed a reservoir of thinking on nationalities issues that could be relevant to China's concerns. Winning the minorities for socialism while curbing Han chauvinism and the majority's lack of sensitivity toward the national needs of "less developed peoples"—these were the tasks the CCP leaders proclaimed as keys to creating a new China.[24]

The Soviet advisers who came to China in December 1949 did not expect much understanding from the Chinese side of the "advanced principles of Marxism" in handling national minorities. Because many of the most important minority groups—Mongols, Koreans, and the peoples of the northwest—lived in the Sino-Soviet borderlands, some of these Soviet experts had observed Chinese relations with the minorities first hand before coming to the PRC, and their experiences prepared them for the worst. Soviet experts often misinterpreted Chinese eagerness to learn as ignorance. Meanwhile, the Chinese suspected that the Soviets wanted to maintain their influence among China's minority peoples even after the PRC had been set up. But overall the Chinese leaders viewed the Soviet Union as holding the solution to one of China's major problems and insisted that CCP cadre should learn from Soviet advisers and extensively study Marxist literature on the topic.[25]

Both Chinese Communists and Soviets were driven by a desire to categorize and label, to count and register, alongside the mission to civilize and transform. Each minority had to be discovered again. The ways that ethnicity had been seen in the past were not suited for a socialist state. The debates in the 1950s on which groups should have the status of recognized minorities on a national scale were fierce and deeply ideological, centering on what constituted a "people" in socialist terms. The debate was even more heated because all sides appealed directly to the views expressed by Stalin in his 1913 *Marxism and the National Question*. The CCP's own past visions of China's different minorities also played a major role in the policies it recommended. The Communist relationship with Tibetans and Muslims had not been easy in the 1930s and 1940s. Many Communists saw the traditional leaders of the communities as sworn enemies of their political project. Their preferred policy, supported by Chinese ethnographers, was to carry out revolutions *within* these groups, through locating and empowering their oppressed peasants, landless workers, and slaves. Soviet advisers generally agreed with this policy, but urged caution and stressed the need for long-term planning in carrying it out. There were clashes early on, in 1951 and 1952, in which Chinese leaders—including quite a few with at least some experience in working in minority areas—argued that the Soviets themselves had not shown much caution in carrying out revolution within minority areas in the 1920s and 1930s. The Soviets, on their side, suspected some of the Chinese Communists of being Han chauvinists, who wanted to subsume all minorities within a greater Han Chinese people.[26]

Preexisting links between the Soviets and some of the groups on China's border complicated the encounter between Soviet and Chinese nationalities policies. The Chinese political leaders at the center were from the very beginning of their rule torn between the perceived need to learn from Soviet political and academic theory on these thorny questions and the desire to advance Chinese, and not Soviet, predominance inside China's borders. Reading through the top-level conversations on nationalities' questions, I have the sense that the Chinese interlocutors often consciously replaced examples from minorities along the Soviet border with those from minorities of the interior (or other borders, such as the Tibetans) when discussing policy with the Soviets. But while sometimes embarrassing to both sides—and often inconvenient—the Soviets in China understood CCP sensitivities with regard to the border issues and underlined their desire to help the Uighurs, Kazakhs, and Mongols living in China find their place within the new Chinese community of peoples.[27]

Sometimes these policies could have unintended consequences. The CCP's insistence on "re-cataloguing" its inventory of ethnic groups after their long period of relative autonomy in the early twentieth century made for surprising results in the 1950s. In the great counting of peoples, local agency sometimes combined with the intricacies of Stalinist theory to give opportunities for assertion to groups that had never had such opportunities before. Even though the breakdown into fifty-six nationalities that resulted was haphazard and, in some cases, a mere product of decisions made in Beijing rather than regionally, it still meant that some groups that had never had their own institutions recognized suddenly found themselves as one of China's peoples, with representation all the way up to the National People's Congress, China's parliament. Communist political repression could hit at anyone within China's borders, but recognition as a separate nationality gave some degree of protection from the most vicious aspects of PRC political campaigns, at least up to the Cultural Revolution, which began in 1966.[28]

THE CCP'S VIEW OF THE OUTSIDE world was formed by that of the Soviet Union in its Stalinist phase. The party members felt a deep sense of insult at the exploitation of China by the Europeans, Americans, and Japanese. To this negative mix was added the experience of the Korean and Indochina wars, which lent a strong feeling of living in a dangerous neighborhood and of being on the frontline in assisting other Communist parties liberate their countries. At the center of the threats against China, according to the CCP, stood the United States. Given US support for the PRC's Guomindang enemies both before and after their flight to Taiwan and the bloody warfare against the United States in the Korean War, this enmity should come as no surprise. But if one considers the contribution of the United States to China's development in the prewar era and the crucial support it had given during the war against Japan, the absolute priority put on American villainy may seem remarkable. Two major factors in this animus were the centrality the Soviets gave to the United States as its enemy and the problems the CCP had with rooting out the admiration and curiosity many urban Chinese had for things American.

The Chinese Communists saw themselves as being at the forefront of a global battle against imperialism and capitalism, in an alliance of Communist parties led by the Soviet Union. Even if the party leaders feared any outside influence within their own party, they were eager to find their place as the closest brother-in-arms of the Soviets on the global scene and as the main socialist country in Asia. Mao and his lieutenants welcomed the thaw in international relations that Stalin's successors initiated toward the West, because they viewed it as a welcome respite after many years of war. The Chinese and the Soviets both supported the partition of Vietnam and acted together to prevent Kim Il-sung from planning a new war on the Korean peninsula. For the Chinese these were temporary necessities in an ongoing conflict with the United States and the West. The close coordination with the Soviets also helped promote China as the most respected of the Soviet Union's allies, appealing both to CCP nationalist sentiment and to Mao's ego.

The CCP had supported Ho Chi Minh's Communist-led Vietminh movement in their battles against a French reoccupation of Indochina since 1945. Throughout the postwar period Mao had emphasized to

Stalin that Vietnam (and not, for instance, Korea) was the CCP's foreign strategic priority. After 1949, supporting the Vietminh was given higher priority than even preparing for the takeover of Taiwan. The reasons were obvious. In Vietnam, the Communists stood a real chance of winning, in which case the group that was closer to the CCP than any other foreign Communist party would come to power. PRC support for the Vietminh was stepped up during the Korean War, with Chinese military advisers filling key positions in the Vietnamese forces up to and during the battle of Dien Bien Phu in 1954. During the battle itself, in which the Vietminh routed the French, Mao sent off strategic advice to General Vo Nguyen Giap as he would have done to his own generals in the field in Korea. When the peace arrangements for Indochina were agreed to at Geneva, the PRC was a proud participant at the conference. The Chinese agreed with the Soviets that some form of temporary division line was necessary to secure peace in the region. They helped push the reluctant Vietnamese to accept a settlement. Zhou Enlai told Ho that it would be wise to cease hostilities with the French and consolidate control now, and look to extend the Communist zone later. Referring to left-wing French premier Pierre Mendès-France, Zhou said to Ho, "We should do our best to support the Mendès government, so that we can prevent the warlike elements in France from overthrowing [it]."[29]

The same moderate attitude informed China's approach to other Third World countries. Guided by the USSR's new emphasis on peaceful coexistence as a means of winning postcolonial regimes as allies in the struggle against the West, China signed on to Indian Prime Minister Jawaharlal Nehru's Five Principles of Peaceful Coexistence, basically committing to equality of nations and noninterference in international affairs. China attended the Bandung Conference of Asian and African nations in 1955, praising the principles of nonalignment (from the West, of course, not from the Soviet Union). Secret Sino-Soviet foreign policy planning emphasized that one should support nationalist Third World regimes such as Nehru's in India, Sukarno's in Indonesia, and

U Nu's in Burma, while preparing the Communist parties of such countries to take power. Moderation, the way Mao understood it, was a tactical tool while readying the world for revolution.

The PRC had another reason for a moderate approach to the West in the mid-1950s. Mao and Zhou Enlai hoped that the United States would give up its protection of Taiwan, either because they tired of Chiang Kai-shek or as a result of a grand compromise with the Soviet Union. In 1954, however, the PRC shelled the GMD-held islands next to the Chinese mainland coast, Jinmen and Mazu (Quemoy and Matsu), to remind the Americans that it had not given up on recovering the Chinese islands that were still outside its control.

THE RELATIONSHIP OF THE PRC to the outside world cannot be understood without mention of the seemingly endless series of campaigns the Communist leaders invented for their fellow citizens. In the end, the biggest campaign, the Great Proletarian Cultural Revolution of the late 1960s, would almost consume the Communist Party itself. But up to then the victims were real or imagined enemies of the regime, or party members who were suspected of thinking differently. The campaigns, patterned on Stalin's policies of the 1930s, created a sense of constant crisis and combat, which helped radicalize politics within the CCP. These policies also helped create a society where all kinds of foreign associations were dangerous. For example, in 1958 a seventeen-year-old girl was sent to the labor camps for telling a friend that "shoe polish made in the United States is really good." The accusation against her was "worshipping and having blind faith in foreign imperialist things."[30]

As soon as it gained power, the party set out to erase all real or potential opposition to its rule. Its ruthlessness in doing so far outdid anything seen in China since the early and mid-Qing campaigns against its enemies. For the Qing, the enemies deemed ripe for extermination were mostly groups they defined as non-Chinese. For the CCP, however, the victims were fellow Chinese, most of whom would never have lifted a chopstick against the party's rule. Enemies were defined as those who "oppose proletarian dictatorship, attack the foreign policies of the government, and attack the movement of liquidation of the counter-revolutionaries."[31] The campaigns started as soon as victory on the battlefield was in sight in 1949 and sped up after the Korean War began. In May 1951 Liu Shaoqi explained to the party faithful that

> Once the gongs and drums of resisting the United States and as-sisting Korea begin to make a deafening sound, the gongs and drums of the land reform and suppression of counter-revolutionaries become barely audible, and the latter becomes much easier to im-plement. Without the loud gongs and drums of resisting the United States and assisting Korea, those of the land reform (and counter-revolutionary campaigns) would make unbearable noise. Here a landlord is killed and there another is beaten; there would be fuss everywhere. . . . Things would then become difficult.[32]

The effects of the large-scale killing that took place during these early campaigns have often been underestimated in our views of China's international policies. Far from being more lenient than the Soviet Union in the treatment of domestic enemies, as some have believed, the PRC became a throwback to the height of Stalin's terror, with quo-tas set in each province for how many counterrevolutionaries should be found and shot. Mao stipulated that the target be 0.1 percent of the population, but in some provinces local Communist enthusiam for killing far exceeded this figure. "Collaboration with imperialism" headed the list of capital crimes, which also included the offense of illegal border crossing. In Guangdong province more than 10,000 people were exe-cuted in April 1951 alone. By the end of May 1951 the south central region (Henan, Hubei, Hunan, Guangdong, and Guangxi provinces) had executed 200,000. It is impossible to calculate how many Chinese died or were sent to labor camps during the first five years of Communist rule, but the Chinese historian Yang Kuisong finds that the figure was much higher than the 700,000 killed and 2.5 million arrested that Mao admitted to in 1957. A reasonable estimate is somewhere between four and five million deaths, with more than half of these being executions, for the 1949–1955 period.[33]

By the late 1950s, the party's policies began to turn ever further to the left. The population was scared into obedience to such a degree that immediate submission to the latest party directive seemed the natural order of things, even to people who had fought against oppression or imperialist control in the 1930s and 1940s. Actions taken out of fear—the denunciation of a friend, the attendance at a public execution—were often justified by nationalist pride or ideological loyalty that seemed extreme even to Soviet observers. Most Chinese—way beyond the Communist Party—*wanted* to believe in the new regime and in its plans for a rapid transformation of the country into a modern, efficient state. Even though people's thought processes are always complicated in these kinds of situations (what accounts for more—fear, pride, or nationalism—is as hard to say in Mao's China as it was in Hitler's Germany or Stalin's Soviet Union), there is no doubt that the willingness to sacrifice for the common good, a notion always strong in China, came into play among victims and perpetrators. There was in the 1950s a genuine belief that terror and extreme discipline were necessary to create a new China. Some Soviet advisers found it frightening that just as Moscow was moving out of the Stalinist mode of terror, China seemed to be moving toward it. As the surviving Soviet camp inmates were returning from Siberia, the Chinese camps started to fill up, in northern Manchuria and in the far west, in Gansu, Qinghai, and Xinjing, where the camps still are. In some cases Chinese prisoners fled across the border to the Soviet Union. They were promptly sent back.

G IVEN WHAT MAO'S CHINA was trying to do and the methods it was willing to use, it was to be expected that foreign reaction would be divided. In the United States, the terror, the close alliance with the Soviets, and the sense of futility and loss in the American decade-long support for China came together to construct a view of the country as the most vicious son of the depraved Communist family of nations. The US sense of unfulfilled expectations for China was particularly strong and helped feed a McCarthyist hysteria that blamed left-wing Americans for China "going Communist." The subtext of many of these accusations, often against leading US experts on Asia, was racist. The Chinese could not possibly have decided for Communism themselves; they would have had to be pushed into accepting it by American Reds and Soviet evildoers. Many Americans feared that the Chinese, a bit like children, having accepted the Communist creed, would take it to extremes both domestically and internationally.

After a period of openness to the outside world, China was back where it had been around 1900 in terms of its foreign relations. "Red China," the US Assistant Secretary of State for Far Eastern Affairs Walter Robertson claimed, was "hostile, aggressive, and building up its military capabilities. . . . By every standard of national and international conduct [it was] under its present regime . . . an outlaw nation."[34] Whereas the Qing had been a failed regime that increasingly allowed its people to in-teract with the world, the CCP was attempting to close its people in, prevent travel and contacts, except with the Communist states, and even there under strict control. The lack of knowledge about what was really going on inside China helped fuel Western paranoia. Because it was an Asian country, which in the Western mind predisposed it to collectivism, it was seen as succeeding in implementing Communism even in areas where the Soviets had failed. It was aggressive toward the world, as shown in Korea, and was preparing aggression in Southeast Asia, a region key to Western interests, which another Asian nation, Japan, had tried and failed to dominate in the previous decade. In the longer run, when China's power had expanded, what would prevent even the Japanese from joining up with the winning alliance in Asia?

These kinds of nightmarish visions helped prevent an effective American policy toward China in the 1950s. Instead the three administrations that followed Truman's employed an increasingly stale approach, based in part on fear of domestic political repercussions, to their China policies: economic embargoes, diplomatic isolation, and support for the GMD on Taiwan. In a way, US policies made Mao's job easier. The CCP leaders *wanted* to isolate China and were afraid of any foreign influence within the country. When the British Labour government tried to recognize the PRC in 1950, Mao would have nothing of it until London had closed down all of its representation on Taiwan. And when Conservative British Prime Minister Anthony Eden himself wanted to come to China to break the ice in February 1955, Mao bragged to the Soviet ambassador that "the PRC intentionally gave an answer that meant Eden would refuse to come." When the Eisenhower administration showed a less belligerent approach to China in 1959, the Chairman immediately interpreted it as an attempt to subvert the country from the inside. Mao told his aides that US Secretary of State John Foster Dulles "wants to change a country such as ours. He wants to subvert and change us to follow his ideas. . . . Therefore, the United States is [still] attempting to be aggressive and expansionist with a much more deceptive tactic. . . . In other words, it wants to keep its order and change our system. It wants to corrupt us through peaceful evolution."[35]

Race played an important role in how the outside world viewed new China, and in how China viewed the world. The American leaders (and the Europeans to a lesser extent) were concerned that China as a nonwhite country stood a better chance than European Communists in seducing and subverting countries in Asia and Africa that were emerging from colonialism. In a mirror image, the Soviets, from Stalin on, thought that the Chinese could and should act in Third World contexts where it would be more difficult for the Soviets themselves to operate. Many Third World leaders in the 1950s saw China as a potential ally—its presence at Bandung was crucial in this regard—or even as representing a non-European variant of socialist development that they themselves wanted to follow. For Mao Zedong, all of these approaches were problematic. He agreed with Moscow that China had a particular role to play in the Third World on behalf of world Communism, but not that it stood for a specific model. It stood for Marxism-Leninism, pure and simple. China wanted global influence, but the Americans, according to the Chairman, were chasing ghosts if they believed that China would involve itself deeply outside the socialist camp. And finally the CCP welcomed Third World radicals to Beijing and would be happy to develop relations with them, but on the clear understanding that Marxism-Leninism was the only possible solution to the ills of the developing world. There was no third way, and China in ideological terms most definitely did not want to develop one.

The CCP's views on religion also created difficulties in how others saw China. During 1950 all Christian missionaries were expelled, and their medical and educational institutions taken over by the state. Some foreign missionaries were incarcerated, including an American Catholic bishop, James E. Walsh, who spent twelve years in prison. Almost all of the Chinese Catholic hierarchy was arrested. The archbishop of Guangzhou, Dominic Deng Yiming, was held for twenty-two years. Ignatius Cardinal Gong Pinmei spent thirty years in a labor camp. Christian denominations were broken up and reorganized into "patriotic" religious organizations. Tibetan or Mongolian Buddhist or Muslim leaders in Xinjiang, Gansu, or elsewhere in China fared little better. For the Chinese government these persecutions were ways of controlling the country. But for many foreign fellow believers of those persecuted in China, the actions of the CCP made them loathe and distrust the Chinese regime.

Overall the views held in the outside world of China in the early phase of Communist rule may have been uninformed but not necessarily wrong. China had embarked on an experiment that had a tremendous human cost and that would ultimately fail. But foreigners criticizing the PRC made some Chinese even more convinced that they had to persist in their course. To them, the most important thing was that Maoism was Chinese, and that the Communist Party had succeeded in uniting the country and given the majority of its people a sense of purpose. After one hundred years of state weakness, China seemed finally to be building a state that would provide its people with a good standard of living and be respected in the outside world. For most Chinese in the 1950s that was enough to know.

O N ITS OWN TERMS, the CCP had reason to be proud of its achievements during the 1950s. It had fought the United States to a standstill in the Korean War. It had carried out comprehensive campaigns against its domestic enemies, had collectivized agriculture and nationalized all key industries, and had, with massive Soviet assistance, completed the First Five Year Plan of production with satisfactory results. Within the fields emphasized in the Plan—iron and steel manufacturing, coal mining, cement production, electricity generation, and machine building—growth had been significant, at around nine percent per year. Even so, the leadership, and Mao especially, were still worried about the future. In spite of showing growth in output, agriculture could not keep up with industrial expansion or even the increase in population. There were signs that even industrial growth was slowing toward the end of the period. And, most importantly, Mao and some of his advisers were not satisfied with China's overall growth, because they felt that the country had so much ground to cover before catching up with the advanced nations. By 1956 a wedge in terms of policy was starting to develop between Mao and some of the younger members of the leadership on the one hand and more traditional Marxist leaders, such as Liu Shaoqi and Zhou Enlai, on the other. The former stressed innovation and speedy transformation in the economy, while the latter emphasized the need to rely on the Plan and learn from the successes and mistakes in the Soviet experience.

In February 1956 Soviet leader Nikita Khrushchev shocked all those around the world who had drawn inspiration from the Soviet Union. In a speech to the Twentieth Congress of the Soviet Communist Party, he revealed at great length the extent of Stalin's terror. Khrushchev's revelations unsettled the CCP leadership, as it did Communists everywhere. Mao's own first reaction, however, was that the condemnation of Stalin improved his own chances of becoming the ultimate arbiter of Communist doctrine in Asia and eventually around the world. As he later told the Soviet ambassador, to him Stalin's death had been like getting out of a straitjacket. The CCP leaders liked Khrushchev's insistence that Stalin had promoted "Russian chauvinism" in relations with other parties, from Yugoslavia to China. Hereafter the CCP would be freer in setting its own policies and in moving faster toward socialism. But the Chairman grew increasingly concerned after workers in Poland and Hungary attempted to overthrow their Communist regimes later in the year, using the revelations of the Twentieth Congress as evidence that Communism could not work. Mao and many Chinese leaders began sensing that the Soviet criticism of Stalin's infallibility and the cult of the individual could be directed against the CCP and its cult of the Chairman. "You see what Stalin's mania for greatness led to," Khrushchev had said. "He completely lost touch with reality."[36] In China, Mao wanted to make sure that such a verdict could not be passed on him.

The Polish and Hungarian events in the autumn of 1956 marked the first time the CCP gave advice to the Soviets on key foreign policy issues. Mao warned the Kremlin that an armed intervention in Poland would be seen as a case of "serious big-power chauvinism, which should not be allowed in any circumstances."[37] But after Communists were lynched in the streets in Budapest, the CCP came to support, indeed urge, a Soviet invasion there. By the end of the year, Soviet and Chinese Communists alike were attempting to rebuild their badly dented authority. According to a Chinese statement much lauded by the Soviets,

The sole aim of socialist democracy is to strengthen the socialist cause of the proletariat and all the working people, to give scope to their energy in the building of socialism and in the fight against all anti-socialist forces. . . . Criticism should be made only for the purpose of consolidating democratic centralism and of strengthening the leadership of the Party. It should in no circumstances bring about disorganization and confusion in the ranks of the proletariat, as our enemies desire.[38]

The ghost of Budapest frightened the CCP leaders with some reason. In the autumn and winter of 1956, China itself saw open opposition against the CCP's policies and its lack of democracy for the first time since 1949. In many provinces public demonstrations for better conditions for workers, more democracy, and freedom of speech were observed and reported on by the secret police. A report to the Politburo noted that some of these rallies were even joined by party members, who helped chant "'we will fight to the end' and '[we will] denounce the low ranking [officials] and then turn to the higher ones.' A few workers were even heard to proclaim, 'As [we] see, there's no other way for us than learning lessons from Hungary!'"[39] When the party, on the defensive, decided at Mao's suggestion to launch a campaign for greater openness, the Hundred Flowers Campaign, it was precisely to identify its opponents and later destroy them. By the end of 1957, hundreds of thousands of "bourgeois rightists" had been arrested and sent to labor camps.

In foreign policy, too, the late 1950s was an unstable period. As Mao struggled to regain the initiative within China through driving the revolution toward a more radical phase, he also set new and more aggressive policy aims in international affairs. This was the time, Mao thought, for a Communist offensive against the United States and its allies throughout the Third World. Washington had spurned the moderation of the socialist camp. Hungary and the continued "occupation" of Taiwan showed how the United States would treat what it perceived as Communist weakness. Visiting Moscow on his second and last trip abroad, Mao exhorted his hosts to confront imperialism. "It is my view," the Chairman said, "that the international situation has now reached a new turning point. There are two winds in the world today, the east wind and the west wind. There is a Chinese saying, 'Either the east wind prevails over the west wind or the west wind prevails over the east wind.' It is characteristic of the situation today, I believe, that the east wind is prevailing over the west wind. That is to say, the forces of socialism are overwhelmingly superior to the forces of imperialism." There was no reason to fear a war with the imperialists, Mao said:

> If worse came to worst and half of mankind died, the other half would remain. Imperialism would be destroyed, and the whole world would become socialist. In a number of years there would be 2.7 billion people again and definitely more. We Chinese have not yet completed our [socialist] construction, and we desire peace. However, if imperialism insists on fighting a war, we will have no alternative but to make up our minds and fight to the finish before proceeding with construction.[40]

The international meeting of Communist leaders whom Mao addressed sat in shocked silence as the Chairman's remarks were translated. One young Russian delegate who was present in the hall that night later told me that to him it was as if Stalin had come alive again. He did not cherish the thought, or that of half the world's population perishing.

After returning from his politically disastrous trip to the Soviet Union, Mao began considering how China could make a great leap forward, intensifying production in heavy industry and in agriculture at the same time. In Moscow, Mao had boasted that China's economy would overtake Britain's in fifteen years. As he began discussing new production aims with his colleagues in the spring of 1958, he pushed for increased quotas in most parts of the economy. Other leaders, cowed by Mao's prestige, optimism, and revolutionary spirit, were eager to tell him that China could outdo the British in steel production in seven years, some said five or even three years. Obsessed with steel as the constructor of modernity, Mao told them that China needed to make its great leap into the future, to show doubters within the country, the Soviets, and the imperialists, what socialist man was capable of. It was a world of struggle, the Chairman insisted, and China had to catch up quickly or be annihilated.

B Y THE LATE 1950s, China and its foreign relations were transformed from what they had been a decade before. The Communists had introduced a new political and economic order, patterned on that of the Soviet Union. Most of the ties with the rest of the world that had been built cautiously and gradually over the previous century had been severed and those who represented them had been killed, sent to labor camps, or otherwise silenced. China's isolation was going to get a lot worse as Mao began putting in place policies that would lead to a break with the socialist countries as well. But the foundation for China's isolation was laid in the 1950s, when socialism was first constructed.

It is not difficult to understand why the CCP opted for a break with the international orientation of the late Qing and Republican eras. Its own foreign experience was limited, having spent twenty years fighting the GMD in the Chinese countryside. Based on its reading of history, the party saw past foreign involvement in China as purely negative. From more modern times, it copied the full break that USSR had had with the West since its founding. It did not understand that this break, from Lenin's perspective, had been forced on the country by relentless Western hostility rather than actively sought. But most importantly the isolation of the PRC came from the sectarian aspect of CCP politics. The party was extremely disciplined, narrow-minded, and inward-looking, with Mao as an increasingly prophet-like leader for whom no constraints existed. Together with the continued ideological hostility shown by the United States, Japan, and Western Europe toward new

China, the CCP blend of isolationist policies and attitudes ensured that the new state would grow up outside any internatonal framework except the one created by its alliance with the USSR.

Many Chinese hoped for more interaction with the outside world in the future—reconnecting with relatives and friends outside the PRC, on Taiwan, in Hong Kong or Macao, in Southeast Asia or elsewhere in the Chinese diaspora. But they had enough pride in their country's achievements to create mass support for the CCP's hatred of foreign things and ideas. As the Chinese learned more about the CCP's use of mass executions and labor camps, most simply hid the party's excesses from outsiders. They believed that these methods, though terrible, could be justified in the building of a new and modern China, which, eventually, would be able to meet the rest of the world on equal terms. Some may even have believed that China was in the process of surpassing other countries in the competition for modernity. They were in for some big shocks in the decade that followed.

CHAPTER 9

CHINA ALONE

URING THE 1960s, China went through a period of isolation and increasing irrelevance in international affairs. Its break with the Soviet Union drove the country away from its few remaining international contacts. The radicalism and eccentricity of Mao's policies at home and abroad made China look like what we today would call a failed state, a chaotic, self-referential, and extreme polity with few links to the outside world. Although there were small offshoot groups of so-called Maoists in industrialized countries (even in places such as New Zealand or Norway), they were more about social protest than Mao's doctrines, and never got close to real political influence. And in the Third World those movements China supported became fewer and increasingly isolated. China's leaders expected them to conform closely to their own domestic policy preferences whatever twist or turn Chinese politics took during these tumultous years. Even for those who sincerely wished to remain China's allies, the task was not easy.

The self-centeredness of China during the Great Proletarian Cultural Revolution—the campaign that Mao Zedong launched in 1966 to radicalize Chinese politics and destroy perceived enemies—knew almost no bounds. The Chinese were led to believe that only China possessed the right road to revolution and that the country therefore was the enviable center of all human development, that it carried the key to the future. This key was the person of Mao Zedong and the political road he devised for China. Mao's own obsession, after the failure of the Great Leap, was to create a new generation of Chinese who were not held back by what he saw as convention and conformity, including ethics, family, and friendship, and therefore could dedicate themselves fully to carrying out the revolution even after he himself was gone. They should be ruthless, strong, and brave, uncontaminated by foreign or bourgeois influence, and able to take losses on China's road to full Communist development. Mao's new dream was a China entirely purged of its past, its people a blank slate on which a superior form of modernity could be inscribed. He saw a road to a bright future, paved with the corpses of those who had erred or simply got in the way. Mao's final ladder to paradise, his Cultural Revolution, rose among heaps of bodies, the way Stalin's and Hitler's had done in the past and Pol Pot's would do in the future.

China's isolation in the 1960s was largely self-imposed, but it did not have to be this way. After its break with the Soviets, China received considerable goodwill in the Third World, mainly for racial reasons. It was seen as a progressive anticolonial Asian power, and the break with the (European) Soviets initially made China more attractive as a partner for Third World radicals. The war with India in 1962—an unnecessary war, if ever there was one—held many of the more moderate Asian and African regimes back from working closely with the Chinese. But as late as 1964 or 1965 China could shine on the Third World stage, as it did through Premier Zhou Enlai's visit to African countries or the agreement to help build a railway between Tanzania and Zambia. By the late 1960s, however, China had turned away from these achievements, and most of its Asian and Third World potential was gone. Formerly radical countries from Ghana to Indonesia turned to the right and expelled the Chinese representatives. Even North Korea sided firmly with the Soviets, though it continued to receive Chinese aid—with great *schadenfreude*, one must assume. By 1970 only one Chinese alliance was fully intact, that with North Vietnam, and that would collapse, with a vengeance, as soon as Saigon collapsed in 1975. The PRC was dangerously isolated—mostly by choice, it should be added—and its increasingly frenzied regime reckoned that war, this time with the Soviets, was right around the corner.

H OW DID REVOLUTIONARY CHINA get to this pretty pass? The catastrophes were mainly due to Mao's hubris, China's ill-conceived development plans, and its international isolation. By the summer of 1958, the CCP center in Beijing had ordered massive improvements in production in all fields. Through a Great Leap Forward, China would rapidly enter a new stage of development, Mao believed, and his enthusiasm carried the day within the party, even among economic experts who knew better. In the countryside all private property was abolished and peasants grouped into people's communes in order to improve production. Within the communes all services were collective, including child care and care for the elderly. In many provinces children spent six days a week in care, only returning to their parents on Sundays, so that men and women could dedicate their lives fully to production. Peasants were ordered to carry out gigantic land reclamation campaigns, while their own produce was sent to the cities and sometimes abroad. Lack of fertilizer was made up for by demolishing barns, outhouses, and latrines—and in the end the peasants' own dwellings—for the building material to be ground up and spread on the fields.

Large numbers of people wanted to believe in Mao's new revolution and worked themselves to exhaustion for its success. Rumors of production miracles abounded: Watermelons as big as houses had been produced in Shaanxi, there had been a 600 percent increase in potato growing in Henan. Worse, the government set quotas for agricultural produce that could be exported out of the provinces based on entirely inflated production figures. Local CCP leaders lied about output to curry favor with their bosses. In some parts of the country villagers were led to believe that they could help steel production by setting up back-yard furnaces where they melted their household goods and, in the end, their tools, to present to the Communist leadership. By the late autumn of 1958 it was already clear that parts of the country were going hungry as result of these excesses. In the winter of 1958–1959, peasants started dying. By the time the Great Leap campaign was over in 1961, an estimated 45 million people, mostly peasants, had died from hunger, illness, and exhaustion. It became the greatest man-made catastrophe in human history, mainly because Mao and the other leaders would not beat a retreat even when the results of their campaign were plainly visible.[1]

The Soviets had observed the beginning of the Great Leap with much concern. Even if some of their experts sympathized with the methods the CCP wanted to use to force a new modernity onto China, the more level-headed reporting to Moscow predicted in the spring of 1958 that the human toll of Mao's methods would be considerable. In private, Soviets advisers began warning their CCP colleagues of the potential results from the Leap. The Soviet attitude infuriated Mao. He decided to use a Soviet request for greater military coordination, along the lines of what NATO was doing in Europe, to vent his anger and to make his policy a question of Chinese national interest. The long-suffering Soviet ambassador Pavel Iudin—a Marxist philosopher who had been sent to China at Mao's request to be on hand to discuss theoretical questions with the Chairman—was called to Mao's new residence in the CCP leadership compound in the middle of the night to listen to Mao's outpourings. "You only trust the Russians," the Chairman shouted.

> You never trust the Chinese. [To you] Russians are first-class, while we Chinese are inferior people, who are stupid and careless. . . . You think you are in a position to control us [through having] a few nuclear bombs. . . . You have never had faith in the Chinese people. Stalin was among the worst. The Chinese [Communists] were re-

garded as second Titos; [we] were considered a backward nation. You have often stated that the Europeans used to look down on the Russians. I think some Russians now are looking down on the Chinese.[2]

In the summer of 1958, Mao tried to use foreign affairs to drive domestic mobilization for his Great Leap. When the Soviet leader, Nikita Khrushchev, rushed to Beijing to clear up the "misunderstanding" on military cooperation, Mao treated him gruffly and with visible contempt. The Chairman listed all of his complaints against the Soviets, from the 1920s on. Not commenting on the amount of assistance the Soviets were providing, Mao instead criticized the behavior of some Soviet advisers. "You can bring complaints about the follies of our specialists, and we do not have your specialists. Therefore, it turns out that only we commit follies," an exasperated Khrushchev sighed. "History is to blame for this," Mao responded. "And we have to answer for it?" "You made a revolution first." "And should we be blamed for this?" "That," Mao said, "is why you have to send specialists." At their second meeting, Mao received the Soviet leader poolside, in his swimming costume, fully aware that Khrushchev could not swim. With his visitor struggling to stay afloat at the back of the pool, Mao calmly did laps while lecturing the Soviets on Communist strategy. Upon Khrushchev's return to Moscow, many Soviet leaders started wondering, for the first time, whether their treasured alliance with China was going to last.

Immediately after Khrushchev left, Mao decided to again attack the GMD-held islands near China's coast. This time the aim was not so much to put pressure on the United States and Chiang Kai-shek as to create an international crisis in order to strengthen support at home. The Soviets were not informed before the attacks began but still gave the Chinese full diplomatic support. The second Taiwan Straits crisis blew over, but by 1959 Mao still seems to have reached the conclusion that his domestic aims were simply incompatible with keeping the original version of his Soviet alliance in place for much longer. When

Khrushchev again went to Beijing in October 1959 to attempt to straighten things out in the wake of mounting Chinese criticism, Mao would have nothing of it. He attacked the Soviet leader for being capitulationist toward the United States, for supporting India and other non-Communist countries, and for refusing to fully share nuclear weapons technology with China. Khrushchev shot back that the Chinese were extremist, militarist, and unwilling to cooperate. Marshal Chen Yi, the Chinese foreign minister, called Khrushchev a time-server to his face. "If you consider us time-servers, comrade Chen Yi, then do not offer me your hand," Khrushchev replied. "I will not accept it. . . . You should not spit from the height of your Marshal title. You do not have enough spit. We cannot be intimidated. What a pretty situation we have: On one side, you use the formula 'headed by the Soviet Union' [about the international Communist movement], on the other hand, you do not let me say a word."[3] Khrushchev left in the middle of his official visit. Sino-Soviet relations were in tatters.

But the confrontation between Mao and Khrushchev was only the beginning of the Sino-Soviet split, not its conclusion. In the winter of 1959–1960 Mao began to prepare for an open polemic against Soviet views on international affairs and Communist doctrine. A small group, headed by Deng Xiaoping, was assembled to prepare a series of articles attacking Khrushchev's views, thinly disguised as those of Marshal Tito and the Yugoslavs. In April 1960, on the ninetieth anniversary of Lenin's birth, the CCP fired the first barrage. Placing themselves in the position of determining what modern-day Leninism amounted to, the Chinese exhorted Marxist-Leninists worldwide to "thoroughly expose the absurdities of the imperialists and modern revisionists on these questions, eradicate their influence among the masses, awaken those they have temporarily hoodwinked and further arouse the revolutionary will of the masses."[4] In June 1960 the two parties clashed openly at the congress of the Romanian Communist party, displaying to the world that all was not well in the Communist camp. In the wake of the congress

Khrushchev's temper got the better of him, as Mao may have hoped for. On 18 July the Soviet leader ordered the majority of the 1,400 Soviet advisers in China to return home immediately, and most left within three weeks.

In just two years Mao and the CCP had created a massive economic disaster at home and come close to breaking with all of its allies abroad. Mao proclaimed that it was all good for China; his policies, according to the Chairman himself, ensured national independence and political purity, and therefore laid the foundation for China's future transformation. But by the autumn of 1960 cooler heads began to prevail. Looking at the staggering death toll of the Great Leap, Liu Shaoqi and Deng Xiaoping, on occasion helped by Premier Zhou Enlai (when he found the courage to do so), began to reverse some of the worst excesses of the party's policies. The Chairman himself was happy to sit back and let others begin to clear up the mess he had created, though he kept close watch to avoid political deviations. He even allowed a reduction in tension with Moscow, permitting the Soviets to send new advisers in to complete ongoing projects and send food supplies to help alleviate the hunger in some provinces. Mao had no problem with receiving further assistance from Moscow. As late as the spring of 1962 it is doubtful whether he had envisaged a complete break with the Kremlin. He wanted to strengthen his own position in the world Communist movement and gain the freedom to take China in whatever direction he thought best. If the Soviets were willing to accept that, he might not break fully with Khrushchev even in the future, he told his subordinates.

Throughout the early 1960s, limited forms of cooperation between Beijing and Moscow continued. In April 1961, the two countries signed a new and comprehensive trade agreement, and in the international negotiations on the future of Laos, the Soviets and Chinese worked quite closely together, at least up to the spring of 1962. In some fields, such as intelligence sharing and acquisition of military technology, a bilateral relationship continued to exist up to mid-1964. By then, however, Mao had decided to make the final break with the Soviet Union. To him and his closest supporters, the danger to the Maoist project was clear. The new forms of cooperation with the Soviets taken together with the consolidation in the Chinese economy implied an inherent criticism of the Great Leap Forward. In the summer of 1962, Liu Shaoqi, whom Mao a few years earlier had made president of the People's Republic, openly castigated the Leap. "We had many flaws and mistakes in implementing the general line, organizing the people's communes, and conducting the Great Leap Forward, even grave flaws and mistakes," Liu told the party's inner circle. "I think it is high time that we look back to examine and draw lessons. We can no longer continue to go on like this."[5] On foreign affairs, the head of CCP International Department Wang Jiaxiang, the Soviet-educated first PRC ambassador to Moscow and a key CCP intellectual, recommended a return to the principle of peaceful coexistence and a continuation of the Sino-Soviet alliance.

Mao was furious. At two meetings in late summer 1962 he struck back against those he saw as his opponents within the party. "I think that right-wing opportunism in China should be renamed: it should be called Chinese revisionism," he told his shocked colleagues. The Chairman insisted that the Soviet case showed that class struggle continued under socialism, and that China was engaged, domestically and internationally, in a "struggle against bourgeois ideas, which is identical with the struggle between Marxism-Leninism and revisionism." "On whether or not revisionism will emerge in our country, one [answer] is yes and the other is no. Now some cadres can be bribed with a pound of pork or a few packs of cigarettes." Making doubts about the Great Leap a matter of class struggle was tantamount to taking methods earlier employed against the party's class enemies and using them on party members. It meant that hereafter nobody was safe. Zhou Enlai, eager to please the Chairman and unable to understand the long-term consequences of Mao's views, immediately fell into line. "The struggle against revisionism has entered a new stage," the Premier now found, in which "class struggle has become a fundamental issue in our relations with fraternal parties." Zhou continued, "The truth of Marxism-Leninism and the center of the world revolution have moved from Moscow to Beijing. We should be brave and not shrink from our responsibilities."[6] Mao, as he often did, composed a poem about his own feelings of increasing megalomania:

> On this tiny globe
> A few flies dash themselves against the wall,
> Humming without cease,
> Sometimes shrilling,
> Sometimes moaning. . . .
> The world rolls on,
> Time presses.
> Ten thousand years are too long,
> Seize the day, seize the hour!
> The Four Seas are rising, clouds and waters raging,
> The Five Continents are rocking, wind and thunder roaring.
> Our force is irresistible,
> Away with all pests![7]

AS THE SINO-SOVIET CONFLICT ESCALATED, the search for allies in the Third World intensified. The mid-1950s saw a Soviet charm offensive toward non-Communist regimes such as India and Indonesia. In response, China established as a top priority the developing of good relations with its neighbors in Asia, India included. At the 1955 Afro-Asian conference in Bandung, Indian premier Nehru and Chinese premier Zhou embraced and promised eternal friendship between the two countries. By the end of the decade, however, the Sino-Indian relationship was in tatters. As China's domestic priorities drifted toward the left, the CCP became less tolerant of the character of the Indian leaders, whom the party saw as the bourgeois successors to British imperialism. China also became more security-minded about its border areas and regretted even the very limited form of de facto autonomy that had been given to Tibet in 1950. When the more radical Chinese policies in Lhasa led to a rebellion in Tibet in 1959 and to the flight of the Dalai Lama, the Tibetan religious leader, Mao Zedong concluded that India was behind the unrest and that New Delhi sought to benefit from it. By the early 1960s the relationship between the two countries was at the breaking point.

Both the Soviets and the CCP's own nationalities experts had recommended that the new PRC government go easy on Tibet after Chinese soldiers entered Lhasa in 1950. While local CCP reports from Tibet from the beginning condemned the feudalism and oppression of peasants that they saw in Tibetan society, Mao Zedong and the leadership intially wanted to carry out reform in such a strategically important area gradually and carefully. When smaller uprisings against land reform broke out in the Tibetan borderlands in 1956, the PRC increased its security presence in Lhasa step by step. In the spring of 1959 a rumor that the Chinese were planning to kidnap the Dalai Lama brought hundreds of thousands of Tibetans onto the streets in Lhasa. The PLA crushed what they saw as a rebellion in the Tibetan capital with an iron fist, but in the mêlée that followed Dalai and some members of the Tibetan religious leadership managed to flee across the border into India. Before the Dalai Lama's flight, the PRC authorities had been complaining to the Soviets for more than a year about what they saw (probably correctly) as Indian and CIA assistance to the Tibetan fighters. With the Tibetan refugees welcomed south of the border, the CCP leaders were certain that they faced an enemy in New Delhi that was intent on stirring up trouble along China's frontiers.[8]

The conflict with India was made worse by Soviet unwillingness to condemn Delhi outright and by China's increasingly hard-line domestic policies. By the summer of 1962, when Mao turned on those who had been trying to sweep up after the crash of his Great Leap, policy toward

India was pulled into the framework of isolation and siege. India choosing this precise time to begin forward patrolling into the disputed border areas of course contributed to the pressure on the authorities in Beijing. Even Mao did not want a war with India; on the contrary, he wanted to limit the border issue in order to concentrate on the Tibetan problem. But when Delhi turned down the Chinese appeal for negotiations, the Chairman saw a direct challenge and was ready to react:

> We fought a war with old Chiang [Kai-shek]. We fought a war with Japan, and with America. We feared none of these. And in each case we won. Now the Indians want to fight a war with us. Naturally we are not afraid. We cannot give ground; if we give ground it would be the same as letting them seize a big piece of land equivalent to Fujian Province. . . . Since Nehru sticks his head out and insists on us fighting him, for us not to fight him would be discourteous. Courtesy means reciprocity.[9]

The Chinese attacked on 20 October 1962 along two fronts six hundred miles apart, east of Bhutan and in the western sector south of the Kunlun mountains, near the border with Pakistan. On both fronts the Indian forces were defeated, and when China declared a ceasefire a month later all of the disputed territory was under Chinese control. For India the outcome of the war was a profound shock: Not only were its forces routed, but the international sympathy and assistance that it had counted on had been of little help. The Soviets stayed neutral in practice, while rhetorically supporting the Chinese position. Mao was not impressed, believing that Khrushchev was simply trying to gain China's help in the Cuban Missile Crisis, which was taking place at the same time. Most importantly, the war created a sense of enmity and confrontation between Asia's two biggest countries, a situation that has lasted up to today.

By 1963 Mao Zedong had, almost singlehandedly, managed to wreck the Sino-Soviet relationship. This had been his purpose, at least since the decade began, but it would have been much more difficult if it had not been for the stupendous arrogance of the Soviet political leadership and the political blindness of his colleagues in Beijing. Mao wanted to destroy the relationship to Moscow because he needed to be free, in ideological terms, to take China further to the left, in what came to be called the Great Proletarian Cultural Revolution. Always a wily operator, Mao made sure that the Chinese leaders he most suspected of disagreeing with his increasing radicalism should bear the brunt of the confrontation with the Soviets, and do so both on ideological and nationalist terms. Deng Xiaoping, who was one of these, was sent to Moscow as head of a CCP delegation in the summer of 1963, with the implicit purpose of attacking the Soviets. Deng was put in a hopeless situation: On the one hand he did not much care for the Soviets at the personal level, but on the other he knew how dependent China's technology and its whole economic development were on collaborating with Moscow. Still, Deng fulfilled the Chairman's instructions to the full, as he always did as long as Mao was alive. He told his Soviet hosts that they had created "a split in the ranks of the international Communist movement and, moreover, have done so in an increasingly sharp, increasingly extreme form, in an increasingly organized [way], on an increasingly large scale, trying, come what may, to crush [the CCP]." He added with a wry smile, "I would like to note that using such methods is a habitual affair for you."[10] Not surprisingly, there were no further meetings.

Instead there was an escalation of conflict between the two Communist giants bordering on war. From 1962 on, Chinese spokesmen had claimed that the Soviets were putting military pressure on their common border. The defection of large numbers of people from Xinjiang, China's westernmost province, to the Soviet Union only confirmed to the CCP faithful that the Soviets were now their sworn enemies (even though it is more likely that it was a combination of Great Leap–induced hunger and Soviet blandishments that produced the mass decampment). In the summer of 1964 Mao said, "We cannot only pay attention to the East [the United States] and not to the North, only pay attention to imperialism and not revisionism, we must prepare for war on both sides." And at the same time he made his most ominous statement vis-à-vis the Soviets. "About a hundred years ago," he told a visiting group of Japanese, "the area east of Baikal became Russian territory, and since then Vladivostok, Khabarovsk, Kamchatka, and other points have become territories of the Soviet Union. We have not yet presented the bill for this list."[11]

Mao now took a major step in breaking with both superpowers. After the 1962 Cuban Missile Crisis, the Soviet Union and the United States had begun edging back from the brink. In August 1963, along with the United Kingdom, they signed the nuclear test ban treaty, lowering the temperature of the Cold War. Mao would have none of it. In October 1964 he took his country out of interaction with most of world society with the first successful Chinese nuclear test. Now China had its own nuclear capability, and the security that went with it, Mao believed. By the end of the year the Chairman began to speak darkly about enemies of the revolution and "capitalist roaders" within the Chinese Communist Party. During 1965 the preparations for a major purge were visibly underway. Mao criticized the CCP Secretariat and the Central State Planning Commission as independent kingdoms outside his control. Whenever there was an opportunity, he beat the drums of war—against the Americans in Vietnam, against the Soviets in the north, against all comers who wanted to destroy China. In October 1965 he told a startled group of party officials that "we must prepare for war. . . . Do not be afraid of mutiny or rebellion." He added, "What will you do if revisionism emerges in the Central Committee? In that event, you must rebel. . . . Now you must remember, whatever one says, be it the Central Committee, its bureaus or the provincial party committees, you can refuse to implement it if it is not correct."[12] Very soon afterward Mao left Beijing for secret locations in the provinces, not to return until the summer of 1966, when the Great

Proletarian Cultural Revolution—as he called his new campaign—was washing all over China.

Mao had engineered China's isolation so he could prepare for his great purge. But he also attempted to use his theories about people's war to appeal to Third World countries and radical groups to align with China and create a new center in international affairs. Marshal Lin Biao, who had reemerged to become Mao's chief henchman in the military, the most obsequious singer of the Chairman's praise, and, eventually Mao's chosen successor, had put his name to a text entitled "Long Live the Victory of People's War" in September 1965. In it, he hailed Mao as a genius whose "great merit lies in the fact that he has succeeded in integrating the universal truth of Marxism-Leninism with the concrete practice of the Chinese revolution and has enriched and developed Marxism-Leninism by his masterly generalization and summation of the experience gained during the Chinese people's protracted revolutionary struggle." Lin reminded people around the world that Mao's "theory of the establishment of rural revolutionary base areas and the encirclement of the cities from the countryside is of outstanding and universal practical importance for the present revolutionary struggles of all the oppressed nations and peoples, and particularly for the revolutionary struggles of the oppressed nations and peoples in Asia, Africa and Latin America against imperialism and its lackeys."[13] In other words, China would support revolutionary groups in other countries, but only if they recognized Mao's strategic genius first.

For the revolutionaries next door, China's new turn to the extreme left could not have come at a worse time. Both North Vietnam and North Korea had learned to navigate the choppy waters created by the Sino-Soviet split and become quite accomplished at getting support from both. Now Mao insisted that they had to choose, just at the point when both were most in need of foreign assistance. US ground troops had landed in Vietnam in 1965, and the Vietnamese Communists had to design a strategy to defeat them to achieve their aim of re-unifying their country under their party's leadership. In North Korea, Kim Il-sung had been hoping that the American involvement in Vietnam would allow him to put more pressure on the South, but instead found himself facing a Chinese regime that insisted on total loyalty to its ideals.

The leaders in North Vietnam and of the National Liberation Front in the South had used the widening ideological split between the Chinese and the Soviets to push a more aggressive strategy for reunifying the country. In the early 1960s, the Chinese had, in most respects, supported the Vietnamese policy, while the Soviets had called for patience and negotiations in order to avoid a further US involvement. Even Beijing, though, had advised the North Vietnamese to not move too fast, out of fear of dragging China into another direct confrontation with the United States similar to what had happened in Korea fifteen years earlier. Mao knew, of course, that without Soviet aid, China stood no chance in a war against the Americans. Instead China limited itself to sending advisers and limited amounts of materiel to support North Vietnam, while building a close political relationship with its leaders. By 1964 North Vietnam was close to joining China outright in its ideological attacks on the Soviet Union, in spite of still receiving Soviet aid. The Vietnamese, especially Ho Chi Minh and his successor Le Duan, were inspired by the Chinese road to socialism. They genuinely believed that the Chinese methods of great leaps and extreme collectivism were better suited for Vietnam's modernization than what they saw as the more moderate Soviet ways. Linked to their ideological predilections were the cultural closeness with China and the long and intimate relations between their two Communist parties. Finally, they knew that theirs would be a long struggle, and that China was a next-door neighbor, the only likely candidate to furnish the support they needed over time. Though there were still Vietnamese Communists who, for historical reasons, feared China's long-term influence, the relationship between the two in the first half of the 1960s was over-whelmingly positive.

The US ground intervention in Vietnam in the spring of 1965, just as Chinese politics were moving toward the Cultural Revolution, changed the strategic picture both for Hanoi and Beijing. The North Vietnamese leaders now had to fight a rapidly escalating war directly against US forces, and were in desperate need of weapons and economic support. The Soviets, who had already reacted angrily against the US bombing of North Vietnam, which began in the autumn of 1964, started a large-scale program of supplying Hanoi with what they needed most: aircraft, tanks, and air defenses. Mao wanted China to take a more differentiated position. China's military advisers and support troops, who were already in the North, should be augmented but not engage in the fighting. China should step up its material assistance to North Vietnam, but mainly in terms of basic supplies, thereby not de-pleting stocks that China would need for its own defense. Covertly, China should warn the Americans that an invasion of North Vietnam would mean war with the PRC (thereby avoiding a Korean War sce-nario, where Chinese troops first intervened when US troops were near-ing their border). And—first and foremost—Chinese representatives should guard against Soviet perfidy and deceptions. Mao speculated that Moscow might be planning to attack China under the guise of bringing advanced weapons to Vietnam or might want to provoke a devastating Sino-American war.

Mao's instructions led to a Chinese foreign policy disaster in Viet-nam. China managed to stay out of the war, but Mao's policies de-stroyed the country's close relationship to the Vietnamese leaders that had been carefully built over two generations. Le Duan, who had been a supporter of Chinese views, could not understand why Beijing seemed to put all possible hindrances in the way of urgently needed Soviet aid reaching Vietnam through Chinese territory. He and the other Viet-namese leaders also resented Chinese beratings on tactics and strategy, which became increasingly shrill and Sino-centric as the Cultural Revolution progressed, attempting to push Hanoi to choose between Soviet or Chinese aid. As the Soviet program of increased military aid to the Vietnamese Communist forces got going in 1965, Zhou Enlai told the Vietnamese that Soviet help was "not sincere." Such aid served US interests, he said, and Vietnam would be better off without it.[14] In 1966, Deng Xiaoping, himself soon to be purged in the Cultural Revolution, yelled at Le Duan, who had mentioned concerns about Chinese propaganda inside Vietnam:

> What are you still afraid of? Why are you afraid of displeasing the Soviets, and what about China? I want to tell you frankly what I now feel: Vietnamese comrades have some other thoughts about our methods of assistance, but you have not yet told us. . . . It is not only the matters concerning our judgment on the Soviet aid. Are you suspicious that China helps Vietnam for our own intentions? We hope that you can tell us directly if you want us to help. The problem will easily be solved. We will withdraw our military men at once. We have a lot of things to do in China. And the military men stationed along the border will be ordered back to the mainland.[15]

By 1969, the Communist Vietnamese leaders were convinced that China was not acting in their country's best interests. They now believed that the PRC planned to dominate a future reunified Vietnam and that the Chinese wanted the war to go on for as long as possible to take strategic pressure off China itself. Some even suspected that by prolonging the war, China hoped to force the United States into some kind of modus vivendi with the PRC. In other words, China was willing to fight the Vietnam War to the last Vietnamese. It was a relationship in which something had to give.

If things were bad in Vietnam, they were not much better across the border in comradely North Korea. Like his North Vietnamese comrades, Kim Il-sung had at first sided with the Chinese in their disputes with the Soviets. Mao Zedong, Kim believed, was much closer than the new Soviet leader Leonid Brezhnev to the kind of socialism Kim wanted to create in Korea: authoritarian, intense, and rapidly progressing. But by 1966 Kim had begun to have his doubts. Having Chinese advisers and students in his own capital Pyongyang shout slogans about the greatness of Mao Zedong Thought and against the revisionists was a step too far, in his view. Having attempted and failed to rein them in through his "advice" to the Chinese embassy, Kim denounced Beijing for its "superpower chauvinism" and called Mao's cherished Red Guards "kids who know nothing about politics." Kim had hoped for a reinvigorated alliance that could help him stage an offensive against South Korea. But now he had suddenly a new security concern on his northern border. Over loudspeakers set up along the entire frontier with North Korea, China began agitation against the "Korean revisionists." Drawing closer to the Soviets, Kim furiously condemned what he called the idiocy of the Cultural Revolution. In Beijing, the Red Guards warned "Kim Il-sung and his breed that those who collaborate with the U.S. or with revisionism, and continue with anti-Chinese policies, will come to a bad end. Sooner or later the Korean people will rise up and settle scores."[16]

B Y THE MID-1960S, China had only one remaining foreign policy strategy. It was based on Mao's insistence that his country was heading an undefined and unorganized Third World front against both American imperialism and Soviet revisionism. Countries such as Indonesia, Algeria, Ghana, and Cuba, Mao asserted, were part of the front and would, in the end, join with China in overcoming Western dominance. War was coming, the Chairman said, and the Third World, led by China, would be the victor. "The Soviet Union came out of the First World War," Mao told an Indonesian visitor. "China and many other socialist countries came out of the Second World War; and imperialism will perish in a Third World War."[17] But the problem for Chinese policies was not only that difficulties abounded in its relations with putative Third World allies but also that the radical leaders in these countries seemed to be losing influence. By the late 1960s all of China's Third World allies were gone, because their leaders had been overthrown, they had joined up with the Soviets, or simply because they had tired of China's know-it-all attitude and self-centered militancy.

Indonesia had been a top Chinese priority since the 1950s. By far the biggest country in Southeast Asia, Indonesia was led by Sukarno, a radical anti-imperialist and eclectic socialist with increasingly close relations to the local Communist party. As we have seen, Indonesia also has a large ethnic Chinese population, some of which was influential in the country's trade and industry. The PRC was, in turn, embarrassed by the Sino-Indonesian petit bourgeoisie and motivated by the wish to be seen as the protector of all Chinese living abroad. Still, Mao's main aim was to ally himself with Sukarno's regime and with the Indonesian Communist Party as part of it. In his meeting with the Indonesian leader in June 1961, Mao hailed Sukarno as the leader of the nonaligned world, implying that the untrustworthy Nehru was trying to steal the crown off him. In January 1963, Liu Shaoqi proclaimed that Indonesia had replaced India as the fulcrum of Third World anti-imperialism and anticolonialism.[18]

But as China's own policies turned ever leftward, the leaders in Beijing became increasingly preoccupied with what they saw as the Indonesian regime's bourgeois character. From 1962, Indonesia was involved in an undeclared jungle war against Malaysia in Borneo. China supported Indonesia, and its leaders were shocked when Sukarno in 1964 went to the negotiating table. The Chinese thought Sukarno had fallen under the influence of the Americans. US Attorney General Robert Kennedy, brother of the recently assassinated president, had just met with Sukarno to discuss peace. The Chinese saw the Indonesian decision as "instigated by Robert Kennedy" and reflecting "the dark side and the double-dealings of bourgeois nationalists." China therefore increasingly prioritized its support for the Indonesian Communist Party and its militia, which they began to supply with arms and training from early 1965.[19] There is little doubt that China's support encouraged those Indonesian Communists and sympathizers who attempted to carry out a coup in October 1965 and thereby facilitated the army's subsequent crushing of the left in Indonesia. The result was a new anti-Communist regime, as well as thousands of Indonesians of Chinese descent killed in the massacres the coup leaders instigated.

In Africa the trajectory of China's involvement was similar. In Ghana, the radical president Kwame Nkrumah had been happy to receive Chinese aid. But in 1964–1965, his country became a center for Chinese guerrilla training of various left-wing movements. The Chinese advice to set up a people's militia helped trigger the army coup that overthrew Nkrumah. In Algeria, the relationship between the new revolutionary government of Ahmed Ben Bella and the Chinese had been very close immediately after Algerian independence in 1962. But by 1965 it had soured, in part because of Algeria's increasing cooperation with the Soviet Union. According to the Chinese Foreign Ministry, Ben Bella's anti-imperialism was just "tough talk, weak action." The Chinese embassy in Algeria questioned whether he had the courage to use "revolutionary means" to overcome Algeria's economic difficulties: "the Algerian ruling group is very arrogant and conceited, but its tiger's ass can still be petted."[20] When Ben Bella was overthrown by a military coup in June 1965 the Chinese breathed a sigh of relief and immediately recognized the new government. It was the first of many Chinese recognitions of military regimes in the Third World in the 1970s and 1980s simply because they were seen (wrongly, in the Algerian case) to be anti-Soviet. China's Third World policy was nearing both its intellectual and political bankruptcy.

The slap that smarted most in Beijing was Cuba's turn toward the Soviets. Although Fidel Castro and Che Guevara undoubtedly were closer to much of the fine print in the Chinese elaboration of socialism, the Soviet economic model was more manageable and Soviet assistance had fewer strings attached. China wanted Cuba to allow dissemination of Chinese propaganda on the island. It asked for a more balanced approach to themselves and the Soviets. When in 1966 the Chinese threatened reductions in Sino-Cuban trade, Castro exploded. He publicly charged China with committing "a criminal act of economic aggression against our country" and joining the US-led embargo of Cuba. China's actions, Castro said,

> can be explained only as a display of absolute contempt toward our country, of total ignorance of the character and sense of dignity of our people. It was not simply a matter of more or less tons of rice, or more or less square meters of cloth, which were also involved, but of a much more important and fundamental questions for the peoples: whether in the world of tomorrow powerful nations can assume the right to blackmail, extort, pressure, attack, and strangle small peoples; whether in the world of tomorrow, which the revolutionaries are struggling to establish, there are to continue to prevail the worst methods of piracy, oppression, and filibusterism. . . . Our revolutionary state could not allow such an attempt to influence military and administrative cadres by acts that constitute a betrayal of the trust, friendship, and brotherhood with which our country receives the representatives of any socialist state.[21]

China's Third World influence was for all practical purposes a thing of the past.

THE GREAT PROLETARIAN Cultural Revolution was by far the largest and most intense government campaign in Chinese history. It killed fewer people than the Great Leap and it affected the economy less, but in terms of people's daily lives and of lives ruined and made meaningless it was far worse. All over China, people—mostly innocent of any crime or dissent—were hauled before impromptu tribunals and kangaroo courts, publicly humiliated or tortured, with their families and friends in attendance. Many of the victims had built their lives on serving the revolution and the CCP, and all of the most prominent victims were leaders of the Communist Party. Liu Shaoqi, China's president, was tortured and left to die in prison. At public rallies, Peng Dehuai, the commander of Chinese troops in Korea, was beaten until his back was broken. The young people who carried out the killings and torture were empowered by the Chairman himself, whom they revered as a godlike figure. When Mao told them to "bombard the headquarters" and condemned his closest colleagues as revisionists and China's Khrushchevs, the Red Guards took the kind of action the Chairman expected of them. Mao and his new circle of assistants made sure that nobody stood in their way and encouraged the violence when necessary. It was Mao's final attempt to isolate China and to perpetuate his revolution.

During the Cultural Revolution, almost all of China's relations with the outside world came to a standstill. Chinese diplomats and students abroad were called back home to make self-criticisms and undergo training in Mao Zedong Thought. Foreign students in China were expelled and some of the embassies attacked. The British embassy was stormed and set on fire in August 1967. Foreigners in China compared the situation to that of the Boxer uprising sixty years earlier. As we have seen, the North Koreans and the North Vietnamese, China's only remaining allies in the region, complained about the treatment their staffs received and about the eagerness Chinese advisers in their countries had to spread Cultural Revolution propaganda, including the ubiquitous Little Red Book of Mao quotations. The Cubans were eager to pull out; one returning group told a Soviet diplomat that "it is hard to imagine, to what type of idiocy the ranks of the 'Red Guards' and the people led by them reach. The Hitlerites could have learned something from them." Meanwhile in Beijing, the Soviet embassy was put under siege by Red Guards and Soviet and East German diplomats were beaten up on the street. When they tried to issue a complaint with the Chinese Foreign Ministry, the Soviets were told that the ministry "resolutely supports the revolutionary activities of our people."[22] In Moscow, Chinese diplomats only shouted slogans from Mao's little red book when the Soviet foreign minister asked for an urgent meeting.

The anti-Soviet and anti-Western rhetoric increased as the Cultural Revolution progressed. The Americans and British were accused of planning to wage war on China, and they would be helped by the Soviet Union. "The Soviet Union has changed character," claimed the CCP paper *The People's Daily* in June 1967. "A dictatorship of the bourgeoisie has replaced the dictatorship of the proletariat and the bourgeoisie has effected counter-revolutionary restoration through its agents." Kang Sheng, the head of the party's security and intelligence bureau, who had thrown his lot in with the Cultural Revolutionaries, saw foreign agents at work everywhere within China. "The Soviet revisionists have trained many secret agents now operating in our country," he told the Red Guards. "The Mongolian revisionists are promoting treasonous activities among our people and so are the Korean revisionists. . . . You must heighten your vigilance."[23]

At its height, the Cultural Revolution turned increasingly xenophobic. All that was foreign was viewed with suspicion. Friends of mine remember being beaten up because a foreign-language book was found when Red Guards ransacked their homes, or, on the street, for wearing glasses (an assumed accoutrement of foreignness). Meanwhile, some foreigners living in China tried their best to join the new campaign. The Polish-born journalist Israel Epstein, a veteran Communist survivor of many purges and a member of the CCP since 1964, wrote of "living through tremendous days, weeks, months that do indeed 'shake the world'—rejuvenating, revivifying, scraping all the barnacles off the mind (and scraping off those who have themselves become barnacles on the cause)." Epstein and his boss, Sidney Rittenberg, set up a Red Guard "rebel group" to criticize other foreigners who were not quick enough to catch the political winds. But Epstein was himself relegated to the position of "barnacle" in 1968 and spent five years in prison. Rittenberg got ten. Posters put up by other foreigners after Rittenberg's arrest proclaimed in big Chinese characters, "He has climbed so high and fallen so low" and "Rittenberg shows all the qualities we have long been accustomed to finding in the Jew."[24]

In a world where leading figures were publicly tortured, with their families forced to watch, all was possible. The wife of President Liu Shaoqi, Wang Guangmei—a Communist since age sixteen—was kidnapped from her official residence by Red Guards from Qinghua University. She was beaten up, forced to put on the thin silk dress she had worn during an official visit to Jakarta and was paraded in public. According to the official interrogation record of Wang Guangmei, the students shouted at her:

> You are being struggled against today. We are at liberty to wage struggle in whatever form we may want to, and you have no freedom. . . . We are the revolutionary masses, and you are a notorious counter-revolutionary old hag. Don't try to confuse the class demarcation line! . . . By wearing this dress to flirt with Sukarno in Indonesia, you have put the Chinese people to shame. . . . ([Red Guards] reading in unison [from Mao's *Little Red Book*]: "Everything reactionary is the same; if you don't hit it, it won't fall.")[25]

Among those inside the CCP who were set to handle China's foreign relations, all was in chaos. Zhou Enlai tried to guess in which direction the Chairman wanted to go, and then adhere to it in order to save himself and those around him. When Chen Yi, the tough veteran Communist who was now foreign minister, questioned the Red Guards' handling of foreign affairs, Mao exploded. The Central Cultural Revolution Group (CCRG), he said, was "97 percent correct. Whoever opposes CCRG, I firmly oppose him! If you want to negate the Cultural Revolution, you will never succeed." Diplomats in the Foreign Ministry scurried to set up their own Red Guard groups (the one in the Department of the Americas and Oceania called itself the Beat Drowning Dogs Brigade) and raised the slogan "Bombard Chen Yi, and completely lift the lid off the class struggle in the Foreign Ministry."[26] Chen Yi was publicly humiliated at struggle meetings, before being sent for re-education to a factory in Hebei province. Bizarrely, he kept the title of foreign minister until he died in January 1972.

To THE EXTENT THAT CHINESE foreign policy continued to exist after the onset of the Cultural Revolution, its energy was directed toward condemning the Soviet Union. By the late 1960s Moscow had become China's number one enemy. The Soviet invasion of Czechoslovakia in August 1968—though unrelated to Sino-Soviet relations—frightened the Chinese leaders. They knew how weak their country had become as a result of the Cultural Revolution, which, by then, had degenerated into chaos, with bands of Red Guards fighting each other with heavy weapons in the streets. The Soviet deployment of armed forces to Mongolia—at the request of Mongolian authorities, who feared the bedlam next door—also fueled Beijing's paranoia. Even though the US war in Vietnam still preoccupied Mao and the CCP leaders (those, that is, who were still at large), the Soviet Union was an increasingly open and direct threat of a kind that the United States was not, at least for the time being.

In 1968, Mao increasingly called the Soviet Union "social-imperialist." The term implied that the Soviets would at some point attack China in a repeat of Russia's past imperialist aggression. Mao defined social-imperialism as a particularly virulent form of great power expansionism, thereby grouping Moscow with Washington and London as "Western" imperialists. In his last meeting with a Soviet leader back in 1965, when Soviet premier Alexei Kosygin had come to Beijing, Mao harangued his visitor: "The United States and the USSR are now deciding the world's destiny. Well, go ahead and decide. But within the next 10–15 years you will not be able to decide the world's destiny. It is in the hands of the nations of the world, and not in the hands of the imperialists, exploiters or revisionists."[27] Three years later the Soviet Union had become the most dangerous Western imperialist power as far as China was concerned. But although Mao's language was becoming increasingly racial, China's only remaining ally was a European country, Albania, whose Communist leaders had fallen out with all of its neighbors. Mao was quick to hold up Albania as a beacon of world revolution, but for many in Beijing the very mention of the Albanians served as a reminder of how isolated China was in international affairs.

In Beijing the top leaders were preparing for war. The increasing worry about having to confront the outside world led to a bizarre program of moving key parts of China's industry to what was regarded as safer areas in the western parts of the country. These were generally the same areas where the Guomindang had survived the Japanese onslaught after 1937. Now, whole factories were dismantled and transported to what Mao called the Third Line, a big stretch of land from Gansu in the north to Yunnan in the south. Begun in 1965—as the US war in Vietnam intensified—the Third Line, increased in significance as the conflict with the Soviets intensified. The waste and dislocation of the process was significant and the damage done to China's economy was severe. In some cases, however, the challenges of being dumped (and sometimes forgotten) in the back of beyond during the chaos of the Cultural Revolution taught industrial managers skills that they were to use to their advantage during the capitalist revolution in later decades. The policy of creating a "secure rear base area" continued up to the early 1980s, and may have consumed as much as a third of China's total investment program for this period.[28]

During the Cultural Revolution, as it built bases for war inside the country, the PRC neglected its own Chinese periphery. Hong Kong remained important as a conduit for China's foreign trade, and Taiwan served as a tangible reminder of China's division and therefore its national humiliation. But Beijing had no active policy toward either region. Among overseas Chinese fear ran rampant. Having listened to the few stories that got out from a small number who visited China, almost none had a wish to go back. They knew, of course, that some of those who were persecuted during the Cultural Revolution were returnees who had come back to serve China. In minority areas, Mao's final campaigns were especially disastrous. In Tibet, temples were destroyed along with religious symbols and paintings, while monks and nuns were hauled off to be struggled against by Red Guards flown in from Beijing and Shanghai for the purpose. In Inner Mongolia at least 16,000 were killed while CCP leaders and Red Guards were hunting for a separatist party that turned out to be a chimera. In Guangxi, which the CCP had defined as an autonomous region for the Zhuang people, the Cultural Revolution descended into a murderous frenzy, with politically inspired cannibalism as one ingredient.[29]

The main components of the Cultural Revolution—the xenophobia, the relocations to the interior, and the terror against minorities— served Mao Zedong's purposes well. The mass hysteria in Beijing, where millions of young people from all over the country rallied before him at Tian'anmen Square, appealed to his limitless ego. The sending of youth from the cities to the countryside, where they were supposed to learn from the peasants, appealed to his sense of politically motivated development. To the Cultural Revolution leadership, China's international isolation helped create a new China and save the revolution. Even after he had used the army to end the worst of the chaos on the streets in late 1968, Mao saw the processes as continuing. As he told the new party leadership in early 1969,

> We are talking about victory. This means that we must guarantee that we should unite the vast masses of the entire country to pursue victory under the leadership of the proletariat. The socialist revolution must continue. There are still unfinished tasks for this

revolution to fulfill, such as to conduct struggle, to conduct criticism, and to conduct transformation. After a few years, we will
probably need to carry out another revolution.[30]

A MAIN REASON WHY MAO ZEDONG, assisted by Zhou Enlai and the
army, pulled China back from almost total chaos of the cultural
revolution in 1968 was the increasing fear of war with the Soviet Union.
While there is no evidence of the Soviets having prepared such an attack,
it is easy to see how such a fear could come out of the Cultural Revolution frenzy and the Chairman's own rhetoric. Having put China and
its revolution squarely at the center of world history, as the envy of all
peoples, it was only logical that their enemies should try to destroy them
through military force. Other scenarios than a Soviet attack were contemplated as well. There could be a Soviet-American war, which China
could be drawn into. The Americans could attack from the south, if the
war in Vietnam went badly for them. Mao ruminated to his visitors:

> Since Japan's surrender in 1945, 23 years have passed. In another
> five years, 28 years will have passed. Without a war in 28 years? In
> reality, all kinds of wars have occurred since the end of World War
> II. According to Lenin, capitalism is war, and capitalism cannot
> exist without war. There are two superpowers in the world today.
> They not only have conventional weapons, but also have nuclear
> weapons. This is something that is not easy to deal with.[31]

In order to suss out Soviet intentions and assure himself of the
army's loyalty, Mao agreed to a limited military operation against Soviet
forces. The March 1969 attack was on Zhenbao/Damanskii island in
the Ussuri river, part of the north Manchurian border zone claimed by
both countries. About thirty Soviet soldiers were killed in the initial
strike. While fighting continued in the area, Soviet Premier Kosygin
desperately tried to speak to Mao by phone. The Chinese operator re-

fused to connect the call, shouting slogans against the revisionists. For a few days the question of war or peace hung in the balance. The Soviets considered an attack on Chinese nuclear installations as a preventive measure. While Mao quickly backtracked, allowing negotiations to begin on the border issue, tension along the frontier remained. In August new clashes took place in the western sector, along the Xinjiang border. There were heavy casualties on both sides. This time the Chinese leaders believed that the Soviets were planning a large-scale attack on China, in spite of a visit by Kosygin to Beijing, where he tried to negotiate. Lin Biao, acting on Mao's behalf, issued his "order number one" in October 1969, putting the army on emergency alert and evacuating the senior leaders (and their most prominent Cultural Revolution victims) from the capital.

Although the war never came, the situation in China remained tense up to the early 1970s. The war scare of 1969 convinced Mao that China's isolation was dangerous and ineffectual. Now he wanted more order and less revolution at home, at least for a while. His mobilization orders attempted to suspend most of the Cultural Revolution excesses:

> All factional struggle by violent means should be stopped unconditionally and immediately. All professional teams for struggle by violent means should be dissolved. All strongholds for struggle by violent means should be eliminated. All weapons should be handed back. If any team for struggle by violent means continues to occupy a stronghold and stubbornly refuses to surrender, the People's Liberation Army can surround the stronghold by force, launch a political offensive toward it, and confiscate the weapons [held by the team] by force.[32]

But the genie of disorder was not easily to put back in the bottle. Mao, after all, refused to give up his Cultural Revolution ideals and inner-party politics remained as frenzied as ever. In September 1971 Lin Biao, Mao's putative successor, attempted to flee to the Soviet

Union as the Chairman prepared to purge him from the leadership. Lin's plane crashed in Mongolia.

From the summer of 1969 on, Mao sought the advice of the old heads of the army (many of whom he had allowed to be tortured and imprisoned in the previous three years) about how to handle an international crisis he himself had created. In their report, the marshals emphasized that the Soviet Union was the main enemy, now and in the future. Soviet power was growing, they wrote, while American power was waning. They asserted that "the Soviet revisionists have made China their main enemy, imposing a more serious threat to our security than the U.S. imperialists. . . . [But] both China and the United States take the Soviet Union as their enemy, thus the Soviet revisionists do not dare to fight a two-front war." In a personal memo to the Chairman, Chen Yi—still with the title of foreign minister, but in reality under house arrest—discussed his "wild ideas": "It is necessary for us," Chen wrote in September 1969, "to utilize the contradiction between the United States and the Soviet Union in a strategic sense, and pursue a breakthrough in Sino-American relations." He suggested unconditional high-level meetings with Washington. Over the two years that followed, Mao took up many of Chen's "wild ideas" while sticking to his Cultural Revolution agenda and condemning Chen himself as a "sham Marxist" and "anti-party careerist."[33]

M AO'S CAMPAIGNS, begun in the late 1950s, isolated China and made it vulnerable to attack. Inside the country the violent attempts to purge all outside influence and reorient party policy to center on Mao alone held back the country's development and created a cynical generation, whose initial idealism had been drowned in blood and broken promises. For some Chinese historians, the collapse of the Sino-Soviet alliance was a good thing, because it made China more independent and nationally oriented. In reality, however, Mao wanted freedom from Soviet influence precisely so that he could undertake the disastrous campaigns that set China's progress back by decades. To the CCP of the 1960s, Cultural Revolution and isolation went together. Both aims would make the country stronger.

Since the early part of the nineteenth century, China had never been more isolated in international affairs than it was during the 1960s. The CCP revolution, which had promised to make China rich and strong had, it seemed, ended up making it poor and weak. True, China under Communism had kept its territorial unity and made huge advances in technology and in areas such as public health. It had also carried out a social revolution which had eliminated private control of agriculture and industry, thereby making all Chinese (except the surviving party elite) more equal. But this equality, in the 1970s, was a question of being equally *poor* and visibly helpless in an international context. No wonder that some Chinese were starting to ask themselves questions that were distinctly similar to those of the 1920s: How could China be saved from poverty and stagnation? How could China be made modern and successful? What was the meaning of being Chinese in a world where those who had left the country prospered, while those who stayed at home suffered and failed?

CHAPTER 10

CHINA'S AMERICA

THROUGHOUT THE TWENTIETH CENTURY, Chinese have had a complicated but almost obsessive relationship with the United States. It is a place many Chinese would like to go to, in order to visit, to sojourn, or to settle. But it is also a threatening and confusing zone, where politics, values, friendships and even the landscape itself are in constant flux. America challenges much of what Chinese think of as their values: tradition, family, and concern for the collective. It is also suspect because Americans are believed by some to look down on the Chinese, viewing them as inferior and that is why Americans locked their country's gates to them. It is impossible for most Chinese to understand how the United States, which is a nation of immigrants, could have any other reason for Chinese exclusion than prejudice. History matters a great deal in China, and in terms of memory, the negative in Chinese historical relations with the United States often outweighs the positive.

But then there is also the endless fascination with things American, with American wealth, and with American ideas. Although few Chinese today see it this way, the United States and China have had much in common during the twentieth century. Chinese often laud their traditions, but they have spent most of the past hundred years throwing them away and transforming—endlessly, it seems—into something different. Much of this transformation has been inspired by the United

States: Technology, business, culture, and political concepts with American origins have been ubiquitous in China, even when the Chinese state has been most preoccupied with rooting out all American influence. What connects, though, goes further than simple exchanges. It has to do with the speed of change itself and with dissatisfaction with things as they are. It also has to do with accepting change. Even though the political trajectories of China and the United States in the twentieth century could hardly be more different, both peoples have been primed to accept rapid transformation of their daily lives. The intense drive toward modernity that has motivated both American and Chinese elites may have come about for different reasons—for the Chinese the urgency of reviving the past, for the Americans the necessity of recreating the future. Still, both have a teleological purpose for entering into modernity, and a firm belief that only their country can fully possess it.

In 1970, Mao Zedong made the decision to "ease," as he put it, the overall conflict with the United States. China was exiting from the most disastrous phase of the Cultural Revolution, but this reorientation in China's foreign policy had nothing to do with any reevaluation by Mao of his political ideals. For the rest of his life he remained wedded to China's complete revolutionary transformation. The reason for his turnaround was China's increasing conflict with the Soviet Union and the fear of a Soviet attack. Most of this fear was born of the ideological conflict with Moscow in the 1960s, a conflict that grew in the minds of the Chinese leadership to a cataclysmic contest that could end in nuclear war. But the opening to the United States had unintended consequences that Mao could not foresee and which would have horrified him if he had been able to. The final part of the twentieth century became America's decades in China, a time when one foreign country dominated the sense most Chinese had of "abroad" in a way that had never happened before and probably will never happen again. American influence was everywhere: in the economy, politics, arts, and consumer patterns. For a while it seemed that all that mattered in China's relations with the world was the relationship, for good and bad, with the United States.

At the start of the twenty-first century, the fascination with America persists, even if diplomatic relations are sometimes problematic. The Chinese Communist leadership may talk a great deal about their troubles with the United States and about extending their cooperation with other powers so as to balance the predominance of Washington within the international system. But the CCP has accepted that system more or less the way it was created, first by Britain and then by the United States, on all matters from the framework for trade to the functions of the UN Security Council. A rising China may want to be seen as an alternative to the United States in international affairs. But while rising, its domestic social and economic system has been transformed in America's image to an extent that even Europeans and Latin Americans sometimes find puzzling. China's American dream may be discordant, but it is still very intense.

WHEN MAO ZEDONG, at the height of the crisis with the Soviets in 1969, issued orders to begin easing relations with the United States, few among his top colleagues were surprised. The CCP heads had worked themselves into a frenzy over the conflict with Moscow. Because ideology was the only significant aspect of life during the Cultural Revolution, all attention was on political divergence among Communists, be it outside or inside China. Those of his colleagues who had survived the purges saw that the Chairman's move was a tactical one, similar to his contacts with the Americans during the war with Japan: When a great danger is threatening, every deflection helps. None among the leaders thought that China's willingness to work with the Americans to confront what they saw as the growth of Soviet power would influence the course of the revolution at home. And only the most well-informed among them knew how desperately weak China was in military terms after the ravages of Mao's political campaigns and how important it therefore was for it to break out of its isolation.

Mao was exceptionally lucky with the timing of his American overtures. Richard Nixon, who became president in 1969, was the only US Cold War leader who believed that the United States needed broad alliances outside Europe and Japan in order to prevail in the competition with the Soviet Union. The war in Vietnam and domestic unrest had convinced Nixon, and his national security adviser, Henry Kissinger, that an opening to China was an option for American diplomacy, in addition to working with anti-Soviet Third World powers such as Brazil, South Africa, Iran, and Indonesia. The intensification of the Sino-Soviet conflict accelerated Nixon's wish for a dialogue with Beijing. In October 1969 he asked the Pakistanis to facilitate such contacts and for them to tell Mao that "the US would welcome accommodation with Communist China." It frustrated the new leaders in Washington that Beijing was so slow to respond. But in spite of Mao's willingness to ease relations, the chaos of the Cultural Revolution had created near paralysis in Chinese diplomacy and ensured that any new initiative would take time to materialize. When the two sides finally, in February 1970, agreed to a meeting in Beijing, the intense and prolonged US attack in mid-1970 on Cambodia set the tentative negotiations back by several months. And when Mao, finally, in October 1970 decided to send a personal signal, he did not exactly find the easiest route. Receiving his old American acquaintance, the left-wing journalist Edgar Snow, atop Tian'anmen for the national day celebrations, and telling him that Nixon himself would be welcome to China, was not the best way of contacting a Republican president.

In the end, it was Nixon himself who cut to the chase and decided on the greatest political gamble of his career. He was, he told Zhou Enlai in a secret message in May 1971, willing to come to Beijing if a secret trip by Kissinger could be arranged first and a suitable format for the visit could be found. The Chinese interpreted the proposal as a sign of US weakness. The Politburo speculated that Nixon acted mainly on account of pressures from "the broad masses of the people" who were against the "Vietnam War and racial discrimination." But China's leaders concluded that "since there is no way to be sure that an armed revolution would break out in the United States," Nixon's offer should be accepted. Kissinger arrived in Beijing for a secret visit in July 1971, after having feigned illness during a trip to Pakistan. Nixon followed for an official visit in February 1972. For Mao, ill and politically weakened after his second in command, Lin Biao, had broken with the regime and died while trying to flee to the Soviet Union, Nixon's visit was a true godsend. In the eyes of many Chinese, the leader of the most powerful Western country recognized China's centrality by himself coming to Beijing to sit with the Chairman and listen to his political wisdom. The Americans were full of praise for their new acquaintances. Kissinger said that Mao's chief diplomat, Zhou Enlai, was "the most impressive foreign leader I have ever met. We spoke for 20 hours, he completely without notes. . . . Those 20 hours were the most impressive conversations I have ever had." Mao was less fulsome. "Kissinger is a university professor who does not know anything about diplomacy," he told the North Vietnamese.[1] As could be expected, everyone agreed that Nixon in China was the week that changed the world. But no one could say how it had actually changed.

It took Chinese and Americans almost the rest of the decade to decide the content of what Kissinger had called Sino-American "rapprochement." The Chinese wanted trade, which got underway quickly, and military technology, which was slower in coming. The two countries began a limited cooperation against the Soviets, especially in the Third World, with the Chinese helping the CIA get in touch with small Maoist or anti-Soviet groups in southern Africa, the Middle East, and Latin America. Most importantly, Beijing helped the United States get out of the Vietnam War. The moment the North Vietnamese leaders heard of Nixon's visit to China, they knew that they had better settle fast. The Vietnamese, alongside the great majority of the world's left-wing movements, saw Mao's willingness to work with Washington as treason, and the most important effect in the Third World was probably to drive radical regimes and movements closer to working with the Soviets. China was no longer an alternative for those who wanted world revolution.

Despite the hopes for a quick normalization of Sino-American relations after Nixon's visit, another seven years would pass before full mutual recognition took place. The main reason for this delay, which gave the Soviets time to mobilize against Chinese and US collusion in the Third World, was the political turbulence of the 1970s in both Beijing and Washington. On the Chinese side, much of the political madness of the Cultural Revolution continued up to Mao's death in 1976, and uncertainty reigned afterward. On the American side, Nixon was forced to resign in disgrace in 1974 because of the Watergate scandal, and his successors, Gerald Ford and Jimmy Carter, shared neither his political bravery nor his brutality against political enemies. The relationship to Taiwan became a major irritant. Most Americans were unwilling to give up the old alliance with the rump Guomindang regime (with Chiang Kai-shek, now in his mid-eighties, still president) in order to normalize fully with Communist Beijing. Despite increases in trade and technology transfers, the complete lack of dynamism in the state-run Chinese economy prevented strong links from being developed. Inside China, after years of anti-American propaganda, Mao's about-face contributed to the dominant political cynicism, in spite of the leadership's lame explanations that the Americans had finally come to their senses and realized the strength of the Chinese people. Among Americans who visited, such as the US representative in Beijing, George H. W. Bush, the Maoist dictatorship was orientalized into an expression of the collectivism and regimented will of the Chinese. Meanwhile the Chinese leaders' gnomic statements on international strategy were taken as ultimate examples of the realist wisdom of an ancient civilization, instead of the ignorance about the world that they really represented. The main advantages China had in the first years of its renewed relationship with the United States were probably the chance it now got to normalize relations with other US allies—Japan, Indonesia, Thailand, and the West European countries, for instance—and the increased security it received vis-à-vis the Soviet Union.[2]

MAO ZEDONG DIED ON 9 September 1976. In spite of the chaos and confusion he had created over the last part of his rule, most Chinese looked upon Mao as a once-great leader who had united the country and made it strong. Just as after Stalin's death in the Soviet Union, many people felt bereaved and uncertain, and it took time for the immensity of Mao's misjudgments and crimes to become known. In fact, the CCP government has never admitted them fully, and, absurdly, Mao's portrait still dominates the vista at the central square in Beijing, Tian'anmen. In terms of foreign as well as domestic policy, all cards were off the table once the Chairman had died. China could have moved further to the left and become a genocidal hell not unlike Pol Pot's Cambodia (Pol Pot was China's closest foreign ally when Mao died) or it could have moved toward a more open and pluralistic form of socialism. Mao's chosen successor was the recently appointed Premier Hua Guofeng. His main attraction for the Chairman, beside his oafish loyalty, seems to have been that he was from Hunan, Mao's home province, and therefore could better understand what the party leader said. Hua did not have much of a vision of his own, but after weeks of uncertainty he allied himself with the military and carried out a coup d'état in which the Chairman's radical allies on the Politburo were arrested. The military, afraid of a return to the chaos of the height of the Cultural Revolution, insisted that old leaders such as the party's former general secretary Deng Xiaoping and Chen Yun, the planning expert, both purged by Mao before his death, be brought back into power. All over the country those who had been sent away, purged, or arrested began coming back to their homes. For the Communist Party old guard, and for many ordinary Chinese, especially in the cities, it was as if a nightmare was over.

Deng Xiaoping, given his third chance to set China's course, did not waste time. More than any other Chinese leader, Deng realized that his country's isolation and endless political campaigns had cost it dearly in terms of development. He wanted to experiment in order to advance. First he wanted to go back to using material incentives to increase production in agriculture, along the lines of what he and Liu Shaoqi had proposed in the early 1960s, before Mao had purged Deng and killed Liu. He was looking at the more liberal socialist economies of Hungary and Yugoslavia as possible models for China. Then, as his power grew within the leadership, Deng began considering more radical reforms. While exiled in the south in 1976, Deng had noticed attempts by factories and collectives to import technology through Hong Kong or use surpluses to barter for materials or equipment they needed. In 1978 he began asking whether all of China now needed such reform and opening. Deng told the CCP that instead of being denounced as smugglers and traitors, those who wanted to develop fast and test political theory against practical results were heroes of the four modernizations that China needed. By 1981, with Mao's successor, Hua Guofeng, demoted and the military firmly behind a policy of growth, Deng was ready to go further. In agriculture, industry, technology, and military affairs China was still a backward country, he declared, and the party had to throw overboard Mao's errors and focus on "modernization centering on economic construction." In that process, "some people may get rich first, through hard work."[3] That did not matter, as long as the Chinese economy could grow.

Upon returning to the frontline of Chinese politics, Deng made it clear that the United States would serve as the model for China's technological needs. After he had been purged for a second time, Deng had spent much time thinking about the significance of the change that was taking place in science and technology in the 1970s. In a conversation with the Chinese-Belgian writer Han Suyin in 1977, he spoke about his concerns over China falling behind.[4]

In the 1960s, the gap between the scientific and technological levels of China and the rest of the world was not very big. However, in the late 1960s and the early 1970s, the . . . levels of the rest of the world improved tremendously. All fields of science developed quickly. The improvement made in one year amounted to that of several years; we might even say the improvement made in one day amounted to that of several years. In 1975, I once said, China was fifty years behind Japan in science. At the time, I had wanted to pay more attention to scientific study, but, in the end, I could not do so, since I myself was under house arrest. If we do not take the newest scientific achievements as our starting points. . . , I am afraid there is no hope for China.[5]

For Deng, the easing of tension with the United States could be made to serve China's economic development. Visiting several American cities in 1979, the Chinese leader was bowled over by the technology, the productivity, and the consumer choices he found. After returning home, he told his colleagues that he could not sleep for several nights, thinking about how China might achieve such abundance. One thing was clear to Deng: Working with the United States on foreign affairs opened gigantic opportunities for US technology transfers to China, both military and civilian. America was the world's leading power, and opposing it made no sense, even if the Taiwan issue remained unresolved. Deng often said that there would be a time for China to take a more prominent position in international affairs. But that time was not now, when China was weak and needed to grow fast.

B Y 1979, THE YEAR DENG visited the United States, the relationship between the two countries had begun to look like an alliance. Full diplomatic relations were restored that year, and Washington cut off all formal ties with its former clients on Taiwan, now led by Chiang Ching-kuo after the 1975 death of his father, Chiang Kai-shek. But even more important than diplomacy was the increase in economic and military cooperation between the two sides, directed against the Soviet Union and its allies. "Wherever the Soviet Union sticks its fingers, there we must chop them off," Deng told President Jimmy Carter during his visit. Deng said that he was certain a war with the Soviets would break out, but he hoped to postpone it as long as possible. The 1978 Vietnamese invasion of Cambodia and the 1979 Soviet invasion of Afghanistan were harbingers of things to come, Deng believed. Deng's short 1979 war with Vietnam, in response to the latter's removal of the Pol Pot regime in Cambodia, proved a dismal failure. China would have to rely on the United States to supply what was needed for China's military modernization. General Zhang Aiping, a revolutionary veteran who had been badly tortured during the Cultural Revolution and whom Deng put in charge of modernizing the military, spoke with the visiting US secretary of defense, Harold Brown. Zhang said, "we are glad you want to help us develop our military capability. With your help we can develop faster. . . . We want to develop our weapons not only for China but also for the interests of the world and perhaps of the US." Deng himself put it plainly to Carter's cabinet: "I hope all of you present will provide, in your corresponding area, the very best. Of course, you do not have things that are of 1950s vintage. We still have many facilities of that period. I wish that you would provide us with the 1970s rather than the 1960s. I hope you will provide us with the late 1970s rather than the early 1970s. Do you understand?"[6]

The Chinese strategy was to get as much as possible out of the Americans by telling them what Beijing assumed they wanted to hear: that the Soviet Union was a threat to world peace and that only a strong China could dam up Soviet advances in Asia. During Ronald Reagan's hard-line administration, starting in 1981, the Chinese message was even more welcome than it had been to Jimmy Carter, despite Reagan's early concerns about not betraying old friends on Taiwan. Throughout the 1980s the United States treated China as a de facto ally, sharing sensitive intelligence information with it and giving it access to much-needed technology that was sometimes unavailable to others outside the United States itself. Reagan's purpose was to build China into a real threat to the Soviet Union, thereby putting pressure on the leaders in Moscow and reducing their capacity to intervene elsewhere. Reagan's friend the film producer Douglas Morrow toured China in 1981 and told the president that the Beijing leaders were "absolutely obsessed about Taiwan" and that any focus on the island's position would effectively prevent the United States from working with Deng and the Chinese leaders. And such cooperation was important, Morrow told the president:

> I sure as hell don't know where they are going. I don't think they know. But they are going. . . . It would be advisable not to be too paranoid, at this stage, about their being a communist state. There are hints that they might develop into some unprecedented hybrid. . . . I think they will bend, twist, and adjust to whatever seems to abet their progress. And perhaps come up, eventually, with a mutant system which neither they nor the world have yet experienced.[7]

Already during its first year in office, the Reagan administration offered China what it called a "strategic association" with the United States. It was in effect a de facto alliance. Reagan also declared himself willing to sell sophisticated weapons directly to Beijing. As the Cold War grew colder in the early 1980s, Sino-American security cooperation expanded. US anti-Communist campaigns in Afghanistan, Angola, and Cambodia were closely coordinated with the Chinese and intelligence sharing increased. China never became a big importer of US weapons, which were not needed to build China's military prowess. What Beijing wanted was access to US weapons technology, and the Chinese got a lot of that in the 1980s, including aviation and missile technology. China then set out to produce its own weapons. Deng's plan was to make China into one of the world's top military powers within twenty years. That way, he calculated, a Soviet attack could be prevented or defeated, with a bit of luck and US assistance.

The Taiwan issue remained an irritant in Sino-American relations into the 1980s, but already in August 1982 the Chinese side achieved a breakthrough. Pushed by the increasing global confrontation with the Soviet Union, Washington agreed to issuing a joint statement with China on US weapons sales to Taiwan. The statement committed the United States to phase out its policy of arms supplies to the Guomindang regime:

> the United States Government states that it does not seek to carry out a long-term policy of arms sales to Taiwan, that its arms sales to Taiwan will not exceed, either in qualitative or in quantitative terms, the level of those supplied in recent years since the establishment of diplomatic relations between the United States and China, and that it intends to reduce gradually its sales of arms to Taiwan, leading over a period of time to a final resolution. In so stating, the United States acknowledges China's consistent position regarding the thorough settlement of this issue.[8]

At the same time, Deng attempted to get negotiations going to facilitate reunification across the Taiwan Strait, on conditions that were more favorable to Taibei than anything that had been offered before. Deng's attempts failed, not least because of the continued US commitment to Taiwan. And the weapons compromise, the core part of which all later US presidents have ignored, still casts a shadow over Sino-American relations. But during the 1980s, as the Cold War first intensified and then moved toward its end, the joint communiqué on Taiwan contributed to a framework that ensured some form of stability in relations between Washington and Beijing.

None of the Chinese leaders at first gave much thought to what would happen if the Sino-American alliance actually succeeded in reducing or destroying Soviet power. This lack of strategic thinking originated in the uncritical acceptance of Mao's dogmas and Deng's own incomplete understanding of the international situation. By 1983, however, it had started dawning on Beijing that some form of balance in the Cold War might actually be to its advantage. By that time it was much too late to secure any form of breakthrough with the Soviets, and in 1985—the year Gorbachev came to power in Moscow—the Soviet Union, strategically weakened by the Sino-American alliance, began seeking a settlement with its strongest opponent, the United States. By teaming up with the Americans, China had contributed to the death wounds of the *weaker* superpower while helping the *stronger*, the United States, achieve global hegemony. In the long run this transformation would not be to the benefit of Chinese foreign policy. But from the vantage point of the 1980s almost all contact with America seemed to be to China's advantage.

I N 1980 I VISITED SHENZHEN for the first time. Back then the area was a typical grouping of small and very poor Cantonese fishing villages in the Pearl river delta, tantalizingly close to Hong Kong. That year Deng decided to make this area the showcase in China's new opening to the world. As a special economic zone (SEZ), Shenzhen would attract foreign investment to build new plants that would be foreign-owned and operated. Any surplus could be freely sent overseas, and the companies had duty-free privileges, concessionary tax rates, land made freely available, and the ability to set their own wage levels. In return, the foreign investors agreed to technology transfers and training programs, as well as long-term schedules of investment. Almost all the products were made for export. Shenzhen, so different from anything any Chinese could have imagined only a few years before, turned out to be a huge success. Today it is a city with more than fourteen million inhabitants, the fourth largest city in China in terms of economic output. Tens of thousands of people now commute from Hong Kong to Shenzhen for work each day.

More than 20,000 international partnerships with a total value of more than $26 billion were signed by China in the 1980s. They helped the Chinese economy get going again, first in and around SEZs that sprang up all over the country, especially near where the foreign concessions had been in the early part of the century, and then elsewhere in the south and along China's eastern seaboard. As property rights were gradually restored, private Chinese companies began to emerge, very often in the SEZs. Even some state-owned industries relocated to SEZs in the south. Together with the end of collectivization in agriculture, it was a remarkable transformation. Already by 1983 Chinese economic growth had hit double digits, and GDP almost quadrupled over the course of the decade. Deng told his critics: "It does not matter if it is a black cat or a white cat; if it catches mice it is a good cat." Deng's cat theory belonged to another universe than the empty Marxist theorizing of the 1970s. It symbolized a counterrevolution in economics and political orientation the likes of which the world had never seen.

The relationship with the United States stood left, right, and center in Communist China's initial market revolution. Even though much of the capital came through Hong Kong, the experts, the methods, and the technology were often American. It was the United States, more than any other country, that lobbied for China's entry into international institutions. It was also the United States that took the largest share of the PRC's exports, on which China's beginning prosperity depended. While many Americans worried about Japanese and European competition in the 1980s, very few worried about China. Most assumed that it would take generations before China's economy got off the ground and believed, with the US government, that strengthening China was in the national security interest of the United States. As Western Europe, Japan, and Taiwan did at the beginning of the Cold War, China at the end of the Cold War benefited from the American security imperative in more senses than one.

Life in an SEZ, and increasingly in China's cities, in the 1980s was a curious affair. Foreign experts and businessmen, often American, mingled with Chinese with very little mutual comprehension. The foreigners had no way of understanding the dismal conditions that Chinese had got accustomed to living under, and most Chinese were too ashamed, or too afraid, to tell. Capitalist practices had to be cloaked in Marxist terminology. In these games of charade the Chinese had the advantage of being accustomed to using "correct" terms to cover widely varying practices. The cynicism that was the main legacy of late Maoist China served some of those who entered into the new economy well. The most cynical, always those with the right Communist Party connections, did get rich first. For the vast majority, however, the beginning change in the Chinese economy meant very little. They were mostly preoccupied with scraping a living out of the wreckage of the Maoist campaigns, and they were grateful that under Deng there were a few more ways of keeping their heads above water than there had been before.

As limited forms of private wealth in the cities increased, the taste for foreign consumer goods also rose. A number of American companies invested in China—Coca-Cola, Heinz, and General Foods were among the first. Others helped facilitate the remarkable rise in Chinese exports to the United States, which already by 1990 amounted to almost twenty percent of China's total. The first foreign fast food restaurant inside China opened in 1987, a Kentucky Fried Chicken on a busy street corner in central Beijing. Tens of thousands of people walked slowly past, just to get a glimpse of what was going on inside. Almost nobody could afford to eat there, and over the first few weeks the Beijing authorities had to dole out special "foreign exchange certificates"—the only money foreign businesses were authorized to accept—to its senior cadre in order to ensure a minimum of trade. KFC became a symbol of the West in China, resented by some for its American brashness but admired by many more for its business acumen. Led mostly by Taiwan-born US executives, KFC's Chinese expansion became hugely successful, and today there are 2,500 outlets in the PRC.

Some historians today exaggerate the changes that took place in China by the end of the 1980s. In economic terms, the vast majority of workers were still employed in state-owned companies that functioned according to planned economy principles. After leaving school, people were assigned to a work unit where they were supposed to stay for life. Their wages were negligible, but all services, from housing to health care, from nurseries to care for the elderly, were supplied by the state-run work unit in which they were employed. There was no labor market. There was no capital market. Bank loans were out of reach for ordinary people. In Beijing, in the evening, if you walked past the new KFC toward the Forbidden City, you were looking toward the new neon lights at Wangfujing, the main shopping street. But the reason you were looking toward them was that everywhere else was dark. In a tiny speck of land in the center of the old imperial capital a new world seemed to be emerging, but it had so far done little except whet people's appetite for a new kind of life.

A S CHINA'S ECONOMY BEGAN to change, ordinary people and some leaders within the party began to clamor for political change as well. The debates about China's political system in the 1980s took place in a society still traumatized by the mass murder of previous decades and in a state still run according to tight Marxist-Leninist principles. Those most preoccupied with political reform were students and intellectuals, and some party officials who had glimpsed how people elsewhere were able to live their lives. But the old guard of the CCP did not favor such change. They were afraid of a return to the political chaos of the Cultural Revolution. They also believed that the massive process of economic reform needed their leadership (though it is hard to tell how a lifetime spent in the most extreme of Marxist-Leninist parties prepared them for this). More than a few were also worried about losing the privileges that their connections gave them, including the privilege of making their families very rich indeed. By the late 1980s no political reform was in sight. When in 1987 the CCP general secretary, Hu Yaobang, a man Deng Xiaoping himself had appointed, voiced support for a more open debate, Deng had him fired.

Many of the ideas of political reform were drawn from abroad and especially from the United States. China's opening to the West occurred at the same time as the rise there of individualistic and personal rights–oriented thinking symbolized by Ronald Reagan and Margaret Thatcher, and Chinese students abroad were influenced by these trends. The strength of the United States, Chinese liberals claimed, lay in its political system, and especially in how the rights of citizens were observed. If China wanted to get rich and strong, it also had to become free. The crises in the Soviet Union and Eastern Europe in the late 1980s seemed to confirm this point of view: Marxism, in all its forms, was a thing of the past, and the CCP's rule was therefore outdated. When the disgraced former general secretary Hu Yaobang died in the spring of 1989, many students felt that he had died a martyr to the cause of political freedom. Demonstrations broke out in the cities. The students urged the party to memorialize Hu properly and move toward opening up the political system. Deng Xiaoping feared that the demonstrations would turn to chaos and had the prime minister, Li Peng, impose martial law in Beijing and other cities where the students were organizing large rallies. But the attempts at sending soldiers into the cities increased popular support for the students and created a mass movement for democracy. In one of its key texts, Liu Xiaobo (who went on to win the Nobel Peace Prize in 2010) and his co-signatories drew their lineage back to the calls for democracy in the 1910s and 1920s:

> For several thousand years, Chinese society has been living in a vicious cycle of a new emperor replacing an old emperor. History has proven than the stepping down of some unpopular leader and the assumption of power by some very popular leader cannot solve the essential problems of Chinese politics. What we need is not a perfect savior, but a perfect democratic system. . . . The whole society should use every means to establish legal and popular autonomous organizations, and gradually form popular political power to counterbalance the government's decisionmaking . . . because the essence of democracy is checks and balances. We would rather have ten mutually balancing devils than one angel with absolute power.[9]

The crackdown on 4 June 1989, in which several hundred demonstrators were killed around Tian'anmen Square, split the Communist Party and humiliated it before a global audience. A government shooting unarmed students in the center of its capital is never a popular image abroad, and the Beijing killings came just as Communism elsewhere seemed headed for either political reform or oblivion. The demonstrators in Tian'anmen Square had erected a thirty-three-foot-tall papier-mâché effigy, the Goddess of Democracy, which looked remarkably similar to the Statue of Liberty. They placed it facing Mao's portrait. A tank knocked it over and crushed it. For the army, the Goddess was a symbol of foreign influence. Walking through town a few days later, I came across a figure of Colonel Sanders from outside the Beijing KFC. It had been "executed" with a single bullet through the head. The Tian'anmen crackdown was very much about what kind of relationship China should have with foreigners, foreign ideas, and foreign products.

The regime's brutal suppression of student protesters destroyed in one swoop the outside world's image of China as being at the forefront of global change. Almost all elected governments condemned the use of force, and many of them, including the United States and the European Union, imposed sanctions on China. But the new administration of President George H. W. Bush, the former US representative in Beijing who had succeeded Reagan as president in January 1989, also tried its best to keep the relationship with Deng Xiaoping intact. Less than a month after the massacre at Tian'anmen, Bush sent his national security adviser, Brent Scowcroft, on a secret mission to Beijing. Scowcroft told the Chinese that

> President Bush recognizes the value of the PRC-US relationship to the vital interests of both countries. Beyond that, he has a deep personal desire to see the friendship between the Chinese and the American people maintained and strengthened. This commitment derives from his experience in China and his personal friendship for so many

of China's leaders. How the G[overnment of the] PRC decides to deal with those of its citizens involved in recent events in China is, of course, an internal affair. How the USG[overnment] and the American people view that activity is, equally, an internal affair. Both will be governed by the traditions, culture, and values peculiar to each.[10]

A Reagan moment it was not. But Bush had his reasons. The United States, he felt, could not continue the pressure on the Soviet Union without at least tacit Chinese support. It was a sign of China's importance for the United States in international affairs that the president would risk sending signals to the Chinese leaders that so contravened what most Americans thought and felt.

THE EVENTS AT TIAN'ANMEN set political reformers within the party against those who opposed changes in China's political structure. Among the latter—those who preferred the existing patchwork of Leninist ideas and authoritarian practices—there were some who were also against the economic and social reforms (which they termed a counterrevolution) that were being carried out by Deng's supporters. Having summarily dismissed the party leader, Zhao Ziyang, who wanted political reform, Deng after 1989 turned on his leftist critics. In a tour of the southern provinces in 1992 the leader spurred on the turn toward a market economy and more interaction with the world.

> We should be bolder than before in conducting reform and opening to the outside and have the courage to experiment. We must not act like women with bound feet. Once we are sure that something should be done, we should dare to experiment and break a new path. That is the important lesson to be learned from Shenzhen . . . where conditions permit, some areas may develop faster than others; those that develop faster can help promote the progress of those that lag behind, until all become prosperous.[11]

But Deng also warned against the effects of the increasing foreign influence in China. He cited the example of the collapse of the Soviet Union in 1991. "The imperialists are pushing for peaceful evolution towards capitalism in China, placing their hopes on the generations that will come after us. Hostile forces realize that so long as we of the older generation are still alive and carry weight, no change is possible. But after we are dead and gone, who will ensure that there is no peaceful evolution?"[12] Deng's answer was to strengthen the dictatorship through a new generation, while making sure the country became rich and strong.

The Tian'anmen massacre did frighten off all sorts of internal dissent for two decades or more. But without the massive opening up of the economy that happened in the 1990s—and the prosperity that it gave all sorts of elites in China—it is unlikely that the dictatorship could have reimposed itself as easily as it did. Deng's final bargain with his people—he died in 1997—was the prospect of a good life in return for party control of politics. At the regional level, many CCP leaders threw themselves into the government-inspired dismantling of the old socialist system, in part as repentance for the political repression they had gone along with in the post-1989 crackdown on dissidents. The 1990s did not become the decade of political change at the top that some had hoped for. But it did become the decade of economic and social change on an unprecedented scale. By 2000 the country was integrated into the global economy to an extent that it had not been since the 1920s, and the socialist state was becoming submerged by networks of private, and often international, enterprise.

When foreign investment returned to China in the early 1990s, after the shocks of the Tian'anmen events, it was at a pace and level never seen before in China's history. The combination of a dedicated and cheap workforce and the foreign hope of buying into China's own domestic development led to the country leap-frogging all others in terms of foreign direct investment (FDI). Over the course of the decade, China was second only to the United States in attracting FDI—

a remarkable change, given that foreign investment of any kind had not existed in Communist China prior to 1980. Up to today the changes in China's economic system have to a large extent been driven by the needs created by foreign investors. For instance, a legal framework of ownership had to be created to serve those who wanted to invest in China. The same framework could then serve China's own embryonic capitalists. Similarly for stock exchanges, insurance arrangements, and quality control. China's bid to join the World Trade Organization (WTO), which finally succeeded in 2001 (very much thanks to the goodwill of the United States), was intended to serve China's export potential, but also made the country sign up to stringent regulations concerning state subsidies (or rather the absence thereof), industry standards, copyright protection, and not least opening the Chinese market to foreign competition. The international drove the domestic in terms of economic change.

By 2000, the socialist economy in China had lost out to a market economy encouraged by a party dictatorship that was still Communist in name. For China's population it was clear that they were living in a new society in which market forces were dominant. State-owned enterprises were sold off, down-scaled, or allowed to go bankrupt (at least 5,000 such companies have gone bankrupt each year since 2000).[13] Those that survived are publicly listed and under the same management regulations as all other Chinese companies. For ordinary people this re-arrangement means that employers that may not have paid them much money, but otherwise looked after them and their children from the moment the state assigned them to the factory to the day they died— now such employers were a thing of the past. No more free health care, kindergartens, schools, housing, holidays, or homes for the elderly. Instead, people had to—gingerly—enter a private housing market, search for a good job, and save for their children's college education. Millions of people had to travel elsewhere to find work. China's capitalism, when it finally broke through in the 1990s, was very unlike the European and the Japanese variants, with their safety nets and entitlements, but remarkably like that of the United States, with its emphasis on mobility, opportunity, and personal responsibility.

B UT IT WAS NOT ONLY the Chinese population that had to learn a new way of living in the 1990s and 2000s. The state had to learn, too. Having given up direct ownership of the economy, it had to create new instruments of indirect control, most of them borrowed wholesale from the West and based on legislation, regulation, and fiscal and monetary policy. It was, in many ways, a return to China's preoccupations of the interwar period, only with a much larger segment of the population involved in the industrial economy. Some critics called it a counterrevolution, since the state increasingly saw its main task as serving market-led economic growth. By the 2000s the Chinese Communist state had adopted concerns about inflation, interest rates, credit flows, and property rights that sounded very similar to those of Reaganite America or Thatcherite Britain in the 1980s. Capitalism was in the driver's seat, even if CCP leaders would not admit it, and the role of the state in advanced capitalist economies—minus electoral democracy— was what Beijing was aiming for. China's capitalist revolution of the past twenty years has brought the country closer to the outside world— and especially to the United States—in terms of the aims many people set for themselves or how the Chinese state operates than ever before, or at least since the Mongol dynasties of the thirteenth century.

Why did the party do it? The CCP was founded on an anticapitalist creed in a China in which many people—not only Communists—felt that capitalism had brought nothing but suffering, exploitation, and humiliation. Now, the move from Maoism to market demanded a remarkable turnaround not just in ideology but also in mentality. For critics of the CCP inside and outside of China, the answer is simple: The party's much-lauded "flexibility" was a consequence of its long history of manipulating the truth and deceiving those who believed in it.

Party leaders embraced capitalism to enrich themselves and their families, and because the plans for the future they had once promoted had utterly failed. There is obviously some truth to these assertions, but they are far from the whole truth. The main reason why the CCP chose the market was that from the position of the early 1990s there seemed to be no other way out. Modernity was capitalist. The USSR had—very unexpectedly for the Chinese—collapsed, as had the socialist states in Eastern Europe. The United States led the way toward an increasingly integrated capitalist world economy, and those who opted out of it would fall behind. The risk of falling behind was what first and foremost animated China's leaders from Deng Xiaoping to Hu Jintao. If the race to modernize could be better run with Nike trainers, then the Chinese Communists would put them on (especially if the shoes themselves were made in China).

The new generation of returned students played a big role in China's capitalist transformation. Even though, as we have seen, a very large number of Chinese who had studied abroad wanted to remain abroad into the 2000s, those who did go back to China had the expertise and the status to begin introducing new practices, first, in private enterprise, and, later, in the state and even in the party. By the late 2000s one could get the impression that the CCP itself had taken over many of the management methods of foreign enterprises. Quantifiable results for young party brass were all the rage among top cadre. One high-level CCP member I spoke with in 2009 described his training at the party academies in terms that anyone with an MPA or MBA from Harvard or LSE would recognize. At the same time foreign-educated academics are transforming China's own higher education. Research output is crucial to promotion, and the output is supposed to be of international standard. Student concerns are increasingly taken seriously by their professors (since they are paying customers). When party control and academic ambition collide, it is as often the latter that wins out as the former.

Although consumer choice meant nothing in China before the late 1980s, it now means a lot to most Chinese, even those who live far from the main cities. The preoccupations are very similar to those of the pre–World War II era. How can modernity—preferably of an international kind—be best expressed in terms of products? Young people in China today are among the most fashion- and brand-conscious in the world. Foreign-produced goods generally have the edge, even though some Chinese brands are beginning to catch up. Music is often American, with liberal doses of Canto-pop thrown in. Clothes styles and hairstyles are Western, mediated through Hong Kong and Taiwan. For other products, concerns such as environmentalism or sustainability are beginning to find their way in, but not on key issues that really matter to the Chinese consumer, such as buying a car. In China—the world's largest market for new cars in 2010—the American habit of buying the biggest engine your pocketbook can afford is still the rule (with foreseeable consequences: China today has twenty of the thirty most polluted cities in the world).[14]

Mass consumption is only one part of China's capitalist revolution at the ground level. The other is the way people invest in the new economy. The main aim for many in China today is to buy their own house or apartment. In the cities a young couple can only do it through immensely hard work, because property prices are almost at European levels and salaries are much lower. Even though the Chinese savings rate is still very high, more and more of it—within an extended family—contributes in one way or another to paying off debt. Meanwhile many Chinese are investing directly in the market and have sometimes found that their investments can earn them as much as their salary. There is an increasing number of Chinese investors in property and stocks. Even though they are not likely to be more democratic or less nationalistic than their fellow citizens, they have, quite literally, bought into a development pattern for China that is quite similar to that of Western nations, Japan, and South Korea.

The one area in which China stands out from other East Asian states, including Taiwan, in terms of development is—ironically enough, given the pretensions of its Communist government—the matter of equality. While the early Communists had dreamed about a China that was modern and strong and socially just—and Mao had pursued the topic of equality endlessly in his campaigns—China today is one of the most socially stratified societies on earth. While more than a third of the population—those who have not joined the industrial economy—live on slightly more than $2 income per day, China has 128 billionaires and half a million millionaires.[15] Its Gini coefficient (the standard used for measuring levels of income inequality) is higher than that for any other country in its region, and just slightly lower than the most unequal countries on earth, such as Brazil.[16] While presiding over increasing levels of inequality, CCP leaders defend themselves by quoting Deng's maxim that some people have to get rich first. In some areas of the country, social unrest is increasing, with local organizers claiming that the party is a tool of foreign exploitation of China. For minorities, in Tibet and Xinjiang but also in the south, the same party that tried to drown their identity in blood during the Cultural Revolution, now drowns it in consumer products and market adjustments, while increased mobility leads to ever more Chinese in minority areas. Capitalism, though victorious in China, is in no way uncontested.

T HROUGHOUT THE LATE TWENTIETH CENTURY, Taiwan remained the main irritant in Sino-American relations and the main reason for China's unease in international affairs. In the early 1980s, Deng Xiaoping had tried to come to an arrangement with Taiwan's new president, Chiang Ching-kuo, Chiang Kai-shek's Russian-educated son. But the talks came to nothing, mainly because the Guomindang leaders on Taiwan knew that they would continue to receive US support even after Jimmy Carter broke formal relations with the Taibei regime in 1979. Deng had to play the Taiwan issue very carefully. China's modernization was vastly more important than reunification with Taiwan. Deng's personal attitude was that reunification would happen anyway, in its own good time, if China succeeded in its domestic and international transformation. He was also aware of how important the pro-GMD constituency still was in the United States, especially after Ronald Reagan became president in 1981, and he did not want a conflict over Taiwan to ruin the overall relationship with the Americans. What irritated Deng was that Taiwan's separation from the mainland was a domestic Chinese issue that the Americans could work in whatever way and at whatever time suited them. He was also well aware that the new generation of Chinese leaders who were trying to reestablish the CCP's legitimacy after 1989 were substantially more nationalist and substantially less fastidious in policy terms than he himself was.

On Taiwan itself politics were also in flux after Chiang Ching-kuo took over in 1975. The younger Chiang was a reflective man, who had lived under two authoritarian regimes, Stalin's and his own father's, and had not liked either of them very much. And so he set out to liberalize Taiwan politics. In spite of his formidable political pedigree, Chiang's reforms were slow and spasmodic. He was hindered by opposition within his own GMD and fear of a rebellion on Taiwan against the rule of mainlanders like him who had come over after the civil war. But in 1986, ill with heart disease, Chiang sped the process up. He abolished martial law and de facto allowed opposition parties to function. He selected the Taiwan-born Li Denghui as his vice president and successor. It was Li who, as president in 1990, responding to massive student demonstrations, set a timetable for the introduction of full democracy. In 1996 Li became the first democratically elected president of the Republic of China on Taiwan, and the island became the first modern Chinese democracy, with a constitution that inscribed the people's right to freedom of organization, speech, and political participation and a freely elected parliament that made sure the executive practiced what it preached.

For the leaders of the PRC the situation on Taiwan had gone from bad to worse. The 1979 Taiwan Relations Act, passed by the US Congress, seemed to cement US influence on the island. It was officially entitled "An act to help maintain peace, security, and stability in the Western Pacific and to promote the foreign policy of the United States by authorizing the continuation of commercial, cultural, and other relations between the people of the United States and the people on Taiwan"—which about says it all. The democratic reforms of Chiang and Li convinced some CCP leaders—including Jiang Zemin, who had taken over as party general secretary in 1989 and president in 1993—that Taiwan was heading for full independence from China. Jiang was especially suspicious of Li Denghui, since Li was Taiwan-born and had become a convinced democrat. Beijing saw democracy there, the dismantling of the fiction that the GMD government there represented all of China, and even Li's declaration that his government would never use force to "retake" the mainland as steps on the road to full separation. The CCP preferred fighting with the GMD over who really represented one China to confronting the islanders on the issue of Taiwanese independence.

When Congress forced President Bill Clinton to admit Li Denghui into the United States in 1995 in order to give a speech at Cornell University, his alma mater, annoyance in Beijing boiled over into action. For the first time since 1958, the PLA fired missiles near Taiwan-held islands and carried out amphibious landing exercises nearby. It even mobilized its infantry divisions in Fujian province, across the strait from Taiwan. On Taiwan itself, people started fearing a PLA invasion. But from a PRC perspective, the saber rattling failed both politically and strategically. Mainland pressure strengthened Li's candidature at the democratic elections in 1996, giving him a greater victory than what he otherwise would have got. It also set off a tough reaction from the United States. The Clinton Administration sent two aircraft carrier battle groups, headed by the USS *Nimitz* and the USS *Independence*, to the Taiwan Strait. It was the largest US military deployment in East Asia since the Vietnam War. The PRC leaders protested US "interference," but there was little they could do to stop the clear message that the United States was still the primary power in the Western Pacific, and it intended to remain in that position on all matters, including Taiwan. The result in Beijing was that military influence on foreign policy making was dramatically reduced. Jiang Zemin was criticized for being careless on foreign affairs by party elders who kept insisting that conflict with the United States was not in China's interest.

Having elected in 1996 a GMD president sympathetic to the separatist agenda, Taiwan voters felt that in 2000 they might as well go the full distance. And so they elected a non-GMD president who had been an open supporter of Taiwanese independence. Chen Shuibian, who was in office to 2008, was the first non-GMD president of the Republic of China, and his party, the Democratic Progressive Party (DPP), had separatism as part of its policy platform. Though Chen muted these views while in office, the leaders in Beijing were increasingly desperate. Having made opposition to any move toward "splitting" Taiwan from China a staple of party-sponsored nationalism in the 1990s, they had to devise a better strategy to counter Chen's implicit challenge than the one that had failed so dismally against the more moderate Li Denghui in 1996. This time the PRC was rescued by a combination of the mainland's phenomenal economic growth (which Taiwan companies wanted a part of, especially since Taiwan's own growth figures were lagging), the corruption that emerged within Chen Shuibian's administration, and the American need to have a stable relationship with China after President George W. Bush's war on terror began. By emphasizing the need for prosperity for all Chinese and insisting that a safe economic future for Taiwan could only be found in cooperation with the mainland, the PRC was able to help pave the way for the thorough rejection of the DPP at the 2008 Taiwan elections. Today the relationship between the governments on the two sides of the Taiwan Strait is the best it has ever been. China is Taiwan's largest trading partner, and Taiwan companies are among the biggest investors on the mainland. Gone are the days when all flights between Taibei and the mainland had to stop over in Hong Kong. Now passengers can fly direct from the island to Beijing in three hours or less. Not surprising, perhaps, that the people of Taiwan in 2009 overwhelmingly preferred status quo against all other alternatives: sixty-four percent, against nineteen percent for independence, and five percent for unification.[17]

THE 1990S SET THE DIRECTION of Sino-American relations up to our own day. Both countries had a new generation of leaders in office. In China, Jiang Zemin, a sixty-three-year-old Soviet-trained engineer, was made head of the CCP in 1989 and would keep that office for thirteen years. In the United States Bill Clinton, a domestic policy–oriented Southern governor, served from 1993 to 2001. Both countries were drawing up new priorities, less ideological than before, and centering on rapid market-oriented economic growth. Most important of all, the Cold War had ended with the collapse of the Soviet Union in 1991. No longer were the United States and China tied together in an alliance of convenience against what they had both deemed an ascending and expansionist great power. With the Soviet Union gone, the strategic picture in East Asia changed completely. Suddenly, China and the United States were the main poles of influence in the region. The United States was the dominant power, through its alliances and its military prowess, but China was rising because of its unprecedented economic growth. For both countries the issue was whether these trends would pull them apart or bring them together. Liberal intellectuals hoped for the latter, through increasing economic interdependence. Realists expected the former, through increasing great power rivalry.

What neither side had expected or prepared for was the massively negative fallout from the Tian'anmen crackdown. In the United States the effect was particularly strong. While more than two-thirds of

Americans had viewed China positively before Tian'anmen, less than a third did so in 1990.[18] The lasting change in views among liberal and neoconservative elites in the United States was very strong and influences policymaking even today. Congress decided, with veto-proof majorities in both houses, to impose sanctions on China, some of which are still in place and complicate relations between the two countries. But the United States was in no way unique in its reaction to the use of soldiers against the people of Beijing. Fifty-seven other governments, including the European Union and Japan, introduced sanctions, in most cases as a result of public opinion in their countries. The main issue for many was not just what happened in China in 1989, it was the timing of it. In the span of just a few years, as the Cold War came to an end, much of the world, from Eastern Europe and Russia to South Africa and South America, seemed to move from authoritarianism to forms of participatory democracy. Only the Chinese government had shot at its democrats and survived in power. It created an outcast image for Beijing that the country, in spite of its economic success, found hard to shake off.

Within China itself the new generation of elites who grew up in the 1990s had an almost schizophrenic view of the world's relationship to their country. Even though most of them resented the government's actions in 1989, they took immense pride in China's economic progress and, bizarrely, bought into some of the regime's propaganda about sanctions being imposed as a result of American pressure to keep China down. As Chinese nationalism grew, both officially and unofficially, through the 1990s, many young people began feeling that in spite of their own misgivings about their government, foreigners were condemning it for all the wrong reasons. The regime of Jiang Zemin may have appeared utterly uninspiring to most Chinese in political terms, but it ensured stability, growth, and increasing freedom for people in their daily lives. While 1989 was in no way forgotten, Jiang Zemin and the CCP benefited domestically from presiding over unprecedented prosperity while being more liberal in terms of information and discussion than any Communists had been before.

The relationship between Jiang and Clinton got off to a rough start. The Chinese feared, rightly, that the new president's emphasis on human rights might become linked to China's trade access to US markets, and it took almost three years of Clinton's first term before the two issues were delinked. The US administration also suspected, with some reason, that China was supplying other countries with components for their chemical and nuclear arms programs. For China, arms sales was an issue of sovereignty as much as profit, especially since the United States sold weapons globally (including to Taiwan) and had imposed an arms embargo on Beijing after 1989. Together with the 1995–1996 Taiwan crisis, these tensions stymied progress on the bilateral relationship and fed Chinese popular nationalism. In 1996 the best seller of the year in China was a hackneyed anti-American diatribe entitled *China Can Say No: Political and Emotional Choices in the Post Cold-War Era.*[19]

Many Chinese, including Jiang Zemin, suspected that the weapons embargo and the increased concern over transfers of advanced US technology to China had to do more with the end of the Cold War than with human rights. With the Soviet Union gone, some Americans saw China as their main future rival, and these views were quickly picked up and elaborated in Beijing, especially after knowledge of the overwhelming military preponderance of the United States spread in the wake of the First Gulf War. "China must [now] pay close attention to those countries that are opposed to American interests," one Chinese observer wrote. "China should do all it can to warn and help these countries, and prevent them from being destroyed by the United States as the Soviet Eastern European Bloc was." While the new generation of Chinese leaders was ruing the unipolar world, many Americans of Bill Clinton's generation believed that, in spite of Tian'anmen, China would conform to a US-led international system, while gradually becoming more open and democratic at home. It was, Clinton said over and over again, simply in China's own interest to do so. The US president scored more than one victory. At a remarkable press conference during Clinton's visit to China in 1998, Jiang Zemin seemed even to explain 1989 in terms of expediency rather than principle: "Today the Chinese Government solemnly commits itself to the promotion and protection of human rights and fundamental freedom," Jiang told Clinton and the international press corps. "With regard to the political disturbances in 1989, had the Chinese Government not taken the resolute measures, then we could not have enjoyed the stability that we are enjoying today."[20]

B Y THE BEGINNING OF THE 2000s China's relationship to the United States was contradictory. On the one hand the two countries were growing ever more similar and contacts between them were more extensive than ever before. On the other Chinese nationalism was on the rise, with US policies as its particular target, while American concern about the nature of China's political system was increasing. With the Soviet Union gone, Chinese leaders felt that the West's suspicions about all forms of Communist rule had been automatically transferred to them, in spite of all they had done to conform to a Western-led international economy. On the American side the CCP regime's human rights record and its policies in Tibet came to overshadow much of the epochal transformation that was happening in the Chinese economy. Within China the singular preoccupation with American technologies, style, music, and education continued to overwhelm all impulses that came from elsewhere, but on the international scene the two states increasingly saw each other as rivals.

Three events at the turn of the century symbolized these contradictions. In May 1999, during its war against Serbia, US bombers dropped five 2,000-pound precision-guided bombs on the Chinese embassy compound in Belgrade, killing three Chinese and wounding twenty-one. In April 2001 an American spy plane collided with a Chinese jet fighter that was intercepting it seventy miles off the Chinese coast. The Chinese pilot was killed, and the US crew was held on an airbase in Hainan for almost two weeks before being released. But while these confrontations were taking place, China was also quietly negotiating with the United States and the world community for its accession to the World Trade Organization (WTO). The resulting, unprecedented agreement gave China membership in WTO from November 2001, with full US support for its bid. Mistrust seemed to be driving the two governments apart, while economic interest seemed to be edging them closer.

The US bombing of the Chinese Embassy in Belgrade led to one of the most serious confrontations between China and the United States since Tian'anmen. Although there is no evidence for it, many Chinese believed that the attack was deliberate, rather than a result of miscommunication and outdated maps, as the American air force claimed. China had denounced the US and NATO attack on the Serbian dictator Slobodan Milosevic's regime, saying that it constituted "a flagrant violation of the United Nations Charter." The purpose of the bombing, some Chinese nationalists believed, was to warn China off opposing US international hegemony. The attack led to furious and sometimes violent demonstrations—some instigated by the authorities—in the main Chinese cities. In Chengdu, the US consul general's residence was burned down. President Jiang Zemin stoked the flames, saying that the rallies stemmed from "the great patriotic spirit and cohesiveness of the Chinese nation and their strong will to maintain world peace and oppose hegemony. The great PRC will not be bullied." The main official newspaper, *Renmin ribao* (People's Daily), said that NATO had "become the heir to the evil heritage of Western culture" and headlined an editorial, with clear reference to the Boxer War, "This Is Not 1899 China."[21] A poll of university students in Beijing showed that more than seventy percent thought the US bombing was a deliberate act, and there were some slogans in their demonstration criticizing President

Jiang for being too weak on foreign affairs. A poem, of sorts, published in a Beijing daily caught the nationalist mood:

> *When we are wearing Pierre Cardin and Nike*
> *When we are driving Cadillacs, Lincolns, and going to*
> > *KFC and McDonald's*
> *Do we have a clear conscience?*
> *No!!!* . . .
> *Can we still find glory by using foreign products?*
> *No!!!* [22]

Pollsters working for foreign companies in China found a decided drop in the consumption of Western products immediately after the bombing. But the trend lasted only a week.

The midair collision between an American spy plan and a Chinese jet fighter two years later was interpreted by some Chinese in similar terms as the Belgrade bombing. When the new US administration of George W. Bush asserted that the US plane had been on a routine mission outside Chinese territorial waters, *Renmin ribao* shot back that it "sternly warns the US side that it should not absolve its domineering action with its hegemonic logic." To most Chinese it was a question of fairness. China did not conduct reconnaissance flights up and down US coasts, and Bush's denial of wrongdoing demonstrated what was wrong in international relations: The United States could do as it pleased, while every other country had to behave according to American rules. Chinese intelligence officials, though, were secretly pleased. The Yugoslavs had provided them with access to parts of a downed US stealth fighter from its war with NATO, and they had several months to dismantle and study the surveillance aircraft stranded on Hainan.[23]

But although the embassy bombing and the spy plane incident indicated increased conflict between China and the United States, the November 2001 US-sponsored Chinese accession to the WTO pointed to a different kind of future. The concessions the Chinese government had to make to achieve their much-publicized aim of fully joining the world's trade mechanisms were more staggering than any nationalist propaganda could imagine. China had to open up its domestic markets to foreign imports and foreign capital in all areas of production and services. Thus, the Chinese financial, telecommunications, distribution, and legal services sectors were now accessible to foreign firms. It had to stop preferential treatment for its state-owned enterprises. It had to eliminate quotas on most agricultural goods and to eliminate export subsidies for any of them. It had to build transparent financial regulations and laws that adhered to international standards. The changes the WTO agreement imposed on China went further than those for any other country, in part because of the complexities created by China insisting on being treated as a developing country. One South Asian WTO negotiator told me that seeing the glittering skyline of Pudong, Shanghai's new financial district, from the negotiating room window did not help convince him of China's "developing" status. The full protocol incorporated thousands of lines of tariffs and specific agreements and was put together after talks between China and every single one of the 142 members of the WTO. Having to negotiate with Haiti on beer and Fiji on sugar taught Chinese diplomats something about how international affairs worked beyond great power consultations. They learned from it. Even though top Chinese leaders were divided on the outcome, most of them agreed that WTO accession allowed them to do what they wanted to do anyway: abolish transfers to lossmaking agriculture and industry and reduce tariffs on imported goods. As in other countries, it was easier for the Chinese leaders to blame foreign pressure for such unpopular decisions than to take the responsibility themselves.

When the new century began, Chinese and Americans were eyeing each other warily. Many Chinese, including some who had lived abroad, were surprised at the influence pressure groups on human rights issues or on Tibet had on the US political system and the American public. Most Americans saw China, under its current government, as a future threat to the United States because it was undemocratic and oppressive. The fact that its economy was growing at more than twice the rate of the US economy, even through the boom years of the 1990s, began to worry some Americans. They did not realize the significance of the fundamental change that was taking place as China decided to accept integration into a US-led world economy. There was, in 2001, as George W. Bush was installed as US president and Hu Jintao was preparing to take over from Jiang Zemin (the first ever peaceful transition of power in mainland China), a sense that the Sino-American relationship was at a watershed, from where wild torrents threatened on one side and a slow but steady current flowed downriver on the other. But when the course was to be set, it was under very different winds of change than anyone had imagined in early 2001.

IT MAY NOT BE TRUE, as some historians claim, that the 9/11 terrorist attacks on New York and Washington changed everything in international affairs. But they certainly changed the Sino-American relationship almost overnight. George W. Bush had attacked his election opponent, Vice President Al Gore, for having been complicit in what Bush called the Clinton Administration's coddling of the Chinese Communists. But the authorities in Beijing had become used to such rhetoric during US election campaigns from whomever were not in office, and largely disregarded what Bush had said. Instead they chose to remember George W.'s long-standing ties to China, from when he came to stay with his father—the later president George H. W. Bush—when Bush *père* was US representative in the Chinese capital in 1974–1975. The spy plane crisis soon caused real concern for the Beijing leadership. But it was the new president's insistence on referring to China as a "strategic competitor" and as the main challenge to US security that upset Jiang Zemin and Hu Jintao most. Then came 11 September. The Bush administration turned to fighting a "war on terror" in the Middle East and at home, which not only took its attention away from China but made that country's regime a partner in another US global campaign. For the Chinese leadership it was a welcome break from the tensions in the relationship and from the US focus on the CCP's human rights violations. Jiang called Bush by telephone on 12 September and told the US president that "China is ready to strengthen dialogue and co-operation with the United States and the international community in the joint efforts in combating all sorts of terrorist violence."[24]

China supported the US attacks against terrorist bases in Afghanistan after 9/11. It accepted the overthrow of the Taliban regime because of the support Kabul had given to Osama bin Laden. In fact, Beijing was happy to see the Taliban go because of their suspected links to Islamist organizations in China's own Muslim-populated northwestern province Xinjiang. The long lead-up to the US war against Iraq put more strains on the Sino-American relationship, but even in the case of a US invasion not supported by the UN Security Council the Chinese leaders saw their interests best served by not opposing it too strongly. As things turned out, China could verbally dissent from the invasion and occupation of Iraq from a safe distance, while leaving to Russia and the Americans' own European allies Germany and France to provoke Washington's ire by attempting to block military action. The new Chinese president, the buttoned-down bureaucrat Hu Jintao, did not want to take any risks over a war he believed was coming whatever China said or did. No surprise, then, that Bush's Secretary of State, General Colin Powell, in September 2003 characterized relations with China as "the best they have been since President Nixon's first visit."[25]

Leaders in Beijing used the break from the attention of an aggressive and nationalistic new US administration to further build their economy and their military power. While the United States pursued its wars in Afghanistan and Iraq, China's GDP almost tripled. In 2010 it became the world's second largest economy, after the United States, but ahead of all others, including Japan and Germany. It is the largest exporter and the second largest importer of goods in the world, and will soon become the largest trading partner of the United States and the European Union. It is already the main trading partner of many leading countries, from Japan and Australia to India and Brazil. As could be expected, China's trade surplus is massive, and Chinese investment is starting to flow outwards. During the 2008–2009 economic crisis, Chinese companies bought car manufacturers (Sweden's Volvo and Britain's Rover, for instance), financial companies, and technology firms abroad. Chinese institutions are the largest buyers of US government securities, holding an estimated twenty percent of the total.[26]

But not all is well with the Chinese economy. As we will see in the final chapter, China's economic outlook is in no way certain, and the extensive links with the world economy bring risks as well as opportunities. Other countries, most importantly the United States, are complaining about Chinese currency manipulations and state interventions in the domestic economy, and want to see the Chinese trade surplus reduced. Inside China many people are concerned about rising inequality, atrocious labor conditions in some industries, and the need to create new jobs for the millions who enter the industrial job market every year. In terms of GDP per capita, China is still number 101 of all the countries in the world. Its $7,400 is right behind Albania, Ecuador, and Algeria. The US figure is $47,500.

China's military modernization started, as we have seen, from a very low level. When the reform period began in 1980, China had a large conscript army of 4.5 million men and little combat effectiveness, as its war against Vietnam had shown. The PLA's technological level was atrocious compared to armies elsewhere; its mechanized divisions were in disarray; its air defenses were mostly unserviceable; its air force and navy near nonexistent for purposes of modern warfare. It has taken China a generation to catch up, and its military capabilities today are still far behind those of the United States or even Japan. It does, however, now for the first time since the fifteenth century have a blue-water navy, with fifty submarines (ten nuclear) and seventy major warships. In 2011 the Chinese air force tested a new stealth fighter, similar to the American F-117. While the PLA is extraordinarily proud of this achievement, it must jar a bit that its testing came two years after the US air force began retiring their F-117s, first tested in 1981. The chances for China to catch up with the United States in military terms for another generation are slim as long as the present pattern in military investment continues. US defense spending was at least one trillion dollars in 2010. The Chinese was one-tenth that, from a much lower starting point in terms of training or military hardware. China's military power today is therefore much more comparable with that of Japan or Britain than that of the United States.[27] What will happen to China's emphasis on its military development will primarily be shaped by events in its own region, East Asia, which we will look at in the next chapter. But there is no doubt that China's complicated relationship with the United States in the past will cast its shadow over all Chinese thinking about national security in the future.

THROUGHOUT THE LATE twentieth century, China viewed the United States eagerly. It did so simply because America was the dominant force on most matters from medicine to music to military power. Many foreigners who visit China for the first time are astonished by the significance young Chinese give to the United States, for good or bad, and by the contradictory view of the world that this imagining of US positions creates: US global predominance is certainly visible all over the world, but people in Berlin or Buenos Aires pay less attention to it than do people in Beijing. Maybe this is because some Chinese think that the United States is occupying a global position that rightly belongs to China. Or is it because so many young Chinese want to become more like Americans as they see them—modern, independent, goal-driven, and wealthy, with a fair amount of ruthlessness (soap opera style) thrown in for good measure? Whatever the reason for China's current US obsession, it is influenced and shaped by the history the two countries share, not only in diplomatic and military terms, but in terms of how people think and behave. It is probable that in the future China will become more similar to what the United States looks like now. But political relations and the two people's perceptions of each other will likely be strained.

CHAPTER 11

CHINA'S ASIA

THE MOST REMARKABLE ASPECT of China's international development over the past thirty years has been its reengagement with the rest of Asia. Until three decades ago China suffered a self-imposed exile from the continent of which it is a part. Its only close relationship was with North Korea, and even in Pyongyang, the dirt-poor capital of the northern Korean state, Beijing had to compete for position with Moscow. As if the diplomatic isolation were not enough, China had territorial issues with all of its neighbors, including North Korea. Along the northern border, Chinese and Soviet troops were facing each other along 3,000 miles of closed frontiers. In the south, China had just fought a war with Vietnam, in which it lost at least 20,000 soldiers, and the other Southeast Asian states understandably viewed China with suspicion. India, along China's southwestern frontier, was politically close to the Soviet Union and, since the 1962 war regarded China as a diehard enemy. It was an Asian world that seemed to have expurgated China from its midst. The central kingdom was no longer central, but distinctly peripheral to the rest of the continent.

The main cause of China's marginality was its own contrary politics, but another key reason was economic. While other Asian economies were making strong gains, China's stagnated. Japan had of course been the pioneer of development in the region, with substantial growth rates even in the early twentieth century. But from 1950 to 1973, the

Japanese economy grew by an average of ten percent a year, as did Taiwan's. Singapore, South Korea, and Hong Kong grew by eight percent annually. In the PRC, GDP per capita in 1973 was around $800. In Japan it was $11,500, in Hong Kong $7,000, in Singapore $6,000, and in Taiwan $4,000. China was falling further and further behind the leading economies in Asia, and even though most Asians would have liked to see China open up to their exports, they did not actually believe that it was going to happen anytime soon.[1]

Then look at the situation today. China's own economic growth since 1980 has been spectacular, averaging near ten percent a year, and it has rejoined an integrated East Asian system of trade, finance, and investment. What is more, this growth has taken place in a country of 1.3 billion people, more than double the population of the rest of East and Southeast Asia put together. The journey that China has been on over the past generation has been intimately linked with its relationship to its neighbors, first those next door and then into the southern and western parts of the continent. Indeed, China's rise would have been impossible without it revitalizing these links. China is now an economic powerhouse that all of the rest of Asia orients itself toward, and its policies on all matters are of crucial importance for the whole region.

In order to understand China's interplay with its neighbors today we need to look at its immediate history. More has changed over the past thirty years than during any other generation in this region's development, and it is an ongoing process. In 1991 the Soviet Union suddenly collapsed. New Russia in the north and the other post-Soviet states bordering China in the west are no security threats, except as far as terrorism is concerned. In the south, instead of being a Soviet ally, Vietnam is now a part of an increasingly integrated community of states in Southeast Asia, ASEAN (Association of Southeast Asian Nations). In the east, Japan has become more independent in its foreign policy, although it is still a close US ally. As far as Korea goes, China is now South Korea's most important export market, and Koreans invest more in China than they do anywhere else. The whole region's relationship with China has changed profoundly, but so has the relationship the other countries have with each other. As Eastern Asia has become the center of world economic development, the region itself—and China's place in it—has been in constant flux.

THE MOST STRIKING CHANGE in China's foreign relations has taken place in the south. China's most recent border war was with Vietnam, a country Maoist China had supported in its struggles for reunification against France and the United States. The 1979 war left deep scars in China. To most Chinese, its course demonstrated Vietnamese ingratitude, Soviet perfidy, and Chinese military weakness all in one. I visited the border areas not long after the war ended, and the shock was palatable. It was no secret to local people that China had lost the war, or at least not won it. In Beijing Deng Xiaoping must have thought about the wars in Vietnam two hundred years earlier, and how the Qianlong emperor's inability to win had eroded his legacy. He may also have given some thought to the Americans' unhappy experience of fighting the Vietnamese. Deng's response, as we have seen, was to end the war, sideline the military politically, while streamlining and improving the country's fighting capacity, which, it was hoped, would prevent similar disasters from occurring in the future.

It was Chinese diplomatic ineptitude that brought about the brief but disastrous Sino-Vietnamese war of 1979. Throughout the late 1960s and 1970s, the Maoists had supported the radical Cambodian faction, the Khmer Rouge, especially after it took power in 1975 and introduced a Maoist-type state. When the Khmer Rouge leader Pol Pot repeatedly attacked Vietnamese territory, Beijing stuck by him because of its concerns over Hanoi's increasingly close relationship with the Soviets. Throughout the 1980s China and Vietnam carried out a war by proxy in Cambodia, with Vietnamese troops keeping a new government in place in Phnom Pen. China supported the Khmer Rouge, the former regime whose claim to lasting infamy is that it carried the only known genocide against its own population. Although China was not the only country that supported directly or indirectly the Khmer Rouge remnants fighting from the jungles of western Cambodia after the Vietnamese forces had thrown them out of the capital in 1979, it was the only one that kept a close political relationship with Pol Pot's group. Kaing Khek Eav, or Duch, who went on trial in 2009 for torturing and murdering 14,000 people in Tuol Sleng prison during Khmer Rouge rule, spent a year in China in the mid-1980s. Pol Pot himself spent two years there, ostensibly for medical treatment. China supplied considerable amounts of weapons and funds to the Khmer Rouge both before and after 1979. Vietnam withdrew from Cambodia in 1989, as the Cold War was coming to a close, but the terror of the Khmer Rouge continued up to the movement's self-destruction in 1997, when Pol Pot killed his second-in-command and then either died or was killed himself. In the meantime, Cambodia could begin its slow journey back from the nightmare it had experienced.

The end of the Cold War had a deep impact on the Sino-Vietnamese relationship. With the Soviet collapse and with the war in Cambodia won by the Vietnamese (although at a terrible cost), both Hanoi and Beijing were eager to find a modus vivendi. As China's economy expanded, the Vietnamese Communist leaders became convinced that Vietnam had to reform its own economic sector. By the early 2000s, much inspired by the Chinese example, Hanoi had transformed its sluggish planned economy into a market-led expansion that in relative terms in Asia was second only to that of its northern neighbor. But the worries the Vietnamese leaders had over what they saw as Chinese attempts at controlling their country did not abate, and they were wary of Chinese investment, including that by returning Sino-Vietnamese who had fled during the war. Even so, China has become Vietnam's largest trading partner, and all forms of economic exchanges are increasing rapidly.

Despite good economic links and decent overall bilateral relations, some of the Sino-Vietnamese tension that we have seen through history continues today. Hanoi is particularly concerned over China's territorial claims in the South China Sea. As we shall see later, this is a conflict that is threatening to overshadow much of China's relations with its neighbors to the south. But for Vietnam, having fought a recent war with China, these claims have a direct security relevance as well as economic implications. If Vietnam accepted the Chinese position, even in part, then almost all of its coast would be alongside waters controlled by the Chinese navy. It would also, many in Hanoi believe, be left out of the exploration of rich natural resources under the seabed and rich fisheries in the sea above. Having joined ASEAN in 1995 and dramatically improved its relations with the United States, Australia, and Japan, Vietnam is trying to multilateralize the issue, in order to balance China's growing power. China, on its side, is worried that Vietnam is spurning its offers of friendship and cooperation and that the country might become a cornerstone in a US-led containment policy toward China.

China has come a long way in normalizing its relations with what is probably, in the long term, its most important neighbor in the region. But issues from history stand in the way of a full partnership. Still led by two Communist parties, the two countries go through frequent spats over historical issues. Both set of leaders insist that the other should censor nationalist sentiments on Internet sites or blogs. At the heart of the matter is the view, never completely forgotten or lost in Beijing or Hanoi, that China is the central state in the region, and therefore expecting, or demanding, subservience by others. The Sino-Vietnamese agreement on the exact land borders between the two countries, signed in 1999, took ten years to implement, amid accusations that both sides were moving century-old border markers in the dead of the night to gain advantage.[2] It will not be easy for the two to achieve a balanced relationship.

THE MOST COMPLICATED of China's relationships in the region is with Korea. Even more than Vietnam, Korea was linked to the

Qing-centered system of states in eastern Asia up to the late nineteenth century, and Chinese culture and political ideals have had a lasting impact on the country. Since 1947, Korea has been divided in two separate and inimical states as a result of the Cold War and the ideological dissensions among Koreans. Communist China fought its bloodiest war to save the Communist North Korean state, the Democratic People's Republic of Korea, from its southern enemies and their American allies in the early 1950s. To many Chinese it is still a point of pride that China fought the most powerful country on earth to a standstill in that war. What China got in return, though, was an unreliable North Korean ally, led by the dictatorial Kim Il-sung and his offspring, over which it for a long time had to compete with the Soviet Union for influence. When the Soviet state collapsed in the early 1990s, the DPRK's economy went into freefall, creating a man-made hunger disaster during which at least a million people died. Only Chinese aid kept it from being much worse. Today leaders in Beijing privately call the DPRK an albatross around China's neck rather than a strategic asset. But, like Coleridge's bird, it has proven exceptionally hard to get rid of without unleashing a curse that will send the region toward conflict and potentially war.

Meanwhile, the Republic of Korea, South Korea, has transformed itself into one of the world's leading economies and one of the region's most advanced industrial states. China was slow to recognize South Korea's increasing importance in its own right—partly for ideological reasons and partly because the CCP viewed it as being under US control. Even after reform began in China it took fifteen years for Beijing to recognize the government in Seoul and begin to deal with it directly. After mutual recognition in 1992, the relationship developed very slowly at first, because of intense resistance from China's ally North Korea and Beijing's worries about Seoul's close alliance with Washington. But by the late 1990s both economic exchange and political contacts flourished, especially when South Korean president Kim Dae-jung and his successor, Roh Moo-hyun, tried to carry out a policy of détente toward the North between 1998 and 2007. Not only is China South Korea's most important trading partner, but more than half a million South Koreans live in the PRC, more people than from any other country. This South Korean presence is a result of significant Korean investment in China's industrialization process. Koreans feel a cultural and historical closeness with China. In opinion polls in South Korea in 2005, China was ranked equally with the United States—South Korea's long-term ally—as a country South Koreans viewed favorably. Among those under forty, China had a clear lead in terms of being seen as friendly.[3]

Over the past twenty years, China's big headache in its relationship with Korea has been North Korea. Financially insolvent, internally oppressive, and aggressive toward its neighbors, North Korea symbolizes those flaws with which China does not want to be associated as it attempts to expand its regional reach. Ruled until December 2011 by the dictator Kim Jong-il, who inherited the position from his father in 1994, the secretive North Korean regime has, over China's protests, developed nuclear weapons and is threatening to use them if its leaders feel under pressure. So why, may one ask, does China not simply disassociate itself from the Kim regime, now led by Kim Jong-il's son Kim Jong-un, and build on its good relations with the prosperous South? The answer is complicated, but may be worth dwelling on if one is to understand China's biggest foreign relations dilemma.

The first part of the answer is about history. As we have seen, China has had close links with its Korean neighbor for millennia. Its soldiers fought and died there in the mid-twentieth century in order to preserve the North Korean state and prevent—as they saw it—American aggression. The regime in Pyongyang still declares itself to be Communist and stresses the PRC's role as its older brother. Even when it ignores China's advice, it pays enough obeisance to the older brother to make the relationship work in vaguely Confucian terms. Even though the

Chinese leadership knows that it is running the risk of doing what the Soviets did with East Germany—preserving it until it is too late to bargain it away—even the Hu Jintao generation of leaders in Beijing find it very hard to criticize North Korea or be seen as acting against it, especially alongside South Korea, Japan, or the United States.

Another part of the answer is about risk. The Chinese leaders simply believe that North Korea and its nuclear weapons are much more controllable if there is a close relationship with China than if there is not. A third part of the answer is linked to China's strategic rivalry with the United States in the region. The PRC leaders are afraid that if North Korea were to go, they would find a reunified Korea under US tutelage. And finally the answer is connected to discussions about the future influence of China in whatever settlement is reached on the Korean peninsula. We will look more closely at this question in the next chapter. But to understand China's position on Korea it is essential to see that both the past and the future weigh heavily on the present and prevent China from solving its main foreign policy problem.

Meanwhile, since about 2007 China's relationship with South Korea has started to deteriorate. Today an increasing number of young South Koreans find it difficult to remain friendly toward China as long as Beijing props up an aggressive dictatorship in the north of the country. As the South Korean electorate swung to the right in 2008, choosing a more hard-line president, some of the relationship with China— painstakingly built by both sides over almost two decades—seemed to be in freefall. Even controversies about ancient history have come into play. South Korean academics accused China of portraying the Koguryŏ kingdom from two thousand years ago as Chinese, although for most Koreans it is the foundation state of the Korean nation. More than a few politicians, including some who had been close to the Chinese in the past, began fearing that the Koguryŏ controversy was a signal that China intended to preserve North Korea as a Chinese vassal state whatever Seoul said or did.[4] Whatever happens next in North Korea, Chinese leaders will have a real task on their hands in convincing the South Korean public that China stands on their side in their wish to reunify their country.

A S WE HAVE SEEN throughout this book, China and Japan have had a complicated and unsettled relationship for most of the past 150 years, sometimes close, sometimes in violent conflict. There has always been a formalistic or even ritualistic quality to their mutual affairs, based on Chinese suspicions that Japan's real aim has been and still is to replace China as the central power in the region. This, most Chinese feel, would be against the nature of things. In spite of their strong admiration for Japanese capabilities and skills, Japan to them remains a peripheral island kingdom, which ought never to aspire to take China's place. The normative aspect is very important here. Increasingly the Sino-Japanese relationship has become more about who is right or wrong (or who are using the correct terms), than about the potential for cooperation and mutual benefit. There is something rather Confucian in this, in a quite negative sense, and it has left both countries looking diplomatically helpless. The only power to benefit in a strategic sense is the United States, which can use Chinese and Japanese fear of each other to its own advantage. Despite the ongoing controversies, however, the dealings between the two have been more stable over the past generation than they have been at any other time since the mid-nineteenth century, and both sides are at present benefiting from significant economic and technological exchange.

The new relationship between China and Japan began in 1971, after what the Japanese press referred to as the *Nikuson Shokku*, or Nixon shocks. First there was the US decision to open a dialogue with Beijing. And then Washington rushed to implement a more self-centered economic policy to deal with its balance-of-payment problems. The Japanese government had not been told beforehand of either of these decisions, and their effects hit the country hard—the first one in foreign policy and the second in exports. The new Japanese prime minister, Tanaka Kakuei—a tough-minded nationalist from the Liberal Democratic Party's right wing, who had long wanted less Japanese dependence on the United States—seized the opportunity. He began his own negotiations with Beijing, resulting in a 1972 joint communiqué between the two countries. In it, the Chinese side got almost all it wanted: diplomatic recognition, acceptance of Taiwan as part of China, and a clause that committed both sides to work against "efforts by any other country or group of countries" to establish "hegemony" in Asia—the latter obviously aimed at the Soviet Union, but with an implicit warning to the United States as well. Japan, on its side, got an opening to the China market, slowly to begin with, but increasingly intense after the reform era began in China in the late 1970s.

The decade of the 1980s was the golden age of Sino-Japanese collaboration. It was in many ways similar to the first decade of the century, when people on both sides of the East China Sea saw immense opportunities in cooperation. In the 1980s, trade increased significantly, with Japanese technology being easily and freely imported into China. Travel and exchanges of all sorts picked up, and in intellectual terms the trend from three generations before was continued. Soon the largest number of foreign students in Japan was Chinese. Today the Chinese student population accounts for two-thirds of all foreign students in Japan. In the 1980s seventy percent of all Japanese felt an affinity to China, far more than for any other nation. The positive emotional impact of normalization was strong in both countries, but probably stronger in Japan. Japanese opinion polls showed that a large majority hoped that the two countries could put the past aside and start over again as friends and partners. Both governments managed public views on their new relationship very closely. The CCP did not allow any anti-Japanese protest in China, and the Japanese authorities made sure that newspapers carried only positive stories about China.

It was a make-believe relationship that could only be set up for a fall. In the 1990s economic interaction continued to grow, but it was not accompanied by a growth in the sense of community. Quite the contrary: By the end of the decade citizens of both sides felt considerably more negative about the other than they had done ten years earlier. First, the Japanese reaction to the 1989 events in China was strong. (It was difficult, however, to tell whether Japanese in China reacted more strongly to government suppression or simply to "disorder" in general.) The number of Japanese who saw China as a potential threat shot up. On the Chinese side, as access to the public sphere increased, more negative views about Japan came to the fore, most of them centering on history. Japan had never publicly apologized for its occupation of China, or paid proper compensation, some people wrote, and the atrocities Japanese soldiers had committed during the war had not been properly exposed. Interestingly, more of these views were held by young Chinese, who had not experienced the war, than by those who had. Both governments moved away from managing the relationship toward exploiting its negative aspects for their own advantage. When the CCP needed to focus attention away from its own shortcomings, it allowed public criticism of Japan. When a Japanese government needed support for unpopular initiatives at home or abroad, it appealed to Japanese concepts of uniqueness and willingness to sacrifice, sometimes symbolized by a prime ministerial visit to the Yasukuni shrine, where vast numbers of fallen Japanese soldiers are commemorated alongside fourteen convicted war criminals. The era of "historical issues" in the Sino-Japanese relationship had started in earnest. In the decade that followed, concentration on such disputes threatened to derail a relationship that the previous generation had so painstakingly built.

No issue that has done more damage to Sino-Japanese relations over the past ten years than how history is taught in schools. The truth is that history books used in Japan's schools are uncertain or dishonest in portraying World War II and its causes, including Japan's atrocities against civilians during the occupation of China. School history books in the PRC are terrible for all of the modern period, serving a mishmash of nationalist-infused lies in order to please what is seen as government policy. A Chinese historian and philosopher, Yuan Weishi, pointed out in 2006 that in Chinese history books "if there is a conflict between China and others, then China must be right; patriotism means opposing other powers and foreigners. In the selection and presentation of historical materials, we will only use those that favor China whether they are authentic or not."[5] Chinese textbooks still talk about sneaky missionaries, patriotic Boxers, and Japan's permanent expansionism helped by cowardly GMD leaders. For post-1949 history it gets worse. The death toll of Mao's campaigns is never mentioned. Nor are the effects of the Great Leap Forward. According to these textbooks, China broke with the Soviets for patriotic reasons only and the Cultural Revolution was the result of a set of misunderstandings combined with the deranged ambition of a woman, Mao's wife, Jiang Qing. In Chinese school textbooks the Korean War is painted in black and white. In a chapter entitled "Resisting America, Supporting Korea, Protecting the Homeland and Defending the Country," the best-selling history textbook for Chinese high schools gives the following account:

> Not long after the founding of New China, the country faced the threat of external invasion. In the summer of 1950 the Korean Civil War erupted. The United States rushed to use military force to interfere in Korean internal matters, forming an American dominated "Allied Army" to invade Korea. They crossed the 38th Parallel and took the flames of war right up to China's border. At the same time, the US 7th Pacific Fleet entered the Taiwan Straits and so interfered in China's internal affairs. The situation in Korea was grave and imperiled China's security and safety. . . . Faced with such a dire situation, the government of the Democratic People's Republic of Korea requested that the Chinese government send troops to their aid. On October 10, 1950, in order to resist America, support Korea, and to protect and defend the country, a Chinese volunteer army under the leadership of Peng Dehuai entered Korea. Standing shoulder to shoulder, the Chinese volunteers and the Korean army and people beat back the American invaders, pushing them past the

38th Parallel, after which a stalemate ensued between China/Korea
and the American invaders. Due to fierce resistance by the Chinese
and Koreans, in the summer of 1953 the United States had no
choice but to sign the armistice. With their defeat of the American
army and victory in the War to Resist America and Support Korea,
the Chinese Volunteer Army disbanded triumphantly.[6]

Likewise, Japanese textbooks do a great disservice to the country's
young people by lying about its attacks on and occupation of China
and other Asian countries in the twentieth century. The attempts to diminish and qualify the suffering of the people of Nanjing in 1937 is
particularly galling. According to one textbook, published in 2005, "At
this time, many Chinese soldiers and civilians were killed or wounded
by Japanese troops (the Nanking [Nanjing] Incident). Documentary
evidence has raised doubts about the actual number of victims claimed
by the incident. The debate continues even today."[7] The book also portrays the attack on Pearl Harbor as the result, rather than the cause, of
war. It documents moments where Japanese troops were seen as liberators in Southeast Asia but has no similar texts on Japanese atrocities.
These nationalist textbooks, and the controversy that surrounds them,
keep mobilizing young people for antiforeign movements, especially in
China, where many youngsters are only too eager to spot the mote that
is in Japan's eye, rather than the beam that is in their own country's.

Alongside textbook controversies come clashes over territory and
over redress for wartime mistreatment. The disagreement over the dividing line in the East China Sea became more acute when in the early
2000s Chinese companies began drilling for gas in the disputed areas.
The Diaoyu/Senkaku islands at the center of the dispute are claimed by
both countries, though historically China has the stronger claim. With
regard to redress, since 1995 Chinese have been suing the Tokyo government and companies in Japanese courts for compensation arising
from wartime crimes. These cases have been big news in both countries.

Chinese papers claim that the processes are moving too slowly. Japanese papers criticize the size of the compensation demands, even in cases where Japanese courts have agreed with the plaintiffs. So far the courts have awarded the plaintiffs more than 800 million yen.[8] The irony is, of course, that Chinese citizens are still unable to take their own government (not to mention the CCP) to court, and that nobody has issued an apology for the millions killed in the CCP's atrocities in the 1950s and 1960s. Instead nationalists in both countries use cases that involve citizens from the other country to prove the continuing evil intent of the opposing side.

The lack of imagination in Sino-Japanese relations has cost both countries dearly, and is likely to continue to do so in the future. What is striking in the relationship today is the complete failure of strategic vision on both sides. Leaders in Beijing and Tokyo *know* that they have nothing to gain from further demonizing the other. In fact, each is increasingly dependent on the other to succeed: China in its great power ambitions and Japan in its need to overcome economic stagnation. But nobody has so far been able or willing to give the relationship the priority it must have by putting the past to rest.

As CHINA BEGAN EMERGING from years of isolation, its leader, Deng Xiaoping, focused on forging closer links with Southeast Asia. That region is full of not only Chinese migrants who have done well but also companies and individuals who could contribute to China's modernization through trade and investment. Deng thought their involvement in the PRC would be less politically problematic than that of Americans, Japanese, and Koreans. The problem China faced was that most Southeast Asian states had leaders who saw China as a threat. They feared the political influence of the Chinese minorities in their own countries. And they resented the PRC because for almost a generation it had sponsored Communist parties opposed to their governments. In countries like Malaysia, Thailand, Burma, and the Philippines, China had supplied Communist-led guerrillas with money, weapons, and training to carry on civil wars. It was not an ideal starting point for opening up relations with the existing regimes.

In more ways than one, China got very lucky in its attempts to reach out to old elites in Southeast Asia. It could benefit from contacts with the Huaqiao, the Southeast Asian Chinese. Some of these connections had not even been broken during the Cultural Revolution. China could also build on the general assumption among the wealthy in the region that China would be a gigantic market for Southeast Asian goods if they could get in before other and more powerful foreigners were able to establish themselves there. From the early 1980s on, very much driven by the Chinese diaspora, Southeast Asian companies became a significant presence in China. Some of them, such as Thailand's Charoen Pokphand (Zheng Dai in Chinese), are now among the largest foreign investors there. The Vietnamese overthrow of the Pol Pot regime in Cambodia in 1979 also helped China in this regard. The PRC could stand as a de facto ally of the conservative Southeast Asian regimes against what they feared would be Vietnamese and Soviet attempts at controlling the whole region. Singapore's anti-Communist leader, Lee Kuan Yew, told Western visitors that "if the Chinese had not punished Vietnam, all of Southeast Asia would have been open to Soviet influence. Now it has gained 10 to 15 years. The Thai premier, for instance, is a new and relaxed man after the Chinese punitive expedition." China's attempts at "teaching Hanoi a lesson" may have been a disaster from a Chinese military perspective, but the stunned praise it brought Beijing from countries further south gave Deng time to quietly shelve his country's support for Communist insurgencies outside its own borders.[9]

As a Chinese-majority state and the most dynamic economy in Southeast Asia, Singapore has played a particularly important role for China. Deng Xiaoping visited there in 1978. It was his first foreign

visit after having retaken the reins of power in Beijing. Deng, the pro-
ponent of "muscular growth" as he called it, was most impressed with
what he saw. Deng had last visited Singapore in 1920, when it was a
colonial backwater where the Chinese existed to do the work for British
authorities. In the late 1970s Singapore was a powerhouse. It was in
most respects everything Deng wanted China to become. After returning to Beijing, Deng stressed the need to learn from Singapore's social
order and stability, from its economic versatility, and from the role the
government had in promoting and steering growth. For three generations of Chinese Communists, Singapore had been everything there
was reason to hate: capitalism, class oppression, and closeness to the
United States. In the 1980s and 1990s it became an object of emulation,
especially as social and political unrest in 1989 threatened to derail
Deng's plans. It also became an economic partner. Singapore is now
the fifth largest investor in China and a primary conduit for the import
of technology, including forms of technology that China finds it difficult to obtain elsewhere.

Lee Kuan Yew, the Singaporean leader, taught the new Chinese
leadership much about the region he operated in. By the 1990s he
stressed the importance of the regional organization, ASEAN. Originally
set up in 1967 as a framework for cooperation among anti-Communist
governments, ASEAN soon took on a much broader significance in
terms of regional integration. After the Cold War it began a set of ambitious programs for deepening cooperation among member states. And
it added new members: Vietnam in 1995, Burma and Laos in 1997,
and Cambodia in 1999. Today's ASEAN states, which together have
almost 600 million people in them, are aiming for an economic community not unlike the European Union.

For China the emergence of ASEAN was both a threat and an opportunity. Lee and other Southeast Asian leaders were at first told that
China preferred to deal with individual states, not regional organizations. Then, as it became clear that ASEAN would not accept a divide-

and-rule approach and that the organization was an increasingly integrated force for regional stability, the Chinese government changed
tack. Since the late 1990s, cooperation between China and ASEAN has
gone from strength to strength, with real practical progress underlying
the often fuzzy language about Asian values and common heritage. On
economic issues, the big northern neighbor has come to be seen more
as a partner than a threat through a number of new formal and informal
mechanisms. China's support for regional currencies during the economic crisis in 1997–1998 convinced even those who had been critical
of Chinese policies in the past that Beijing now had no interest in economic dislocation to its south. An ASEAN-China Free Trade Area came
into force in 2010, but there are still difficulties in the trade relationship
that need to be sorted out.

As we have seen in the case of Vietnam, now a key member of
ASEAN, institutional cooperation does not always translate into security
perceptions. If one speaks with leaders from the Southeast Asia region,
the overarching problem of living next to a giant is always present, in
all its facets. In broad outline, the relationship is not unlike the one between the United States and Latin America. But China's southern
neighbors are, relatively speaking, far more powerful than those of the
United States, not least because they are better organized. Uncertainties
over who will be in a position to develop the resources that border the
Southeast Asian region create mutual suspicions and potential conflict.
ASEAN countries are for instance worried about Chinese links with
Burma, a resource-rich member state that is run by a particularly incompetent military dictatorship. The regional organization has been
pushing for reform in Burma, while China has seemed happy with status quo.

But first and foremost the main ASEAN members are concerned
over Beijing's claims to most of the small islands within the South China
Sea. This vast maritime area holds immense riches—oil, gas, and mineral
ores—and both the ASEAN countries and China want to develop it.

These waters also contain the world's busiest commercial sea lanes. China and Vietnam have already clashed over ownership of some of the islets, with China occupying nine of the Spratly Islands, over which Vietnam also claims sovereignty. Now other ASEAN states are getting increasingly concerned about China's motives and its actions. Chinese maps show Scarborough Shoal, about 120 miles from Subic Bay in the Philippines, as Chinese territory, and claim reefs as far south as thirty miles off the coast of Borneo, all in the name of "historical rights." From 2010 some ASEAN members have leaned heavily toward internationalizing the issue, seeking support from the United States and other powers, such as India. All similar attempts in the past have met with a stern reaction from Beijing, which has now begun speaking of the South China Sea as a Chinese "core interest." There is obviously much that still can go wrong in the Sino-ASEAN relationship, in spite of a hopeful beginning.

Within ASEAN, the biggest economy and the most powerful military are both Indonesian. With a rapidly growing population of close to 250 million people, Indonesia has now become the key power in the region, and, as we have seen, its relationship with China has not always been easy. The CCP had supported the Indonesian Communist Party, which was crushed in a military crackdown in 1965. In the massacres that followed the military takeover, Chinese-Indonesian communities were targeted and thousands of innocent people killed. The Indonesian constitution contained anti-Chinese restrictions all the way up to the reintroduction of democracy in 1998. People of Chinese ancestry are still underrepresented in politics and military affairs but massively overrepresented in business; it is often said that Chinese-Indonesians control up to two-thirds of the Indonesian private economy.[10] There is much uncertainty in the relationship between Beijing and Jakarta, although the two *are* working together within an ASEAN framework.

The contradictory form of the Sino-Indonesian relationship came to the fore in 1998, a year many Indonesians celebrate as the beginning

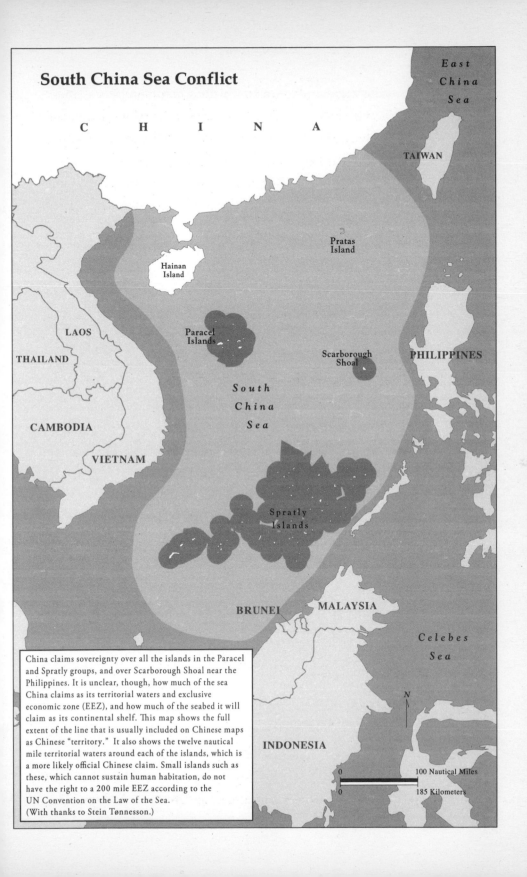

South China Sea Conflict

East China Sea

C H I N A

TAIWAN

Pratas
Island

Hainan
Island

Paracel
Islands

Scarborough
Shoal

PHILIPPINES

*South
China
Sea*

LAOS

THAILAND

CAMBODIA

VIETNAM

Spratly
Islands

BRUNEI MALAYSIA

*Celebes
Sea*

N

China claims sovereignty over all the islands in the Paracel
and Spratly groups, and over Scarborough Shoal near the
Philippines. It is unclear, though, how much of the sea
China claims as its territorial waters and exclusive
economic zone (EEZ), and how much of the seabed it will
claim as its continental shelf. This map shows the full
extent of the line that is usually included on Chinese maps
as Chinese "territory." It also shows the twelve nautical
mile territorial waters around each of the islands, which is
a more likely official Chinese claim. Small islands such as
these, which cannot sustain human habitation, do not
have the right to a 200 mile EEZ according to the
UN Convention on the Law of the Sea.
(With thanks to Stein Tønnesson.)

INDONESIA

| 0 | | 100 Nautical Miles |
| 0 | | 185 Kilometers |

of their country's democracy. As the strongly anti-Communist Suharto dictatorship ended, Indonesians of Chinese descent were attacked in many parts of the country by mobs that accused them of amassing illicit wealth during the dictator's rule. For older Chinese, who had had relatives killed thirty years before by the dictator's forces on suspicion of being Communists, the wanton murders and rapes in 1998 were signs that if you were of Chinese descent in Indonesia you were in constant danger whatever you did. One report described the ordeal of a Sino-Indonesian family who ran a little corner store in a suburb of Jakarta: "Among the looters were people known to the family, including the local meatball seller, who made off with a television set. Others stole the photo-copier from the store and then later tried to sell it back to the family for a high price. A year after the attack the family were operating their store again, supplying basic goods to the neighborhood." Unlike after 1965, the PRC government's reaction was measured. It stressed that Sino-Indonesians were, above all, Indonesian citizens who should be protected by their own government. Student protests in Beijing were quelled by the authorities, who wanted a good relationship with the post-Suharto regime in Indonesia.[11]

China's fear today is that Indonesia will increase its cooperation with the United States as a result of Beijing's economic rise and more powerful international position. Military and diplomatic planners whom I have spoken with see such a development as quite likely. The United States had a close strategic relationship with Indonesia during the Suharto dictatorship from 1965 to 1998, and most of the Indonesian leaders are oriented toward the United States culturally and educationally. They are also aware of the positive impact in the country of President Barack Obama having spent four years there as a child. Beijing is trying to use its new economic muscle to be seen by Jakarta as an equal to the United States. Right before Obama's first visit to Jakarta as president in 2010, China offered investments of $6.6 billion in desperately needed infrastructure improvements. But such forms of economic cooperation are just turning the existing situation around very slowly, especially as the United States will likely pay more attention to the region after the end of its wars in Iraq and Afghanistan.

The South China Sea issue is less of an immediate concern to Indonesia than to some of the other ASEAN members, but Jakarta has made a point of full ASEAN solidarity on the matter. Unfortunately for both countries, especially in the longer run, the Chinese ocean claims overlap with Indonesia's economic zone in one area, which happens to be part of the world's largest gas field off the Natuna Islands. The Indonesian government has reacted very negatively to what it sees as Chinese attempts at intimidating its neighbors. When some ASEAN states tried to raise Law of the Sea concerns at the ASEAN regional forum meeting in 2010, the Chinese foreign minister reminded his counterparts very sharply about the difference in size between China and its southern neighbors. The Indonesians will not have it; a former top foreign policy maker told me afterward that "Indonesia is a serious country that will not be bullied."

It is not surprising, then, that the Indonesian armed forces in 2009 carried out a joint exercise with the United States, code-named Garuda Shield. They, and other ASEAN militaries, stress that they believe a US presence in the region is needed in order to balance the growing power of China. The Indonesians have also sought closer relations with India, China's rival further west. China's response has been halting. Most Chinese leaders believe that a gradual and measured approach to Southeast Asia, combined with China's rising economic power, will prevent great power rivalries in the region. They tend to stress China's historical ties to the area, and their peaceful development over a long period of time. But Beijing is in no mood to barter away what it sees as Chinese rights in return for a stable relationship. In 2010 China held its biggest naval exercises ever in the South China Sea, with ships from all three main Chinese fleets participating. For the first time since the fifteenth century, China has a predominant naval presence in the southern seas.

NOTHING SYMBOLIZES THE CHANGE in China's international fortunes better than its relationship with Russia. When our story began, back in the eighteenth century, Qing China was predominant along its northern borders. Then, for almost two hundred years, Russia expanded and China retreated. Now, in the early twenty-first century, China is back in the driver's seat and sets the terms for how interaction with its northern neighbors will take place. All of this change has happened in little more than thirty years. While China strengthened its economy and its state, the Soviet experiment collapsed, leaving Russia in political chaos and economic free fall. But while China's newfound strength sets the tune, the links with the Soviet successor states are far from unproblematic as seen from Beijing. Their political disorder means uncertainties in many aspects of relations with China, from access to raw materials to antiterrorism. It is difficult to see easy ways forward for China's northern policies.

During the last years of the Soviet era, China spent almost two decades in a stale relationship with Moscow. It was mostly driven by an exaggerated and ideologically based fear of Red Army power. Deng Xiaoping tried to limit the conflict in the mid-1980s, mainly because of a growing concern that the United States could be getting too preponderant in international affairs. But very little came out of the détente with the Soviets, even after Mikhail Gorbachev became general secretary of the Soviet Communist Party in 1985. The Chinese leaders feared that Gorbachev was out to cut a deal with the United States and Western Europe, leaving the Soviet Union free to step up its military presence in eastern Asia. In 1988, as it became clear that the USSR was not only planning to withdraw from Afghanistan but also wanted the Vietnamese to withdraw from Cambodia, Deng increased diplomatic contacts with Moscow. These contacts culminated in Gorbachev's visit to China in the spring of 1989. The visit had a great symbolical importance. Mao Zedong had gone to Moscow right after becoming leader of the PRC. Gorbachev came to visit Deng in Beijing.

Gorbachev's visit should have been a triumph for Deng Xiaoping. It completed Sino-Soviet normalization on criteria put forward by China. But the summit in Beijing could not have come at a more awkward moment. In May 1989, as Chinese and Soviet leaders met in The Great Hall of the People, tens of thousands of students occupied Tian'anmen Square right outside. Many held banners in support of Gorbachev's democratic reforms. Deng would not be distracted. At eighty-five, he lectured the Soviet leader on the need to put the past behind them. "Looking at the past," Deng said, "many of the expressions that were used by both sides were empty. . . . The question was not [about] ideological differences. We too were wrong." The problem had not been different views on Communism, Deng maintained, but Moscow accepting China's position. "Read my speech [at the Moscow meeting in 1963] . . . its leitmotif is [that] the Soviet Union wrongly imagined the place of China in the world." Deng listed a series of Russian land grabs from China in the past, ending with "the Chinese province of Outer Mongolia, which today is called the Mongolian People's Republic."[12] Deng was willing to let the past be past, but only on conditions of historical memory set by Beijing.

The rapid collapse of the Soviet Union in 1991 came as a complete shock to the Chinese leaders. They simply could not imagine that a Communist Party general secretary could accept, first, the banning of the party and, then, the dissolution of the Soviet state, almost without a shot being fired in anger. Whereas the Chinese had used massive force to crush unarmed protest in 1989, Gorbachev had accepted change from below, and allowed the Soviet republics to secede peacefully after first dismantling Moscow's control over Eastern Europe. Three main explanations developed in the CCP, all of which would have significance for the future: Gorbachev was a fool, seduced by US charms and his own ego into leaving the Soviet peoples defenseless against foreign exploitation. Or the Soviet version of socialism had been so unproductive and behind the times that it had dug its own grave. Or the Soviets had been overextended; they had tried to do too much abroad and when they finally got to domestic reform, it was too late. None of these explanations were mutually exclusive, but where leaders put the emphasis signaled how they wanted to approach China's own development in the future. Even today the Soviet collapse is a hotly discussed topic among Chinese leaders. They want to learn from the Soviet disaster so as not to follow its example.

After the Soviet Union was replaced by fifteen separate republics in 1992, the Chinese leaders struggled to keep up with the rapid changes along their northern borders. Eager to portray itself as the epitome of stability in a chaotic world, the CCP in the late 1990s pointed to two examples of what not to do. The wars in the former Yugoslavia demonstrated that post–Cold War Europe was unstable. The chaos in the former Soviet Union showed what could go wrong if large states collapsed. Very soon, though, China began trying to set up mutually beneficial links with Russia. Jiang Zemin and his successor Hu Jintao despaired of working with the first Russian president, Boris Yeltsin, who disliked the CCP for being autocrats, and whom they excoriated as a drunk. But the Chinese leaders found it much easier to work with Yeltsin's successor, the former KGB officer Vladimir Putin. Putin made no secret of his admiration for China's authoritarian government, social order, and economic success. In July 2001 Russia and China signed a new agreement of Good-Neighborliness and Friendly Cooperation, to replace the treaty that had lapsed under much acrimony in 1979. The new pact underlined mutual consultations and economic cooperation, in fields such as energy and military technology. The text had a vague anti-US tint, promising to cooperate against countries "interfering in the internal affairs of a sovereign state under all sorts of pretexts." It also prohibited any support to "terrorists, splittists and extremists" in each country. Finally, Russia recognized Taiwan as part of China and China affirmed that it had no territorial claim against Russia. It was a creaseless treaty, symbolizing a new era in the relationship, but forcing either side to do very little that it did not want to do or preventing it from doing what it had the power to do already.[13]

China's main interest in Russia after 1991 has been economic. With a large population, high growth rate, and limited access to resources, China's leaders see Russia—with its smaller (and shrinking) population, low internal growth, and an abundance of raw materials—as a supplier of resources China will need for its modernization. Chinese leaders tend to think of such a relationship as mutually beneficial and to be irritated by Russian concerns about growing Chinese influence and physical presence in the eastern parts of Russia. Chinese businessmen are also horrified by the complexities of doing business in and with Russia: The bureaucracy, the corruption, and the amount of time needed even for the simplest of transactions hold back business links, the Chinese think. From a Western perspective watching some of these exchanges is truly instructive: The Chinese—often themselves accused of unconventional business methods—lecture Russians and Central Asians on proper financial conduct, responsibility, and international standards. China is increasingly aware of Russia's centrality for any future Chinese development plans, but the development of economic interaction has been slow. China's acute energy needs may put an end to the lethargy, however. The two countries have been negotiating massive new oil and gas pipeline deals, although both construction and exports are so far hampered by disagreements on prices and volume.

UNTIL 1991, CHINA'S CONCERN with Central Asia was exclusively about the Soviet Union, an inimical power that was the main threat to Chinese security. At that time the Muslim regions in the west were part of the Soviet state, and in the east the People's Republic of Mongolia was firmly under Soviet control. China itself controlled Tibet and the southern parts of Mongolia. The vast territory from the Korean borders to the Caspian Sea—a distance almost half the circumference of the globe—seemed frozen in time. Then the Soviet Union collapsed, and everything thawed. The change took the CCP leaders entirely by surprise. Even more than in their relationship with the new Russian state, Beijing hesitated and procrastinated in forming clear policies for the Central Asian region. It is only since the early 2000s that China has begun to expand its power and influence among its Asian neighbors to the north.

The PRC's first concern as the USSR collapsed was with military and security issues. Beijing had two main aims. First, it wanted to make sure that the sudden dissipation of authority over sophisticated weapons systems—including nuclear weapons, in the case of Kazakhstan— would not endanger China or its regional interests. Second, it aimed to avoid any support being given by the new states to their secessionist-minded ethnic brethren inside China's own borders or to those who supported cross-border political projects built on Muslim or Buddhist identities. By the late 1990s both of these threats seemed to have been averted. China cooperated with a US-led program to peacefully rid Central Asia of the weapons of mass destruction its states had inherited from the Soviet Union. It also cooperated with Russia to curb secessionism. In 1996 the two signed an agreement with Kazakhstan, Kyrgyzstan, and Tajikistan on Deepening Military Trust in Border Regions. Out of that treaty came the Shanghai Cooperation Organization (SCO) five years later. SCO's charter binds the members to seek "multipolarity" (read: avoid a US-dominated world), to combat "terrorism, separatism and extremism," and to support the "territorial integrity of States and inviolability of State borders." China, Russia, and the authoritarian leaders who had taken power in the new states were exquisitely lucky with the timing of their new initiative. After the 9/11 attacks on the United States, the Bush administration was willing to ignore the anti-American foundation of the organization and concentrate on working with it to fight real or perceived Islamist threats. In all matters, China was the main beneficiary of the organization named after its economic capital. The SCO helped secure China's borders and defeat internal opposition. Under it, China became open to settlements of disputes over territory and water with the smaller member states. And the SCO underscored China's central role in Central Asia. After a century, Beijing was back in the driver's seat in the region.[14]

China's relations with Mongolia are even more complicated than those with the post-USSR republics. Mongolia is a vast country, half the size of India but with less than three million inhabitants. For seventy years, as the People's Republic of Mongolia, it was a de facto part of the Soviet Union. The Soviet presence had a fair amount of support among Mongolians. The ethnically homogeneous population is strongly anti-Chinese, mainly because Qing rule in Monglia had been deeply unpopular toward the end of the empire and because a very large number of Mongolians believe that China has never really given up its claim on their territory. Even so, China's economic pull has proven irresistible to the democratically elected governments in Ulaanbaatar, and China is today the largest investor in the country. The Mongolians, however, are trying to compensate for their increasing economic dependence on China. They are inviting US and Russian companies, as well as companies from elsewhere in Asia and Europe, to help develop their country's phenomenal natural resources. They may succeed in this strategy, not least because China for internal reasons has to be careful how it treats Mongolia, since there are at least twice as many Mongols inside China as in the independent republic to the north.

Economic plans and needs are increasingly taking over as drivers in the relationships between China and all of the Central Asian states. They are giving this region a much greater importance to China than it had in the wake of the Soviet collapse. The 2008 economic crisis concentrated the minds of many Chinese planners, public and private, on the need for access to Central Asia's abundant natural resources. Chinese companies have invested heavily in the oil and gas sectors in Kazakhstan and Turkmenistan, with massive loans to those crisis-ridden governments in return for the deals. One of the world's longest pipelines now transports gas from Turkmenistan to China. All other great powers, including India, view China's increasing economic predominance in Central Asia with suspicion. But there is little they can do about it, as long as China can and will invest more in the region than any others.

L IKE TODAY'S CHINA, contemporary India was born in the bloodshed and chaos of the 1940s. China took a long time to reach some form of stability, but from the start India developed a democratic and durable political system, which has mostly kept the country on an even keel. During the Maoist years the Chinese Communists looked down on India because they thought its politics and overall development were too closely patterned on the model set by its former colonial masters. Mao himself felt that the lack of revolutionary spirit and its massive size made India a possible threat in the future. In the short run, he relied on the combination of what he saw as Nehru's foreign policy naïveté and Indian disunity to steer the country away from conflict with China. To his associates the Chairman wondered whether the Indian state project was viable; he saw India more as an "abstraction" than a country, he said. The 1962 war was in many ways a shock for China; its leaders had not expected the Indians to take such a forward attitude to the border problems. Despite the Chinese victory, Beijing realized that India—especially as a de facto ally of the Soviet Union—would be more of a problem than it had bargained for.

The Indo-Pakistani war of 1971 proved all of China's suspicions about India's aims. Instead of viewing the entry of Indian troops into East Pakistan in support of a popular rebellion there as an act of liberation, China insisted it was a naked power grab. Deng Xiaoping told the Americans, "It is the dream of Nehru, inherited by his daughter, to have the whole South Asian subcontinent in their pocket."[15] The first Indian nuclear test in 1974 surprised the Chinese, who had not thought that India had such capabilities and suspected the Soviets of having

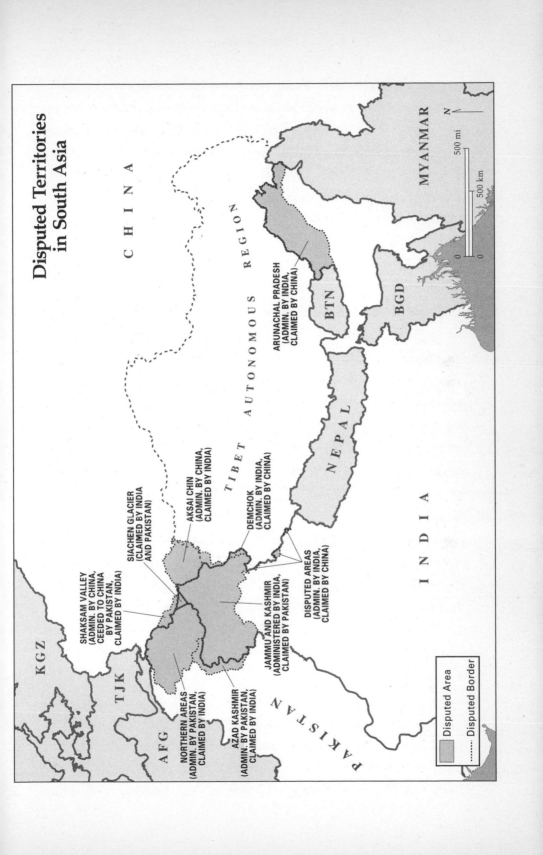

Disputed Territories in South Asia

CHINA

TIBET AUTONOMOUS REGION

MYANMAR

N

500 mi

500 km

0

BTN

BGD

NEPAL

INDIA

PAKISTAN

AFG

TJK

KGZ

ARUNACHAL PRADESH
(ADMIN. BY INDIA,
CLAIMED BY CHINA)

AKSAI CHIN
(ADMIN. BY CHINA,
CLAIMED BY INDIA)

DEMCHOK
(ADMIN. BY INDIA,
CLAIMED BY CHINA)

SIACHEN GLACIER
(CLAIMED BY INDIA
AND PAKISTAN)

SHAKSAM VALLEY
(ADMIN. BY PAKISTAN,
CEEDED TO CHINA
BY PAKISTAN,
CLAIMED BY INDIA)

NORTHERN AREAS
(ADMIN. BY PAKISTAN,
CLAIMED BY INDIA)

AZAD KASHMIR
(ADMIN. BY PAKISTAN,
CLAIMED BY INDIA)

JAMMU AND KASHMIR
(ADMINISTERED BY INDIA,
CLAIMED BY PAKISTAN)

DISPUTED AREAS
(ADMIN. BY INDIA,
CLAIMED BY CHINA)

Disputed Area

Disputed Border

supplied the know-how. Prime Minister Indira Gandhi's assumption of emergency powers in 1975 was also seen by the Chinese as a Soviet ploy, especially since it came right after the Soviet-supported Indian annexation of Sikkim, which China also claimed to have rights over. There was a temporary increase of tension at the border. In 1986, India created a new province out of its northeastern territories called Arunachal Pradesh, which incorporated areas the Chinese thought of as theirs. Tension rose again, but open clashes were averted. Relations between the two giant nations remained as frozen as they had been since the late 1950s.

It was the end of the Cold War that defrosted Sino-Indian relations and set them on a new but still uncertain course. In 1988 Indian Prime Minister Rajiv Gandhi visited Beijing, but it was his successor Narasimha Rao's visit there five years later that really set the relationship on a new course. The two sides began to withdraw troops from their borders and facilitate trade. But even if the diplomatic relationship improved, the strategic rivalry remained. India's new round of nuclear tests in 1998 marked a low point, especially since Indian officials made no secret of the fact that they regarded the improvement of their country's military capacity as directed against a potential Chinese threat. In a letter to President Bill Clinton, India's Prime Minister Atal Bihari Vajpayee summed up his fundamental view of the situation:

> I have been deeply concerned at the deteriorating security environment, specially the nuclear environment, faced by India for some years past. We have an overt nuclear weapon state on our borders, a state which committed armed aggression against India in 1962. Although our relations with that country have improved in the last decade or so, an atmosphere of distrust persists mainly due to the unresolved border problem. To add to the distrust, that country has materially helped another neighbour of ours to become a covert nuclear weapons state. At the hands of this bitter neighbour we have suffered three aggressions in the last 50 years.[16]

China, meanwhile, started transferring its fear of encirclement from the Soviet Union to the United States. It worried about any improvement in Indo-US contacts, especially with Hindu nationalists such as Vajpayee in command in Delhi. Still, China felt strong enough to not let these concerns, and Indian rhetoric, bring relations back to where they had been during the Cold War. When India fought elements of the Pakistani army, which had infiltrated the Indian held zone in Kashmir, in 1999, Beijing attempted to rein in its Pakistani ally to avoid an all-out war. Mutually beneficial trade continued to increase in the 2000s, with China becoming India's largest trading partner in 2010. With this expansion, however, has gone an increase in India's trade deficit with China, which now stands at almost fifty percent of total trade. China is pushing for a further opening up of trade, but many Indians are skeptical, fearing that it will disadvantage producers in their own country.

The Indian public's attitudes to China are among the biggest problems in the relationship today. Only twenty-two percent of Indians see China's growth as positive. Despite India's own phenomenal economic growth, they worry about the possibility that China expanding first will mean less room for India in the global economy. Indians, including their security officials, also remain concerned about the security implications of a more powerful China. It is not any longer just Pakistan and the border that are problems but also Burma and Nepal, both bordering India, where Chinese influence has been increasing. In Beijing there is less worry about the relationship, and a growing understanding of the need to take India's security concerns into consideration. But even so, Chinese leaders are concerned about the increasingly warm relations between Delhi and Washington and about India's growing closeness with Indonesia. Indian public support for Tibetan causes also irritates the Chinese, who cannot come to terms with the pluralism of Indian society. Symbolically, and perhaps ominously, China is now the only permanent member of the UN Security Council that has not endorsed India's wish for membership of that select group.

THE CRISIS IN THE MUSLIM world that began with the Soviet collapse and is continuing today across the Middle East and North Africa has deeply affected China's foreign relations in the new century. The US-led interventions in Afghanistan and Iraq convinced Chinese leaders of the inherent aggressiveness of the United States, even if most Chinese sympathized with the US predicament after 9/11. The problem was (and is) that China has no alternative international strategy to recommend to deal with the crisis, except emphasizing peaceful negotiation to resolve all problems. It does not explain how such negotiations could have delivered the al-Qaeda terrorists from Afghanistan in 2001 or prevented Saddam Hussein from developing weapons of mass destruction (which the Chinese, like their US counterparts, believed that Saddam was trying to do in 2003). In the aftermath of these conflicts, China appears not so much as an alternative superpower as a fearful power obsessed with stability and sovereignty. In place of a grand strategy to change the world, China seems to offer little but a firm belief in free trade and the inviolability of borders. Such a deeply conservative doctrine might have suited some in the wake of George W. Bush's acutely unpopular wars. But China's many abstentions on crucial votes in the UN Security Council have left the impression of a power that wants to abdicate responsibility in the international community rather than assume it.[17]

The Chinese leadership was concerned about the implications of US troops in Afghanistan after 9/11, but it realized that opposing the invasion would have few benefits for it internationally. Instead, Beijing restricted itself to recommending the establishment of a broad-based coalition government under UN supervision to replace the Taliban. China was happy to see the end of the reactionary religious-inspired regime, which had also promised to support Islamist groups from Xinjiang. But its leaders worried that a Western presence in Afghanistan would make the whole region more unstable. China's main concern was with Pakistan, a traditional ally of Beijing's, whose government chafed under pressure both from Washington and from its own increasingly anti-American population. While the CCP leaders's analysis of Afghan matters was not very wrong—and significantly more accurate, to be sure, than that in Washington—China did not want to take an active role there. It preferred strengthening its ties with Pakistan while engaging in limited aid programs and commercial activities across the border.

The big dividing line in international affairs in the early twenty-first century was President Bush's decision to go to war against Iraq. President Hu and his advisers had seen the war coming for some time. By October 2002 Beijing was sure that the United States and its coalition would attack even if there was no agreement at the UN to do so. China had to position itself carefully. On the one hand, there was no doubt that China would oppose a UN Security Council resolution authorizing an attack on Saddam Hussein's regime. On the other hand, China did not want to be seen as the main opponent of unilateral US action and was happy to leave that task to Russia and the Americans' own European allies, France and Germany. In the wake of the invasion, China secretly cooperated with the United States at the UN to enable a resolution that, postfactum, found the foreign occupation of Iraq "legal," so that oil exports could continue. At the time, China was Iraq's main foreign debtor. It was in the PRC's interest to provide an income for the new occupation government and to keep Iraqi oil flowing, including to China itself. Although other powers that had opposed the war admired China's Realpolitik, they were irritated that Beijing was not willing to be louder in its opposition to US policies. For China, however, confronting the United States over Iraq simply made no sense. Instead, as we have seen, it used Washington's post-Iraq diplomatic dependence on Beijing to eke out concessions on East Asian issues, such as North Korea and Taiwan.

Hu Jintao's foreign policy team also concluded that the Iraq and Afghanistan wars were weakening the United States, rather than making it stronger. Even though the military capacity of the Americans impressed PLA observers in Beijing, they were not shocked at the extent of US capacity as they had been after the last war against Iraq, the Gulf war of 1991. China had caught up in terms of its knowledge of military technology, though not always in its implementation. But the main conclusion Beijing drew was that the wars in the Muslim world would distract the United States from attempting to contain China's own rising power. The global financial crisis that began in 2008 underscored this perspective for Beijing. The US federal budget deficit was described as a form of imperial overstretch, and the US trade deficit as a lack of public and private prudence in consumption. By 2010 China's critique of America's wars sounded increasingly like a defense of moderation and free trade, more Adam Smith than Karl Marx, more "Let do and let pass, the world goes on by itself" than "History needs a push."

But the crisis in Muslim countries also reminds the Chinese leaders of the problems they may have to face in their own region. If China wants to be the regional leader in Asia, it will have to do more than letting matters be, even if it does not want to copy US and Soviet interventionisms. The potential for meltdown in North Korea or Burma is great, and Beijing is very uncertain as to how such situations should be approached. At the moment, China is comfortable positioning itself as a country that wants to learn from more advanced countries on matters concerning administration, management, finance, production, technology, and education. It is much more uncomfortable attempting to deal with chaos in places such as Afghanistan and Iraq. Many public voices in China advocate disengagement from "failed states," for three main reasons: They kill and injure Chinese. They are the responsibility of the Western powers, who created the chaos there in the first place. And China has no business alleviating disorder in foreign and wild territories—better concentrate on reform at home. Whichever way one views such anti-interventionist creeds, the echoes of China's past are unmistakable.

MODERNITIES

CHINA'S TRANSFORMATION over the past 250 years has been part of its internationalization. For a long time foreigners took advantage of China, a process that unsurprisingly bred resentment among most Chinese. But at the same time, some of those who lived in the country made use of what came from the outside to change China and change themselves. The country today has become a hybrid of what has developed internally for centuries and what has come from abroad. Quite a number of Chinese, as we have seen in this book, are well equipped to handle these forms of hybridity. They are resourceful beyond their means, both because they stand in a long tradition and because they have learned—sometimes the hard way—the value of flexibility when confronting major challenges. China is on its way to developing distinct forms of modernity, connected to what has been happening in North America, Europe, and Japan, but still separate, because it comes out of a very particular Chinese past.

The problem for the historian in discussing Chinese modernities and their future is that what went before threatens to overwhelm the present. China, as its inhabitants are fond of reminding us, has so much past, so much perceived continuity, that it sometimes becomes a perceptual barrier against dealing effectively with what goes on today. One key argument in this book has been that even as one should respect the Chinese preoccupation with the past, one should not be daunted by it. China has a very long history, and some of it may be seen as continuous, in a way that Europe's and certainly America's are not. But the most important aspect of China today is how it has taken on a set of changes that were happening globally in the nineteenth and twentieth centuries and made them part of what the country is now. It has embraced change, not always for the good, but with effects that put it right next to the United States in terms of inconstancy and changeability. For a rather old-fashioned European like myself, China today is distinctly, and sometimes embarrassingly, about the rapidity of change, about uncertainties, willingness to copy, and the impermanency of all things.

Even if China were to transform its political system into something more like that of the United States or, for that matter, Japan, it would remain a hybrid society in terms of its relationship with the outside world, just as it has been from the beginning of our story. One part would be outward-looking, seeing opportunity. Another would be looking inward, sensing danger. Believing that the first one is good and the second bad would be a mistake for Chinese and foreigners alike. History does not break down as neatly as that. Some of those who have been looking outward, such as Mao Zedong or, for that matter, the wartime collaborator Wang Jingwei, have seen opportunities that have turned into nightmares for Chinese and foreigners alike. And some of those who have looked inward and been mostly afraid have attempted to reestablish that domestic congruence and balance that both China and the world's relationship to China have sorely needed.

Our final chapter will look at how China's relations with the rest of the world will likely develop, based on what we know today. As all predictions it is grounded on guesswork. As we observed at the beginning of this book, a number of current estimates have postulated that China sometime toward midcentury will be the world's largest economy and the world's mightiest state. But even if that were so, it would not help us predict China's behavior as it is reaching these exalted positions. Some knowledge of the past may help, at least as far as direction and possible choices are concerned. The contradictions that are built into China's modern experience will not go away as its status grows, and some of them will become more acute. The amount of transformation that China and the world watching China are yet to see will be mind-boggling. Some of it—such as minority relations or class readjustments within China—have the potential for becoming violent and controversial. Other parts will, I believe, be less confrontational than what most people think. The relationship to Taiwan, or even to a reunified Korea, a more independent Japan, or a more assertive Vietnam, will be based less on confrontation than compromise as long as the development inside China itself makes that possible. The central problem for China's foreign affairs in the future is that it is an enduring empire that increasingly behaves like a modern nation state. It may, in the long run, turn out to be more like the United States, integrating its minorities and controlling its neighbors, or like Britain, France, or Russia, giving up its imperial pretensions based on principle or economic necessity. Whatever way it turns, it will be impossible to separate the internal from the external in China's search for modernities of its own.

WHOEVER WANTS TO UNDERSTAND China's options must begin with Singapore, Taiwan, Hong Kong, and Macao, the four Chinese societies that are not directly ruled by the CCP. While the latter two are now parts of China, they retain their own judicial system and governmental arrangements, and these have proven quite resistant to PRC attempts to change them. Singapore is, of course, an independent multiethnic state, located far away from China, but with a majority Chinese-ancestry population. Taiwan is a democratic Chinese republic, located right off the mainland of China, which—by an accident of history—has been independent of the People's Republic on the mainland for sixty years. All of these are Chinese states, and they are always at the core of Chinese thinking about the PRC's future, whether your Chinese interlocutors will admit it or not. The PRC is in need of ideas on good governance, and its leading men and women believe that they can get such ideas from other Chinese, as rulers in Beijing have so often done in the past.

The advice given by those who look at the external Chinese world goes in very different directions. Those who stress the need for elite control, usually point to Singapore and its experience under Lee Kwan Yew. Singapore is today a very well-regulated society with authoritarian traits, and many Chinese who go there from the PRC remark—in astonishment, if it is their first visit—on how much better it works as a model for stability and organization than China does. Lee and his men got much right—not least in poverty alleviation and growth economics but also in planning for the future: Singapore's sovereign wealth funds are the envy of the world. But Singapore is a city state, no easy model for a country that contains a fifth of humanity. Singapore therefore is an ideal for some within the CCP, but not a reality that is easily adhered to. And even if the Lion City today—with its ban on chewing gum and its "managed" democracy—shocks many Westerners with its censoriousness, it is still a big stone throw's away from the PRC, where people are executed for what in Singapore would lead to a stiff fine, and where debates are utterly suppressed that would not raise a wrinkle in Singapore today.

Hong Kong and Macao are the strange cases, colonial remnants within China itself, though taken over by the PRC with much fanfare in 1997 and 1999 respectively. But takeover did not mean political and juridical subjugation. Beijing was very aware that Hong Kong, especially, was the hen that laid the golden eggs. It connected trade and industry, above all in south China, with international markets, and its British colonial justice and order was conducive to its role as a center for finance that contributed to China's growth. Beijing is less enamored by the traces of democracy that the British attempted to add to their colony almost as an afterthought in the 1990s, after they had negotiated its return to China. But while the PRC has been eager to avoid a furthering of political pluralism in Hong Kong, the Communists have respected the former colony's unique position as a city that in essence is ruled by English common law within the borders of a Communist state.

According to the US State Department, as of 2011, "Hong Kong remains a free and open society where human rights are respected, courts are independent, and there is well-established respect for the rule of law."[1] Although Shanghai is moving to become the commercial capital of China, Hong Kong is likely to retain much of its position because of its laws, its good administration, and its relative freedom of speech. At the moment of writing, the market capitalization of the two is about equal; their stock exchanges are fifth and sixth in the world, respectively.

The big comparer for China, however, is none of these former colonies, but Taiwan. The rump Republic of China, situated a hundred miles from the mainland coast, has an almost fully Chinese population, high income levels, social stability, and a democratic form of government. As we have seen, the military and political tension across the Taiwan Strait has abated in recent years, and many people—both on the mainland and on the island—are hoping for some form of slow, peaceful integration of the two sides. But it is highly unlikely that the people on Taiwan would be willing to give up their own good institutions—developed through two generations of struggle—in return for some form of reunification with the mainland. On the contrary, more and more people in China are looking to Taiwan for inspiration in how to reform corrupt, unresponsive, and laggard institutions on the mainland. As increasing numbers of people from the PRC get the chance to visit the island, they will be struck by the massive qualitative differences between public administration there and at home, not to mention by the full freedom of speech that exists on Taiwan. Some will still claim that Taiwan is an American colony, or contend that China is too big to take over models that may fit one small island. There are even those who are venturesome (and brave) enough to say that the different traditions Taiwan took up during Japanese colonial rule lay the foundations for a different development today, one that China cannot easily copy. But increasingly these will become small groups compared to the many who will be wondering why China, with all its resources—

human and economic—cannot deliver what the Taiwan government can give its population.

High levels of individual freedom and political pluralism are some of the main aspects of what Chinese today see when they look at how other Chinese live outside the PRC. But—even more importantly—they also see stable, well-organized societies of the sort that they wish for in China, after all the chaos of the past four generations. The PRC government is trying to tell them that if they do not stick with the CCP, the alternative is disorder. But, when they look at Chinese states elsewhere, it is not far-fetched for PRC citizens to conclude that *theirs* is the chaotic state, with a predatory market system, laws that cannot be enforced, and rules of behavior that change on the whim of the government. Listening to some young people in Beijing discussing the arrest and imprisonment of a former Taiwan president on charges of embezzlement and corruption, I heard only a couple viewing Chen Shuibian's arrest as a sign of things going badly on Taiwan. Most were marveling at a society and a state where such measures were possible against the high and mighty.

THE DEVELOPMENT OF CHINA'S economy will be at the center of the country's international affairs for the next generation, irrespective of the twists and turns in its domestic politics or its diplomacy. The reason for this is not only that China is now the second largest economy in the world, but also the roles it has taken on for this to be possible. China is today the world's workshop, the zone where things are made, which then end up on the consumer lists of Americans, Europeans, and Asians, and which nearly everyone else aspires to own. This is the country's current role, and it has achieved it by being willing to play the global market game according to the rules that were set up first by Britain in the nineteenth century and then by the United States in the twentieth. In spite of its government's nominal Communism, China has in practice become the champion of free market capitalism, internationally if not always internally. It is working hard to take on the rules of the game and is increasingly concerned that others, be it in Africa or Europe, are themselves not always doing so. Seen from a Western perspective it is hard not to conclude that China is now "playing our game."[2]

But as China emerges as the master player of international capitalism, it is also obvious that the rules of the game are being remade in China. In spite of observations by Sino-skeptics, these Sinified rules so far rarely go in the direction of corporatism or state control, but, at best, toward collective decisions and compromise, and, at worst, corruption and nepotism. It is very unclear how Chinese capitalism is going to influence practices in other countries, especially in cases where there are great cultural differences with China. Because of the massive amount of foreign investment that has flowed into the country over the past decade it is a given that Chinese financial practices over time will influence the foreign companies that do business there. But at the moment the Chinese are busy implementing foreign rules, for instance on managerial and labor relations, in ways that are profoundly changing Chinese society.

The Chinese government today wants to play a strong regulatory role in the development of the country's economy. Because China is a political dictatorship, all institutions, including private companies, pay generous attention to government instructions. But in reality the state's ability to influence private decision making is limited, in spite of the repressive means at its disposal. In South Korea or Taiwan, the regimes could set directions because they controlled credit and capital flows, and because they—and only they—facilitated access to foreign markets. The amount of foreign direct investment in their industrialization processes was minuscule, their credit companies were under state control, and their main firms invested nationally for export abroad. In China these crucial aspects of industrialization are turned upside down. Foreign investment has driven significant parts of the process, foreign banks are operating in China and Chinese banks have plentiful means to resist government pressure, and the biggest Chinese companies have already become multinationals with large investments abroad. The domestic Chinese growth process since 1990 has been governed not by national priorities or five-year plans but by the chaotic interplay of market forces. All of this has happened while the state has kept its investments in profitable industries, owning or part-owning many of China's biggest companies. But, as one economic planner told me recently, state-owned companies are increasingly behaving like privately owned companies in the market; they recruit their managers from the same pool of talent and they are equally responsible for profits and losses. They may listen to what the government says, but only if it provides a sound bottom line for their company.

At the moment quite a few global investors and corporate executives are agreeing with the general direction of this book: that China will reinvent global capitalism rather than ruin it. In the wake of the crisis of 2008/2009, Chinese officials and businessmen alike began lecturing Western countries on the need for market and currency stability, and for avoiding corporate greed, bad loans, excessive deficits, and extravagant consumption. Some of this sounds laughable, given the amount of bad business practices in China itself. But it does signal that many elite Chinese now see themselves as stakeholders in an international economic system, on the success of which their futures depend. Many people in China (and quite a few outside) dream about a future Sino-capitalism that will be better organized, more balanced, and less destructive than its Western inspirators. So far there is little that tells us that will be the case. But, as has often happened in the world economy before, those who are the generators of global growth innovate as well as imitate. Future Chinese leaderships, public and private, may be stimulated by the crises they have gone through to opt for more regulation and government design than what we have seen in previous versions of world capitalism.

The 2008/2009 global financial crisis showed a China that had arrived as a key player in the world economy. At the World Economic Forum in Davos in 2010, Chinese Premier Wen Jiabao placed the blame for the crisis on the "inappropriate" macroeconomic policies of Western countries . . .

> and their unsustainable model of development characterized by prolonged low savings and high consumption; excessive expansion of financial institutions in a blind pursuit of profit; lack of self-discipline among financial institutions and rating agencies and the ensuing distortion of risk information and asset pricing; and the failure of financial supervision and regulation to keep up with financial innovations, which allowed the risks of financial derivatives to build and spread.[3]

Quite a handful: The apprentice was taking the past masters to task for their excess. But the medicine the CCP itself prescribed did not imply that there was anything wrong with capitalism as such. Instead it implemented the largest stimulus program of government spending in history, thereby attempting to stave off the worst consequences of the crisis for Chinese companies and for the Chinese population. Post-crisis growth for China will most likely not be of the same scale as before, because of international competition and, eventually, the country's aging population. But even with *only* six percent annual growth on average, China will probably still become the world's largest economy sometime in the mid-2030s.

C HINA'S INTERNATIONAL POSITION in the twenty-first century will be determined as much by what happens inside China as what happens outside its borders. The country's biggest domestic problem is that uneven growth has left large regions behind and that the lack of a proper welfare system and protection for workers against exploitation has led to an extremely high level of inequality. While Premier Wen and others are lambasting the West for its excesses, inequality in China is at least twice as high as in the United States and Britain, with higher ratios to relatively equal societies such as Germany and France. While slowly and uncertainly trying to deal with its worst consequences—for instance by reintroducing some forms of subsidized education and health care—the Chinese government is defending itself by saying, with Deng Xiaoping, that in a developing society "some people have to get rich first." The problem with this "rising tide lifts all boats" scenario is that there are no signs that Chinese inequality is abating; on the contrary, the situation in the poorer regions is getting worse and worker unrest over low pay and atrocious working conditions in many factories is on the increase.

Despite receiving credit for China's overall economic growth, there is little indication that the CCP as a party is capable of dealing with some of the social tensions this growth is creating. The party's steady refusal to allow increased political pluralism, which could have acted as a safety valve against discontent, will make Chinese politics more unsettled over time. The CCP today is unable to act with massive brutality against its own urban population, as it did during the Mao era, not least out of fear that such atrocities could unsettle the country's economy. A leading party member told me that he thought that even a repeat of 1989 would be unthinkable now: "Just imagine," he said, what would happen to the country's credit rating!" But at the same time the party's leaders gamble all on the general economic growth keeping their people from taking action against them. As we have seen, in history such gambles rarely pay off.

A main reason why China is viewed with such suspicion abroad is that it is led by a Communist party. But today's Chinese regime is a far cry from Communists of the past. In reality, the regime itself has become much more like Taiwan or South Korea before democratization—authoritarian, and sometimes ugly and brutal, but not capable of atrocities on the scale of those of the past even in its own defense. While it is impossible to predict what will happen in Chinese politics, I would not be surprised if China follows a similar pattern of democratization to the other main states in the region, only stretched out over a longer period of time. Whatever happens, the CCP will not be around forever, and those foreign observers who today equate the party with the country are making a major mistake. History shows that China is as capable of political change as it has recently been of economic and social change, and there is no set of ingrained values or attitudes that will necessarily put the country at odds with its neighbors or with the West. As before in its history, China's direction will ultimately be a matter of its leaders' political choice.

One issue that will be intriguing to follow is the development of civil law in China. The rule of law has always lagged in China's modern transformations, and the Communist Party likes to believe that this is still the case, so that it can abduct and imprison its enemies at will. But as in the surrounding countries two decades ago, the deficiencies of civil law are coming under increasing pressure from rapidly developing commercial law. Foreign and Chinese investors alike are eager that their money be protected, and they have reaped a great harvest from the seeds they have sown. Today's business law in China is remarkably similar to its Western parentage on crucial issues such as contract law, company law, banking law, and commercial dispute resolution. What is more: Commercial law is not only accepted, but adhered to within China, with court decisions usually not discriminating against foreign companies or foreign investors, or by definition ruling in favor of state-owned companies against others. While the argument that emerging middle classes are more democratically inclined than other groups rarely holds up in history, the need to protect investments is, as Karl Marx observed for Europe in the nineteenth century, one of the reasons why the bourgeoisie generally create the rule of law. And, at least in most cases, it becomes hard over time to defend the principle that money has more rights than men.

As this book has shown, China is manifold, and only those who respect its pluralism are likely to stay in power long. The Qing ruled for a long time because they learned that China is a pluralistic society and has to be governed according to its discongruity. The Guomindang did not realize this and fell quickly. The CCP has not realized it either but is so convinced that the modern condition means congruity and homogeneity that it expects history to come to its rescue. Its leaders also believe that the homogenization of China is in accordance with the real wishes of the majority population and therefore part of a Chinese tradition. They are probably wrong on both counts. The Chinese want stable and predictable government, but they also want respect for their own predilections and practices and do not want a state that meddles unnecessarily in their business or, unjustly, enriches its leaders' sons and daughters. Like the Guomindang before them, in a period of tremendous change the Communist leaders run the risk of maximizing the number of their enemies just when they are most in need of acquiring allies.

THE CURRENT LEADERSHIP in Beijing is obsessively fearful of political deviance and ethnic or religious dissonance. Maybe because they know that their power to govern the economy is limited, they insist on controlling the political sphere. At the moment there are no political alternatives in China, and although workers' movements and professional organizations pressure the government from many different directions, the number of political dissidents is very small. Even so, the CCP overreacts—with disastrous consequences for its regime's international reputation—whenever it feels challenged by opposition. When the soft-spoken dissident Liu Xiaobo, already sentenced to eleven years in prison for peaceful protest, won the Nobel Peace Prize for 2010, he was demonized by Chinese authorities as a criminal and an insult to the prize. The vaguely millenarian and transcendental Buddhist movement Falun Gong was banned in 1999, with the CCP condemning its "feudal superstitions and decadent ideas."[4] Thousands of its members ended up in prison. The CCP seems inherently incapable of dealing with criticism and therefore appears to be afraid of anyone or anything outside the economic sector that the party itself has not explicitly sanctioned.

The two most important issues concerning the CCP's treatment of minorities—political, religious, ethnic, and cultural—will be its policies toward Tibetans and Uigurs, and toward religious revivalists. These policies will of course be linked. Part of the reason why the party is so afraid of regional autonomy is that it fears such freedoms would be used by religious extremists within China. Internationally, its harsh treatment of the Tibet and Xinjiang opposition is among the regime's biggest problems—more important, according to recent polls, than any other single issue for US, European, and Muslim views of the country. Many Chinese, and not just those who support the government, think this criticism is unfair: China's economic transformation is surely more important, they think, and Tibetans and Muslims in western China have benefited at least as much as the majority of Chinese from the growth in the economy. What these defenders of the status quo fail to realize is that it is the CCP's tone-deafness to the natural religious and national aspirations of minority groups that is creating China's problems on these issues at home and abroad. As we have seen, the Communists are not the only leading group in recent Chinese history who have had trouble understanding China's minority populations. But spreading the leadership's retrograde views through modern media is rapidly making matters worse.

There are very clear signs that China is running out of time to start allowing more autonomy and less interference for its main minorities. At the moment, most Tibetans and Xinjiang Muslims would be satisfied with being allowed to run their own religious affairs (mainly because outright independence seems chimerical). But with the Communists denigrating the Tibetan religious leader, the Dalai Lama, as a "wolf in monk's robes" and calling the exiled Uighur leader Rebiya Kadeer "a housewife who has used her illegal fortune to conduct secessionist activities," the future does not look bright.[5] The younger generation of Tibetans and Uighurs will want increased recognition of their own identity within China, and will not be satisfied with less. Sending political education teams to be stationed in Lamaist Buddhist monasteries and closing Xinjiang mosques for so-called preservation and repair will mean only more tension between minorities and non-Tibetans/non-Muslims in the western provinces. The CCP government will then be forced to intervene on behalf of immigrants from other parts of China, and the negative consequences of such confrontations for China's image in the world will be great.

The international reputation of the CCP and the PRC is also challenged by a revival of religion within the main parts of China itself. The Falun Gong phenomenon may just be a beginning of Buddhist, Muslim, and Christian resurgences and metamorphoses. As we have seen, the Chinese state has been—from its perspective—cursed with such "superstitious sects" for the last 250 years. But today the challenge seems greater than ever, simply because the state itself gives its people so little to believe in—except material progress, which rarely has stirred people's hearts. I sometimes visit a Christian congregation in the Beijing suburb of Haidian. It is not registered with the authorities, because its members want to avoid outside control, but still counts more than 1,000 members. The congregation is evangelical Protestant, and its members are young, white-collar Chinese with good educations and little political ambition, but a lot of interest in money and finance. As with other congregations, irrespective of religion, the authorities face a choice in how to treat this group of Christians. If they are smart enough to leave them alone, there is little reason to expect trouble. But if they do not, then there is little doubt that these people will follow what they see as the will of God rather than the will of the Communist Party.

The same pattern holds up for other groups in society as well. Some young Chinese may believe CCP propaganda about foreign interference being behind arrogant Tibetans or disloyal Muslims. But the very same people get embarrassed if they have to talk about the CCP's Internet censorship to friends or relatives from abroad. In all my years of teaching history in China, the most embarrassing moment I have witnessed for a Chinese student was not discussing, say, Mao's purges or the 1989 crackdown. The worst moment came when the student had to explain to newly arrived foreign classmates that Facebook is blocked in China. Young people in China are seething over not having access to the same forms of networking or simple fun as kids elsewhere. Despite the government's best efforts to build a Great Firewall of China, the country's youngsters know better. They know what they are missing out on, and they resent the authorities for blocking it. Some observers will say that easy access to games or chatrooms is of minor importance in a country that still imprisons people for their beliefs. But no government in recent Chinese history has gone on annoying its young people for very long without paying a price. In this sense the Great Firewall may be more a symbol of the regime's impotence than a protection against foreign seditious influences.

BECAUSE OF ITS RAPIDLY EXPANDING economy, China's future international position will to a large extent be set by how well its acquisition of knowledge keeps up with that of other countries. So far China is not doing well in this respect. Young Chinese are exceptionally good at reading and algebra: Shanghai high school leavers are the best in the world on both scores, according to recent statistics. But China's institutions of higher education often let them down, and they have to go abroad for their advanced training. Very often the best young Chinese then excel at their foreign universities and remain abroad for long periods of time. This dichotomy is particularly true for the humanities and social sciences but is also notable in science and technology.

China's top universities suffer in comparison to the best American or European institutions. They have a very large number of talented people in them, but they are run in ways very similar to Soviet institutions of old. Conformist mediocrity is rewarded above unsettling brilliance. The party and its views hover over everything, and hiring and promotion are decided by patronage rather than by talent. The problem is not censorship by itself. Debates and discussions at the top institutions are today free to an extent unthinkable only a few years ago. The problem is the conformism that institutions of higher education produce, and the lacunae in innovative knowledge, which descend from that. China today is simply not, by itself, producing enough top thinkers within various fields of knowledge to sustain its future growth.

This failure is a serious problem for China's engagement with the world. To overcome it, the Chinese government needs to rework its higher education system, or—a less likely prospect—allow these institutions to reform themselves profoundly from within. Given the centrality of education in the government's own development plans, it is remarkable that not more is done already. In the meantime China is, in fact, shedding talent at a high rate. Newspapers and the universities and research centers themselves often publish major articles about how world-famous scholars who were born in China or have Chinese ancestry return to teach at Chinese institutions. But there are few of these, and they are usually at the end of their careers. Young scholars who are trained abroad sometimes go back, although, as we have seen, only in small numbers. But then they only stay for a few years if they are so good that they have the chance for a job abroad. The encounter with the problems and intricacies of the Chinese higher education system defeats them. They felt they fitted in at Yale or Cambridge or CalTech but feel marginalized at Chinese universities.

It is possible that foreign-trained scholars who return and remain in China will, eventually, change the system. There are examples of real centers of excellence in Chinese research, and they are sometimes found in surprising places. One such example in my field is the Central Party School of the CCP. Here there are no limits to discussion (even though little of it can be repeated outside the school's compound in northwestern Beijing), and it attracts first-rate minds to teach the party's future leaders. There is also the possibility that the establishment of foreign universities in China will transform the Chinese landscape of higher education, as it did in the late nineteenth century. The largest of these at the moment, the British-run University of Nottingham campus in Ningbo near Shanghai, can take up to 8,000 students and teach them in a university setting that is similar to what they would encounter outside China.

Over time, perhaps the biggest problem in China's search for knowledge is its failure to recruit first-rate talent from abroad. More than a third of all US Nobel Prize laureates in medicine in the postwar period were born outside the United States.[6] In China, one would be hard pressed to find a handful of full professors of foreign origin in all fields at the country's top universities. One reason for this is that China is not yet an attractive enough place of residence for the world's top scientists. But it also has something to do with attitudes in China today. While many people around the world can imagine themselves reinvented as Americans, few think in the same way about China, even after its economic growth has put the country at the center of attention. Unlike the situation when our story began back in the eighteenth century, Chinese authorities and institutions seem to go out of their way to narrow the concept of what it means to be Chinese. If such attitudes persist, China will find it difficult to compete in innovation and knowledge the way they are now competing very successfully in production.

AS WE HAVE SEEN, nationalism in anything approaching its Western form is a very recent phenomenon in China. It is largely a product of the tumultuous twentieth century. Today, however, different forms of nationalism thrive in the Chinese political landscape, in variants that would be easily recognizable to nineteenth-century Europeans. Not all of this is negative. A sense of pride in being Chinese and in the long history of the Chinese people can be a counterweight to regime *diktat* or to the insecurities that have marred China's relations with the outside world. The problems begin when nationalism is manipulated by the regime for political gain, or when it creates resentment against foreigners or people who look different or behave differently. Most dangerous of all is the nationalism that says, "The world hates us, but we don't care," because it may provide license to behave in ways that are truly inhumane against those who are defined as outsiders.[7]

Related to (but not equal with) the problems of nationalism is the increasing Chinese preoccupation with ethnic or racial characteristics. Again, as we have seen earlier, this is a recent fixation of some Chinese, and it has been stimulated by the Communist Party's need to find an argument for its continued rule. The Chinese, the line of reasoning goes, are different from other peoples—oriented toward collective gain, coherent policies, and admirable aims. They are adverse to chaos and uncertainty, and in favor of analytical approaches and accurate predictions. Where other peoples are easily led astray into indolence or inconstancy, the Chinese are earnest, hard-working epitomes of common sense. They are also, because of their long history, more authentic and more righteous than others. All of this nonsense stands in the way of developing a reasonable foreign policy for the People's Republic and deflects its people from dealing with its own problems, most importantly the democratic deficit within China itself.[8]

On occasion, the CCP borrows the terminology of the small number of Chinese who are extreme nationalists. But the party is also afraid of them, aware that its own imported ideology and adherence to open international markets could make it the focus of ultranationalist attacks. Indeed, both in 1989 and more recently, nationalist slogans have been used against the party and its rule. The CCP wants to use nationalism as legitimacy for its continued control of China, but it is not quite sure how to employ it without risk. It must be said, though, that some of the party's propaganda about special Chinese characteristics for development has struck a chord with youth who are eager for something to believe in. A student I was talking with in 2010 explained it succinctly. Even though most people of her generation are aware of the deficiencies created by one-party rule, she said, they are less and less willing to discuss it, especially with foreigners present. In a China that is becoming increasingly internationalized, there must, some of them think, be a part that is truly and uniquely Chinese, and not just an imitation of foreign models, something that helps explain China's current stride to the fore. The West already has prosperity and democracy. Maybe prosperity *without* democracy could be something for Chinese to be proud of, since it has created unprecedented economic progress. But my student friend was quick to add that her group only thought that way when thinking about China in comparison with other countries. As soon as the conversation turned to China itself, the party's many failings in governance provoked broad condemnation.

The existence of this dual view of China's relations with the outside world is supported by recent opinion polls. One has to be careful with data collected under a dictatorship, but some general trends are visible. Younger people feel more threatened by the outside world than older people. In a recent poll, almost two-thirds of all eighteen-to-twenty-four-year-olds agreed that the United States posed a threat, but only a third of those over fifty-five felt the same way. Men and those with higher education were more likely to find Americans (and Japanese and Indians) threatening. All groups, however, agreed that global processes such as climate change or water or food shortages were more threatening than any foreign military force. When asked *why* the United States posed a threat to China, the whole sample answered that it might seek to restrain China's growing influence in the world; it might support separatist elements in China; it is more likely to take the side of Taiwan in a cross-strait dispute; and it has a more powerful military than China's own.[9]

Those pessimistic about China's future on the international stage focus on its growing nationalism, but some who are more optimistic dwell on a countercurrent. China's interest and orientation, they say, are closely linked to the development of international law and to harmony and balance in international affairs. Such a search for a better-organized international community that can accommodate China's international economic expansion has, as we have seen, as deep if not deeper roots in Chinese history than today's nationalism. It is striking how often Chinese foreign policy analysts and diplomats use the term "international society" when they describe the conduct of international affairs that they are looking for. Wang Jisi, the influential dean of Peking University's School of International Studies, argues that "China will serve its interests better if it can provide more common goods to the international community and share more values with other states."[10] But, as Wang would be the first to agree, it can only do so if it throws overboard the concept of a "special path" to modernity for China and the belief that outsiders are inherently hostile to China's rise.

S OME HISTORICALLY INFORMED commentators think that Asia, or at least its eastern parts, is on its way back to the international system that existed when our story began: a China-centered world, where other countries conformed to the symbols of Chinese power. I do not think that is the case, even if there may be some similarities between the situation 250 years ago and today. China is undoubtedly becoming *the* central power in its region and the economic powerhouse that will define Asia's growth for at least the next two generations. But it is not likely to be easily able to bend others to its will, except in extreme crises. Even during the Qianlong emperor's reign there was, as we have seen and contrary to a widely held view, no set tribute *system* through which China could enforce its control. Today, the country would face insurmountable obstacles if it were to try to dominate and control its neighbors. Today's China is nationalist, not universalist. Its nationalism is up against other nationalisms in the region that are at least as powerful in domestic ideological terms as China's own; think only about Korea or Vietnam. The United States will not disappear as an Asian power. And, in cultural terms, China is singularly lacking in soft power: No young person of sound mind in Tokyo or Seoul, or even in Taibei or Singapore, is looking to the PRC for music to download, films to watch, or ideas to latch on to.

China's centrality in Asia will therefore increasingly be expressed in economic terms, as a place not just of production but also of consumption. One of the big stories of the early twenty-first century will be the increase in intra-Asian trade, as economies within the region continue to grow very fast, but not in parallel or even in the same manner. The concept that Asian states have little to trade among themselves has been a myth for almost all historical periods. Even when the Chinese state was at its weakest—from 1880 to the 1910s—trade within Asia grew faster than East-West trade, within what economic historians call an informal Chinese commercial sphere.[11] Unless political disasters intervene to stop it, one may think of a significant part of Asia's future growth as a relay, in which technologies, production, and markets in different countries take over from each other decade after decade. If we use the past as evidence, no Asian nationalism, however virulent, has been able to stop this process.

In the short run, China's most important regional relationship will be with Japan. In spite of the recent steep worsening in perceptions of the other, there is reason to believe that the two countries will grow closer in their bilateral relationship, especially on economic issues. Each of them needs the other. Japan's aged population needs Chinese markets for its products and, increasingly, as a place of production. China needs Japan's technology and its *dégagé* approach as China's military power grows. There is no doubt that over time China's power seems to be waxing as Japan's wanes. But it is unlikely that Japan will try to balance China in any way as this process continues, except through keeping its alliance with the United States. It is also quite possible that the negative rhetoric in the Sino-Japanese relationship will be kept up from both sides as their mutual dependence grows. Such disconnects between terms of abuse and terms of trade are not uncommon in Asian history.

Korea, once it is united, will probably maintain its military alliance with the United States. Of course, China, through some spectacular diplomacy, might be able to manage the coming North Korean breakdown and offer the South Koreans reunification on terms that it can heavily influence. The latter scenario is very unlikely, however, mainly for historical reasons that we have explored earlier in this book. It is much more likely that Pyongyang simply will run out of time to reform, the North Korean state will collapse from the inside, and South Korea will be faced with a rapid and largely uncontrollable reunification whether it wants it or not. What China does in such a situation will be of decisive importance for its future position in the region. If its leaders realize that a united Korea whose leadership freely chooses its foreign policy orientation may be of more use to China than anything that can achieved by coercive diplomacy, Beijing will truly have come of age in international affairs.

Southeast Asia may turn out to be the easy success story of Chinese international policies, if Beijing plays its cards right. ASEAN is the great experiment in regional cooperation for our times. Although it probably will never be supernational, like the EU, it is setting up a framework for cooperation among postcolonial states that is unique both in format and depth. The main test for China will be whether it is willing to accept a deepening of the integration process in Southeast Asia, which deliberately places Beijing outside the regional framework. In private, policy makers in Beijing very often admit that they much prefer to deal with individual states rather than regional organizations. They are also, of course, aware that despite all kinds of agendas set up to make China a partner in Southeast Asian development and security, ASEAN's remarkable success has at least in part been due to a fear of the consequences for the region of China's rise. There is also the potential for increased cooperation between ASEAN, the United States, and India. But if it plays its cards right—emphasizing economic synergies instead of territorial rivalries—China does have a real chance to form lasting ties with the region, ties that will survive both political changes in China and the ups and downs of Southeast Asian integration.

China's biggest foreign challenge in the future will be India. It is a very big challenge. We have already seen how the relationship has been pestered by border problems and negative views of one another. Over the past decade, China and India have increasingly become rivals for influence in international organizations. China is well ahead in terms of economic development at the moment, but India has its advantages. While China's population is aging because of the one-child policy ("China," some demographers say, "will be old before it is rich"), India has a young and increasingly healthy and well-educated population. By 2050, its population will be fifty percent larger than its northern neighbor's. India also has a stable political system, and outlets for dissent. It uses English as one of its administrative languages. India already has a fully convertible currency, and, though its market capital is smaller, the transparency and predictability of its capital markets are much greater than China's. So is its labor mobility.[12]

While many economists today argue that for these reasons India in fifty years will have overtaken China in terms of GDP, China will probably be able to keep up. It will do so if it deepens reform, especially of the political sector, and gets rid of the disastrous one-child policy. China is today investing wisely in infrastructure, public health, and education, with significant improvement in its citizens' quality of life as a result. Infant mortality in India is twice as high as in China, and Chinese children on average go to school almost twice as long as children in India do (7.5 years and 4.4 years, respectively). China also has a manufacturing base that is way ahead of India's. If China keeps attracting investment, the level and quality of its industrial output will, on average, remain considerably higher than that of India. But first and foremost the relationship between the two will depend on whether each can accept the near simultaneous rise of the other. India will have to tread carefully with regard to its involvement in the Himalayas, and especially in Tibet. But China has the bigger challenge. Being a close ally of Pakistan, which India with some justification regards as the root of most of its foreign policy problems, Beijing can easily be held hostage to whatever conflict with India Pakistan ends up in. In 2011 Pakistan's president described the closeness of his country's ties with China as "not matched by any other relationship between two sovereign countries."[13] If this remains so, it will be difficult for Beijing to avoid future rivalries with Asia's other rising power.

CHINA'S INTERNATIONAL FUTURE depends not only on China itself. It also depends on how others treat China. The power with the greatest ability to influence the future of China (and the world) is the United States. When China becomes the world's largest economy sometime in the 2030s, the United States will still be the world's leading military power, and it is set to remain so for another decade or more after that. Even more importantly, at the moment when China does become the world's largest economy, around forty percent of its population will still be poor by international standards. Its per-capita income will be less than half that of the United States (and less than a third of Singapore's, which around that time is projected to take over from Norway as the world's richest country per capita). The United States will, because of its wealth and its power, be able to influence China's rise in ways that no other country can. The big question is whether the United States will be willing to accommodate an increase in China's status or will attempt to frustrate it.

Despite Chinese suspicions—historically grounded, as we have seen—that the United States wants to contain China because its majority population dislikes the Chinese, there is little contemporary evidence of such prejudice. On the contrary, surveys show that all groups of Americans rate Chinese and Chinese Americans very highly on most variables, although some ethnic stereotypes persist. But when it comes to attitudes toward the current Chinese government, the picture changes. About two-thirds of Americans believe that it will be difficult for US leaders and the CCP regime to get along in the future. The key issues for conflict are seen to be human rights, Tibet, and trade.[14] The majority believes that China could be a partner of the United States if Beijing became more democratic, but they also worry that the US government is not doing enough to preserve US jobs and wealth against Chinese competition. Just like nationalist views in China of other countries, the latter concern is really a criticism more of Washington than of Beijing. But the preoccupation with China's lack of democracy and how it treats its own people is more fundamental and harder to overcome even if a US administration wanted to work with a CCP regime.

As we have seen, the Chinese fascination with the United States is nearly boundless. It mixes fear with attraction and admiration with disgust. Most Chinese can distinguish criticism of a government from criticism of a people, a nation, or even a state, but China's new nationalism often gets in the way of a cool-headed appraisal of US policies. So does the Taiwan issue, where a vast majority of Chinese in the PRC believe that the United States is to blame for the lack of reunification, now as in the past. It is quite possible that popular Chinese views of the United States will turn more negative in the future, almost irrespective of what the US government says or does.

Anti-American attitudes among Chinese citizens are a double-edged sword to the CCP. Despite its hope that such attitudes can be used to solidify domestic support for current Chinese leaders, any rise in popular sentiment on the issue leaves Beijing with a problem. The CCP does not want a sustained confrontation with the United States, because it is convinced that would hinder China's economic expansion. At the moment the PRC government is, as we have seen, quite happy for the country's economy to function within a US-led global economic system. The United States is after all acting in ways that, broadly speaking, promote growth in China. The last thing the PRC needs is a long-term strategic face-off with the most powerful country on earth, of the kind that destroyed the Soviet Union in the 1970s and 1980s.

China is therefore not headed for a form of Cold War with the United States. Despite what leaders in Beijing and Washington sometimes claim, there is simply not enough distance between the two sides in terms of how they believe the world is supposed to work to create a Cold War. There will be incidents and rivalries to be sure, and there is always the risk that Korea or Taiwan—the two perennials in the Sino-American relationship—may upstage any attempts at building strategic trust. But a long-term and systematic attempt at destroying each other with any means short of all-out war, such as Washington and Moscow mobilized around in the postwar era, is simply not in the cards. Being able to create distinct forms of cooperation, though, is quite another matter. For that to happen, China must become more than a spoiler of US policy in international affairs, and it is uncertain whether that can happen under its current regime. At its rhetorical core, Chinese foreign policy is concentrated on concepts that strike many Americans as rather old-fashioned: sovereignty, of course, but also honor, sincerity, and international respect. While general invocations of these concepts win China friends overseas, their specific use to protect petty dictators such as Zimbabwe's Robert Mugabe, Sudan's Omar al-Bashir, or the Burmese junta plays badly internationally, and is disastrous in relations with Washington, where both liberals and conservatives feel that China's only aim in so doing is to assist America's enemies, whomever they may be. China has to learn that sticking it in the eye of the world's hyperpower may bring short-term gratification, but it does not amount to a grand strategy in international politics.

CHINA'S FOREIGN AFFAIRS in the new century are quickly moving beyond its old horizons. A main challenge for any future Chinese leadership will be how to develop a *global* foreign policy and respond to concerns in regions that historically are little known in China, but that, to an unprecedented degree, will affect and be affected by the country's economic growth. Africa, Latin America, and the Middle East need a policy by Beijing that goes beyond trade and resource extraction. But it will be very hard for the CCP or any other Chinese leaders to create such effective policies. The Chinese population is relatively uninterested in foreign affairs and less and less interested the more foreign these affairs become. Besides, China so far has had little to contribute outside its key economic role. As one African official said to me, China is not going to be an inspiration for good governance or anticorruption measures. Unlike the United States, China seems uninterested in peace plans, regional cooperation, or ethnic reconciliation. On the contrary, it seems intent to limit its political role as its economic importance increases. Such an approach is unlikely to serve China well.

The world may be tired of US interventionism, but it is certainly not ready to welcome an abstemious superpower. Most people, when crises occur, expect great powers to *lead*. The Middle East is bound to be a troubled region for decades, and China needs a policy that addresses the causes of the trouble and that will use economic clout to put such a policy into practice. China also needs to respond to those African leaders who will be saying, over the coming decades, that Beijing is simply following in the footsteps of the imperialists. It simply offers its own sorts of sweeteners to get access to natural resources, instead of forming partnerships with Africa and investing in poverty reduction. In order to improve its act China needs to draw on the expertise of the Chinese diaspora and strengthen its knowledge centers at home, making them more free and more open to the public. It needs policies and instruments for policy making that go beyond the simple purposes of securing China's gains.

Some of my Chinese friends shake their heads at these arguments. How can China, they ask, develop such policies when it has so many unsolved problems at home? China cannot teach others about pluralism and tolerance, because it has a political regime that is dictatorial and intolerant. It cannot solve ethnic and religious conflict abroad, because it has no solution to such controversies within China. The Chinese people may want a state that is a great power but is itself immature in foreign affairs, often reducing other societies to simple caricatures of themselves. The counterargument is straightforward: Besides the rather obvious historical point (for someone who lives in Britain) that solving one's own problems is not a prerequisite for developing policies for the world, China does not have a choice. No country with an economy that increasingly affects almost every human being can turn away from problems as they arise, even outside its own region. Sensible Chinese foreign policy leaders say that China does not want to have an American-style approach to the world, with its built-in conviction that all the world's problems can and should be solved by the United States. That may be right, but it cannot be an invitation to put one's head in the sand and then gloat over the mistakes of others. Such an approach may help achieve minor aims, but it is not a foreign policy, and far less a strategy.

One of the biggest ironies of Chinese foreign policy is that while Beijing has begun to realize that Baghdad and Buenos Aires matter, Brussels and Berlin are largely ignored. Although the European Union is now the PRC's biggest economic partner, China's relationship to the EU has been concentrated almost exclusively on narrow issues of trade and technology transfer. Chinese diplomats justify this, rather lamely, by saying that China traditionally prefers to deal with individual states rather than regional groupings. But as the ASEAN example has shown, this policy has not been very successful in the past and is even less likely to succeed toward a behemoth that is increasingly unified in international affairs. Even the Chinese policy toward individual European countries has been, mainly, a nonpolicy, limited to stimulating economic exchange interspersed with the occasional and increasingly ritualistic condemnation of visits by the Dalai Lama or other *bêtes noires* in Beijing's political bestiary.

This neglect of the third big concentration of power in the world will be problematic for China unless it dramatically changes its approach. Smart people in the Chinese foreign policy leadership are already strenuously arguing this point. It is possible that China will adjust its European policy over the coming decades, and that the two will draw closer. While China is more like the United States in its acceptance of change, it is more like Europe in its adversity to risk. This duality may seem contradictory but is not. Change, deemed to be internal, is viewed as controllable. Risk, containing at least elements of the external, is seen as uncontrollable. The Chinese and Europeans may turn out to be, on the whole, entirely wrong in their views of how best to interact with the outside world, but there is little doubt that their approaches have something in common, which may connect them further over time.

A S WE HAVE SEEN, China still has a lot of catching up to do in its approaches to the outside world. Some of this readjustment will be difficult to achieve until China gets a government that is more representative of its people. The Communist leaders at present argue that China has special characteristics that endorse the continued rule by its self-appointed elite. Sustaining this arrangement in the long run will be next to impossible. The Chinese are not more cloddish than other people at governing themselves, or more deserving of having decisions made for them by a small group. Because of China's history, it is reasonable to assume that only a broadening of participation in political discussion and in government can help overcome the current deficiencies in Chinese foreign policy. But even when such a change happens, it is important for outsiders to remember that China's foreign affairs will for a long time be run by people who are groomed and trained within the current political system. This almost certain continuity means that the more that is done today to engage and debate the Chinese foreign policy elite, the better the chances are for future policies that reflect the rest of the world's interests and not just China's, irrespective of politics within the country itself.

Even when it becomes the world's largest economy, China will be in no position to take the lead in global politics. The more probable scenario is a slow deterioration of US power, during the span of which we move toward a more multipolar world. The period in which the global economy will be centered on China, while the United States remains the world's most powerful state, will be a dangerous one, in which both countries will have to tread very carefully to avoid conflict. Wise leaders will be helped in their efforts by the many ways in which the two countries will depend on each other for their people's welfare and by the existence of other and different forms of powers, Europe and India first among them, which will remind leaders in Beijing and Washington that the stakes are high in their bilateral relationship. An emerging multipolar world may push China and the United States toward collaboration, or at least tolerance of each other, despite differences in political systems.

It is unlikely that China will get a Western-style form of government within the average lifetime of the readers of this book. But it is also unlikely that the CCP will remain in power the way it is today for several decades to come. The most plausible outcome is a fairly authoritarian government at the center, which will grudgingly allow some more provincial self-rule and more cultural autonomy for minorities. Such a blend—even if it is not what most foreign friends of China would like to see—could keep the country in political shape for a long time to come, and frame its relations with the outside world in a nonconfrontational manner. But these are the views of a historian who cannot predict the future any better than others who know the country and its people well. What is certain, though, is that those who expect

China to remain for a long time as it is today will be proven wrong. Its turbulent past points toward a changeable future, during which both locals and foreigners will be surprised at the continuous resourcefulness and adaptability of the Chinese people.

SUGGESTIONS FOR
FURTHER READING

THE LITERATURE ON CHINA'S INTERNATIONAL AFFAIRS in English has expanded massively over the past few years. When I began studying the country, there were only a handful of general texts available, many written by academics who had barely visited China. Now there are thousands, on every possible aspect of China's dealings with the world. Even though quality has improved significantly overall, quite a few leave a bit to be desired, as one can imagine when publishers worldwide are rushing to get texts on China into print. The following is a brief overview of where to start one's reading, with suggestions for each part of this book. Take it for what it is worth: It is a small selection, and there will be new work appearing by the month. A visit to a bookstore may land unexpected treasures.

To begin with, get hold of a book on China's general history over the past 250 years. There is nothing better than Jonathan Spence's *The Search for Modern China* (2nd ed; 1999). For the twentieth century, there is also Rana Mitter's magnificent *A Bitter Revolution: China's Struggle with the Modern World* (2004). It would be worth having a look at a book that puts Chinese history into a larger regional perspective; try Charles Holcombe, *A History of East Asia: From the Origins of Civilization to the Twenty-First Century* (2010).

On the foreign affairs of the Qing empire, see William T. Rowe's splendid overview, *China's Last Empire: The Great Qing* (2009); Joanna

Waley-Cohen's dissection of the Qing's military pretensions, *The Culture of War in China: Empire and the Military Under the Qing Dynasty* (2006); Peter Perdue's outstanding account of Qing expansionism, *China Marches West: The Qing Conquest of Central Eurasia* (2005), and Mark Elliott's telling portrait, *Emperor Qianlong: Son of Heaven, Man of the World* (2009).

On foreign imperialism in China, see Ulrike Hillemann's exploration of the links between China and the British Empire, *Asian Empire and British Knowledge: China and the Networks of British Imperial Expansion* (2009); James Polachek's discussion of the effects of the British attacks on China, *The Inner Opium War* (1991); Robert Bickers's overview *The Scramble for China: Foreign Devils in the Qing Empire, 1832–1914* (2011), and the first two volumes of Frank King's excellent *The History of the Hongkong and Shanghai Banking Corporation* (1987; 1989).

On relations between China and Japan up World War II, see W. G. Beasley's magisterial *Japanese Imperialism 1894–1945* (1991); Joshua Fogel's instructive exploration *Articulating the Sinosphere: Sino-Japanese Relations in Space and Time* (2009); the edited survey collection by Akira Iriye, *The Chinese and the Japanese: Essays in Political and Cultural Interactions* (1980); Douglas Reynolds's analysis of the impact Japan had on the first Chinese republic, *China, 1898–1912: The Xinzheng Revolution and Japan* (1993), and Parks Coble's *Facing Japan: Chinese Politics and Japanese Imperialism, 1931–1937* (1991).

A good overview of the foreign affairs of the Chinese republic and its contexts is Frederic Wakeman's and Richard Louis Edmonds's edited collection, *Reappraising Republican China* (2000); William Kirby's exploration of *Germany and Republican China* (1984) is highly instructive, as is Arthur Waldron's intriguing account *From War to Nationalism* (2003). The best biography of Chiang Kai-shek is Jay Taylor, *The Generalissimo: Chiang Kai-Shek and the Struggle for Modern China* (2009); the most in-depth critical biography of Mao Zedong is Jung Chang and Jon Halliday, *Mao: The Unknown Story* (2006).

On China's beginning transformation, see Benjamin A. Elman's overview, *A Cultural History of Modern Science in China* (2006). David Wright explains the Chinese understanding of new knowledge in *Translating Science: The Transmission of Western Chemistry into Late Imperial China, 1840–1900* (2000). Frank Dikötter discusses the myriad transformations through consumerism in *Things Modern: Material Culture and Everyday Life in China* (2007). Zhaojin Ji explains the significance of new financial practices in *A History of Modern Shanghai Banking: The Rise and Decline of China's Finance Capitalism* (2003). In *Sisters and Strangers: Women in the Shanghai Cotton Mills, 1919–1949* (1986) Emily Honig explains how the Chinese working class came into being.

On foreigners in China, see the background in David Mungello, *The Great Encounter of China and the West, 1500–1800* (2nd ed.; 2006). Jonathan D. Spence's *To Change China: Western Advisers in China, 1620–1960* (1969) shows the bravery and folly of some foreigners. Adrian Bennett's *John Fryer: The Introduction of Western Science and Technology into Nineteenth-Century China* (1967) is an excellent overview of the life of perhaps the most important transmitter of Western thinking into China in the nineteenth century. Marie-Claire Bergère, *Shanghai: China's Gateway to Modernity* (2009) presents the role of foreigners in China's most international city.

On Chinese abroad, an excellent overview is *The Encyclopedia of the Chinese Overseas* (1999), edited by Lynn Pan. The best analysis of different forms of Chinese migration is Adam McKeown, *Chinese Migrant Networks and Cultural Change: Peru, Chicago, Hawaii, 1900–1936* (2001). The grand old man of Chinese migration studies, Wang Gungwu, has collected some of his key contributions in *The Chinese Diaspora: Selected Essays* (1998). Philip A. Kuhn, *Chinese Among Others: Emigration in Modern Times* (2009) is an outstanding reinterpretation of the motives behind Chinese emigration.

China in World War II is, remarkably, a study that is just coming of age. For an overview, see Diana Lary, *The Chinese People at War: Human Suffering and Social Transformation, 1937–1945* (2010). The beginning of the war is covered in Stephen R. MacKinnon, *Wuhan, 1938: War, Refugees, and the Making of Modern China* (2008). Christian Henriot et al., eds., *In the Shadow of the Rising Sun: Shanghai Under Japanese Occupation* (2004) deals with the situation in China's largest city, while Mackinnon et al., eds., *China at War: Regions of China, 1937–45* (2007) discusses other parts of the country. The often overlooked military dimensions are discussed in Mark Peattie et al., eds., *The Battle for China: Essays on the Military History of the Sino-Japanese War of 1937–1945* (2010). An often inflammatory issue is ably dealt with in Timothy Brook, *Collaboration: Japanese Agents and Local Elites in Wartime China* (2005).

The origins of the foreign affairs of the Communist Party are delineated in an outstanding account by Michael H. Hunt, *The Genesis of Chinese Communist Foreign Policy* (1996). I explore the developments during the Civil War in *Decisive Encounters: The Chinese Civil War, 1946–1950* (2003). Chen Jian's *China's Road to the Korean War* (1994) is a modern classic. My edited collection *Brothers in Arms: The Rise and Fall of the Sino-Soviet Alliance* (2000) discusses the development of the Sino-Soviet alliance. Two excellent books—Lorenz M. Lüthi, *The Sino-Soviet Split: Cold War in the Communist World* (2008), and Sergey Radchenko, *Two Suns in the Heavens: The Sino-Soviet Struggle for Supremacy, 1962–1967* (2009)—present new findings on the collapse of the Sino-Soviet alliance and its effects.

On High Maoism and its disasters we are lucky to have a set of fine recent books: Frank Dikötter's superb *Mao's Great Famine: The History of China's Most Devastating Catastrophe, 1958–1962* (2010); Michael Schoenhals and Roderick MacFarquhar's useful overview *Mao's Last Revolution* (2006); Ma Jisen's *The Cultural Revolution in the Foreign Ministry of China* (2004); and not least Feng Jicai's edited *Ten Years of Madness: Oral Histories of China's Cultural Revolution* (2007).

On China and the United States see William Kirby et al., eds., *Normalization of U.S.-China Relations: An International History* (2005);

James Mann's excellent *About Face: A History of America's Curious Relationship with China, from Nixon to Clinton* (2000); Henry Kissinger's own idiosyncratic summing up at eighty-eight: *On China* (2011); Simon Shen's *Redefining Nationalism in Modern China: Sino-American Relations and the Emergence of Chinese Public Opinion in the 21st Century* (2007); and S. Mahmud Ali, *U.S.-China Relations in the "Asia-Pacific" Century* (2008).

On China and Asia see Jonathan Holslag, *China and India: Prospects for Peace* (2010); Vinod K. Aggarwal and Min Gyo Koo, eds., *Asia's New Institutional Architecture* (2008); Claude Meyer, *China or Japan: Who Will Lead Asia?* (2011); and Hasan H. Karrar, *The New Silk Road Diplomacy: China's Central Asian Foreign Policy Since the Cold War* (2010).

On China's international future there are a number of useful starting points: William A. Callahan, *China: The Pessoptimist Nation* (2010) provides a snapshot of Chinese attitudes at the start of the twenty-first century; Martin Jacques, *When China Rules the World: The Rise of the Middle Kingdom and the End of the Western World* (2009) presents a stark view of a coming power shift; Scott Wilson, *Remade in China: Foreign Investors and Institutional Change in China* (2009) shows how China is changing and is changed by international capitalism; and, finally, two sharply differing views of the significance of China's new position: Edward Steinfeld, *Playing Our Game: Why China's Economic Rise Doesn't Threaten the West* (2010) and Stefan Halper, *The Beijing Consensus: How China's Authoritarian Model Will Dominate the Twenty-First Century* (2010).

ACKNOWLEDGMENTS

I AM DEEPLY INDEBTED TO ALL THE SCHOLARS and writers whose work I draw on for this book of synthesis. Having accepted the need to limit the use of notes in a book that is primarily intended for a general reading public, I feel guilty that ideas borrowed from so many of my colleagues and friends are not properly acknowledged. I can only offer the weak excuse that the book may hopefully stimulate the reader's interest in further reading on the topic, and that the English-language works to which I am in most debt are listed for such purposes here.

I do need to note a special thanks to a few friends who have stimulated my interest in Chinese history over twenty-five years. My teacher Michael H. Hunt opened the world of Chinese history for me, and has been the source of lasting inspiration and friendship. This book is for Michael and Paula, for so much warmth and fun over the years. My close friends and colleagues Chen Jian, now at Cornell, and Niu Jun, in Beijing, have greatly advanced my understanding of China (and of many other things). Together with hundreds of other scholars in China and abroad they have remade the study of Chinese history over the past generation.

Other friends from various walks of life have also helped out by reading the manuscript or parts of it. I am particularly grateful to Antony Best, Michael H. Hunt, Emmanuel Roman, Dominic Lieven, Maurice Pinto, Munir Majid, and Stein Tønnesson.

Lastly, I need to thank my colleagues at the London School of Economics, my intellectual home for the past fifteen years, for their support during the research and writing of this book. A particular thanks goes to Michael Cox, Svetozar Rajak, Emilia Knight, and Tiha Franulovic—makers of IDEAS.

NOTES

EMPIRE

1. **It is often predicted that:** See, for instance, Willem Buiter and Ebrahim Rahbari, *Global Growth Generators: Moving beyond "Emerging Markets" and "BRIC"* (New York: Citigroup Global Markets, 2011) or Karen Ward, *The World in 2050: Quantifying the Shift in the Global Economy* (London: HSBC Global Research, 2011). **The Chinese Academy of Sciences anticipates:** See, for instance, *China Modernization Report 2006*, at Zhongguo xiandaihua wang [China Modernization Network]: http://www.modernization.com.cn/.

2. Benjamin I. Schwartz, *China and Other Matters* (Cambridge, MA: Harvard University Press, 1996), 114.

3. Jonathan Spence, *The Search for Modern China* (New York: Norton, 1990).

4. James Legge, *The Chinese Classics: With a Translation, Critical and Exegetical Notes, Prolegomena and Copious Indexes*, vol. 1 (London: Trubner & co., 1861), 9.

5. But if you do want to study it, Ralph Sawyer's is by far the best edition on the market: Sun Tzu, *The Art of War*, 9th ed. (New York: Basic Books, 1994).

6. See Peter C. Perdue, "Strange Parallels across Eurasia," *Social Science History* 32, no. 2 (June 1, 2008): 263–279; and Victor Lieberman, "The Qing Dynasty and Its Neighbors: Early Modern China in World History," *Social Science History* 32, no. 2 (June 1, 2008): 281–304.

7. In this book I will be using their *reign names* to identify Chinese emperors: The emperor whose reign name is Kangxi was at birth given the Manchu name Hiowan Yei (Xuanye in Chinese) of the Aisin-Gioro clan.

8. An excellent overview of these processes is Kenneth Pomeranz, *The Great Divergence: China, Europe, and the Making of the Modern World Economy* (Princeton: Princeton University Press, 2000).

9. On **"the eighteenth-century genocide par excellence":** see A. Dirk Moses, *Empire, Colony, Genocide: Conquest, Occupation, and Subaltern Resistance in World History* (Oxford: Berghahn Books, 2008), 188. **Then he incorporated:** see Peter C. Perdue, *China Marches West: The Qing Conquest of Central Eurasia* (Cambridge, MA: Harvard University Press, 2005).

10. Marcia Yonemoto, *Mapping Early Modern Japan: Space, Place, and Culture in the Tokugawa Period, 1603–1868* (Berkeley: University of California Press, 2003).

11. Gerbillon and Pereira both spent most of their working lives in China, dying there in 1707 and 1708 respectively. On the Russian side, incidentally, the main advisers on China were the Croat Iurii Krizhanich (Juraj Križanić) and the German Gerhard Friedrich Müller; see Michael B. Petrovich, "Juraj Krizanic: A Precursor of Pan-Slavism (ca. 1618–83)," *American Slavic and East European Review*, Vol. 6, No. 3/4. (Dec. 1947): 75–92; and L. Maier, "Gerhard Friedrich Müller's memoranda on Russian relations with China and the reconquest of the Amur," *Slavic and East European Review*, 59 (1981): 219–240.

12. Not just wanton destruction; a visit to the Sir Percival David galleries at the back of the British Museum in London, recently renovated through a donation from the Anglo-Chinese

Sir Joseph Hotung, shows that the British knew enough about imperial Chinese porcelain to steal it rather than destroy it.

CHAPTER 1: METAMORPHOSIS

1. "Han Chinese" is a tricky concept. Until very recently, Chinese people's main identification would be with their province or home area, and the term "Han" has been most often used to distinguish non-Chinese ethnic groups living in the PRC from the Chinese, but since "Chinese" is now used as a term for all citizens of the PRC, "Han" has been added as a signifier for the majority group. New DNA evidence shows a clear north-to-south spread of the Chinese population over the last two millennia and establishes a reasonable degree of genetic cohesiveness of the (Han) Chinese; see Jieming Chen et al., "Genetic Structure of the Han Chinese Population Revealed by Genome-wide SNP Variation," *The American Journal of Human Genetics* 85, no. 6 (December 11, 2009): 775–785.

2. Wang Kaixi, *Gemo, chongtu yu qutong: Qingdai Zhongwai liyi zhizheng touxi* [Lack of Understanding, Conflict and Convergence: Divergence of Rites During the Qing Dynasty] (Beijing: Beijing shifan daxue, 1999), 200.

3. **Although Asian geography had been mapped:** Matteo Ricci, *Il mappamondo cinese del p. Matteo Ricci, S. I. (3. ed., Pechino, 1602) conservato presso la Biblioteca Vaticana* (Vatican City: Biblioteca apostolica Vaticana, 1938). This is Ricci's *Kunyu wan'guo quantu* [Complete Map of the Myriad Countries on the Earth] (Beijing, 1602), the most complete (and most beautiful) of these *mappae mundi*. It was mainly based on the Flemish scholar and geographer Abraham Ortelius's *Typus Orbis Terrarum* from 1570. The best overview of early Chinese mapmaking is *Zhongguo gudai dituji* [Chinese Ancient Maps], 3 vols. (Beijing: Wen wu, 1990). **A masterful cultural compromise:** *Da Qing tongshu zhigong wanguo jingwei diqiu shi* [Model of the Myriad Tributary States of the Great Qing from Around the Globe].

4. See Jürgen Osterhammel's magnificent *China und die Weltgesellschaft: Vom 18. Jahrhundert bis in unsere Zeit* (Munich: C. H. Beck, 1989).

5. Governor of Guangdong to Imperial Court, 30 November 1814 in Lo-Shu Fu, ed., *Documentary Chronicle of Sino-Western Relations (1644–1820)*, 2 vols. (Tucson: University of Arizona Press, 1966), vol. 1, 394.

6. Jiaqing Emperor decree to Grand Council, 14 June 1818, in ibid. vol. 1, p. 413.

7. Zheng Yangwen, *The Social Life of Opium in China* (New York: Cambridge University Press, 2005), 58.

8. Echoing a prohibition—never enforced—against opium smoking from 1729.

9. *Chinese Repository*, Vol. 8 (February 1840), 497–503.

10. Later Chinese historiography often portrays the Manchus as cowards who ran away while the local ("Chinese") people stood and fought; in almost all cases of serious battle the exact opposite was true.

11. Ng Chin-keong, "Shooting the Eagles: Lin Changyi's Agony in the Wake of the Opium War," in *Maritime China in Transition, 1750–1850*, ed. Wang Gungwu and Ng Chin-keong (Wiesbaden: Harrassowitz, 2004).

12. Ibid.

13. The episode in the spring of 1847, when Hong took a two-month break from his incipient insurgency to study the Bible with the American Baptist missionary Issachar Jacox Roberts (from Sumner County, Tennessee), is a farcical case in point: Roberts thought that he had finally made a Chinese convert, only to be told that he was in fact presented with the son of God.

14. The battle is described in *Supplement to The London Gazette*, 27 November 1860, p. 4771.

15. Quoted from Bernard Brizay, *Le Sac du Palais d'Été: L'Expédition Anglo-Française de Chine en 1860 (Troisiéme Guerre de l'Opium)* (Monaco: Rocher, 2003), 268.

CHAPTER 2: IMPERIALISMS

1. Wen-hsin Yeh, *Shanghai Splendor: Economic Sentiments and the Making of Modern China, 1843–1949* (Berkeley: University of California Press, 2007).

2. Bryna Goodman, *Native Place, City and Nation: Regional Networks and Identities in Shanghai, 1853–1937* (Berkeley: University of California Press, 1995), 14–32.

3. Frank H. H. King, *The History of the Hongkong and Shanghai Banking Corporation* (Cambridge: Cambridge University Press, 1987), vol. 1, 504.

4. Madeline Zelin and Andrea McElderry, eds., "Business History in Modern China." Special issue, *Enterprise & Society* 6, no. 3 (2005).

5. Daniel H. Bays, ed., *Christianity in China: From the Eighteenth Century to the Present* (Stanford: Stanford University Press, 1996), 65.

6. See Evelyn Sakakida Rawski, *Education and Popular Literacy in Ch'ing China*, Michigan Studies on China (Ann Arbor: University of Michigan Press, 1979).

7. John K. Fairbank, ed., *Cambridge History of China*, vol. 10 (Cambridge: Cambridge University Press, 1978), 583.

8. John C. Ferguson, "The Abolition of the Competitive Examinations in China," *Journal of the American Oriental Society*, vol. 27 (1906), 79.

9. Benjamin A. Elman, *A Cultural History of Civil Examinations in Late Imperial China* (Berkeley: University of California Press, 2000), 596–597.

10. Ruth Rogaski, *Hygienic Modernity: Meanings of Health and Disease in Treaty-Port China* (Berkeley: University of California Press, 2004), 84–85.

11. Fryer, born in England in 1839, lived in China for over thirty-five years, before becoming the first professor of Chinese at the University of California, Berkeley, in 1895.

12. David Wright, *Translating Science: The Transmission of Western Chemistry into Late Imperial China, 1840–1900* (Leiden: Brill, 2000), 168; see also James Reardon-Anderson, *The Study of Change: Chemistry in China, 1840–1949* (Cambridge: Cambridge University Press, 1991).

13. For this and other stories of the encounter with Western learning in the late nineteenth century, see Guo Moruo, *Quanji* [Complete Works] (Beijing: Renmin wenxue, 1985), vol. 11.

14. Wu Tingfang, *America, Through the Spectacles of an Oriental Diplomat* (London: Anthem Press, 2007), p. 60.

15. Zhigang, *Chu shi taixi ji* [First Mission to the Far West] (Beijing: Shishutang, 1877) quoted from R. David Arkush and Leo O. Lee, eds., *Land Without Ghosts: Chinese Impressions of America from the Mid-Nineteenth Century to the Present* (Berkeley: University of California Press, 1989), p. 27.

16. Liu Xihong, Yingzhao siji [Private Notes on England], in Zhong Shuhe, ed., *Zouxiang shijie congshu* [A Collection of Books on Setting out into the World] (Changsha: Yuelu shushe, 1986), 48–49.

17. Suebsaeng Promboon, "Sino-Siamese Tributary Relations, 1282–1853" (PhD thesis, University of Wisconsin, Madison, 1971), 292.

18. Rune Svarverud, *International Law as World Order in Late Imperial China: Translation, Reception and Discourse, 1847–1911*, Sinica Leidensia 78 (Leiden: Brill, 2007), 90–91.

19. Ibid., 136.

20. *Zhongguo jindai duiwai guanxi shi ziliao xuanji (1840–1949)* [Selection Materials from the History of Modern Chinese Foreign Relations (1840–1949)], book 1, vol. 1 (Shanghai: Shanghai renmin, 1977), 241–43.

21. Zeng Jize, *Chushi Ying Fa E guo riji* [Diary of Embassies in England, France, and Russia], ed. Zhong Shehe (Changsha: Yuelu shushe, 1985), 178.

22. *Qingyibao*, 45 (May 1900).

CHAPTER 3: JAPAN

1. Harry Harootunian, "The Functions of China in Tokugawa Thought," in *The Chinese and the Japanese: Essays in Political and Cultural Interactions*, ed. Akira Iriye (Princeton: Princeton University Press, 1980), 12.

2. J. Mason Gentzler, *Changing China: Readings in the History of China from the Opium War to the Present* (New York: Praeger, 1977), 70–71.

3. Edwin Pak-Wah Leung, "The Quasi-War in East Asia: Japan's Expedition to Taiwan and the Ryūkyū Controversy," *Modern Asian Studies* 17, no. 2 (January 1, 1983): 260.

4. Norihito Mizuno, "Early Meiji Policies Towards the Ryukyus and the Taiwanese Aboriginal Territories," *Modern Asian Studies* 43, no. 3 (May 1, 2009): 683–739.

5. Peter Zarrow, "Anti-Despotism and 'Rights Talk': The Intellectual Origins of Modern Human Rights Thinking in the Late Qing," *Modern China* 34, no. 2 (January 2008): 186.

6. Han Fuqing, *Qingmo liu Ri xuesheng* [Chinese Students in Japan in the Late Qing Period] (Taibei: Zhongyang yanjiuyuan, Jindaishi yanjiusuo, 1975), 127–128.

7. Yi Manson et al., "Memorial Submitted by Ten Thousand Men," in Peter H. Lee, ed., *Sourcebook of Korean Civilization*, vol. 1 (New York: Columbia University Press, 1992), 335.

8. **"It is obvious":** Choe Ik-hyon, "Memorial against Peace," 1876, Peter H. Lee, ed., *Sourcebook of Korean Civilization*, vol. 2 (New York: Columbia University Press, 1992), 333. **"But the plan to assassinate":** Seo Jae-pil, one of the young coup-makers who fled to Japan, later went to the United States, where he took the name Philip Jaisohn, trained as a medical doctor, and became a political mentor to Syngman Rhee and, after World War II, to the young Kim Dae-jung. Seo died at eighty-seven in 1951.

9. Ki-Baik Lee, *A New History of Korea* (Cambridge, MA: Harvard University Press, 1984), 284.

10. The Chinese suffered at least 35,000 dead and wounded soldiers and sailors, seven times more than the Japanese; see Zhang Mingjin, *Luori xia de longqi: 1894–1895 Zhong Ri zhanzheng jishi* [The Setting Sun of the Dragon Banner: A True Record of the 1894–95 Sino-Japanese War] (Beijing: Beijing Yanshan, 1998).

11. Wm. Theodore de Bary and Richard Lufrano, eds., *Sources of Chinese Tradition*, vol. 2, 2nd ed. (New York: Columbia University Press, 2001), 275.

12. Ibid., 269–270.

13. Isaac Taylor Headland, *Court Life in China: The Capital, Its Officials and People* (New York: F. H. Revell Co., 1909), 357. All of Guangxu's edicts are in Zhongguo diyi lishi dang'anguan. *Guangxu Xuantong liang chao shangyu dang*, 37 vols. (Guilin: Guangxi shifan daxue chubanshe, 1996).

14. Bary and Lufrano, *Sources of Chinese Tradition*, vol. 2, 312.

15. Ibid., 317–318.

16. Sushila Narsimhan, *Japanese Perceptions of China in the Nineteenth Century: Influence of Fukuzawa Yukichi* (New Delhi: Phoenix, 1999), 181.

17. Geoffrey Jukes, *The Russo-Japanese War 1904–1905* (Oxford: Osprey, 2002), 21.

18. Harry J. Lamley, "Taiwan under Japanese Rule," in *Taiwan: A New History*, ed. Murray A. Rubinstein (Armonk, NY: M.E. Sharpe, 2006), 223.

19. Ibid.

20. Herbert P. Bix, "Japanese Imperialism and the Manchurian Economy, 1900–31," *The China Quarterly*, no. 51 (July 1, 1972): 425–443.

21. Sun Yat-sen, *China and Japan: Natural Friends—Unnatural Enemies* (Shanghai: China United Press, 1941), 150–151.

CHAPTER 4: REPUBLIC

1. Loren Brandt, "Reflections on China's Late 19th and Early 20th-Century Economy," in *Reappraising Republican China*, ed. Frederic Wakeman and Richard Louis Edmonds (Oxford: Oxford University Press, 2000), 28–54.

2. Philip P. Pan, "'Saints' in Rome Are 'Henchmen' to Beijing," *Washington Post*, September 30, 2000; *Christian Century*, 18 October 2000.

3. I remember, as a child in Norwegian Lutheran Sunday school, seeing blood-curdling pictures of Christians being hacked to death by the heathen Boxers; a fair number of the missionaries killed were Scandinavians.

4. Philip W. Sergeant, *The Great Empress Dowager of China* (London: Hutchinson & Co., 1910), 241.

5. **In one town near Beijing:** Joan Judge, *The Precious Raft of History: The Past, the West, and the Woman Question in China* (Stanford: Stanford University Press, 2008), 180; see also Joan Judge, "The Politics of Female Virtue in Turn-of-the-Century China: The Case of Tongzhou," paper delivered at the annual conference of the Association for Asian Studies, San Francisco, April 2006. **"There are things that I";** George Lynch, *The War of the Civilisations, Being the Record of a "Foreign Devil's" Experiences with the Allies in China* (London: Longmans, Green, and Co., 1901), 142. **A major Japanese newspaper:** Editorial, *Yorozu Choho*, December 1901; quoted from Robert A. Bickers and R. G. Tiedemann, eds., *The Boxers, China, and the World* (Rowman & Littlefield, 2007); see also Bickers, "Boxed Out: How the British Museum Suppressed Discussion of British Looting in China," *Times Literary Supplement*, 5129 (2001): 15.

6. Victor Purcell, *The Boxer Uprising: A Background Study* (Cambridge: Cambridge University Press, 1963).

7. **The *Philadelphia Press* declared:** *Philadelphia Press*, 11 April 1898. **In notes outlining:** *Papers Relating to the Foreign Relations of the United States: With the Annual Message of the President Transmitted to Congress, December 5, 1899* (Washington, DC: Government Printing Office, 1901), 129–130.

8. Quoted in Walter LaFeber, *The American Age: United States Foreign Policy at Home and Abroad Since 1750* (New York: W. W. Norton, 1989), 209.

9. Samuel Isaac Joseph Schereschewsky, the founder of St. John's University, was born in Lithuania in 1831, went to Germany to study for the rabbinate, there became a Christian, emigrated to America, trained for the priesthood, and in 1859 was sent by the Episcopal Church to China, where he began translating the Bible into Chinese. Schereschewsky later developed Parkinson's Disease, was largely paralyzed, resigned his position as Bishop of Shanghai, and spent the rest of his life completing his Bible translation, the last two thousand pages of which he typed with the one finger that he could still move. He died in Tokyo in 1906.

10. Jacobson to Reichmarineamt, 27 January 2005, quoted in Klaus Mühlhahn, *Herrschaft und Widerstand in der "Musterkolonie" Kiautschou: Interaktionen zwischen China und Deutschland, 1897–1914* (Munich: Oldenbourg, 2000), 238.

11. Governor of Jiaozhou, Meyer-Waldeck, to Tirpitz, 14 October 1912, quoted in Mühlhahn, *Herrschaft und Widerstand in der "Musterkolonie" Kiautschou*.

12. Von Falkenhausen's China link came back to save him after he in 1951 was sentenced to twelve years in prison for having been military governor of Belgium during World War

II. One of his key defendants was Qian Xiuling, a Chinese chemist who had settled in Belgium before the war, and who had served as a conduit between the German commander and the Belgian resistance. Von Falkenhausen served only three months of his sentence. Qian's life was made into a sixteen-episode television series in China in 2002 (see *Beijing qingnian bao*, 11 December 2001). The best overview of Germany's role in republican China is William C. Kirby, *Germany and Republican China* (Stanford: Stanford University Press, 1984).

13. *The Times*, 20 July 1909.

14. Issued 29 January 1901; quoted from Richard S. Horowitz, "Breaking the Bonds of Precedent: The 1905–6 Government Reform Commission and the Remaking of the Qing Central State," *Modern Asian Studies* 37, no. 4 (October 2003): 775–797.

15. E-Tu Zen Sun, "The Chinese Constitutional Missions of 1905–1906," *The Journal of Modern History* 24, no. 3 (September 1952): 251–268.

16. Edwin John Dingle, *China's Revolution, 1911–1912* (Shanghai: Commercial Press, 1912), pp. 49–50.

17. *Minbao*, April 1906, p. 8.

18. Tsou Jung [Zou Rong], *The Revolutionary Army: A Chinese Nationalist Tract of 1903*, introduction and translation with notes by John Lust, Matériaux pour l'étude de l'extréme-orient moderne et contemporain, textes; 6 (The Hague: Mouton, 1968).

19. Edward J. M. Rhoads, *Manchus & Han* (Seattle: University of Washington Press, 2001), 188–192.

20. Michael Gasster, "The Republican Revolutionary Movement," in *The Cambridge History of China*, ed. John K. Fairbank and Kwang-ching Liu, vol. 11: Late Ch'ing, Part 2 (Cambridge: Cambridge University Press, 1980), 494.

21. Su Quanyou, "Yuan Shikai yu Zhili gongye [Yuan Shikai and Zhili Industry]," *Lishi Dang'an*, no. 1 (March 2005): 77–82.

22. Marie-Claire Bergère, *Sun Yat-sen*, trans. Janet Lloyd (Stanford: Stanford University Press, 2000).

23. B. L. Putnam Weale, *The Fight for the Republic in China* (New York: Dodd, Mead and Company, 1917), 229–230.

24. See for example Frank J. Goodnow, "The Adaptation of a Constitution to the Needs of a People," *Proceedings of the Academy of Political Science in the City of New York* 5, no. 1 (October 1914): 36–37.

25. K. S. Liew, *Struggle for Democracy* (Berkeley: University of California Press, 1971).

26. Angus W. McDonald, "Mao Tse-tung and the Hunan Self-Government Movement, 1920: An Introduction and Five Translations," *The China Quarterly*, no. 68 (December 1976): 751–777.

27. Urgunge Onon and D. Pritchatt, *Asia's First Modern Revolution: Mongolia Proclaims Its Independence in 1911*, illustrated edition (Leiden: Brill Academic Publishers, 1997). For Russian policy, see Nakami Tatsuo, "Russian Diplomats and Mongol Independence, 1911–1915," in *Mongolia in the Twentieth Century: Landlocked Cosmopolitan*, ed. Stephen Kotkin and Bruce A. Elleman (New York: M. E. Sharpe, 1999), 69–78.

28. Russo-Chinese Agreement concerning Outer Mongolia, 5 November 1913, in Putnam Weale, *The Fight for the Republic in China*, 248.

29. Tsepon W. D. Shakabpa, *Tibet: A Political History* (New Haven: Yale University Press, 1967), 246–48.

30. Melvyn C. Goldstein, *The Snow Lion and the Dragon: China, Tibet, and the Dalai Lama* (Berkeley: University of California Press, 1999).

31. Sheng even joined the Soviet Communist party in 1938; for a biography, see Cai Jinsong, *Sheng Shicai wai zhuan* [An Unofficial Biography of Sheng Shicai] (Beijing: Zhonggong dangshi, 2005).

32. Guoqi Xu, *China and the Great War* (Cambridge: Cambridge University Press, 2005), 245.

33. Quoted in ibid., 252.

34. As a result of the protests, China became the only major country that refused to sign the Treaty of Versailles. Cao Rulin, the minister who had his house burned down, survived the ordeal and later moved to Detroit, where he died at the ripe age of ninety-one. His memoirs are in Cao Rulin, *Cao Rulin yisheng zhi huiyi* [Cao Rulin Remembers His Life] (Taibei: Zhuanji wenxue, 1970).

35. Quoted from Spence, *The Search for Modern China*, 303.

36. Lu Hsun, "A Happy Family," in Lu Hsun, *Selected Stories of Lu Hsun (Beijing:* Foreign Languages Press, 1960).

37. Liang Qichao, "Travel Impressions from Europe," in William Theodore De Bary and Richard Lufrano, eds., *Sources of East Asian Tradition Volume 2: The Modern Period*, 2nd ed. (New York: Columbia University Press, 2000).

38. Li Dazhao, quoted in Jerome Ch'en, "The Chinese Communist Movement to 1927," in *The Cambridge History of China*, ed. John K. Fairbank, vol. 12: Republican China 1912–1949, Part 1 (Cambridge: Cambridge University Press, 1983), 513.

39. Sun Yat-sen, *The International Development of China* (New York: GP Putnam's Sons, 1922), 237.

40. "Sun Yat-sen Appeals," *New York Times*, 16 May 1921, 14.

41. Joint Memorandum by the Secretary of State for Foreign Affairs and the Secretary of State for the Colonies, June 1925, CAB/24/174, UK National Archives, London.

42. S. C. M. Paine, *Imperial Rivals: China, Russia, and Their Disputed Frontier* (Armonk, NY: M. E. Sharpe, 1996).

43. *Xiangdao*, 31 (July 1923).

44. Alexander Pantsov, *The Bolsheviks and the Chinese Revolution, 1919–1927* (Honolulu: University of Hawaii Press, 2000).

45. Arthur Waldron, in his excellent *From War to Nationalism* (Cambridge: Cambridge University Press, 2003), emphasizes the effects of the civil wars in the north as being especially conducive to GMD success (pp. 246–274); he is undoubtedly right.

46. Kuo Mo-Jo and Josiah W. Bennett, "A Poet with the Northern Expedition," *The Far Eastern Quarterly* 3, no. 1 (November 1943): 5–36.

47. Kuo Mo-Jo and Josiah W. Bennett, "A Poet with the Northern Expedition," *The Far Eastern Quarterly* 3, no. 4 (August 1944): 362–380.

48. Clarence Martin Wilbur and Julie Lien-ying How, *Missionaries of Revolution: Soviet Advisers and Nationalist China, 1920–1927* (Cambridge, MA: Harvard University Press, 1989), 250.

49. Quoted in Christopher Andrew, *Her Majesty's Secret Service: The Making of the British Intelligence Community* (New York: Viking, 1986), 328.

50. British Foreign Secretary, CAB/23/54, UK National Archives.

51. Sir William Tyrrell to the Committee on Imperial Defense, 28 July 1926, CAB/24/181, UK National Archives.

CHAPTER 5: FOREIGNERS

1. *Renmin ribao*, 4 April 2006.

2. **In Taiwan, the younger generation:** In 2010 fifty-two percent of Taiwanese still saw Japan as their favorite country (the People's Republic of China scored five percent); "Japan Taiwan's Favorite Country, Survey Reveals," *Taipei Times*, 24 March 2010. **In spite of war:** Frank Dikötter, *The Age of Openness: China before Mao* (Berkeley: University of California Press, 2008).

3. Harry Alverson Franck, *Roving Through Southern China* (New York: The Century Co., 1925), 75–76.

4. Frederic E. Wakeman, *Policing Shanghai, 1927–1937* (Berkeley: University of California Press, 1996), 215–216.

5. **Across the street the Cathay Hotel:** The lavish structure is now known as the Peace Hotel—Heping fandian. **In Beijing new public buildings:** It is now the "internal information" office of the official Chinese news agency Xinhua (see Sang Ye and Geremie R. Barmé, "A Beijing That Isn't [Part I]," at http://www.chinaheritagenewsletter.anu.edu.au/features .php?searchterm=014_BeijingThatWasnt.inc&issue=014).

6. Valery Garrett, *Chinese Dress: From the Qing Dynasty to the Present* (North Clarendon, VT: Tuttle Publishing, 2008), 126–155 on the republican era.

7. The name itself has a fascinating foreign background: While in Japan, Sun began using the Japanese surname Nakayama, central mountain, which in Chinese is pronounced Zhongshan. He kept it, in its Chinese form, as a nom de guerre after he returned to China.

8. When Cheng tried to reestablish his paper in Taiwan after 1949, the Guomindang government immediately closed it down.

9. Lu Hanchao, *Beyond the Neon Lights: Everyday Shanghai in the Early Twentieth Century* (Berkeley: University of California Press, 2004).

10. Qi Jianhong and Zhou Jieqiong, *French Direct Investment in China: A Survey Report*, East Asia Economic Research Group Discussion Paper (Brisbane: School of Economics, The University of Queensland, January 2006).

11. Osterhammel, *China und die Weltgesellschaft: Vom 18. Jahrhundert bis in unsere Zeit*, 255.

12. Norman P. Grubb, *C. T. Studd: Cricketer and Pioneer* (London: Religious Tract Society, 1933). Studd had played for England in the first test match against Australia (the origins of the Ashes series) and believed sports would help convert souls for Jesus.

13. Because of Mao's scathing valedictory to the US presence in China (entitled "Farewell, John Leighton Stuart" in Mao's *Selected Works*), Stuart became the most reviled foreigner in China after 1949. Before he died in 1962, he told his family that he wished to be buried at the university he had constructed, when such an act became politically possible. But, in a final slight, when the PRC government finally agreed to his ashes being interred in China in 2008, they insisted that it happen in Hangzhou, his birthplace, rather than at the campus he had created.

14. Watchman Nee was imprisoned soon after the Communist takeover; he died in prison in 1972. Membership in his Little Flock and other groups that have grown out of it now numbers more than 100,000 in China and is rapidly growing. Lian Xi, *Redeemed by Fire: The Rise of Popular Christianity in Modern China* (New Haven: Yale University Press, 2010).

15. Madeleine Chi, *China Diplomacy, 1914–1918* (Cambridge, MA: Harvard University Asia Center, 1970), 53–54.

16. **But as important were:** Julia C. Strauss, *Strong Institutions in Weak Polities: State Building in Republican China, 1927–1940* (Oxford: Oxford University Press, 1998), 75. **The Frenchman Jean Monnet:** Hungdah Su, "The Father of Europe in China: Jean Monnet and Creation of the C.D.F.C. (1933–1936)," *Journal of European Integration History* 13, no. 1 (2007): 9–24.

17. **For understandable reasons Stennes:** Stennes's chances of survival in Nazi Germany would have been low; he had testified against Hitler in a 1931 court case and Hitler had later sued Stennes for copyright infringement. In 2000 it was claimed that Stennes had been a Soviet agent through much of the 1940s; *Trud*, 14 March 2000, no. 46. **Chiang's older son, Chiang Ching-kuo:** Bernd Martin and Susanne Kuss, eds., *Deutsch-Chinesische Beziehungen 1928–1937: "gleiche" Partner Unter "ungleichen" Bedingungen: Eine Quellensammlung* (Berlin: Akademie Verlag, 2003).

18. Walter J. Boyne, *Air Warfare: An International Encyclopedia* (ABC-CLIO, 2002), 126–127.

19. Vasilii Chuikov, *Missiia v Kitae: zapiski voennogo sovetnika* (Moscow: Vostochnoilit-ry, 1981).

20. Almost all of the chief Comintern advisers came to a sorry end: Sneevliet was shot by the Germans in 1942, Borodin and Stern died in Stalin's purges.

21. **"Will Moscow," she wrote:** Anna Louise Strong, *China's Millions: The Revolutionary Struggles from 1927 to 1935* (New York: Knight, 1935), 412–413. **Strong married a Russian:** *The New Soviet Constitution, a Study in Socialist Democracy* (New York: H. Holt, 1937). Strong also wrote a book about Poland's liberation by the Soviets in 1945, *I Saw the New Poland* (Boston: Little Brown, 1946); about the Chinese liberation of Tibet in 1959, *When Serfs Stood Up in Tibet* (Beijing: New World Press, 1960), and, as if this were not enough, an explanation of why Mao's Great Leap Forward would save China, *The Rise of the People's Communes in China* (New York: Marzani and Munsell, 1960).

22. Hyun Ok Park, *Two Dreams in One Bed: Empire, Social Life, and the Origins of the North Korean Revolution in Manchuria* (Durham, NC: Duke University Press, 2005).

23. **Books on law:** See Zou Zhenhuan, Yingxiang Zhongguo jindai shehui de yibai zhong yizuo [The One Hundred Translations That Have Had the Strongest Influence on Modern Chinese Society] (Beijing: Zhongguo duiwai fanyi, 1996). **By the 1910s China:** Ishikawa Yoshihiro, "Chinese Marxism in the Early 20th Century and Japan," *Sino-Japanese Studies* 14 (n.d.): 24–34.

24. Zhang Ping, "Sherlock Holmes in China," *Perspectives: Studies in Translatology* 13, no. 2 (2005): 106; Xiaoqing Cheng and Timothy C. Wong, *Sherlock in Shanghai: Stories of Crime and Detection* (Honolulu: University of Hawaii Press, 2007).

25. Joys Cheung, "Chinese Music and Translated Modernity in Shanghai, 1918–1937" (PhD dissertation, University of Michigan, 2008); Andrew F. Jones, *Yellow Music: Media Culture and Colonial Modernity in the Chinese Jazz Age* (Durham, NC: Duke University Press, 2001).

26. He Libo, "1929 de Xihu bolanhui," *Jiangcha fengyun*, 6, 2010: 6–70; Ai Xianfeng, "1929 de Xihu bolanhui shulun [An Overview and Discussion of the 1929 West Lake Exposition]," *Huazhong shifan daxue xuebao, renwen shehuikexue ban*, 4, 2009: 84–89.

27. *Xin qingnian* 6, 1 (January 1919): 10–11.

28. Suzanne Pepper, *Radicalism and Education Reform in 20th-Century China: The Search for an Ideal Development Model* (Cambridge: Cambridge University Press, 2000).

29. Monlin Chiang, *Tides from the West, a Chinese Autobiography* (New Haven: Yale University Press, 1947).

30. Hu Shi, "Baihua wenyan zhi youlie bijiao [A Comparison of the Good and Bad in the Vernacular Language], *Hu Shi liuxue riji* [Hu Shih's Diary from Studying Abroad], *Minguo congshu*, 2nd series, vol. 2 (Shanghai: Shanghai shudian, 1990), p. 943; quoted from Elisabeth Kaske, *The Politics of Language in Chinese Education, 1895–1919* (Leiden: Brill, 2008), 424 (amended translation).

31. "The Question of Miss Zhao's Personality" (1919), *Mao's Road to Power: Revolutionary Writings 1912–1949*, ed. Stuart R. Schram, 7 vols. (Armonk, NY: M. E. Sharpe, 1992), vol. 1, p. 422.

32. Robert Bickers, "Shanghailanders: The Formation and Identity of the British Settler Community in Shanghai, 1843–1937," *Past & Present* 159, no. 1 (May 1, 1998): 161–211, 188.

33. Kate Bagnall, "Golden Shadows on a White Land: An Exploration of the Lives of White Women Who Partnered Chinese Men and Their Children in Southern Australia, 1855–1915" (PhD dissertation, University of Sydney, 2006), 245–297.

34. Esther Cheo Ying, *Black Country to Red China* (London: Cresset Women's Voices, 1987), 12.

CHAPTER 6: ABROAD

1. Lee Kuan Yew, "A Tale of Two Cities: Twenty Years On," Li Ka Shing Lecture, University of Hong Kong, 14 December 1992, in (Singapore) *Ministerial Speeches*, 16, no. 6 (November-December 1992), p. 55.

2. *The Labor Agitators, or, The Battle for Bread: The Party of the Future, the Workingmen's Party of California: Its Birth and Organization: Its Leaders and Its Purposes: Corruption in Our Local and State Governments: Venality of the Press* (San Francisco: Geo. W. Greene, 1879).

3. Bayard Taylor quoted in Committee of the Senate of California, ed., *Chinese Immigration: The Social, Moral and Political Effect of Chinese Immigration* (Sacramento, CA: State Printing Office, 1877). Taylor's book, which the quote is from, was published in 1855.

4. Chinese American Demographics, at http://www.ameredia.com/resources/demographics /chinese.html.

5. Vincent Peloso, "Racial Conflict and Identity Crisis in Wartime Peru: Revisiting the Cañete Massacre of 1881," *Social Identities* 11, no. 5 (September 2005): 467–488.

6. Lisa Yun, *The Coolie Speaks: Chinese Indentured Laborers and African Slaves in Cuba* (Philadelphia: Temple University Press, 2008).

7. Gregor Benton, *Chinese Migrants and Internationalism: Forgotten Histories, 1917–1945* (London: Routledge, 2007).

8. Ibid., p. 91.

9. Wieland Wagner, "Chinese Tourists Do Europe," *Der Spiegel*, 17 August 2007.

10. Quoted from Adam McKeown, *Chinese Migrant Networks and Cultural Change: Peru, Chicago, Hawaii, 1900–1936* (Chicago: University of Chicago Press, 2001), 127.

11. Benton, *Chinese Migrants and Internationalism*, 67.

12. Quoted from the PBS documentary *Becoming American: The Chinese Experience. Program Three: No Turning Back*. First broadcast in the United States in 2003.

13. *The Times*, 27 December 1917.

14. Xu, *China and the Great War*, 134.

15. Aleksandr Larin, "Krasnye i belye: krasnoarmyeitsy iz podnebesnoi" [Red and White: Red Army Soldiers from the Celestial Empire]," *Rodina*, 2000; Lewis H. Siegelbaum, "Another 'Yellow Peril'?: Chinese Migrants in the Russian Far East and the Russian Reaction Before 1917," *Modern Asian Studies* 12, no. 2 (1978): 307–330. See also Benton, *Chinese Migrants and Internationalism*, 20–29.

16. Linqing Yao, *The Chinese Overseas Students: An Overview of the Flows Change*, paper at the Australian Population Association's 12th biennial conference, September 2004, at http://www.apa.org.au/upload/2004-6C_Yao.pdf.

17. Weili Ye, *Seeking Modernity in China's Name: Chinese Students in the United States, 1900–1927* (Stanford: Stanford University Press, 2002), 19.

18. **The CCP told them:** Elizabeth McGuire, "Between Revolutions: Chinese Students in Soviet Institutes, 1948–1966," in *China Learns from the Soviet Union, 1949–Present*, ed. Thomas Bernstein and Hua-yu Li (Lanham, MA: Lexington Books, 2010), 366. **As late as in 2002:** He Li, "Returned Students and Political Change in China," *Asian Perspective [S. Korea]* 30, no. 2 (2006): 5–30.

19. *Renmin ribao*, 27 January 2010.

20. Allen F. Damon, "Financing Revolution: Sun Yat-sen and the Overthrow of the Ch'ing Dynasty," *The Hawaiian Journal of History* 25 (1991): 166–167.

21. Li Lisan's Russian widow, Elizaveta Kishkina, still lives in Beijing at the age of ninety-six under the name Li Sha; she spent eight years in prison during the Cultural Revolution.

Her autobiography, *Wo de Zhongguo yuan fen: Li Lisan furen Li Sha huiyilu* [My Fateful Encounter with China: The Memoirs of Li Lisan's Wife Li Sha] (Beijing: Waiyu jiaoxue yu yanjiu, 2009) is worth reading as a warning for foreigners who get too involved in Chinese affairs.

22. "The Man Who Saw It All," *Time*, 5 December 2005.

23. Nien Cheng, *Life and Death in Shanghai* (New York: Penguin, 1995), 105.

24. Hua published his somewhat unreliable memoirs in 1981; Leon Hoa, *Reconstruire la Chine: trente ans d'urbanisme, 1949–1979* [Reconstructing China: Thirty Years of Urbanism] (Paris: Moniteur, 1981).

25. Cheng Li, "Foreign-Educated Returnees in the People's Republic of China: Increasing Political Influence with Limited Official Power," *Journal of International Migration and Integration* 7, no. 4 (September 1, 2006): 493–516.

CHAPTER 7: WAR

1. The Land of the Manchu, also spelled Manzhouguo.

2. Although it is notoriously difficult to estimate overall numbers of war casualties, Rudolph J. Rummel, *China's Bloody Century: Genocide and Mass Murder Since 1900* (New York: Transaction Publishers, 1991) is a very trustworthy source. See also Guo Rugui, *Zhongguo kangri zhanzheng zhengmian zhanchang zuozhan ji* (Nanjing: Jiangsu renmin, 2006) and Werner Gruhl, *Imperial Japan's World War Two, 1931–1945* (New Brunswick, NJ: Transaction Publishers, 2007).

3. Prasenjit Duara, *The Global and Regional in China's Nation-Formation* (Abingdon: Routledge, 2009), 51.

4. **On 30 July he declared:** James Crowley, *Japan's Quest for Autonomy: National Security and Foreign Policy, 1930–1958* (Princeton: Princeton University Press, 1966), 339. **Addressing his countrymen by radio:** Statement on a war of self-defense and resistance by the National Government, 14 August 1937, at http://mil.news.sina.com.cn/2005-06-19/1841298670 .html.

5. **In a speech on 5 October 1937:** http://www.vlib.us/amdocs/texts/fdrquarn.html. **During the first year of the war:** John W. Garver, *Chinese–Soviet Relations, 1937–1945: The Diplomacy of Chinese Nationalism (New York: Oxford University Press, 1988)*, 38. **The Soviets lost 9,000 men:** Alvin D. Coox, *Nomonhan: Japan Against Russia, 1939* (Stanford: Stanford University Press, 1990), 915.

6. Aaron William Moore, "The Chimera of Privacy: Reading Self-Discipline in Japanese Diaries from the Second World War (1937–1945)," *The Journal of Asian Studies* 68, no. 1 (2009): 187.

7. John Rabe, *The Good Man of Nanking: The Diaries of John Rabe*, ed. Erwin Wickert (New York: Knopf, 1998), 77.

8. Dreimächtepakt zwischen Deutschland, Italien und Japan vom 27- September 1940, in *Reichsgesetzblatt*, 2, 1940, p. 280.

9. Chiang, 13 April 1941, quoted in Jay Taylor, *The Generalissimo: Chiang Kai-shek and the Struggle for Modern China* (Cambridge, MA: Harvard University Press, 2009), 181–182.

10. Ibid., 188.

11. Ibid., 190.

12. Bevin Alexander, *The Strange Connection: US Intervention in China, 1944–1972* (Westport, CT: Greenwood, 1992), 16.

13. Roosevelt-Chiang dinner meeting, 23 November 1943, Foreign Relations of the United States, 1943, Conferences at Cairo and Teheran, 324.

14. Dong Wang, "The Discourse of Unequal Treaties in Modern China," *Pacific Affairs* 76, no. 3 (October 1, 2003): 399.

15. Theodore White and Annalee Jacoby, *Thunder out of China* (New York: William Sloane, 1946), 162.

16. Micah S. Muscolino, "Refugees, Land Reclamation, and Militarized Landscapes in Wartime China: Huanglongshan, Shaanxi, 1937–45," *The Journal of Asian Studies* 69, no. 2 (2010): 453–478.

17. One particularly good book on how war made modern China is Hans van de Ven, *War and Nationalism in China: 1925–1945* (London: Routledge Curzon, 2003).

18. Entry for 22 December 1943, *The Diary of Georgi Dimitrov*, intr. and ed. Ivo Banac (New Haven: Yale University Press, 2003), 290.

19. **In the name of national resistance:** Ralph Thaxton, *Salt of the Earth: The Political Origins of Peasant Protest and Communist Revolution in China* (Berkeley: University of California Press, 1997), 256. **In the western Shandong borderlands:** Yung-fa Chen, *Making Revolution: The Communist Movement in Eastern and Central China, 1937–1945* (Berkeley: University of California Press, 1986), 267–269.

20. Parks M. Coble, "Japan's New Order and the Shanghai Capitalists: Conflict and Collaboration, 1937–1945," in *Chinese Collaboration with Japan, 1932–1945: The Limits of Accommodation*, ed. David P. Barrett and Lawrence N. Shyu (Stanford: Stanford University Press, 2001), 135–155.

21. Peter J. Seybolt, "The War Within a War: A Case Study of a County on the North China Plain," in *Chinese Collaboration with Japan, 1932–1945: The Limits of Accommodation*, ed. David P. Barrett and Lawrence N. Shyu (Stanford: Stanford University Press, 2001).

22. **They could also, where needed:** Yung-fa Chen, *Making Revolution*, 116–117. **Hurley also promised US supplies:** Michael Sheng, *Battling Western Imperialism: Mao, Stalin, and the United States* (Princeton: Princeton University Press, 1997), 89–93. See also Odd Arne Westad, *Cold War and Revolution: Soviet-American Rivalry and the Origins of the Chinese Civil War, 1944–1946* (New York: Columbia University Press, 1993).

23. Chiang Kai-shek's victory message, 15 August 1945, at IBiblio, http://www.ibiblio.org /pha/policy/1945/450815c.html.

CHAPTER 8: COMMUNISM

1. Sin-wai Chan and David E. Pollard, eds., *An Encyclopaedia of Translation: Chinese-English, English-Chinese* (Hong Kong: Chinese University Press, 2001).

2. For this, see David Apter and Tony Saich, *Revolutionary Discourse in Mao's Republic* (Cambridge, MA: Harvard University Press, 1994).

3. Quoted from Westad, *Decisive Encounters*, 160.

4. *Selected Works of Mao Zedong*, Vol. 5.

5. **Lin Biao, the civil war hero:** "Ai Yingxu, Lin Biao ruhe duidai kangMei yuanChao: Bu tongyi chubing Chaoxian?" [What Attitude Did Lin Biao Have to the Campaign to Resist America and Assist Korea: Did He Not Agree with the Sending of Troops to Korea?], 9 September 2010, at http://dangshi.people.com.cn, accessed 5 October 2010. **"To enter the war":** Mao Zedong to Zhou Enlai, 13 October 1950, Mao Zedong, *Jianguo yilai Mao Zedong wengao* [Mao Zedong's Manuscripts Since the Founding of the People's Republic], ed. Zhonggong zhongyang wenxian yanjiushi (Beijing: Zhongyang wenxian, 1996), vol. 1, 556.

6. James Z. Gao, "War Culture, Nationalism, and Political Campaigns, 1950–1953," in *Chinese Nationalism in Perspective: Historical and Recent Cases*, ed. C. X. George Wei and Xiaoyuan Liu (New York: Praeger, 2001); Adam Cathcart, "Japanese Devils and American Wolves: Chinese Communist Songs from the War of Liberation and the Korean War," *Popular Music and Society* 33, no. 2 (2010): 203.

7. Lorenz Lüthi, *The Sino-Soviet Split: Cold War in the Communist World* (Princeton: Princeton University Press, 2008).

8. For different estimates, see Shu Guang Zhang, *Economic Cold War: America's Embargo Against China and the Sino-Soviet Alliance, 1949–1963* (Stanford: Stanford University Press, 2002) and Shen Zhihua, *Sulian zhuanjia zai Zhongguo, 1948–1960* [Soviet Experts in China, 1948–1960] (Beijing: Zhongguo guoji guangbo, 2003). My figures are based on conversations with Chinese economists working on the effects of the aid program.

9. For Shanghai, see Li Dehong, ed., *Shanghai shi zhongxue jiaoshi yundong shiliao xuan* [Selected Materials on the Secondary School Teachers' Movement in Shanghai] (Shanghai: Shanghai jiaoyu, 1997).

10. See Cui Xiaolin's fascinating *Chongsu yu sikao: 1951 nian qianhou gao xiao zhishifenzi sixiang gaizao yundong yanjiu* [Remoulding and Rethinking: A Study of the Movement to Transform the Thinking of Intellectuals in Colleges and Universities Around 1951] (Beijing: Zhonggong dangshi, 2005). For *Renmin Daxue*, see Douglas A. Stiffler, "Building Socialism at Chinese People's University: Chinese Cadres and Soviet Experts in the People's Republic of China, 1949–1957" (PhD dissertation, University of California–San Diego, 2002).

11. **The wholesale importing of curricula:** Having observed first hand the same mixture at the (re)introduction of American curricula and teaching methods in China in the 1980s, I can only sympathize with the students on whom all of this was tested out. **There was a fair share:** Eddy U, "The Making of *zhishifenzi*: The Critical Impact of the Registration of Unemployed Intellectuals in the Early PRC," *The China Quarterly* 173 (2003): 100–121; and idem, "The Hiring of Rejects: Teacher Recruitment and Crises of Socialism in the Early PRC Years," *Modern China* 30, 1, (2004): 46–80.

12. See for instance the record of the conversation between Mao Zedong and Soviet Ambassador Iudin, 21 December 1955, 11–19, delo 9, papka 410, opis 49, fond 0100, Russian Foreign Ministry Archive, Moscow (AVPRF).

13. See Stiffler, "Building Socialism at Chinese People's University."

14. Pepper, *Radicalism and Education Reform in Twentieth-Century China*, 224.

15. Odd Arne Westad, *Decisive Encounters: The Chinese Civil War, 1946–1950* (Stanford: Stanford University Press, 2003), 274–276.

16. See for instance James Gao, *The Communist Takeover of Hangzhou: The Transformation of City and Cadre, 1949–1954* (Honolulu: University of Hawaii Press, 2004); for CCP attitudes to Beijing, see Wang Jun's controversial *Cheng ji* [Records of the City] (Beijing: Sanlian shudian, 2003).

17. **That discipline was developed:** Barbara Kreis, *Moskau 1917–35: vom Wohnungsbau zum Städtebau* [Moscow 1917–35: From Living Quarters to City Buildings] (Düsseldorf: Edition Marzona, 1985); Alessandra Latur, ed., *Rozhdenie metropolii: Moskva, 1930–1955. Vospominaniia i obrazy* [Birth of a Metropolis: Moscow, 1930–1955. Recollections and Images] (Moscow: Iskusstvo-XXI vek, 2005); R. A. French, *Plans, Pragmatism and People: The Legacy of Soviet Planning for Today's Cities* (London: UCL Press, 1995). **There had to be a centralized plan:** For an excellent critical review of urban planning as a "modernist movement," see Peter Hall, *Cities of Tomorrow: An Intellectual History of Urban Planning and Design in the Twentieth Century,* third ed. (London: Blackwell, 2003).

18. Wu Hung, *Remaking Beijing: Tiananmen Square and the Creation of a Political Space* (Chicago: University of Chicago Press, 2005) provides an original and entertaining view of CCP attitudes to the city.

19. Several of the reports on Soviet advice, as well as material relating to some of the early CCP discussions, can be found in *Jianguo yilai de Beijing chengshi jianshe ziliao. Di yi juan: Chengshi guihua* [Materials on Urban Construction of Beijing since the Founding of the PRC]. Book 1: Urban planning (internal publication; Beijing: Beijing jianshe shishu bianji

weiyuanhui bianjibu, 1987). The following paragraphs build in part on all seven volumes of this important internal-circulation series.

20. **His notes from that time:** See his writings in *Liang Sicheng quanji* [Collected Works of Liang Sicheng], vol. 6 (Beijing: Zhongguo jianzhu gongye, 2001). **His son remembers:** Quoted in *China Daily,* 1 October 1999. **Whatever Liang's own motives:** Wang Jun, *Cheng ji* is excellent on this, esp. 22–65.

21. **"Apparently, emperors can live in Beijing":** Wang Jun, "1950 niandai: dui Liang-Chen fangan de lishi kaocha" [1950s: A Historical Investigation of the Liang-Chen Proposal], at http://www.cc.org.cn. **There should be complete equality:** See *Jianguo yilai de Beijing chengshi jianshe ziliao. Di yi juan.*

22. Stalin, *Marxism and the National Question,* first published in *Prosveshcheniye,* Nos. 3–5, March–May 1913.

23. Xiaoyuan Liu, *Reins of Liberation: An Entangled History of Mongolian Independence, Chinese Territoriality, and Great Power Hegemony* (Stanford: Stanford University Press, 2006) gives an excellent overview of the development of CCP attitudes.

24. The key documents from the late 1940s and 1950s can be found in *Minzu wenti wenxian huibian* [A Collection of Documents on the Nationalities' Question] (internal circulation; Beijing: Zhonggong zhongyang dangxiao, 1991).

25. I do not have a percentage figure on how much of the Soviet theoretical literature that was translated up to 1955 dealt with minorities' issues, but a rough guess would be as much as thirty percent; see Greg Guldin, "Anthropology by Other Names: The Impact of Sino-Soviet Friendship on the Anthropological Sciences," *The Australian Journal of Chinese Affairs,* 27 (1992): 133–149.

26. **The CCP's own past visions:** For this, see Chen Yongfa, *Zhongguo gongchan geming 70 nian* [Seventy Years of Chinese Communist Revolution], vol. 1, second ed. (Taibei: Lianjing, 2001). **The Soviets, on their side:** See the undated Soviet embassy report (early 1954), pp. 25–35, delo 7, papka 379, opis 417, fond 0100, AVPRF.

27. For a view from the time when the People's Republic was being constructed, see record of conversation, Zhou Enlai—Soviet ambassador Roshchin, 15 November 1949, pp. 57–66, delo 220, papka 36, opis 22, fond 07, AVPRF.

28. A reason why some of my ethnic minority friends like to quip about China's political history as representing "Han's cruelty to Han."

29. Shu Guang Zhang, *Deterrence and Strategic Culture: Chinese-American Confrontations, 1949–1958* (Ithaca, NY: Cornell University Press, 1992), 185; see also Shu Guang Zhang, "Constructing 'Peaceful Coexistence': China's Diplomacy Toward the Geneva and Bandung Conferences, 1954–55," *Cold War History* 7, no. 4 (2007): 509.

30. Wang Ning, "The Great Northern Wilderness: Political Exiles in the People's Republic of China" (PhD thesis, University of British Columbia, 2005), 54.

31. Zhonggong zhongyang wenxian yanjiushi, ed., *Jianguo yilai zhongyao wenxian xuanbian* [A Selection of Important Documents since the Founding of the People's Republic] (Beijing: Zhongyang wenxian, 1992), vol. 10, 613.

32. "Liu Shaoqi's report at the first national conference on propaganda work, 7 May 1951," document no. 123/25/2/5, Archives of Shaanxi Province; quoted in Yang Kuisong, "Reconsidering the Campaign to Suppress Counterrevolutionaries," *The China Quarterly* 193, no. 1 (2008): 105.

33. The democide scholar R. J. Rummel estimates deaths to number almost double this; near eight and half million (see Rummel's website, at http://www.hawaii.edu/powerkills /NOTE2.HTM). My figures are based on estimates put together by PRC historians who are now working on this period.

34. Rosemary Foot, "The Eisenhower Administration's Fear of Empowering the Chinese," *Political Science Quarterly* 111, no. 3 (Autumn 1996): 517.

35. **And when Conservative British Prime Minister:** Mao-Iudin, memorandum of conversation, 25 May 1955, p. 112, d. 9, papka 393, op. 48, f.0100, AVPRF. **Mao told his aides:** Mao conversation with Zhou Enlai and others, 12 November 1959, quoted in Bo Yibo, *Ruogan zhongda juece yu shijian de huigu* [Recollections of Certain Major Decisions and Events], 2 vols. (Beijing: Zhonggong zhongyang dangxiao, 1991), vol. 2, p. 1144.

36. An excellent translation is Nikita S. Khrushchev, *The Crimes of the Stalin Era: Special Report to the 20th Congress of the Communist Party of the Soviet Union*, ed. Boris I. Nicolaevsky (New York: New Leader, 1956).

37. Wu Lengxi, *Shinian lunzhan 1956–1966: ZhongSu guanxi huiyilu* [A Decade of Polemics 1956–1966: A Memoir of Sino-Soviet Relations] (Beijing: Zhongyang wenxian, 1999), 35–36.

38. *Renmin Ribao*, 29 December 1956.

39. "Report Made by the Party Organization of the Chinese National General Labourers' Union on the Situation of the Strikes of Workers," vol.141-1-840, p. 16, Hunan Provincial Archives, Changsha. See also Zhu Dandan, "The Double Crisis: China and the Hungarian Revolution of 1956" (PhD thesis, London School of Economics, 2009), 180.

40. Mao Zedong, *Jianguo yilai Mao Zedong wengao* [Mao Zedong's Manuscripts since the Founding of the People's Republic], vol. 6, 630–644.

CHAPTER 9: CHINA ALONE

1. Frank Dikötter, *Mao's Great Famine: The History of China's Most Devastating Catastrophe, 1958–1962* (New York: Walker, 2010).

2. Mao Zedong, *Mao Zedong waijiao wenxuan* [Selected Diplomatic Papers of Mao Zedong] (Beijing: Zhongyang wenxian, 1994), 223–224.

3. "Memorandum of Conversation of N. S. Khrushchev with Mao Zedong, Beijing, 2 October 1959," *Cold War International History Bulletin*, no. 12/13 (2001): 269.

4. "Lieningzhuyi wansui! [Long Live Leninism!]," *Hongqi* (April 22, 1960).

5. Tang Zhennan et al., *Liu Shaoqi yu Mao Zedong* [Liu Shaoqi and Mao Zedong] (Changsha: Hunan renmin, 1998), 357.

6. **The Chairman insisted:** Stuart R. Schram, *Chairman Mao Talks to the People: Talks and Letters, 1956–1971*, first American ed. (New York: Pantheon Books, 1975), 192. **"On whether or not revisionism":** Xiao Donglian et al., *Qiusuo Zhongguo: "wenge" qian shinian shi* [Exploring China: The History of the Ten Years before the Cultural Revolution] (Beijing, 1999), 1000. **Zhou continued:** Zhou Enlai's speech at the Tenth Plenum, 26 September 1962, quoted in Yang Kuisong, *Changes in Mao Zedong's Attitude toward the Indochina War, 1949–1973*, Cold War International History Project Working Paper 34 (Washington, DC: Cold War International History Project, Woodrow Wilson International Center for Scholars, 2002).

7. Mao Zedong, *Mao Zedong Poems* (Beijing: Foreign Languages Press, 1998). The poem was completed 9 January 1963.

8. John Garver, "China's Decision for War with India in 1962," in *New Directions in the Study of China's Foreign Policy*, ed. Alaistair Ian Johnston and Robert S. Ross (Stanford: Stanford University Press, 2006).

9. Shi Bo, ed., *ZhongYin dazhan jishi* [Record of Events in the Big China-India War] (Beijing: Dadi, 1993), 189.

10. Deng Xiaoing's introduction 8 July 1963, in Records of meetings of the CPSU and CCP delegations, Moscow 5–20 July 1963, Aktenband 696, Bestandssignatur DY J IV 2/201, Stiftung Archiv der Parteien und Massenorganisationen der ehemaligen DDR im Bundesarchiv, Berlin.

11. Sergey Radchenko, *Two Suns in the Heavens: The Sino-Soviet Struggle for Supremacy, 1962–1967* (Washington, DC: Woodrow Wilson Center, 2009), 112–113.

12. **Now China had its own:** It took another twenty years, though, before China got missiles that could threaten western Russia or the continental United States, Dongfeng (East Wind) 5, of which there are still about twenty on active service. **In October 1965 he told:** *A Concise History of the Communist Party of China,* ed. Hu Shi (Beijing: Foreign Languages Press, 1994), 318.

13. Lin Biao, *Long Live the Victory of People's War,* at http://www.marxists.org/reference /archive/lin-biao/1965/09/peoples_war/ch08.htm.

14. Record of conversation, Zhou Enlai and Pham Van Dong, 9 October 1965, Odd Arne Westad et al., eds., *77 Conversations Between Chinese and Foreign Leaders on the Wars in Indochina, 1964–1977,* Working Paper 22 (Washington, DC: Cold War International History Project, Woodrow Wilson International Center for Scholars, 1998).

15. Record of conversation, Zhou Enlai, Deng Xiaoping, Kang Sheng, Le Duan, and Nguyen Duy Trinh, 13 April 1966, in ibid.

16. All quotes from Bernd Schaefer, *North Korean "Adventurism" and China's Long Shadow, 1966–1972,* Working Paper 44 (Washington, DC: Cold War International History Project, Woodrow Wilson International Center for Scholars, 2004), 6–9.

17. Record of conversation, Mao Zedong and Head of Indonesian Congress, 9 June 1964, 105-01336-02, Chinese Foreign Ministry Archives (CFMA), Beijing. I am grateful to Zhou Taomo for alerting me to this document and those below.

18. **In his meeting with:** Record of conversation, Mao Zedong and Indonesian President Sukarno, 13 June 1961, 204-01469-02, CFMA. **In January 1963, Liu:** Briefing on Subandrio's visit, 13 January 1963, 204-01504-01, CFMA.

19. **The Chinese saw:** British relations with India and Malaysia, 31 January 1964, 110-01696-03, CFMA. **China therefore increasingly:** Record of conversation, Luo Ruiqing and an Indonesian military delegation, 24 January 1965, 105-01910-07; record of conversation, Yao Zhongming - Subandrio], 11 February 1965, 105-01319-05, both CFMA.

20. **The Chinese advice:** Alaba Ogunsanwo, *China's Policy in Africa 1958–71* (Cambridge: Cambridge University Press, 1974). **The Chinese embassy in Algeria:** Quoted from Jeremy Friedman, "Reviving Revolution: The Sino-Soviet Split, the 'Third World,' and the Fate of the Left" (PhD dissertation, Princeton University, 2011), ch. 3.

21. Statement by Fidel Castro Ruz, *Prensa Latina,* 6 February 1966 at http://lanic .utexas.edu/project/castro/db/1966/19660206.html.

22. **The Hitlerites could:** Quoted from Friedman, "Reviving Revolution," ch. 3. **When they tried to issue:** Radchenko, *Two Suns in the Heavens,* 193.

23. **"A dictatorship of the bourgeoisie":** *Renmin ribao,* 4 June 1967. **"The Mongolian revisionists":** Michael Schoenhals, ed., *China's Cultural Revolution, 1966–1969: Not a Dinner Party* (Armonk, NY: M. E. Sharpe, 1996).

24. Anne-Marie Brady, "Red and Expert: China's 'Foreign Friends' in the Great Proletarian Cultural Revolution, 1966–1969," in *China's Great Proletarian Cultural Revolution: Master Narratives and Post-Mao Counternarratives,* ed. Woei Lien Chong (Lanham, MD: Rowman & Littlefield, 2002), 121.

25. "Interrogation record: Wang Guangmei, 10 April 1967," in Schoenhals, *China's Cultural Revolution, 1966–1969,* 105–106.

26. Ma Jisen, *The Cultural Revolution in the Foreign Ministry of China* (Hong Kong: Chinese University Press, 2004), 108.

27. Sergey Radchenko, "The Sino-Soviet Split," in *The Cambridge History of the Cold War,* ed. Melvyn P. Leffler and Odd Arne Westad, vol. 2 (Cambridge: Cambridge University Press, 2010), 349–372.

28. Barry Naughton, "The Third Front: Defence Industrialization in the Chinese Interior," *The China Quarterly,* no. 115 (September 1988): 351–386.

29. Yang Su, "Mass Killings in the Cultural Revolution: A Study of Three Provinces," in *The Chinese Cultural Revolution as History*, ed. Joseph Esherick, Paul Pickowicz, and Andrew G. Walder (Stanford: Stanford University Press, 2006), 96–123. For a more sensationalist account, see Zheng Yi, *Scarlet Memorial: Tales of Cannibalism in Modern China* (Boulder: Westview Press, 1998).

30. "Mao Zedong's Speech at the First Plenary Session of the CCP's Ninth Central Committee," *Cold War International History Project Bulletin*, no. 11 (n.d.): 163–165.

31. "Conversation between Mao Zedong and E. F. Hill, 28 November 1968," *Cold War International History Project Bulletin*, no. 11 (n.d.): 157–161.

32. "The CCP Central Committee's Order for General Mobilization in Border Provinces and Regions, 28 August 1969," *Cold War International History Project Bulletin*, no. 11 (n.d.): 168–69.

33. **[But] both China:** "Report by Four Chinese Marshals—Chen Yi, Ye Jianying, Xu Xiangqian, and Nie Rongzhen, to the Central Committee, 'A Preliminary Evaluation of the War Situation' (excerpt), 11 July 1969," *Cold War International History Project Bulletin*, no. 11 (n.d.): 166–168. **"It is necessary for us":** Personal Appendix to Marshals' Report, Chen Yi, 17 Sept. 1969. **Over the two years:** Gordon S. Barrass, *The Art of Calligraphy in Modern China* (Berkeley: University of California Press, 2002), 98.

CHAPTER 10: CHINA'S AMERICA

1. **But China's leaders concluded:** Gong Li, "Chinese Decision Making and the Thawing of U.S.-China Relations," in *Re-Examining the Cold War: U.S.-China Diplomacy, 1954–1973*, ed. Robert S. Ross and Changbin Jiang (Cambridge, MA: Harvard University Asia Center, 2001), 346. **Kissinger said that:** Kissinger, Briefing of White House Staff, 19 July 1971, box 1036, China-General July-Oct 1971, NSC files, Nixon Presidential Papers Project, Washington, DC. **Mao was less fulsome:** Mao Zedong and Pham Van Dong, Beijing, 23 September 1970, in Westad et al., *77 Conversations Between Chinese and Foreign Leaders on the Wars in Indochina, 1964–1977*, 175.

2. Uniquely among West European countries, France has had ambassadorial-level diplomatic relations with the People's Republic of China since 1964.

3. **In agriculture, industry, technology:** *Resolution on Certain Questions in the History of Our Party Since the Founding of the People's Republic of China* (Beijing: Foreign Languages Press, 1981). **In that process:** "Muqian de xingshi he renwu [The Present Situation and Tasks]," 16 January 1980, *Deng Xiaoping wenxuan* [Selected Works of Deng Xiaoping], vol. 2 (Beijing: Xinhua, 1983).

4. Han Suyin, ironically, had herself been a chief apologist for Mao's Cultural Revolution; see her two books *Wind in the Tower: Mao Tse-tung and the Chinese Revolution, 1949–75* (London: Jonathan Cape, 1976) and *Lhasa, the Open City: Journey to Tibet* (London: Jonathan Cape, 1977).

5. Li Jie, "China's Domestic Politics and the Normalization of Sino-US Relations, 1969–1979," in *Normalization of U.S.-China Relations: An International History*, ed. William C. Kirby, Robert S Ross, and Li Gong, Harvard East Asian monographs 254 (Cambridge, MA: Harvard University Asia Center, 2005), 79.

6. **"Wherever the Soviet Union sticks":** Record of conversation, Carter and Deng, 29 January 1979, China, box 9, Geographic File, Brzezinski Collection, Jimmy Carter Presidential Library, Atlanta (hereafter JCPL). **Zhang said, "We are glad":** Record of conversation, Zhang Aiping and Harold Brown, 8 January 1980, box 69, Sullivan - Subject File, Staff Material-Far East, Collection 26, National Security Affairs, Presidential Papers, JCPL. **Deng himself put it plainly:** Deng's meeting with the Cabinet, 31 January 1979, China, box 9, Geographic File, Brzezinski Collection, JCPL.

7. Morrow to Reagan, 30 November 1981, Meese Files, box 19, Ronald Reagan Presidential Library, Simi Valley, CA (hereafter RRPL).

8. Statement on United States Arms Sales to Taiwan, 17 August 1982, The Public Papers of the President: Ronald Reagan, 1981–1989, at http://www.reagan.utexas.edu/archives/speeches/publicpapers.html.

9. Liu Xiaobo, Zhou Duo, Hou Dejian, and Gao Xin, "June 2 Declaration," in Suzanne Ogden, *China's Search for Democracy: The Student and the Mass Movement of 1989* (Armonk, NY: M.E. Sharpe, 1992), 358–359.

10. State Department document 29 June 1989, copy held at the National Security Archive, Washington, DC (hereafter NSecArch).

11. *Deng Xiaoping wenxuan*, vol. 3.

12. Excerpts from Talks Given in Wuchang, Shenzhen, Zhuhai and Shanghai, 18 January– 21 February 1992, in *Deng Xiaoping wenxuan*, vol. 3.

13. *Renmin ribao*, 14 September 2009.

14. "China Quick Facts," at http://www.worldbank.org/.

15. *Huanqiu shibao*, 23 June 2010.

16. See UNDP's Human Development Report 2010, at http://hdr.undp.org/en/statistics/.

17. TVBS Poll Center, March 2009, at http://www.tvbs.com.tw/FILE_DB/DL_DB/yijung/200905/yijung-20090508145032.pdf. Accessed February 2011.

18. Robert Suettinger, *Beyond Tian'anmen: The Politics of U.S.-China Relations, 1989– 2000* (Washington, DC: Brookings Institution Press, 2003), 87.

19. Song Qiang et al., *Zhongguo keyi shuo bu: Lengzhanhou shidai de zhengzhi yu qinggan jueze* [The China That Can Say No: Political and Emotional Choices in the Post Cold War Era] (Beijing: Zhonghua gongshang lianhe, 1996).

20. **"China must [now] pay":** S. Mahmud Ali, *U.S.-China Relations in the "Asia-Pacific" Century* (New York: Palgrave Macmillan, 2008), 15. **At a remarkable press conference:** http://www.zpub.com/un/china27.html.

21. **The purpose of the bombing:** UN Press Release 6659, 26 March 1999. The Hong Kong magazine *Qianshao* has reported that Jiang Zemin's unpublished memoirs acknowledge the stationing of Yugoslav intelligence personnel inside the Chinese embassy compound before the attack and close cooperation with Milosevic in the lead-up to the war (*Qianshao*, no. 240 [February 2011]). **President Jiang Zemin stoked:** Ali, *U.S.-China Relations in the "Asia-Pacific" Century*, 94. **The main official newspaper:** *Renmin ribao*, 12 and 13 May 1999.

22. Simon Shen, *Redefining Nationalism in Modern China: Sino-American Relations and the Emergence of Chinese Public Opinion in the 21st Century* (Basingstoke: Palgrave Macmillan, 2007), 63. Shen's book is an excellent introduction to debates about nationalism in contemporary China.

23. **When the new US administration:** Ibid., 73. **The Yugoslavs had provided them:** The PLA also learned to scale down its pursuit of US spy planes to avoid confrontation; see *The Guardian*, 30 July 2001.

24. Press Release of the Chinese UN Mission, 13 September 2001, "Chinese President Jiang Zemin Expressed Condolences by Telegraph over Terrorist Attacks on America and Talked with President Bush on Telephone to Show China's Position against Terrorism," at http://www.china-un.org/eng/chinaandun/securitycouncil/thematicissues/counterterrorism/t26903.htm.

25. US Secretary of State Colin Powell, "Remarks at the Elliott School of International Affairs," September 5, 2003, http://www.state.gov/secretary/rm/2003/23836.htm.

26. Inter-Agency Group on Economic and Financial Statistics, *Principal Global Indicators*, at http://www.principalglobalindicators.org/default.aspx; International Monetary Fund,

Country Information, at http://www.imf.org/external/country/index.htm; US Department of the Treasury, *Major Foreign Holders of Treasury Securities*, at http://www.treasury.gov /resource-center/data-chart-center/tic/Documents/mfh.txt; and European Commission, *Trade: Bilateral Relations*, at http://ec.europa.eu/trade/creating-opportunities/bilateral -relations/. See also JC de Swaan, "China Goes to Wall Street: Beijing's Evolving US Investment Strategy," *Foreign Affairs*, April 29, 2010.

27. For useful comparisons, see the website of the Center for Arms Control and Non-Proliferation, at http://armscontrolcenter.org/. For all countries, I have included that part of payments to veterans that is exclusively used for military veterans' purposes.

CHAPTER 11: CHINA'S ASIA

1. Angus Maddison, *The World Economy: A Millennial Perspective* (Paris: OECD, 2001), 216–217.

2. *Asia Times*, 14 January 2009. When the original agreement was signed in 1999, both sides agreed to give a symbolic one square kilometer of disputed territory more to China than to Vietnam—signaling the images of the traditional relationship (Alexander Vuving, "Grand Strategic Fit and Power Shift: Explaining Turning Points in China-Vietnam Relations," in *Living with China*, ed. Shiping Tang et al. (New York: Palgrave Macmillan, 2009), 229–245.

3. "Dong-A Ilbo Opinion Poll on South Korean Attitudes Toward Japan and Other Nations," 26 April 2005, http://www.mansfieldfdn.org/polls/2005/poll-05-2.htm.

4. See for instance US Assistant Secretary of State Kurt Campbell's conversation with South Korean experts, 18 February 2010, WikiLeaks, at http://213.251.145.96/cable /2010/02/10SEOUL248.html.

5. "Xiandaihua yu lishi jiaokeshu" [Modernization and History Textbooks], *Bingdian*, 11 January 2006. The journal was closed down for its efforts.

6. "On Memories of Violence, Part 2: Chinese Textbooks and Questions About the Korean War 60 years Later," at Jeremiah Jenne's blog http://granitestudio.org/2010/06/25/.

7. New History Textbook (Chapters 4 & 5), 2005 version. Prepared and translated by Japanese Society for History Textbook Reform from *Atarashii rekishi kyōkasho wo tsukuru kai* (The Japanese Society for Textbook Reform), published by Fusosha, Tokyo, at http:// www.tsukurukai.com/05_rekisi_text/rekishi_English/English.pdf. Most Japanese textbooks are more critical toward Japan's wartime guilt.

8. **The Diaoyu/Senkaku islands:** On the background for the dispute, see Unryu Suganuma, "The Diaoyo/Senkaku Islands: A Hotbed for a Hot War?" in *China and Japan at Odds: Deciphering the Perpetual Conflict*, ed. James Hsiung (New York: Palgrave Macmillan, 2007), 155–172. **So far the courts:** Ming Wan, *Sino-Japanese Relations: Interaction, Logic, and Transformation* (Stanford: Stanford University Press, 2008), 304–326.

9. **Singapore's anti-Communist leader:** Record of conversation, Lee and FRG Chancellor Helmut Schmidt, 11 June 1979, in Ilse Dorothee Pautsch et al., *Akten zur auswärtigen Politik der Bundesrepublik Deutschland 1979: 1. Juli bis 31. Dezember 1979* (Oldenbourg Wissenschaftsverlag, 2010), 173–174. **China's attempts at:** Nobody has yet written the history of China's involvement with these insurgencies.

10. **Now other ASEAN states are:** The reader can find excellent maps at http://www.global security.org/military/world/war/spratly-maps.htm. **People of Chinese ancestry are still:** "Indonesia: Chinese, Migrants," *Migration News*, 5, 6 (June 1998), http://migration.ucdavis.edu /mn/more.php?id=1559_0_3_0.

11. **One report described:** Contemporary report, quoted in Jemma Purdey, *Anti-Chinese Violence in Indonesia, 1996–1999* (Honolulu: University of Hawaii Press, 2006), 1. **Student**

protests in Beijing: Nationalist sentiment in China migrated to the internet in the 1990s; the first hacking attack by China's emerging cyber-militia on foreign networks was against Indonesia in 1998, in response to the racist violence there; see Christopher R. Hughes, "Nationalism in Chinese Cyberspace," *Cambridge Review of International Affairs* 13, no. 2 (2000): 195.

12. Mikhail Gorbachev, *Zhizn i reformy* [Life and Reforms] (Moscow: Novosti, 1995).

13. "Treaty of Good-Neighborliness and Friendly Cooperation Between the People's Republic of China and the Russian Federation," 24 July 2001, http://www.fmprc.gov.cn/eng /wjdt/2649/t15771.htm.

14. **SCO's charter binds:** "Charter of the Shanghai Cooperation Organization," at the organization's website http://www.sectsco.org/EN/show.asp?id=69. **After a century, Beijing:** A quick visit to the website of STO (http://www.sectsco.org) shows its name in Chinese throning over smaller versions in Russian and English (with no Kazakh, Tajik, or Uzbek). In practical terms, the organization's influence has so far been limited; its only common institution is the Regional Anti-Terrorist Structure (with the somewhat unfortunate acronym RATS), headquartered in Tashkent.

15. Memorandum of Conversation, Beijing, 27 November 1974, Foreign Relations of the United States, 1969–1976, Volume XVIII, China, 1973–1976, document 97.

16. Jonathan Holslag, *China and India: Prospects for Peace* (New York: Columbia University Press, 2010), 51.

17. China abstained on condemning Yugoslavia over Kosovo in 1998, on sanctions against Burma and Zimbabwe, on a UN mission to Darfur in 2006, and on a no-fly zone in Libya in 2011.

MODERNITIES

1. Bureau of East Asian and Pacific Affairs, US Department of State, "Background Note: Hong Kong, 15 March 2011," http://www.state.gov/r/pa/ei/bgn/2747.htm.

2. **In spite of its government's:** This was of course once the case with the UK and US, too. **Seen from a Western:** Edward Steinfeld, *Playing Our Game: Why China's Economic Rise Doesn't Threaten the West* (Oxford: Oxford University Press, 2010).

3. "Full text of Chinese Premier's Speech at World Economic Forum Annual Meeting 2009," 29 January 2009, http://news.xinhuanet.com/english/2009-01/29/content_10731877 _1.htm.

4. "President Jiang Zemin Comments on Falun Gong's Harms 25 October 1999," http://www.china-embassy.org/eng/zt/ppflg/t36565.htm.

5. "Dalai Lama 'Wolf in Monk's Robes': Official," *China Daily*, 7 March 2011. The comments are by Zhang Qingli, the long-suffering Chinese party boss in Tibet, who is a constant voice within the CCP against "splitters and deviationists."

6. Jan Vilcek and Bruce N. Cronstein, "A Prize for the Foreign-born," *The FASEB Journal* 20, no. 9 (July 1, 2006): 1281–1283.

7. Adapted from a chant by Millwall Football Club (though I in no way hold the Bermondsey Lions responsible for Chinese nationalism).

8. For a good discussion, see Martin Jacques, *When China Rules the World: The Rise of the Middle Kingdom and the End of the Western World* (London: Allen Lane, 2009), 244–252.

9. Fergus Hanson and Andrew Shearer, *China and the World: Public Opinion and Foreign Policy* (Sydney: The Lowy Institute, 2009).

10. Wang Jisi, "China's Search for a Grand Strategy," *Foreign Affairs* (April 2011).

11. For an excellent overview, see the Columbia University site *China and Europe 1500– 2000: What Is "Modern"?* http://afe.easia.columbia.edu/chinawh/web/s6/s6_3.html.

12. See United Nations, Department of Economic and Social Affairs, Population Division, "World Population to 2030" (UN, 2004); Amartya Sen, "Quality of Life," *New York Review of Books* (May 12, 2011).

13. "Pakistan and China: Sweet As Can Be?," *The Economist*, May 12, 2011.

14. "General Attitudes Toward China," WorldPublicOpinion.org, http://www.americans-world.org/digest/regional_issues/china/china1.cfm.

INDEX